THE LEGACY OF HANS W. FREI

THE LEGACY OF HANS W. FREI

Edited by
George Hunsinger

t&tclark
LONDON • NEW YORK • OXFORD • NEW DELHI • SYDNEY

T&T CLARK
Bloomsbury Publishing Plc
50 Bedford Square, London, WC1B 3DP, UK
1385 Broadway, New York, NY 10018, USA
29 Earlsfort Terrace, Dublin 2, Ireland

BLOOMSBURY, T&T CLARK and the T&T Clark logo are trademarks
of Bloomsbury Publishing Plc

First published in Great Britain 2023
Paperback edition published 2025

Copyright © George Hunsinger, 2023

George Hunsinger has asserted his right under the Copyright, Designs and
Patents Act, 1988, to be identified as Editor of this work.

For legal purposes the Acknowledgments on pp. vii–viii constitute an extension
of this copyright page.

Cover image: Rembrandt, *Christ with Two Disciples on the Road to Emmaus*,
c. 1655. Wikimedia Commons.

All rights reserved. No part of this publication may be reproduced or transmitted
in any form or by any means, electronic or mechanical, including photocopying,
recording, or any information storage or retrieval system, without prior
permission in writing from the publishers.

Bloomsbury Publishing Plc does not have any control over, or responsibility for,
any third-party websites referred to or in this book. All internet addresses given in this
book were correct at the time of going to press. The author and publisher regret any
inconvenience caused if addresses have changed or sites have ceased to exist,
but can accept no responsibility for any such changes.

A catalogue record for this book is available from the British Library.

A catalog record for this book is available from the Library of Congress.

Library of Congress Cataloging-in-Publication Data
Names: Hunsinger, George, author.
Title: The legacy of Hans W. Frei / George Hunsinger.
Description: London ; New York : T&T Clark, 2022. | Includes
bibliographical references and index. |
Identifiers: LCCN 2022036242 (print) | LCCN 2022036243 (ebook) |
ISBN 9780567706034 (hb) | ISBN 9780567707870 (epdf) |
ISBN 9780567704863 (epub)
Subjects: LCSH: Frei, Hans W. | Bible--Hermeneutics.
Classification: LCC BS501.F74 H86 2022 (print) | LCC BS501.F74 (ebook) |
DDC 220.6--dc23/eng/20221209
LC record available at https://lccn.loc.gov/2022036242
LC ebook record available at https://lccn.loc.gov/2022036243

ISBN: HB: 978-0-5677-0603-4
PB: 978-0-5677-0607-2
ePDF: 978-0-5677-0604-1
eBook: 978-0-5677-0606-5

Typeset by Integra Software Services Pvt. Ltd.

To find out more about our authors and books visit www.bloomsbury.com
and sign up for our newsletters.

CONTENTS

Acknowledgments — vii

Preface — ix
George Hunsinger

Foreword: On Hans Frei, a Recommendation — xiv
Katherine Sonderegger

Part 1 Personalia

1 Interview with Hans W. Frei, 1980 — 3

Part 2 The Enduring Importance of Hans W. Frei's Work

2 Hans Frei and the Meaning of Biblical Narrative — 13
William C. Placher

3 Hans W. Frei in Context: A Theological and Historical Memoir — 21
John F. Woolverton

Part 3 Theological Themes in Frei's Work

4 Frei's Early Christology: The Book of Detours — 47
George Hunsinger

5 Frei's Later Christology: Radiance and Obscurity — 61
Jason A. Springs

6	The Barthian Heritage of Hans W. Frei *John Allan Knight*	78
7	Hans Frei and Anselmian Theology *Jeffrey Stout*	98
8	Frei and the Project of Christological Reflection *David H. Kelsey*	118

Part 4 Postliberal Hermeneutics

9	Hans Frei and the Hermeneutics of the Second Naïveté *Garrett Green*	137
10	The Gospel of Jesus Christ as a Story to Be Told: Eberhard Jüngel and Hans Frei on "Narrative" in Christian Theology *R. David Nelson*	156
11	The Eclipse of Biblical Narrative: Analysis and Critique *George P. Schner*	172
12	Meaning and Truth in Narrative Interpretation: A Reply to George Schner *Bruce D. Marshall*	198

Part 5 Hans Frei's Achievement

13	Hans Frei, George Lindbeck, and the Objectivity of Scripture *Mike Higton*	207
14	What Can Evangelicals and Postliberals Learn from Each Other? *George Hunsinger*	227
15	On Being Theologically Hospitable to Jesus Christ: Hans Frei's Achievement *David F. Ford*	251

LIST OF CONTRIBUTORS	265
INDEX	267

ACKNOWLEDGMENTS

The publisher and editor gratefully acknowledge permission to reprint the following material.

Preface. From the Foreword by George Hunsinger in *Reading Faithfully,* Volume 1: *Writings from the Archives: Theology and Hermeneutics*, ed. Mike Higton and Mark Allan Bowald (Eugene OR: Cascade Books, 2015).

Interview with Hans W. Frei. *"Hans W. Frei Holocaust Testimony."* Excerpts. Yale – Fortunoff Video Archive for Holocaust Testimonies (April 18, 1980). *https://fortunoff.library.yale.edu*

William C. Placher, "Hans Frei and the Meaning of Biblical Narrative," *Christian Century* 106 (1989): 556–9.

John F. Woolverton, "Hans Frei in Context: A Theological and Historical Memoir," *Anglican Theological Review* 79 (1997): 369–93.

George Hunsinger, "Frei's Early Christology: The Book of Detours," *Pro Ecclesia* 24 (2015): 24–36.

Jason A. Springs, "Frei's Later Christology: Radiance and Obscurity," *Pro Ecclesia* 24 (2015): 37–52.

John Allen Knight, "The Barthian Heritage of Hans W. Frei," *Scottish Journal of Theology* 61 (2008): 07–26.

Jeffrey Stout, "Hans Frei and Anselmian Theology" in *Ten Year Commemoration to the Life of Hans Frei (1922–1988)*, ed. Giorgy Olegovich (New York: Semenenko Foundation, 1999): 24–40.

David H. Kelsey, "Frei and the Project of Christological Reflection" in Kelsey, *Eccentric Existence: A Theological Anthropology* (WJK, 2009): 680–93.

Garrett Green, "Hans Frei and the Hermeneutics of the Second Naïveté" (revised) in *Imagining Theology: Encounters with God in Scripture, Interpretation, and Aesthetics* (Baker Academic, 2020): 73–93.

George P. Schner, SJ, "*The Eclipse of Biblical Narrative*: Analysis and Critique," *Modern Theology* 8 (1992): 149–72.

Bruce D. Marshall, "Meaning and Truth in Narratve Interpretation: A Reply to George Schner," *Modern Theology* 8 (1992): 173–79.

George Hunsinger, "The Carl Henry/Hans Frei Exchange Reconsidered," *Pro Ecclesia* 5 (1996): 161–82.

David F. Ford, "On Being Theologically Hospitable to Jesus Christ: Hans Frei's Achievement," *The Journal of Theological Studies*, ns 46 (1995): 532–46.

PREFACE

GEORGE HUNSINGER

When Hans W. Frei died in 1988, he was hailed as perhaps the leading Anselmian theologian of his generation as well as the foremost historian of modern biblical hermeneutics in his day. He was also remembered, as someone remarked to me at the time, as probably "the kindest man in academic life." Let me begin with a brief word about his personal qualities before turning to his academic accomplishments.

In relations with his students, Hans Frei possessed a rare gift of fatherly warmth and empathy. In particular, he managed to make each of his doctoral students feel affirmed and encouraged without provoking a sense of rivalry among them. As his colleague George Lindbeck noted at his memorial service, what Frei was to each of his students, he was to them all. He so mentored them as to give them "a common bond," one that extended well beyond the classroom. In some cases their camaraderie, fostered by Frei, would persist for decades, as they continued to meet together for scholarly and theological discussion. Frei's generosity, Lindbeck suggested, not only enabled him "to make close friendships with his intellectual opponents, but also helped his students to form themselves into a close-knit community of scholars for whom any natural competitiveness became a secondary matter." Given the nature of graduate schools, Lindbeck observed, this outcome was close to miraculous.[1]

As to kindness, perhaps I may be allowed a personal reminiscence. When my father died during my second year of graduate studies at Yale, to my surprise Mr. Frei (as we all knew him) spontaneously offered to pay for an airplane ticket so that I could fly to California to be with my family. Although that turned out to be unnecessary, it was the kind of gesture one does not easily forget. Nor was it the last time that I (and many others) would be the object of such generosity. Many similar stories began to circulate after Frei's death.

John F. Woolverton, a close friend and former colleague, noted that if one read between the lines, one could discern in Frei a sense of Jesus' "haunting identity." What captivated him about Jesus, Woolverton suggested, was "his compassion, his severity, his ordinary kindness and natural gentleness, his simple, delighted generosity, and his profound humaneness."[2] Frei would recoil if the parallels were pushed too far, but I think it can be stated that, "following at a distance" (to use one of his preferred phrases for the Christian life), Frei himself displayed something of these same qualities. Certainly those who got to know him might realize that his kindness and compassion were not always unmixed with severity.

Although Frei spanned the fields of theology and history, he liked to quip that "to the historians I say that I'm a theologian while to the theologians I insist that I'm a historian." There was something ambivalent in Frei that did not like to be pinned down. Whether as a theologian or as a historian, there could be something tentative in all his explorations. He worried more about being too simple and clearly defined than about being too dense and obscure. His difficult prose, notoriously teutonic and serpentine (though sometimes quite eloquent), seemed to embody this tendency. He admired Barth for his robust convictions without being able to share them completely. He could find something valuable in almost any theological position while still holding something back in reserve. He had a knack for explaining the theology of his teacher H. Richard Niebuhr with unmatched power and sympathy, but in a way that left Niebuhr seeming, ironically, somewhat diminished in the end. Immensely learned and cultured, Frei was a scholar whose sympathies were strong but whose sentiments were hesitant, and finally perhaps a bit troubled.

Whether he was really the leading "Anselmian" theologian of his generation is a nice question. It would depend to some extent on whom we might regard as the contenders. If we restrict ourselves to Protestant theologians of his generation, the names of Jürgen Moltmann and Thomas F. Torrance come to mind. However, while Moltmann was clearly more Hegelian or neo-Hegelin than Anselmian, and while Torrance was more indebted to Cyril than to Anselm, both were clearly more productive as doctrinal theologians than was Frei. In any case, it seems that an Anselmian moment in one of Frei's arguments about Christ's resurrection, which is about all it comes to, would not really be enough to qualify him as a distinctively Anselmian theologian, an epithet that might more properly be applied to Balthasar or to Barth.

What Frei really cared about was the singularity of Jesus and, in particular, about the specific literary way that the gospel narratives (resembling modern "realistic" narratives) set it forth. He therefore worried about modern depictions of Jesus by which that singularity was systematically obscured. These interests establish the common bond between Frei's theological and historical work.

As a theologian, he wanted to show how the gospels, taken as realistic narratives, depicted the identity of Jesus Christ as something irreducibly and unsubstitutably his own. Jesus' narrated identity as the gospels set it forth, and as construed for centuries by the church prior to the seventeenth century, meant that he was not a symbol for anything other than himself. He was a singular human being whose particularity was essential to his universal saving significance. There was no universal significance for Jesus without his stubborn Jewish particularity, and no particularity not fraught with saving significance for the whole world. His universality, we might say, was not grounded in his religious self-consciousness nor in his way of being in the world. It was grounded, rather, in his particularity as the fulfillment of God's covenant with Israel: "... in you all the families of the earth shall be blessed" (Gen. 12:3 ESV). For Frei, in grasping the particular identity and significance of Jesus, the covenantal took precedence over anything merely general or anthropological.

Frei's claim to fame as perhaps the foremost historian of biblical hermeneutics in his day undoubtedly carries weight. He attempted to excavate history in order to show how the gospels came to be misread in modernity. Modern interpreters, whether defenders or detractors of the Christian faith, went astray, he argued, in confusing questions of "meaning" with those of "truth" in reading the gospel narratives. Meaning was made to be dependent on factual truth, or perceptions of truth, rather than the other way around. As Frei demonstrated at great length, no one quite grasped that the narratives *meant* what they said about the identity of Jesus Christ regardless of whether they were assessed as *true*. The literary-theological *function* of the narratives in rendering the singular identity of Jesus in his universal significance and irreducible particularity—their *meaning*—was overlooked all around.

Frei's attempt to rescue biblical narratives from their modern eclipse would receive acclaim even outside the disciplines of theology, capturing the favorable attention of luminaries like George Steiner, Alasdair MacIntyre, and Frank Kermode. The significance of his seminal work *The Eclipse of Biblical Narrative: A Study in Eighteenth and Nineteenth Century Hermeneutics* (Yale University Press, 1974) is still being felt. As Lindbeck wrote: "Frei's work marks the beginning of a change in biblical interpretation as decisive—though in a different direction—as that of Albert Schweitzer's *Quest of the Historical Jesus*."[3]

In conclusion let me mention four themes that it might be helpful for readers to keep in mind.

(i) A distinction between "explanation" and "description," with a clear preference for the latter. If the identity of Jesus was as singular as the gospels claimed it to be, Frei believed, then no independent theoretical or explanatory schemes of interpretation could capture it. Such schemes could only be distorting and reductive. Descriptive hermeneutical strategies—the more formal and less theory-laden the better—were preferable.

(ii) The use of nontheological modes of conceptual analysis to elucidate the logic and content of Christian theology. Frei conscripted secular writers like Eric Auerbach (literature), Gilbert Ryle (analytical philosophy), and Clifford Geertz (cultural anthropology) because they seemed serviceable in avoiding independent theoretical explanations in favor of a less-encumbered literary-theological description.

(iii) A distrust of apologetical strategies because they seemed to eliminate Jesus' radical singularity.

> What I am proposing ... is that we raise the question in a drastically non-apologetic, non-perspectivalist fashion: "What does this narrative say or mean, never mind whether it can become a meaningful possibility of life perspective for us or not." Its meaning on the one hand, and its possible as well as actual truth for us on the other, are two totally different questions.[4]

(iv) Finally, as already indicated, a granting of primacy to the particular over the general. That is, in reading the gospels as "realistic narratives," Jesus' universal saving significance needs to be construed in terms of his unique and unsubstitutable identity. Prior to the rise of modernity, that is how it was regarded by the church. Hermeneutical attempts to do the reverse—i.e. to move from general anthropological ideas to the narrative particularities of the gospels—would be, Frei urged, "first to put the cart before the horse and then cut the lines and pretend the vehicle is self-propelled."[5]

In short, the primacy of the descriptive, the particular, the non-apologetic, and the non-theoretical (in the particular senses I have suggested) was the controlling theme that ran through almost everything Frei wrote as a historian, a hermeneutician, and a theologian.

***

This volume pulls together important essays on Frei's work since his death in 1988, a number previously published, others produced for this volume. It is divided into four parts.

Part 1: Personalia. This includes a new biographical sketch along with excepts from a little-known 1980 interview in which Frei relays anecdotes from his youth growing up as a Jew in Nazi Germany.

Part 2: The Enduring Importance of Hans W. Frei's Work. William C. Placher introduces Frei to a general audience, while John F. Woolverton draws upon interviews he conducted with Frei to place his work in theological and historical perspective.

Part 3: Theological Themes in Frei's Work. Chs. 4 and 5 were presented at a 2013 Princeton conference on Frei and his legacy. My piece (Hunsinger) (Ch. 4) attempts to decipher the elusive argument in his influential book *The Identity of Jesus Christ* (Fortress, 1975). Springs (Ch. 5) then follows up with an assessment of his later christology. Knight (Ch. 6) unearths Frei's important Barthian background. Stout's essay (Ch. 7), a classic in Frei studies, looks at Frei's importance in American theology, while Kelsey (Ch. 8) unpacks Frei's proposals for christological reflection.

Part 4: Postliberal Hermeneutics. Green (Ch. 9) discusses Frei in relation to Ricoeur's vision of a second naïveté, while Nelson (Ch. 10) examines him in relation to Jüngel on the central question of narrative.

In Ch. 11 Schner subjects Frei's argument in *Eclipse* to a strong critique, offering an alternative historical account from a Roman Catholic perspective, while Marshall responds with high intelligence in Ch. 12.

Part 5: Hans Frei's Achievement. In Ch. 13 Higton carefully distinguishes Frei from Lindbeck in a context where they are often conflated. Hunsinger (Ch. 14) then unpacks Frei's understanding of Christ's resurrection over against evangelical-conservative critics, while in conclusion Ford (Ch. 15) commends what Frei accomplished in theology and hermeneutics.

The result is a volume on Frei's legacy that promises to become not only an important point of reference, but also a means of introducing Frei to a new generation of students in theology and religious studies.

NOTES

1. George Lindbeck, "Remarks at Frei's Memorial Service," *In Memoriam, Hans. W. Frei,* Yale University Religious Studies Department, unpublished booklet, 1988.
2. John F. Woolverton, "Hans W. Frei in Context: A Theological and Historical Memoir," *Anglican Theological Review* 79 (1997): 369–93; on 392. Ch. 4 in this volume.
3. George Lindbeck, "Death Notices," *The Christian Century* 105 (1988): 865.
4. Hans W. Frei, "Remarks in Connection with a Theological Proposal," in *Theology and Narrative: Selected Essays*, ed. George Hunsinger and William C. Placher (New York: Oxford University Press, 1993): 26–44; on 40.
5. Frei, "The Literal Reading of Biblical Narrative" in *Theology and Narrative,* 117–52; on 148.

FOREWORD: ON HANS FREI, A RECOMMENDATION

KATHERINE SONDEREGGER

In this splendid collection, George Hunsinger has set out a rich and extensive case for the claim—in David Ford's words—that Hans Frei was the most significant North American theologian in the last quarter of the twentieth century. Here are essays on Frei's life story, with a riveting excerpt from Frei's autobiographical reflections on his childhood as an acculturated Jew in Nazi Berlin; essays on his major scholarly specialties, Christology and hermeneutics; and as a conclusion, large-scale assessments of his work and stature. All these testify to the enduring power, complexity, and influence of Frei's life work. I follow at a distance compared to those who knew him best, but I too consider Frei a scholar of unparalleled analytic power and an unrivalled interpreter of modern Christian thought.

    Nevertheless, to those outside the Yale penumbra, Hunsinger's and Ford's bold claim (and mine) might seem an odd assessment, perhaps exceedingly odd. As Ford himself reminds us in his summary essay, Frei wrote little dogmatic or systematic theology. His early lectures on Christology, later published as *The Identity of Jesus Christ*, stands as his only foray into doctrinal theology published in his lifetime. The work Ford considers the chief article in his defense of Frei's stature, *Types of Christian Theology*, was collated from notes and lectures left in his files, and published only after Frei's untimely, early death. In the decades since Frei's death, scholars have worked through fragments and unfinished essays, letters and lectures, to fill two substantial volumes of posthumous work.

(*Reading Faithfully: Writings from the Archives* of Hans Frei, M. Higton, and M. A. Bowald, eds.) Though he published little, and declared himself a slow, agonized writer, Frei left the substantial remains of an active scholarly life. We gain a taste for those projects from John Wolverton's extensive record of Frei's scholarly preoccupations during many years of friendship. But aside from a single sermon and some brief—though illuminating!—remarks on sections from the Anglican Articles of Religion, the dogmatic material in Frei's corpus is slender indeed. Of course it is not unusual, in an ancien régime, for professors in the Ivy Leagues to publish little and to deliver their reputations into the hands of their doctoral students who advanced their scholarly program. But Frei remains a singular case, all the same, because his stature as theologian diverges sharply, it seems, from the profile gathered from this scholarship.

From the published material, after all, both during Frei's academic career and afterwards, one might well be forgiven for thinking of Frei as an impressive exemplar of the *Germanistik* tradition that flourished in the inter-war years, aligning him with such students of German *belle lettres* as Erich Auerbach, Erich Pryzwara, or Hans Urs von Balthasar. More generally, Frei's reputation rests largely on his study of these pioneers of modernism, *The Eclipse of Biblical Narrative*, a demanding, at times elusive, work of historical and hermeneutical analysis that sets forth the major architectonics of nineteenth-century biblical criticism—problems of faith and history; of meaning and referent; of text and tradents—as a saga of the loss of the singularity and integrity of biblical figures in their words and deeds, enmeshed in the backdrop of covenant and promise. Far less than from the Church nave or seminary corridors, Frei's interlocutors are ordinary language philosophers, cultural anthropologists, sociologists, and secular historians. Though he wrote his dissertation on Karl Barth, and lectured some on Barth's *Church Dogmatics*, Frei did not undertake major studies of prominent theologians, nor did the developments of Protestant dogmatics in the post-war world gain much of his attention. Frei was ordained priest in the Episcopal Church, but as he confessed to John Wolverton, he wore his ecclesial identity lightly, and found a certain air of secularity quite congenial. Like his teacher, H. R. Niebuhr, Frei recognized in himself a kind of "natural theology," as he styles this in an essay on Niebuhr, in which a worldly pessimism and taste for the contingent and the tragic compose his unbaptized view of the world (though not, to be sure, of his Christian vision). None of this is likely to strike the attentive reader as the outline of the premier theologian of his generation.

Contra mundum, I want to support Ford's and Hunsinger's claims here. This wonderful volume, and the two published under Higton and Bowald, will make the extensive literary case for Frei's stature. I want here to point to an elixir in Frei's own person and intellect that makes him an extraordinary theologian of the modern era. It is a small but distinctive sign of this charisma that Frei's former doctoral students—those who knew him best—refer to him still as Mr. Frei. This title might convey the idea that Frei was an old-school Ordinarius, insistent upon his privilege as patriarch in German letters. But I think that would be a complete inversion of the truth. To be in Frei's presence—and one can gather a faint sense of this from the videotaped interview with him—was to encounter an unmatched quality of intellect, mingled with a generosity of spirit we can only call wisdom, the wisdom of one who has watched everything go down to the dust. This personal character, both grave and kindly, gave Frei an angle of vision on the modern that cut across all the conventions of academic study. It made his lifelong title, Mr. Frei, a worthy accolade, at once humble, rather democratic, and deeply reverential.

To hear Frei lecture was to feel the sheer electric current sparked by placing end-to-end and in daring arrays, the mainstays of the modern intellectual tradition, Christian and secular, each made new by this novel arrangement. I studied with Frei only as a Masters student, and then only in his massive lecture survey on Christian thought from 1648 to the present day. But from my seat among hundreds, I too caught the enchantment of an intellect that was brilliant, certainly, but also cultured in a deeply personal way, as if these figures were rudiments of one's own skin, a thought-world broad and deep and novel. Frei brought that amalgam of insight and learning and kindness to his study of theologians, the great ones, but also minor, often overlooked figures that caught his unerring eye. In this way I think Frei's closest companion in the world of letters would be a figure like Wittgenstein: an explosion of intellect in a life that demanded one's attention, and an intensity of creative thought that performed alchemy on the substance at hand. A student of Frei's knew that she or he would be changed by encountering him; the intellectual and moral compass of one's life would swing closer to true north. Of course he had his faults, as a scholar, a teacher, and by his own account as a human being. But he was suffused with a conscience, at once rational and deeply spiritual, that honored the humane, and he knew well how fragile, how ambiguous, and how vital such humanity truly is.

Like many young students of the theology of Karl Barth, I knew Frei's dissertation on Barth's break with Liberalism, and considered it the most demanding, the most instructive, and the most innovative treatment of Barth's early dogmatic formation in all of Barth studies. In my view, it holds that title uncontested. Of similar stature is his assessment of the antecedents and legacy of H. R. Niebuhr, a clarity and incisiveness of analysis unmatched in the Niebuhr literature. These works demonstrate why Hans Frei was unparalleled as a teacher of the modern turn in theology, and why his students found under his tutelage and example a confidence to return *ad fontes* and pursue dogmatic and scholastic doctrine with real verve. He created intellectual freedom in his classroom, and an ambition for serious scholarship that is the fruit of deep study and independence of mind. This, too, is Frei's legacy.

It would not be fitting to leave a tribute to Hans Frei without pausing a moment on his Jewish formation and ancestry. Frei's is not a story of conversion (if this is the right term to use), or if so, only of a fully secularized and acculturated German citizen into a religious refugee. Like many Jews of his professional class, Frei was baptized as a child and, as a young boy, sent to a Quaker school in England. All this was fully compatible with the unshakeable knowledge that one was a Jew, a Jew of German nationality and high *Kultur*. Frei considered his boyhood in Berlin a season of remarkable security and normality, laced with sheer terror. His family left all they had to get out of Germany in time but, once abroad and secure, Frei continued his voracious reading in Christian theology in school, university, and Yale Divinity School. But he had felt the "unrelenting pressure," as he put it in his personal memoir, of a party, then a state that would make Jewish citizenship, then Jewish life impossible wherever Naziism was installed in power. This pressure made Frei a Christian of singular conscience who saw that solidarity with those at risk is the only true path; it opened his eyes to the danger of state power unchecked, and this was an unsleeping gaze. Perhaps someone who comes to the study of modern theology along this steep path remains at once insider and outsider to the life he has chosen. A certain inner emigration may be the inescapable cost of such a life. But all who knew Hans Frei—Mr. Frei—all who heard him, studied under him or now read his work, will know the impress of a scholar and theologian without peer in his generation.

This collection, far more than any foreword I might write, will demonstrate why. I invite you to enter his classroom; it is a school for the intellect, yes, but also, perhaps supremely, for the soul.

PART ONE
Personalia

CHAPTER ONE

Interview with Hans W. Frei, 1980

Hans Frei: Well, I was one of the lucky ones who escaped without having seen anything more horrible than some street clashes in Germany. And I was born in the town of Breslau, which was Southeast Germany, Silesia, now ceded to Poland in 1922.

My family moved to Berlin in 1929, and though I was only seven years old, I got the sense of an extraordinarily powerful city, torn between wealthy and poor. But at the same time, a cosmopolitan and highly varied place, with a lot of *avant garde* literature, film, and so on and so on.

We were very early on in our lives politicized, because some of us, at least, saw—very vaguely, we felt—seeing brownshirts tyrannizing small clumps of people, and clashing with small groups of communists on the streets, we saw something was coming.

Interviewer: Professor Frei, why did you leave Breslau, and what was your father's profession?

Hans Frei: My father was a doctor. He was a professor in a medical school, and he was asked to join the staff of a big hospital. In fact, to direct one of its departments in Berlin in the suburb of Spandau in 1929.

We were thoroughly middle-class. My mother was a doctor too, and so we were really protected. We suffered under the worst of the chaos in Germany. For example, a kind of inflation in 1923, which makes present American inflation look like stability by contrast. But still, we had regular means of sustenance.

My father had a regular salary, so that the oncoming American depression, which had such terrible effects on the German economy, was not really felt by us in any cutting of our standard of living. We were protected. And for just that reason, we couldn't imagine that in 1933 and thereafter, our lives would be completely turned about and just pushed into sheer chaos.

Interviewer: Were you an only child?

Hans Frei: No, I was the youngest—very much the youngest—of three. And that was very fortunate for me, because both my sister and my brother, who were respectively ten and six years older than I, were finishing, or near finishing, the end of their high school career, which ends in Germany at eighteen with the so-called *abiturium*. And my sister was just starting in medical school, and that was simply out. You just didn't do that anymore. And my brother was closing—near to closing—his high school career, and he too found every avenue cut off.

That was the first step, that you simply found yourself professionally no longer able to do a thing, and socially ostracized from the rest of the community. ...

Interviewer: Do you remember conversations with your parents about what was happening?

Hans Frei: Yes. There were some very pathetic things in my family, and it was paralleled by others. My grandmother lived with us. We didn't have the small—tiny, small—nuclear family that we have in America. My grandmother kept repeating that if only the Nazis could have it impressed on them that the Jewish population suffered as keenly in the devastating losses of the First World War as any other sector of the population, surely they would change their policy.

There were a lot of people, a surprising number of Jews, like that. But my parents realized it was different. They had the uneasy feeling that it was the beginning of the end of our citizenship in Germany. And I think, by and large, they were terrified.

They—their first—their first aim was to get us kids out of Germany fast. And their second aim was that as long as we stayed there, as long as we didn't get out, don't make waves. Because if you make waves, you'll disappear. If you don't make waves, you're relatively safe.

Interviewer: Disappear?

Hans Frei: You would disappear. The fear was—by about 1935, you began to hear rumors about something called concentration camps. You began—there was even the rumor of a children's concentration camp. I don't know—I don't believe there was any such thing at that time, but I remember that I was able to get out and go to school in England, beginning in 1935. Though I returned home to Berlin during vacations. And one time I missed a train and came one train late.

And my parents were absolutely panicked when they arrived at the station for the scheduled arrival of the train that I wasn't there, because even though I was an experienced traveler, their immediate reaction was that I must've been grabbed at the frontier between Holland and Germany and stuck away into a concentration camp. So by that time, they were alert.

Interviewer: What was your perception and what was their perception—or more germane—what was their perception of a concentration camp?

Hans Frei: Vague. Vague. We knew it was brutal.

We knew it was confined to Jews, on one hand, and radical political opponents. Left-wing Democrats and Communists of the regime on the other hand. We did not yet know that it was so brutal that it was moving towards the extermination, to the mass extermination of people. That we did not yet know. ... An awful lot of people who were beaten up in the streets, incidentally, were not Jews, because they were thought to look Jewish.

Interviewer: Did you see any of that?

Hans Frei: I saw some of that, but it's amazing how little I saw. I saw some of it with a little Jewish newspaper vendor across the street from us, who on the day of the boycott of Jewish businesses on April 1, 1933, was beaten up by a crowd of brown-shirted ruffians.

When you see an innocent man being beaten up, and you know that he's not being beaten up because the law is powerless, but because the ones who are beating him up really represent the law, then you begin to experience real terror. And that—it is what blacks must feel when they experience police terror in South Africa, and sometimes in this country. Then we experienced the terror in more indirect ways.

For example, there was a day in June of 1934 when Nazis suddenly turned—the Nazis, Hitler, suddenly turned on some of his own followers. It was a power struggle within the party, and he eliminated, in effect, one wing of it. The so-called "SA," the Sturmabteilung, killing its head. But in the process, also wiping out a whole echelon of conservative leaders who were in retirement, but about whom he was still fearful, including some leaders of the Nationalist Party, and some leaders of the so-called Reichswehr, the army.

We didn't know it was happening until it was announced on the radio in a rambling and fierce speech that Hitler made the next day. And so when a very highly-respectable-looking man tried to take refuge with us in our apartment, my parents weren't there, only my grandmother and I, we felt the whole thing was weird, strange. Perhaps he was there as a provocative agent of the party. And anyway, we asked—in any case, we asked him to leave. And then I saw him being led away by the police when he went downstairs. And I looked out of the window. And the next day, I realized that he was probably an opponent of the Nazi regime. It was a—for me and for my conscience, it was a terrible occasion.

Interviewer: When he asked for refuge, what did he request?

Hans Frei: He did a very typical thing in those days. He claimed to be a regimental comrade of my father's from first World War days. The First World War was—had not ended more than fifteen, sixteen years earlier, and was very, very vividly in the mind of all Germans. It was under that pretext that he asked for refuge.

And I realized very soon that first of all, he was not a fellow Jew and secondly, that he did not know what my father's regiment was, because I knew that off by heart. We were all patriotic, and therefore knew what regiments our fathers had belonged to. And we became terribly uneasy.

Interviewer: You were twelve years old. You were—

Hans Frei: I was twelve years old, yes, and we—and my grandmother was in her seventies and somewhat doddery. And I didn't realize. Had I known, had I had the radio on—no, not then! I think that's incorrect.

But as I—as soon as we turned on the radio next day, I realized what had happened. And my parents said, you must stay indoors, because the streets—the street corners—were occupied by police with heavy weapons, as I soon found out. Because as soon as my parents said, you must stay indoors, of course, I found ways of sneaking out and saw the excitement for myself. ...

Interviewer: Did your parents discuss with you your reaction to this man that had come to the door requesting refuge?

Hans Frei: We discussed it. And my parents were very ordinary people in this respect. They were both the highly educated people, but they were scared. And they said that it was a terrible thing, but that I had probably done the right thing. ...

Interviewer: You were sent to England in 1935.

Hans Frei: Yes.

Interviewer: You must have had a different exposure when you were in England, then—and then coming back into Germany.

Hans Frei: Yes. It's a very simple thing. It's a very, very simple thing. As soon as one crossed the frontier, the atmosphere was one of fear. That's all. Just plain fear.

Interviewer: Across the frontier back into Germany?

Hans Frei: Back into Germany. Whereas, as soon as I traveled back across, first into Holland, and then into England. That's usually the way I went, because people were relaxed. You didn't fear your neighbor. As soon as you came back to Germany, you feared your neighbor. …

Interviewer: I have to persist in the question of why they sent you to a Quaker school rather than a Jewish school.

Hans Frei: In England?

Interviewer: Yes.

Hans Frei: Because, like so many other Jewish families, my family was totally secularized. That is to say they had given up their—they—we were—we knew we were Jews, you see? But that meant simply German citizens of Jewish religion until the Nazis came. That was what assimilation meant. We were totally assimilated, and as a result, my parents had us baptized, you see? My parents had all of us children baptized.

Interviewer: Before?

Hans Frei: Before that—long before the Nazis came. It was only when the Nazis came that my father, out of a sense of shame, canceled, if there is such a thing, he canceled his baptism and became—declared himself officially Jewish again. And there were quite a few of us that way. There was a whole population amounting, I think, to about 15,000 German Jews who had become officially Christian.

But even those who hadn't, you see, were so utterly assimilated that, for example, Jewish festivals were not kept. They did not go to special Jewish schools until they were forced, were forced to. And the ideal of assimilation was one that my parents stayed with.

So, first of all, it was the Quakers who were one of the few groups that made us—made it possible for me to come over. For currency regulations reasons, it was very difficult to go to another country. But the Quakers made that possible.

But secondly, I should explain that I personally had participated in a Quaker youth group as a youngster, and that my parents had become acquainted with the Quakers through me, and liked them immensely. But they would not have sent me to a Jewish school in any case. If they had found a school in England where I could become an assimilated Englishman, that's the school they would have sent me to, you see?

Interviewer: Did you go to church services? Christian services?

Hans Frei: Yeah, once in a while. My parents didn't [attend services]. I did. I went to a church school.

And remember that in Germany, at that time, there was religious instruction in the schools. In fact, that was one of the bitterest fights between Nazis and the churches, about religious—release time, religious instruction in the public schools. And I attended the Christian release-time instruction, rather than the Jewish. ...

Interviewer: ... This whole picture, if you can sort of put it together for us, of having been baptized and therefore a Christian by identification, yet Jewish by inheritance. This whole complexity in maintaining the Jewish—the Christian identity later is confusing. And I gather there was a split in the family.

Hans Frei: No, not a split, really. There was a divergence. But my father returned to Judaism. But remember, he didn't do so as a believer on the one hand, nor on the other hand, with any real cultural loyalty.

It was only simply that in the face of Nazism, one did not even try to identify oneself with the Germany one had known before. That was all over. That was all there was. So that my parents really had no investment, I think, in any community other than, on the one hand, an intellectual community, and on the other hand, the nation, the new nation to which they came.

Interviewer: Meaning the United States?

Hans Frei: Yes. But for me there was a more difficult search involved. I had, pretty much to my parents' dismay, become rather religious. And as a result, I found myself gravitating very strongly towards the Quakers. Something they sympathized with, but could not adopt for their own ideology. ...

Interviewer: You yourself, you went to a Quaker school in England. You finally came to the United States. What was your—what was your route? What was your pattern? And how did it all evolve?

Hans Frei: Well, my pattern evolved purely religiously, academically. That is to say, I became very much a member of a Protestant communion. And I really discovered my Jewish heritage, actually, through Christianity, rather than directly.

Interviewer: What does that mean?

Hans Frei: That meant that eventually I discovered the Old Testament. And began to branch out from there into some fascinating study in rabbinic Judaism. And, not that I'm an expert on that, but to some degree on rabbinic Judaism. ... But you see, I came to this only through my having become a Christian theologian, and then a student of the phenomenon of religion generally. ...

Interviewer: Well, that takes us back to you and your family and the relationship between you and your family, which must have been or must be or must have been strained as a result of this departure on your part, even though it was clear why it happened.

Hans Frei: My departure from—towards Christianity, you mean?

Interviewer: Well, yes—not really toward Christianity. But away from the condition that the family found itself in.

Hans Frei: ... The problem, really, for me is that I am, far more than a good many other people, at once an outsider to Jewishness and an insider. And I find that a very difficult way, you see. I mean, for example, if this country were to go officially anti-Semitic, which I don't see coming, but nonetheless, if you know, something like that—I would clearly identify myself with the Jewish community.

Interviewer: Why?

Hans Frei: That's because I think one should always identify oneself with those who are persecuted. I think that's only right. But I think I would do so as one whose persuasion is really one of considerable skepticism at the same time. ...

Interviewer: What is your view of people familiarizing themselves, knowing now and in future times, what happened? In other words, what is your view of remembering this era?

Hans Frei: Well, I'll have to—I'll answer it very candidly. And that is memory is a very curious thing. One has to come to terms with it. And barbarism has to be depicted.

It is an overpowering necessity that we bear witness to that, until we come to the point where it becomes the all-consuming engrossment of our lives. Until the answer to every question about our own disposition, our own outlook on what's going on in the world today, becomes encapsulated in the word Auschwitz—we can't do that. The world will keep going.

We cannot get stuck there. Otherwise, I often think that the tragedy may be that by seeking to concentrate on Auschwitz, we may actually repeat it in another form. So yes, remembering and bearing witness to future generations up to a point. But with some hope, in my mind, of going on to other things from there. ...

Interviewer: In other words, if there is the danger of overfocusing on, as you've just articulated it, on Auschwitz, there is also the danger of acceptance of that bestiality, of that brutality, which creates a circumstance of precedent.

Hans Frei: ... What I would like to see is Auschwitz—and the memory of it—become a warning memorial against the horror of ever doing anything of this sort to any minority or to any group of people, be it Cambodian, be it the Armenians, or be it the Jews.

Interviewer: I'm just burning to ask one last—just one last question. Identifying—people say that we really don't learn from history, despite caveats to the contrary. I'm wondering, whether you from your studies, from your position, your unusual vantage point feels that by bringing up all of this, we can learn to identify evil at its incipient stages, across all ethnic lines. I'm not talking about Jews, particularly. If you were talking to some schoolchildren, if you were talking to young people, what would you say about that matter?

Hans Frei: ... I think the sense that when you find group emotions, especially those of hatred, being played upon, when you find that politicians begin to single out—political leaders in any country, democratic or otherwise, begin to single out individual groups in order to distract their fellow citizens' attention from real problems, you're on your way. You're on your way towards possible, possible brutality.

Interviewer: And what can the average citizen do about noticing that?

Hans Frei: It's easy to say in what is still a democracy. The only thing the average citizen can do to notice it and to help then is to stand by the people who are being brutalized, as some Americans stood by the indiscriminate—though perfectly understandable anger against Iranians after the hostages were taken, Iranians in this country, I mean. I think one simply has to stand by those who are potentially helpless victims as early as possible. And one simply has to say for oneself, well, I'm finally a responsible individual. And my stand must always be on the side of those who are being victimized.

PART TWO

The Enduring Importance of Hans W. Frei's Work

CHAPTER TWO

Hans Frei and the Meaning of Biblical Narrative

WILLIAM C. PLACHER

Hans Frei, who died last September (1988) at the age of sixty-six after a very brief illness, was never famous outside the guild of theologians. He was a perfectionist who wrote slowly and published reluctantly. In over thirty years of teaching at Yale, he devoted himself unstintingly to his students, often at the expense of his own research. And what he wrote was never faddish and often technical. Yet future historians just may consider him the most important American theologian of his generation.

Speaking of a prominent theological figure, Frei once remarked in conversation, "He has all the gifts that make a great theologian except for a central passion—but of course that's the one thing that's indispensable." Frei certainly never thought of himself as a "great theologian," but he did have a central passion, a central idea. That idea emerged through long study, in the 1950s and '60s, of eighteenth- and nineteenth-century ways of interpreting the Bible. He grew convinced that nearly the whole of modern Christian theology, from the radical to the fundamentalist, had taken a wrong turn.

For many centuries before the modem age, most Christian theologians had read the Bible primarily as a kind of realistic narrative. It told the overarching story of the world, from creation to last judgment. Moreover, the particular coherence of this story made "figural" interpretation possible: some events in the biblical stories, as well as some nonbiblical events, prefigured or reflected the central biblical events. Indeed, Christians made sense of their own lives by locating their stories within the context of that larger story.

But somewhere around the eighteenth century, people started reading the Bible differently. Their own daily experience seemed to define for them what was "real," and so they consciously tried to understand the meaning of the Bible by locating it in *their* world.

They did that in—to overgeneralize—two ways. They saw the meaning of the biblical narratives either in the eternal truths about God and human nature that the stories conveyed or in their reference to historical events. The Bible thus fit into the world of our experience either as a set of general lessons applicable to that world or as an extension of that world developed by means of critical history.

Those two ways of interpreting the Bible remain prominent. Those who set out the moral lessons of Jesus' teaching or focus on the insights provided by his parables believe that the real point of the Gospels lies in their general lessons for our lives. On the other hand, fueled by Wolfhart Pannenberg's early arguments for the historicity of Jesus' resurrection and continuing scholarly efforts to establish which of the Gospel sayings were really spoken by the historical Jesus, some Christians still tend to treat the Bible as a historical source whose value lies primarily in its historical accuracy.

Hans Frei argued that both these approaches fundamentally distort the meaning of the text. One of the Bible's most obvious characteristics is that so much of it tells stories. Now any literary critic—or anyone with common sense—knows that the meaning of a realistically told story can never be reduced to a moral. The meaning of a Dickens novel is never simply the general lesson that the poor were ill-treated in nineteenth-century England. The particular characters and episodes of the novel are not dispensable illustrations. Similarly, to reduce to some general principle the Old Testament narratives of Israel's history or the Gospel stories of the life of Jesus misses at least part of their meaning.

On the other hand, if we try to treat these narratives primarily as the raw material for critical history, we again miss the point. To be sure, they sometimes provide that kind of historical information. But the stories themselves, in their indifference to chronology and their occasional inconsistencies, are only loosely related to questions of historical accuracy. Moreover, if we compare the fragments that a modern historian will glean as reliable against, for example, the narrative flow of the passion narratives in any of the Gospels, it is hard to deny that the historian has lost something.

Aspects of character and plot development disappear in the face of the historian's questions.

The initial meaning of a realistically told story is that, within the framework of the story, certain characters did certain deeds and underwent certain experiences. When a text provides a realistic narrative, as much of the Bible does, any interpretation that bypasses this literal reading distorts the text.

Unfortunately, for the past 200 years nearly all Christian theology, Frei argued, has been engaged in such distortion. (Jewish scholars, he thought, have by and large remained more faithful to the narrative tradition.) Frei claimed not only to have identified the distortion but to have explained it: theologians have begun with contemporary human experience and tried to make connections with the biblical message. Paul Tillich defined this approach with particular clarity (and therefore in extreme form) in his "method of correlation": "systematic theology proceeds in the following way: it makes an analysis of the human situation out of which the existential questions arise, and it demonstrates that the symbols used in the Christian message are the answers to these questions." Frei believed that those who develop theology that way, beginning with existential questions arising out of the human situation, will start reading the biblical stories as either historical raw material or timeless truths and moral lessons. Either approach loses sight of the way in which the stories function as realistic narratives.

A Christian theology that respects the meaning of the biblical narratives must begin simply by retelling those stories, without any systematic effort at apologetics, without any determined effort to begin with questions arising from our experience. The stories portray a person—a God who acts in the history of Israel and engages in self-revelation in Jesus of Nazareth. They help us learn about that person in the way that a great novelist describes a character or that a telling anecdote captures someone's personality. They provide insights that we lose if we try to summarize the narrative in a nonnarrative form. No abstract account of God's faithfulness adequately summarizes Exodus. The Gospels surpass any abstract account of God's love.

Still, the Bible is not simply another realistic novel, and its interpreters need to attend to all its special characteristics. As Erich Auerbach, a literary critic Frei much admired, once wrote of the Bible: "Far from seeking ... merely to make us forget our own reality for a few hours, it seeks to overcome our reality: we are to fit our own life into its world, feel ourselves to be elements in its structure of universal history." Christians who tell these stories, stories that are rich, enigmatic, sometimes puzzling and ambiguous, can find that their lives fit into the world they describe—indeed, that our stories suddenly seem to make more sense when seen in that context.

Frei thought that Christian theology ought to be descriptive; it ought to lay out a Christian view of the world. That view will reflect the enigmas and ambiguities of the biblical texts, and it will be a view of the *whole* world. A Christian theologian, Frei explained, will therefore

> do ethics to indicate that this narrated, narratable world is at the same time the ordinary world of our experience, and he will do ad hoc apologetics, in order to throw into relief particular features of this world by distancing them from or approximating them to other descriptions. ... But none of these other descriptions or, for that matter, argument with them can serve as a 'predescription' for the world of Christian discourse.

Letting any such "predescription" set the theological agenda leads to distorting the meaning of the biblical texts.

As I have indicated, Frei distrusted theologies that began with contemporary experience, and he was reticent in discussing his own religious life. He loved to talk, but he rarely talked about himself. When writing about him, one wants to respect that reticence. Still, a word about his life seems in order.

He was born in Germany in 1922, the son of a physician. His family was of Jewish background and had to flee after the Nazis came to power. He received part of his education in Britain before coming to this country and landing a scholarship to study textiles at North Carolina State University. A chance meeting with H. Richard Niebuhr led him to correspond with the theologian and then undertake seminary and graduate study at Yale. (It is fitting that his first major publication, the introductory chapters of the Niebuhr festschrift, *Faith and Ethics,* and his last completed lecture, read for him at Harvard during his final illness, both concerned the work of this teacher he so admired, even when he disagreed with him.)

After briefly serving a New Hampshire parish and then teaching at Wabash College in Indiana and the Episcopal Seminary of the Southwest in Austin, Texas, he returned to Yale in 1957 as a faculty member. Writing came slowly for him. He published the original version of *The Identity of Jesus Christ: The Hermeneutical Bases of Dogmatic Theology* in a Presbyterian adult education magazine called *Crossroads* in 1967, but it did not appear in book form until 1975 (Fortress), the year after he published *The Eclipse of Biblical Narrative: A Study in Eighteenth- and Nineteenth-Century Hermeneutics* (Yale University Press, 1974). *Eclipse* traced his historical argument about the wrong turn in hermeneutics; *Identity* sketched what a Christology based on his principles might look like. Near the end of his life, he published a number of essays, most notably a chapter on D. F. Strauss in *Nineteenth-Century Religious Thought in the West* (Ninian Smart et al., Cambridge University Press, 1985) and an essay on the literal sense of Scripture in *The Bible and the*

Narrative Tradition (edited by Frank McConnell, Oxford University Press, 1986). Plans are afoot to publish a number of lectures he was reworking at the time of his death.

For many of his students and friends, though, nothing on paper quite captures the Hans Frei we knew and loved: the devoted teacher; the faithful friend; a man stubborn about his ideas but genuinely, sometimes unnervingly, modest about himself; prone nervously to stay up the night before a presentation to rewrite his lecture. He was the only person I have ever known who both loved gossip and totally lacked malice.

In the 1950s and '60s, when Frei was developing his ideas, many of his concerns were thoroughly unfashionable. In a number of ways, his work remains out of fashion, but it is striking that at least four of his interests now seem much more in step with the times.

Half a generation or so ago, most New Testament scholars focused on the individual sayings and stories of the Gospels. Some sought the Christian *kerygma,* the call to faith, in individual passages. Others evaluated each brief unit as a historical document: When would this story have been told? What does it indicate about the circumstances of its telling? Does it provide evidence about the historical Jesus? Whatever questions they asked, however, not many scholars turned from particular passages to ask about the narrative sweep or pattern of a whole Gospel.

Today, however, biblical scholars increasingly analyze the plot of biblical narratives, the way the literary forms work, the patterns of climax and tension. They often find they have more to learn from, and discuss with, literary critics than with historians; indeed, the literary analysis of the Bible is becoming a minor industry.

Frei certainly did not by himself cause that shift. It has many sources, from redaction critics who started looking at each Gospel as a whole to literary scholars like Northrop Frye and Frank Kermode who have called renewed attention to the narrative shape of biblical texts. But Frei saw the point early on, and his work remains the deepest probing of the theological implications of such approaches.

In addition to anticipating new conversations between biblical scholars and literary critics, Frei's work also pointed to new conversation partners for theologians. His suspicion of systematic apologetics might at first glance make Frei seem a kind of theological isolationist, retreating from wider circles of intellectual discussion. To those who watched him at Yale with his finger in every intellectual and political pie, such a portrait is unrecognizable.

In addition to having an ongoing interest in literary criticism, he had learned from British philosophers like Gilbert Ryle ways of talking about how the narrative of actions and events defines a person's identity. His concern for the way a community sees and describes its world led to affinities with anthropologists like Clifford Geertz and sociologists like Peter Berger. Frei said on at least one occasion that among theologians he claimed to be a historian and among historians he claimed to be a theologian—but he avoided a complete identity crisis by being consistently clear that he was not a philosopher! On an ad hoc basis, however, he was intrigued by the parallels between his own suspicion of systematic apologetics and the suspicions concerning systematic "foundations" of knowledge growing among deconstructionists and some analytic philosophers. Sometimes the most secular of scholars found that what Frei was doing, with his attention to narrative and his interest in the language that shapes a particular community, made more sense to them than the work of many theologians much more systematically concerned to address other academic disciplines. (Jeffrey Stout's recent *Ethics after Babel* nicely illustrates this.)

Frei's work seems timely in yet a third way. Much of the most interesting recent work in Christian ethics discusses the way narratives shape our understanding of Christian life. Ethicists as different as Stanley Hauerwas, Gilbert Meilaender, and James McClendon (as well as philosophers like Alasdair MacIntyre) propose that ethics is not primarily a matter of making particular decisions in isolation—what Hauerwas calls "quandary ethics." Rather, we make decisions on the basis of beliefs about what sorts of virtues seem important, what sort of human life we believe to be good. To answer that kind of question, a principle or a rule is often less helpful than a story. I may get more help in deciding how to make ethical decisions as a Christian by reading *Pilgrim's Progress* or a biography of Dorothy Day or Martin Luther King, Jr.— or by reading the Gospels—than by reading an academic discussion of medical ethics. Here, too, Frei's interest in the narrative patterns that shape a Christian life now seems prophetic.

Fourth, there is Karl Barth. Frei was not simply a "Barthian" (neither was Barth!), but Barth certainly seemed to him the best exemplar of a "descriptive" theologian who eschewed systematic apologetics and simply tried to lay out a Christian view of the world with attention to its own internal logic. When Frei was writing on these matters in the 1960s, Barth seemed to many obsolete, like a man writing a great defense of Ptolemaic astronomy two generations after Copernicus. There was some interest in his Romans commentary, but the many massive volumes of his *Church Dogmatics* went largely unread.

Much remains unchanged. But at times, in contrast to theologians who try systematically to draw out the "religious" implications supposedly underlying all human experience, Barth seems to be the theologian who has taken radical secularly most seriously. At least the situation has grown more ambiguous. It is possible that, in a crazy, postmodern, thoroughly secular time, Christian theologians might discover that the old man in Basel offered us more help than anyone in thinking about how to do theology. In any event, if we do make that discovery, we will find in this matter, as in many others, that Frei was there before us.

Frei was ironic by nature, and never more so than when thinking about his own "influence." He was sometimes credited with founding a "school" called "narrative theology," but he always doubted that there was such a thing—and would be against it if there were.

He thought the narrative character of the biblical texts had some implications for how those texts ought to be interpreted. But to try to develop some general theory of the narrative shape of human experience as a foundation for Christian theology seemed to him "first to put the cart before the horse and then cut the lines and pretend the vehicle is self-propelled." In a variety of ways, those who offered to agree with him sometimes found that he wasn't sure *he* quite agreed with *them.*

Still, I do not want to overstate that ironic spirit. He had worked a long time without many people expressing much interest in his work. In the last ten years or so of his life, his work drew attention and bore fruit. Though he may have mistrusted the taste of some of that fruit, on the whole he was grateful and happy. He was excited by Alasdair MacIntyre's early and enthusiastic review of *The Eclipse of Biblical Narrative* and later proud and pleased about a new generation of his students beginning in the early 1970s, theologians like Charles Wood and Ronald Thiemann—proud that they had learned from him, pleased that they were independent enough to disagree with him on occasion. He continued to value his relations with colleagues at Yale like George Lindbeck, David Kelsey, Wayne Meeks, and Gene Outka, and he eagerly welcomed the 1984 publication of Lindbeck's *Nature of Doctrine,* with its model of a "postliberal theology," for which Frei's work is the paradigm.

Yet no one was more conscious than Frei that he had left many questions unanswered. The Bible is not just one big story, but a complicated collection of narrative and nonnarrative material. Even with straightforward narratives, in the Bible or anywhere else, a variety of critics from feminists to deconstructionists have reminded us that the meaning of a text can lie as much in what it does not say as in what it says. Frei knew that and, with a modesty as frustrating as it was admirable, was likely to admit that he did not himself know how to solve the problems even as he remained convinced that he had glimpsed an insight that was somehow true.

Beyond even such questions, a more fundamental issue remains. Frei's theology is finally *church* theology: it first of all addresses the Christian community and invites that community to let the biblical narratives shape its vision of the world. To what extent parts of that community will respond to such invitations may be the most important unanswered question regarding Frei's work.

"The most fateful issue for Christian self-description," Frei wrote in the McConnell volume, "is that of regaining its autonomous vocation as a religion, after its defeat in its secondary vocation of providing ideological coherence, foundation, and stability to Western culture." We no longer live in what Kierkegaard called Christendom. But old habits die hard, and Christian theologians had fallen into the habit of trying to delineate the religious dimension of our general culture. Some seem not to notice that our culture, by and large, isn't much interested. Some grow angry at the lack of interest. Some try all the more desperately to make the appropriate connections.

In a post-Christian age, however, Christianity might instead try to regain "its autonomous vocation as a religion." We Christians still have stories to tell—distinctive stories. Stories about how God worked in the life of Israel, and God's self-revelation in the life of Jesus Christ. Stories that define a community different from the world around us because of the way these stories shape our self-understanding, a community that may sometimes be wildly radical politically and on other issues seem conservative, but will not let anyone else's vision set its agenda. Hans Frei called us to be tellers of such tales.

CHAPTER THREE

Hans W. Frei in Context: A Theological and Historical Memoir

JOHN F. WOOLVERTON

In the last decade of the twentieth century Hans Frei (1922–88) has emerged, as one observer judges, as the "most significant figure in North American theology and religious studies during the last quarter of this century."[1] Like the publication of Albert Schweitzer's *Quest for the Historical Jesus* (1906, trans. 1910), that of Frei's *Eclipse of the Biblical Narrative: A Study in Eighteenth and Nineteenth Century Hermeneutics* (1974) and *The Identity of Jesus Christ: The Hermeneutical Bases of Dogmatic Theology* (1975) can be seen to mark a major watershed in the history of biblical studies and of constructive theology.[2] After the appearance of Schweitzer's *Quest* and Frei's *Eclipse*, no one seriously interested in the principles and procedures of biblical interpretation could ignore them. Both studies pointed to the shortcomings of previous generations, both sounded the tocsin at the end of an era, and both dramatically championed a fresh approach to Christian scripture. Both books were in fact milestones,[3] though of rather different character. Schweitzer was more the dramatist, especially at the beginning and the end of his *Quest,* and Frei a Sherlock Holmes who, having read the clues, "confronted us with the largely forgotten history of our own minds, returning us to fundamental questions that had seemed long settled."[4]

But then each book, apart from its startling impact, has, I suspect, remained unread by many professionals and students of theology alike. It is a pity. Perhaps the recent appearance in the 1990s of other works by Frei—*Types of Christian Theology* (1992) and *Theology and Narrative: Selected Essays* (1993)—will encourage greater attention to *Eclipse* as well as to Frei's thought in general.

My knowledge of Frei comes from many conversations, from letters, from thirty-five years of friendship, and from a more or less formal interview which I conducted with him in August 1975. His words deserve to be recorded and remembered. While this essay may not reveal new facets of his thought or add to the assessment of his role in academic theology in America, it may serve to introduce him to Episcopal readers who did not know him, or heighten for those who did, some aspects of his thought and his attitudes. I should also like to provide a context. But as Jeffrey Stout has remarked about those who honored Frei in the *Festschrift, Scriptural Authority and Narrative Interpretation* (1987), "Nobody in this volume even begins to do for Frei what Frei once did for [H. Richard] Niebuhr.[5] That is, nobody ventures an interpretation of his place in the unfolding history of recent theology."[6] Nor do I. This essay is only a very modest beginning.

And then it seems fitting for a member of his own church to write about him, for Hans Frei was a priest in the Episcopal Church and for a time taught at the Episcopal Theological Seminary of the Southwest before returning to Yale University. In Frei's case one does not want to make too much of his association with the denomination or, on the other hand, so little as to fail to mention it. The fact is that while he continued to interest himself in Episcopal theological education and in such voluntary societies as the Episcopal Women's History Project,[7] denominational polemics were not of any great interest to him. At times he was acerbic about certain Anglican attitudes and practices. He was also generous and humane and did not belittle fellow church members for either their words or their deeds.

"How do you know," Frei asked, "that Adam and Eve were not the first man and woman of the human race?" And Frei was quite serious and deliberate. The question did not signal a fundamentalist attitude on his part, only a reticence about dismissing the biblical accounts as incapable of maintaining an integrity of their own or as historically untrustworthy or both. Frei was a theologian who respected the Bible on its own terms and not on those of philosophical, historical, and psychological perspectives which were foreign to its particular ethos.[8] Moreover—if one may paraphrase Ronald Thiemann—Frei himself, like the Bible, did not so much rely on dogmatic assertion as invite and persuade people to neglected and often simple features which lay in particular styles of writing.[9]

At the beginning of his teaching career, Frei taught a course in the interpretation of history, a subject to which he would return at the very end of his life.[10] He had students read, among many others, Thucydides' *History of the Peloponnesian War.* To the work of the fifth-century BC Athenian historian Frei accorded the same focused respect which he gave the Bible. (Both were history-like.) He did not try to fold the one into the other. The point must be made at the outset: while maintaining strong cultural interests, he never tried to force culture into the apologetic arena where the score was always Christians 12, Lions 0, or defend the faith or make it meaningful to someone called "modern man." He sought rather to emphasize the inner consistency of both scripture and Christian faith, on the one hand, and of literature and the arts, on the other. Each had its place; he did not want to make either say what it did not want to say.

By the early 1970s with the deaths of H. Richard Niebuhr (1962), Paul Tillich (1965), Karl Barth (1968), and Reinhold Niebuhr (1971), one heard it said that the age of the theological giants had passed. Certainly there seemed to be few minds on the horizon who could match the general influence of these men either on the churches or on American life as a whole. Henceforth, one colleague told me in the early 1970s, social ethics would dominate the theological scene—or at least the American theological scene. Neither prediction, as it turned out, came true. While in the late 1970s and '80s conservative evangelicals proclaimed their new, self-glorifying Americanism, and while liberal Christians often voiced national self-hate, both opted for a subjective, individualistic appropriation of Christian faith. Both believed that the indispensable moment of either religious awakening or psychological enlightenment *(gnosis)* occurred when the individual's autonomous life journey met divine grace. Such a meeting occurred in the form of either realizing a "personal" relationship with Jesus or exchanging the pain of existence and its estrangements, imagined or otherwise, for the comfort of archetypal, "spiritual" experience. The one wrenched Jesus from his circumstances, the other universalized the circumstances and made Jesus but one example of them. Popularly, both evangelicals and liberals centered their search for that indispensable conjunction of individual quest and divine grace in "liturgical" experience. That experience was now understood, however, not as the "work of the *people,*" that is, as a communal act, but in privatized meanings in ceremony, symbol, and song. At the same time in the churches—and for that matter in the nation—there was an absence of common discourse about important political, ethical, and moral issues.[11] The anticipated dominance of a socially and ethically informed public theology, historically understood and expressed, did not emerge.

It was Hans Frei who in an important address on H. Richard Niebuhr delivered at Harvard University in 1988 (by Ronald Thiemann since Frei was then fatally stricken) provided what could well turn out to be the basis of such common discourse. In that carefully wrought essay Frei did four things: First, he stated that Niebuhr had addressed his country in cautious and circumspect terms. Assuming that the nation was "*the* crucial collective historical agent of the day,"[12] he went on to define its path both historically and theologically. Niebuhr's remarks came at a curious moment (1943) when the present was dark indeed but the future beckoned hopefully. Niebuhr reminded Americans that in the future their duty would be to behave in a restrained and responsible manner as the new, greatest world power. Second, Frei noted approvingly Niebuhr's vision of American Christians as "public citizens rather than private believers" and "that this vision was part of the business of the interpreter of history" as both analyst and involved agent. (It was clear by implication that Frei too, as Niebuhr had done, was quite consciously continuing the tradition of analyst and agent.) Third, Frei called attention to the persistence of the American Puritan tradition for which he had great empathy. And, finally, he was, with characteristic gratitude, rounding out his relationship with the man who had been his greatest theological and personal mentor and with the nation whose history he, as a one-time refugee from Nazi Germany, so manifestly made his own in language and culture.

But in that same, final essay Frei also touched on the fact that the last two decades in theology had been marked, among other things, by "the deadly serious and immensely learned search for a proper [biblical] hermeneutic."[13] And of course he himself contributed significantly to that search. He did so historically in *Eclipse* and elsewhere in his constructive, explanatory study, *The Identity of Jesus Christ,* and critically with his difficult and brilliant essay, "The 'Literal Reading' of the Biblical Narrative in the Christian Tradition: Does It Stretch or Will It Break?" in *The Bible and the Narrative Tradition.* Frei, David Kelsey, Gene Outka, and George Lindbeck have become the leaders of what, no doubt to the embarrassment of all of them, has been dubbed the "New Yale Theology."[14]

Frei did not do theology in the grand manner either as moral philosopher, or as dogmatic church theologian, or, what is least possible given his affinity for Karl Barth, as *systematic* theologian. Rather his penetrating inquiries led him to question the assumptions of his age, mark their weaknesses, and then suggest alternatives. He addressed the great issue of scriptural authority to which the late twentieth-century church had turned and in doing so altered the theological landscape.

He was, first of all as a young person, a refugee and, like Henry Kissinger, a German, Jewish refugee.[15] The parallels between the two men are interesting: both immigrated with their families to America in the same year;[16] each retained a very pessimistic view of life as a result of his early experience.[17] Kissinger's "world view was dark and suffused with a sense of tragedy;"[18] while Frei admitted, "My natural [as opposed to positive religious] bent is very pessimistic."[19] For Kissinger "the holocaust destroyed the connection between God's will and the progress of history."[20] For Frei history seemed a "highly relative process under an overarching, inscrutable fate which is in its own inscrutable way utterly trustworthy and is therefore worthy of worship and trust."[21] Frei had a strong sense of providence. And in this "positive religious bent, the fatedness of history is [for me] a highly Christological providence."[22] How one interpreted history was crucial. The question was whether that interpretation involved the predestining grace of divine governance and responding person, that is, not "totally free or purely originating,"[23] on the one hand, or simply the "uninterrupted freedom of initiatory human action," on the other. In the latter case God's "governance" is only "the inevitability or realism of collective self-interest."[24] These two views were represented by H. Richard and Reinhold Niebuhr, respectively. Frei sided with his mentor, H. Richard Niebuhr, whom he first heard when Niebuhr addressed a Baptist student meeting in the late 1930s at North Carolina State University. It was a relationship which would last, not always easily, for the next twenty-five years.

In the meantime Frei embraced American citizenship with appreciation and enthusiasm; he found the dynamism of the country—and its theological culture—irrepressible. Among the German Jewish, Christian, and liberal intellectuals who found asylum in the United States, many were not as able fully to participate in the American ethos as Frei. Of the generation of emigré German scholars older than he, Theodor E. Mommsen "suffered miserably with the language (to the end of his life he spoke English with a thick foreign accent and had trouble writing clear English prose)."[25] Wilhelm Pauck, on the other hand, a contemporary of Mommsen's, spoke English—as did Frei—with complete confidence and even elegance and enjoyed thoroughly the world of the American church and university. The time of immigration to the United States or the age of the immigrant was not always the deciding factor.[26] While Frei had an American wife and three children, that alone cannot explain his well-affected relation to his adopted country. Tillich, for instance, "was perhaps the one who embraced America most whole-heartedly ... [still] an ambiguity lurked in the background: he too remained more German than his American admirers suspected ... [and never lost that] quasi-pantheist nature mysticism of German Romantic religiosity."[27] Frei, whose parents sent him out of Germany at the relatively young age of twelve,[28] was wholly devoid of nature mysticism. Indeed he came to criticize particularly the most striking examples of the German romantic mindset, Schelling and Schleiermacher.[29]

In 1959 Frei returned to Germany for the first time since 1934. Clearly he arrived as an *American* professor on sabbatical and not at all as a returning German exile. "While we puzzle a good deal about what it is to be German," he wrote, "a lot of people here naturally enough wonder about us Americans."[30] He remarked on the fact that Europe's historic sights were, because of the millions of tourists, just that, "sights and no longer objects hallowed through the accumulation of daily use." He then went on to notice "something in Italy which is wholly absent from Germany: graciousness, lightness, charm of form and humor." In the university library in Heidelberg, he worked next to a professor from Florence who "often complains that the Germans do not know what 'grazia' is, either in the Christian or the classical sense, either as humility or as a form of humor."[31] It was not that Frei and his wife, Geraldine, had met with anything but "great kindness on every side" from the German people. Still the longer they stayed the more the whole question of Nazism seemed "to hover vaguely about in the atmosphere—far more than it had done in the recent past." Frei's characteristic sensitivity to his political surroundings led him to comment at length on German ambivalence about the regime of Adolf Hitler:

> The Germans' recent "unconquered past," as they refer to it here, has suddenly burst in on them. It is not simply the shock registered here over the [recent] anti-Semitic outbursts. Long before that we discovered how similar our reaction to Germany was to that of many other Americans who are here this year. It has in every case been curiously ambivalent. We all felt a certain distance, not to say antipathy toward the Germans, largely for their apparent lack of concern over (or was it shamefaced refusal to come to terms with?) Nazi history. So far as many Germans are concerned that is all in the past.[32]

He went on to say that he agreed with Daniel Boorstin "in regard to the Germans at least," that it has been European history, not American history, which has displayed the most radical breaks in continuity. While he did not believe fascism stood "full blown around the corner," he was critical of Adenauer, "who evidently sets the tone of the government all by himself," for treating latent anti-Semitism and the "casual blinking of the past in government, judiciary, teaching profession, etc., as of little concern." It was in that spirit, he added, that everyone "shed Nazism in 1945 as something indecent, and why not go on from there!" Now he noticed considerable chagrin on the part of Germans at "the inescapable fact that something touching the collective conscience of the whole people can't be dealt with so simply and externally."

The year in Germany was not a particularly easy one for Frei. It had an ironic ending: He managed to get an interview with the Jewish, Nazi historian of Protestant theology and now recluse, Emanuel Hirsch. In return Frei had to agree not to raise any questions about Hirsch's past support of Hitler. And Frei found nothing casual about this evasion of the past.

England was a different matter entirely. Throughout his life he remained grateful to the English. "After all," he once remarked, "they took me in." He admired greatly Isaiah Berlin's essay on Winston Churchill; he spoke highly of Austin Farrer, "an anglo-catholic who toward the end of his life became an evangelical,"[33] and he retained friendships with Anglican theologians such as Maurice Wiles and Stephen Sykes. More particularly "under the influence of Dostoevsky and Søren Kierkegaard," he confided, "in 1945 I came to consider the monastic life." "This moved me in an Anglican direction."[34] But it was William Temple's *Nature, Man, and God* (1934) which he read when he was first out of Yale Divinity School and a Baptist minister in northern New Hampshire. It proved to be *"the book,* and through it I became for a time a Whiteheadian." Frei went on to study such Anglo-Catholic works as Charles Gore's *Lux Mundi* (1889)[35] and *Essays Catholic and Critical* (1926). "I always regarded the Baptists as an ante-room, and knew I would go into either the Lutheran, Presbyterian, or Episcopal ministry."[36] At the time he wanted a "sacramentally centered worship life and a broad doctrinal freedom which came to grips with modern thought."[37] In 1947 he was ordained in the Episcopal Church.[38] But in the end "I became theologically involved without the countervailing force of Book of Common Prayer worship." Later he complained about the excessive number of celebrations of the Eucharist in the Episcopal Church:

> To introduce the whole Eucharistic bit is one thing, but to think it crucial is another. ... Would others, who don't want to go that liturgical route, still have the liberty of the other option?[39]

Frei became critical of the tendency of students at Berkeley Divinity School (which by then had become part of Yale Divinity School) to engage in eucharistic worship by themselves. He wanted them to join with others and not be isolated and self-congratulatory.

As for himself, Frei was quick to admit "I always knew that I would settle for a strong Christian tradition rather than a denomination."[40] He was frank about being a "casual Episcopalian." Early in his career he concentrated on the continental theologians.

Luther [he continued] was an early influence on me at Yale Divinity School, but also More and Cross[41] when I got to New Hampshire. They influenced my Anglicanism. They gave a more successful job of the *via media,* but the book was not a *major* influence. H. Richard Niebuhr drew my attention to the seventeenth-century metaphysical poets, particularly John Donne.[42]

But by 1980 he declared that his "relation to the Anglican communion is really in limbo." He was quick to admit that "there is nothing representatively Anglican at all about my statements." But then he wanted it made very clear that it was not because he taught in a university that he failed to give the fullest allegiance to the Episcopal Church.

Far from wanting to confine my theological thought and writing in and to the university, I am actually thoroughly persuaded that a theologian has to write fully as much in the context of a (or "the") church, but that reinforces my doubts, because in effect my communal Christian context simply isn't Anglican. I'll never change formal affiliation, but my heart simply isn't in the worship or ethos of Anglicanism. This personal movement already began in Austin [Texas] and accelerated thereafter.[43]

Nor was he content with the increasing separation from the denomination he had joined: "I am troubled by it and would like very much to discuss it with you at length—perhaps on a quiet evening next summer." He was, he declared, not at all sure where he stood. "I find Quaker meeting glorious right now, but it won't do in the long run and has little to do with my theological convictions." In any case, he continued,

> I have no worries about writing both in a university and in a church setting. There is no conflict there; what I don't know is where my church is. You can see that when I inquire from you anxiously how the winds are blowing at Virginia Seminary, I am being partially selfish. I somehow thought of Virginia (vaguely and uninformedly) as a link to my residual Episcopalianism. ...[44]

In the meantime, in 1985, when a dozen or so evangelical Episcopalians in the reformed tradition determined to challenge their church to restate its doctrinal position in more up-to-date terms than the Thirty-nine Articles, Frei joined them. He suggested contributors, critiqued manuscripts, and wrote commentaries on three of the Thirty-nine Articles himself.[45]

Over a decade before Frei's admission of his growing distance from Anglicanism, he and his family had spent a sabbatical year at Cambridge University (1966). There the accelerating personal change which had begun in Texas in the 1950s was not slowed by what he observed both about the state of English theology and about the church in the UK. "Theologically there isn't terribly much doing in Cambridge," he wrote at the end of the year, "but then, there isn't terribly much doing in the Church of England anywhere in these emerald isles, so far as I can see."[46] Nonetheless he enjoyed the pace of life, "so utterly relaxed after the hectic and competitive strain of Yale." Frei noted that Norman Pittenger had taken up residence at King's. He himself had the "privileges of Trinity College, ancient, rigid, snobbish and immensely rich—a real anachronism on the current British scene." As always, however, he was touched by the fellow feeling of the English: "They are remarkably courteous and hospitable people. ..."

But then there was the larger context of his theology. Hans Frei was part of the reformed tradition which we have come to associate with a line of march extending from Augustine to Anselm to Calvin and thence to the American Puritans, Edwards, and Karl Barth. "All through the period when I was a Baptist minister,"[47] he recalled, "there was Søren Kierkegaard,

Dostoevsky, Augustine, and particularly the anti-Pelagian Augustine." He liked Augustine's freedom of interpretation of scripture "so long as the love of God and neighbor is enhanced by how you read (as Augustine, for example, stressed)."[48] He became critical of Luther's emphasis on "'all' of God becoming immanent [at the Nativity] in this little child." He preferred Calvin, as he remarked, "because in Calvin there is always something of God which remains transcendent." Calvin's higher estimation of the constructive part of the law in the Old Testament appealed to him strongly.[49] Strongest of all was the fact that for Calvin, "History, doctrine, description of shape of life, all converged for him and were held together by their common ingredience in the storied text of the scriptural world, and by the Holy Spirit's internal testimony to that text through his awakening of the reader's and hearer's faithful beholding."[50] It was a long and telling sentence, not only about Calvin's belief but about Frei's. He quoted approvingly the work of Hans-Joachim Kraus who saw that for Calvin the Bible itself was not inspired and so does not itself inspire but communicates and informs. "The reader, not the text, is to be illumined by the internal or inspiring testimony of the Spirit so that he may discern the written biblical word to be God s own Word, intended for his own and the Church's edification."[51]

Equally important, Frei also saw that for Calvin there was no need for any "systematic scheme for correlating faith as a proposition to be believed and faith as personal life stance...."[52] Modern theologians, Frei judged, created an unnecessary and wearying problem for themselves—and for their readers—by trying to "argue the coherent intelligibility of a divine revelation" which was riveted to a long-gone Christ event, on the one hand, and to "the present personal commerce between God and man," on the other. Both moves, one declaring the Bible *qua* book to be inspired, the other to bid Christians rely on an extra-biblical scheme, demoted the work of the Holy Spirit to a secondary status. (Both moves, of course, represented respectively nineteenth- and twentieth-century fundamentalism and liberalism.) Frei then, in a sentence about Calvin that must stand as a key to his own thought as well as to his debt to the sixteenth-century reformer, wrote, "For Calvin, the coherence of the internal testimony of the Spirit with the meaning of the text was simply part of the same correlation in which promise and fulfillment, law and gospel, Old and New Testament go together; in which history, doctrine, and life description cohere by virtue of the common or joint depiction they receive in the biblical text."[53] There was no need for any other theory.

Frei associated himself as well with Calvin's American followers in New England. The New England Puritans became models for him and played an important part in his appropriation of the American past. Nor was his interest limited to the colonial period:

When you say there is so much in this crazy world that interests Maggie and you, you remind me of the qualities that made not the Puritans but the best of their 19th century inheritors so great, and so essential for all of us. Yes, affirmation first, before all qualifications. Gerry has more of it than I do. I guess I have a rather somber streak.[54]

He himself believed, as he said of H. Richard Niebuhr, that the "Puritan-Protestant tradition provided the chief clue to the long-range continuity between Christian and American identities."[55] He would send off in the mail copies of Yale dissertations on the Puritans with which he was impressed, such as that of David E. Laurence on Jonathan Edwards and the Bible,[56] or Harry Stout's book, *The New England Soul*.[57] And characteristically he was full of praise for such students and colleagues. He also knew, quite correctly, that their ideas were likely to be fed in turn into others' courses! And he was right.

But it was Karl Barth, next to H. Richard Niebuhr, who influenced him the most, together with Augustine: "All through my Baptist period I was reading Barth—and also Schweitzer." While at this time he also liked Bultmann's "apparently strong eschatology" and was "enamoured of radical criticism [of the Bible]—mostly German,"[58] throughout these formative theological years (1945 to 1947) in his Baptist parsonage in northern New Hampshire, there was Barth. "Barth influenced me deeply theologically," he remarked, again without equivalent interest in matters of liturgy and ritual.[59] When Frei completed his doctoral thesis at Yale, "The Doctrine of Revelation in Karl Barth, 1909–1922: The Nature of the Break with Liberalism," such was the size of his accomplishment in the dissertation that Niebuhr thanked him and said, "Either one of them would have done."[60] Frei, breaking away from Kierkegaard as Barth himself had done, judged that

> Karl Barth is the only theologian who has given us a comic vision of reality. … The Christian vision and that of paradox and of suffering are, said Barth, antitheses to each other. The comic looks at man from a transcendent perspective which has no room for tragedy. The problem of death and of non-being is a problem we do not have to face directly. Therefore those ultimate exigencies we do not face: Christ did it for us. Death is the deeply sad side of creation, but it is not tragedy.[61]

Barth had made fun of the existentialists; Frei, acknowledging his debt to Barth,[62] did likewise: "Grace does not come through the ultimate facing of non-being," he declared. "The one who makes this claim is a *poseur*!" First and foremost, Frei went on, he draws inordinate attention to himself, to his fears and to his anxieties, and demands that others listen and sympathize. He hopes by this means to lead others to an appreciation of similar features discovered in the life and experience of Jesus.

Frei had begun in the 1940s to concentrate on late eighteenth- and early nineteenth-century Christology as an area of research and was led into "an ambiguous relation to Hegel and Friedrich Schleiermacher." He began to think that "liberal Protestantism was one of the most magnificent technical accomplishments and at the same time one of the profoundest errors in theology."[63] He found three "errors of faith: first, that the starting point of theology is anthropology; second, the belief that the proper mode of anthropology was to analyze man as self-consciousness, and, third, that out of this one could derive Christology."[64] Drawing attention to the preface of Hegel's *Phenomenology of the Spirit,* Frei saw that

> Through the Middle Ages people believed that their self-consciousness was mediated to them through God. Their self-consciousness was mediate, not immediate. The problem of the modern Christian is that his consciousness is directly of himself. He hopes his self-consciousness will mediate God-consciousness to him. Despite Tillich and Schleiermacher, [I would say that] God as the ground of being is simply not there! [I am in fact] more sceptical than Tillich: Man has no self-consciousness in which a God-consciousness is present. In addition all modern Protestant theology forgot that man is not merely a "self-consciousness"; there is the body of man as well. Man is not simply a self-consciousness but an embodied consciousness.[65]

Austin Farrer, he concluded, saw that humans are *embodied* spirits; "I think he is the greatest [modern] Anglican theologian." Otherwise he remained critical of Anglican theology: "The worst mistake of Anglicanism is the assertion that there can be a normative apologetic which allows one to chart the path from pre-Christian to Christian faith." The Christian's "business is to elucidate as non-existentially and as formally as possible that the ground of moving from unfaith to faith is God's providence," not our self-consciousness.[66]

His criticism of liberal theology in general and of the three errors he detected made him, he declared in 1973, "feel isolated." He professed himself "closer to the common language folk."[67] He was particularly caustic about those who combined "piety and critical dishonesty, who declared that all history is relative to the perspective of the historian and who make no hard claims." Yet he wished it known that "much of what [Van] Harvey speaks against I would too." Among contemporary liberal theologians,

> [Gerhard] Ebeling is the perpetuator of Schleiermacher. On the other hand [among the liberals] I have the greatest sympathy with [Jürgen] Moltmann, but finally not even here for with him the starting point is still anthropology,

that is, the death/resurrection becomes a principle rather than specific [occurrence]. Moltmann still uses [the] death and resurrection as a *motifs*.⁶⁸

Along with "Arthur Danto and Karl Barth, [I would affirm that] there is no substitute for the specific narrative. When one forsakes [that narrative] one forsakes history."⁶⁹ On the subject of the specific narrative, Frei believed that the pre-critical Christian thinkers were right: "As long as one is Christian all one's reading of the whole world has to be taken up figurally in that specific narrative."

On the other hand, the "biblical terminology is not by itself our proper terminology." For Frei there was a close relationship between philosophy and theology: "Philosophy gives us our formal vocabulary,"⁷⁰ though it is, as in Barth, subordinate within theology, and provisional.⁷¹ Thus in distinction from the Pentecostal/Fundamentalist position, he would have us not simply repeat the story, but insofar as "all our language about the Christian story is analogical language, when we use the term 'resurrection' we are, like Paul in 1 Corinthians 15: 35-57, forced to take it out of its own ambiance into our own world views."

In 1975 Frei acknowledged that in 1962 when his reading of Ludwig Wittgenstein began in earnest, "I discovered two things common language philosophy did for me: first, it described how we actually use language in ordinary conversation and so weaned me from a specialized vocabulary and thought form both for philosophy and theology; second, it weaned me away from high-flown ontological reflection in order to understand theology." In addition in 1964 he read for the first time and with the closest attention Erich Auerbach's *Mimesis: The Representation of Reality in Western Literature*.

This remarkable book, poles apart from deconstructionism and more in the tradition of Yale s previous humanism, proved to be crucial to the development of Frei's theology. Like Barth, Auerbach recognized that biblical literature drew the reader into that world—the only real world there was—in which God's rule was autocratic and absolute. Not written to be entertaining as literature, said Auerbach, the Bible was "tyrannizing" in its claim to truth. "Far from seeking, like Homer, merely to make us forget our own reality for a few hours," he judged, the Bible "seeks to overcome our reality."⁷²

But Auerbach supplied for Frei something other than biblical autocracy. His manner of analysis offered another quality which was complementary to but different from Barth's own use of scripture:⁷³ a procedure of stylistic analysis apart from theological interpretation. Who was speaking in a given text, asked Auerbach? What type of character? From what social strata? To what effect? What was left *unsaid*? Finally, what was the intention of the narrative itself? Auerbach asked readers seriously to consider the circumstances and the larger meaning of a comic figure such as Peter in the courtyard of the high priest.

How is it, he asked, that Peter in his denial of Christ appears to carry the destiny of all of us?[74] Frei in "Theological Reflections on the Account of Jesus' Death and Resurrection" went beyond Auerbach and asked the intention of the gospel itself (in this case, that of Luke) with respect to Jesus, his circumstances, and the stages of his emerging identity in the text.[75]

For Auerbach the meaning of the biblical narrative remained latent in the simple and sparse depiction of the most powerful, multilayered thoughts and emotions. The individual reader or the community was left free to interpret the text which at the same time demanded interpretation. For Frei too the text, far from stifling diversity and creativity, as Charles M. Wood has pointed out, "positively mandated them."[76]

Such literary analysis in a sense drew Frei away from pursuing historical theology only, and at the same time provided him with that critical position from which he would come to judge the history of modern theology and hermeneutics. "My interest in literature itself is a side-line," he remarked; "I am more concerned with the relation between literary criticism on the one hand and biblical exegesis and theological thought on the other." From that interest came the "narrative interpretation" of scripture and his emphasis on the "plain sense," understood as the narrative depiction of the identity of Jesus Christ in his particular circumstances. (Others such as Kathryn E. Tanner, Gene Outka, and George Lindbeck have carried the implications of the "plain sense" into other areas such as Christian practice, discipleship, and the church.[77] There will no doubt be others.)

When Anglican theologian Charles Price reviewed Frei's *Identity of Jesus Christ,* he declared, "I begin in a state of radical disagreement with its metaphysical assumption. The assumption of the book, and, I think of theology-of-story in general, seems to be that one can avoid metaphysics by a description or a tale."[78] Here was a popular confusion between the narrative interpretation and theology-as-story which was to plague the American theological scene. Frei responded quickly. He was grateful to Price for a "careful, critical reading," but was anxious to make a clear distinction.

I really disagree pretty completely with "story theology," [he wrote]. The fact that I wrote the essay in the mid-'60s didn't really help me. The "story" fad came up in the mid-'70s, and I knew I was in trouble, that is, in danger of confusion. As I understand "story theology," it rests on the assumption that human experience has certain universal transcendental features that become (universally) expressed or objectified in narrative. And then one goes on from there to draw theological conclusions about the status and meaning of narrative and its ontological theological implications.[79]

Frei found "the whole thing ... intellectually pretty awful and, much worse, it is Christianly quite wrong-headed." His own inquiry, he stated, was about "the meaning of one, unique narrative, in the course of which its logical, aesthetic status as narrative becomes important for me in order to aid in 'locating' its meaning properly & also in order to avoid certain logical errors about placing it."[80]

I agree with him [Charles Price] that story-theology, having an anthropology of a peculiar kind, avoids metaphysics in talking about religion. That's not the case with me at all, even though I think the metaphysical moves I think one ought to make in order to do theology properly may well differ greatly from the way he thinks they ought to be done.[81]

Price suspected that Frei's "use of hermeneutical categories in interpretation which will not distort the story but which will 'let it mean what it says'" was to advance his own "interpretive clues" to the more impressive rank of "'formal' categories." In the end, wrote Price, "Frei analyzes the story by means of these categories and tells us what he thinks it means." Price thought he had given a "good interpretation, but ... not startlingly more persuasive than Tillich's in the second volume of his Systematics. ..." Price thought as well that the "question of historical credibility [with respect to the resurrection] is simply bracketed" by Frei.

Frei thinks it a category mistake to confuse the fact that a story's literal or realistic depiction coincides with its meaning with the claim that the depiction is an accurate account of actual historical facts. I am not sure that the historical question can be dealt with in such a summary way. The theology of the early church was, to be sure, set out in narrative form in the gospels. Yet the church believed that *something* happened. Frei is so preoccupied with understanding "what the story says" that he never indicates whether or not anything in it is historical, or even whether or not the historical question is a significant one in its own right.[82]

"Of course I don't think the question of historical factuality can be ignored," Frei responded,

> But I was at pains to point out that a logical error, to the detriment of both historical & hermeneutical inquiries, is made if the logical distinction between the two is not observed & hence they are made to converge too easily, sloppily & confusedly. That, precisely, has been the problem ever since the Enlightenment in the house of theology, etc., etc.[83]

In the meantime in the spring of 1978, Frei was engaged in reviewing Eberhard Busch's biography of Karl Barth.[84] "It's odd," he confided, "but I found myself far more deeply engaged than I had anticipated, once I started writing. It became a preoccupation for weeks."[85] William Clebsch was not alone when he declared that Frei's review was "Probably the most instructive few pages on Barth as man and theologian that we can find in English."[86] In what became an extended essay Frei not only spoke with frankness and wit of Barth's personality but, more important, of the "increasingly compelling, engrossing quality" of his biblical and dogmatic writing. Not all were pleased with Frei's comment that translations into English lost "the almost colloquial vigor of the German original."[87] Busch himself was delighted with the review. When Frei sent him a somewhat expanded version for comment, Busch replied positively that "the man he had written about seemed to emerge once again recognizably from my [Frei's] miniature representation of his own larger picture. Well, that's good enough any day."[88]

For awhile Frei had difficulty at Yale with his loyalty to Barth, on the one hand, and to H. Richard Niebuhr, on the other. In 1957 when Frei first came on the Yale faculty, "Niebuhr and I parted theologically." It was a painful falling out. "I made a very strong affirmation that the business of Christian theology is to make dogmatic assertions." Niebuhr, on the other hand, "believed that the theologian's task is critical, [is] not to make dogmatic assertions but to comment on the symbolic forms of the religious vision he has."[89] To be sure, Frei appeared at times to side with Niebuhr against Barth as the latter is generally portrayed. At the end of his life in "History, Church and Nation," Frei's comments on Niebuhr's book *The Responsible Self* show deep appreciation for Niebuhr's "central concern, his most powerful persuasion of the prevenient initiatory action of God in time and in human events."[90] Were divine actions to be discerned in Christ alone, as Barth had stated? Or were there "other mysterious forms of the *logos asarkos*, not only in the world's religions but in its philosophies, too?"[91] Barth had "understood all human beings in the light of this one man, Jesus Christ, as portrayed in the Gospels." Niebuhr, on the other hand, sought to state a "fitting universal anthropology of the person as a responding creature." With apparent approval Frei noted that for Niebuhr—and for him?—the two became interlocked.

It is the interlocking synecdoches of Jesus Christ, first as a unique, non-generalizable instance of the image of "responding person," and second as one who in his response is both prophet, priest, and king, that *together* [italics added] become the image of the mediation between God and human beings in history.[92]

It is possible that Frei thought of Barth's "little lights of creation," writes George Lindbeck, as a way of "incorporating H. Richard Niebuhr's concerns in this matter into a basically Barthian sounding statement."[93]

I have of course, along with others, merely scratched the surface. The richness and complexity of Frei's thought call for careful analysis.[94] Whoever attempts to do for him what he did for H. Richard Niebuhr will have to examine the network of ideas woven to include a number of areas of concentration. Preeminent among those areas are, of course, first, the narrative reading of scripture derived from Auerbach and played out against the background of the history of hermeneutics since the Reformation—as well as Frei's later emphasis on the "literal sense" or the "plain sense" of scripture in relation to the modern deconstructionists in general and also to Frank Kermode in particular. Second, historians of theology will want to see Frei's own Christology in the context of his profound knowledge of modern Christology deeply influenced, as it was, by Karl Barth but brought forward and altered by a fresh reading of H. Richard Niebuhr in Frei's "History, Church and Nation."

Third, and perhaps the hardest to come by (it will have to be pieced together from sermons, letters, and such incidental essays as that on the Holy Spirit), will be the reconstruction of his doctrine of sanctification. That doctrine will be seen to steer a very different course from the subjective—often Jungian and even gnostic—spirituality so popular in liberal Christian culture today. Frei's doctrine will, first of all, have to be set in the context of his sense of public service to the nation as "*the* crucial collective historical agent of the day,"[95] as well as to the church and to the church's "constant reconstitution" which occurs in so far—and only in so far?—as it humbly seeks to find the "fit," the concurrence, between the truth of Jesus Christ and the text of the Bible.[96]

Such a study will no doubt begin with Jesus' relation to his disciples and to later followers or, as Frei preferred to call them, pilgrims.[97] The term "pilgrim" was a non-heroic one which he liked and used. Seldom was the pilgrim glamorous or "an aristocrat of the spirit," but quite ordinary. He "always follows his Lord at a distance," much as the disciples followed Jesus to Jerusalem.[98] The pilgrim's track is "mysterious yet directed" and may involve a single person or a whole people who move toward a promised land or a heavenly city. In either case the journey is eschatological; its goal and destiny in the future.

Of that destiny Christ is the fulfillment and the fulfiller. For Frei Jesus does not so much command his disciples, "follow me," as allure and captivate them with that invitation.[99] Jesus is able to do so by self-identifying with them. He is "not *identical* but *identified* with the poor, the undeserving, the spiritual and economic underclass."[100] They may not know it, judged Frei, and "there may be more of them who would laugh at rather than be comforted. ..." The Savior's act of walking incognito among them—or ahead of them—is the act not of a commanding officer but of a friend. Jesus' power in powerlessness together with his concealment led Frei to approve of the remark made by a friend to her theologian husband, "'You didn't really become fully human until you stopped being totally preoccupied with Jesus.'" Frei thought that there could be no textual meeting with the Savior until a person had at the same time met him incognito in a crowd. Frei found Matthew's "identity description" of Jesus (25:40), "Inasmuch as you have done it unto one of the least of these my brethren, you have done it unto me," a haunting one. In his relationship with pilgrims on the way, Jesus' humaneness which "allows us to counter his compassion and severity with each other" caused him to stand out as a very specific person.[101] Frei found "miraculous" Jesus' ordinary kindness, his natural gentleness, his "enjoyment of the neighbor in her or his peculiar character, religion, lifestyle, and work—the enjoyment of just the way she or he is. ..." Such enjoyment was part of the service of Christ.

Frei often spoke of how many professors he knew at Yale University who had come from seemingly strong Christian backgrounds but who had thrown over the faith. Did he sense that commands were not enough in a society increasingly disengaged from the Church? The answer is yes. Obedience remained for the pilgrim, but the accompanying attitude had changed. Frei saw that the call to the apostolate as command more often than not failed to focus on Jesus' own call and was often confined by sacramentalism or born-againism or some other "apostolic succession." Disciples "hounding them [potential converts] with the image of Jesus overstepped the line between devotion in religious service and fanatical religious imperialism."[102] It was to be sure a thin line, "but it is real and deep, and a generous unobsessive love of the neighbor marks that line." Jesus was indeed the caller, gatherer, and upholder of pilgrims, and he called, gathered, and upheld with strange effectiveness, by inviting wonderment and captivation.

Nor should we be surprised that Hans Frei thought in such comprehensive terms. He himself excluded none. He was after all by race Jewish and once a refugee, by birth German, by early baptism Lutheran; he was schooled by English Quakers, attracted at one point to Roman Catholic monasticism, ordained Baptist and then Episcopalian; in nationality American and New England Puritan American at that, in theology reformed, a disciple of Calvin and Barth. For this painstaking, daring Christian intellectual, the relation of Savior to pilgrim was bound to take an appealing—and more biblical?—form. And then, for Frei, these pilgrims, while they tend not to walk in formation, enjoy a very simple consensus: "Jesus of Nazareth has been in all ages at the center of Christian living, Christian devotion, and Christian thought." Further that "the story of Jesus is about him, not about someone else or about nobody in particular or about all of us."[103]

NOTES

1. David F. Ford, "On Being Hospitable to Jesus Christ: Hans Frei's Achievement," *Journal of Theological Studies*, New Series 46, Part 2, October (1995): 532. See chapter 15 of this volume.
2. The comparison was first made by George Lindbeck, "The Story-Shaped Church: Critical Exegesis and Theological Interpretation," in *Scriptural Authority and Narrative Interpretation*, ed. Garrett Green (Philadelphia: Fortress, 1987): 161.
3. Karl Barth's *Der Romerbrief* (1919, 1922, trans. 1935) accomplished the same end. All three books were decisive though, as Lindbeck points out, Schweitzer

took a different—and it should be said finally less radical—course than either Barth or Frei.

4. Stephen Crites, "The Spatial Dimension of Narrative Truthtelling," in *Scriptural Authority and Narrative Interpretation*, ed. Garrett Green (Philadelphia: Fortress, 1987): 98.

5. Hans W. Frei, "Niebuhr's Theological Background," and "The Theology of H. Richard Niebuhr," in *Faith and Ethics: The Theology of H. Richard Niebuhr*, ed. Paul Ramsey (New York: Harper, 1957): 9–116.

6. Jeffrey Stout, "Hans Frei and Anselmian Theology" (unpublished ms, 1987), 4. See chapter 7 in this volume.

7. My wife, Margaret R. Woolverton, was president of the project in its formative years, 1983–9. Frei proved to be a source to her of both interest and support.

8. Stephen Crites, "The Spatial Dimensions of Narrative Truthtelling," in *Scriptural Authority and Narrative Interpretation,* 97 makes the same point with reference to Frei's *theological* attitude.

9. See Ronald F. Thiemann, "Radiance and Obscurity in Biblical Narrative," *Scriptural Authority and Narrative Interpretation*, 28.

10. Hans W. Frei, "H. Richard Niebuhr on History, Church and Nation," in *The Legacy of H. Richard Niebuhr*, Harvard Theological Studies, No. 36, ed. Ronald F. Thiemann (Philadelphia: Fortress, 1990): 1–23.

11. Thiemann, "Radiance and Obscurity," 23. For an alternative view of the church, see George Lindbeck, "The Story-Shaped Church," 161–78.

12. Frei, "H. Richard Niebuhr on History, Church and Nation," 4.

13. Ibid., 4.

14. Perhaps first by Brevard Childs in *The New Testament as Canon: An Introduction* (Philadelphia: Fortress, 1985), 541.

15. Kissinger was born in 1923, Frei in 1922; see Walter Isaacson, *Kissinger: A Biography* (New York: Simon & Schuster, 1992), 20 and Notes for an Oral History, 16 August 1975, Woolverton Papers, Bishop Payne Library, Virginia Theological Seminary, Alexandria, Virginia (hereafter Notes HF/JW), 1.

16. In 1938 when Frei was sixteen, Kissinger fifteen. Isaacson, *Kissinger,* 28; Notes HF/JW, 1.

17. Kissinger in Germany with direct anti-Semitism; Frei with more indirect anti-Semitism but with an additional family financial—and to some degree psychological—depression, neither of which was shared by the Kissinger family.

18. Ibid., 31.

19. Notes HF/JW, 2.

20. Isaacson, *Kissinger,* 30.

21. Notes HF/JW, 2.

22. Ibid.

23. Frei, "H. Richard Niebuhr on History, Church and Nation," 20.

24. Ibid., 21.

25. Norman F. Cantor, *Inventing the Middle Ages: The Lives, Works, and Ideas of the Great Medievalists of the Twentieth Century* (New York: William Morrow &

Co, 1991), 400. Mommsen, however, like Frei in "History, Church and Nation" and like H. Richard Niebuhr, was concerned in the 1950s to warn his adopted country of the great dangers of national pride and arrogance (see T. E. Mommsen, *Medieval and Renaissance Studies* [Ithaca: Cornell University Press, 1959]). Cantor is wrong about Mommsen teaching Latin at Groton School: He taught history only, including American history.

26. Pauck came in 1926, Tillich in 1933, Mommsen in 1937. Both Mommsen and Frei spent time in England, where the former was coldly received, the latter warmly greeted at a Quaker school.

27. H. Stuart Hughes, *The Sea Change: The Migration of Social Thought, 1930–1965* (New York: Harper and Row, 1975), 265.

28. Frei's ancestors were highly placed German Jews. His great grandfather led a desperate charge of Prussian cavalry in 1806 against the French at the close of the day at the battle of Jena. For this he was permitted by King Frederick William III to change the family name from the Jewish Freiberg to Frei. Presumably before and certainly after that event the family were professionals of distinguished position in Germany. During the First World War, an uncle was killed in the first month of the conflict in the Crown Prince's division. As Frei remarked to me, "With typical German thoroughness, the high command put all of the intellectuals in one division—where they would be exposed as a body to death." Hans's parents were both physicians: his mother a pediatrician and his father a urologist who conducted notable research in the area of venereal disease. While Frei can in no way be described as a "converted Jew"—he was baptized as a baby in the Protestant state church of Prussia—his parents early on saw Hitler's anti-semitism for what it portended and sent their sons to the safety of a school in England.

    Jewish life and thought did not play a significant part in either his background or education. (It is probable that the family had been assimilated for some generations.) Still he once remarked to me that he felt guilty in not sharing the sufferings of Jews in Germany.

29. See especially Frei, *Eclipse,* 295–300.

30. Hans Frei to the author, December 1959.

31. Ibid.

32. Ibid.

33. Frei spoke of Farrer's grounding "in the church fathers, in the seventeenth-century English high churchmen (though not in the Book of Common Prayer), and that from these had come an austere philosophy combined with a partly high church piety which changed. ...," Notes HF/JW, 4.

34. Ibid.

35. Gore was the editor as well as the most important contributor to this volume which broke with the older high church biblical tradition of E.B. Pusey and significantly broadened Anglican thought to include historical criticism. At the time this was an important factor in Frei's decision to become an Episcopalian. He also remarked, "I saw little difference between Gore and Temple" Notes HF/JW, 2.

36. Frei had joined a Baptist young peoples' fellowship while at North Carolina State University to which he had received a scholarship in textile engineering. This was not a subject of great interest to him: He had seen an advertisement in the

newspaper! Frei's family in the late 1930s were in financial straits living in New York and his father was ill for some time before his death. It was a dark time for them all, even though they were physically safe in America. Notes HF/JW, 2.

37. Ibid.
38. Frei attended a confirmation class in Lancaster, New Hampshire, which was taught by the Rev. William Crouch. Characteristically he got to know the Crouch family well and kept in touch over the years. When he told his board of deacons in the Baptist church in North Stratford that he had decided to become an Episcopalian, "instead of being asked to leave, they wanted him to stay on" (Conversation with Madge Crouch). Frei also kept up over the years with people in North Stratford where he had taught school as well as being the town pastor.
39. Hans Frei to the author, January 26, 1978.
40. Notes HF/JW, 1.
41. The anthology of P. E. More and F. L. Cross, eds., *Anglicanism* (Milwaukee: Morehouse, 1935; repr., London, 1962).
42. Notes HF/JW, 2.
43. Hans Frei to the author, January 23, 1980.
44. Ibid.
45. They are: Article IV, "Of the Resurrection of Christ," which was first published in *Anglican and Episcopal History* LVIII, no. 2 (June 1989): 139–45 under the title "On the Resurrection." The other two were on Article III, "Of the Going Down of Christ into Hell," and Article V, "Of the Holy Ghost."
46. Hans Frei to the author, December 6, 1966.
47. Frei was pastor of the Baptist church in North Stratford, New Hampshire, from 1945 to 1947. Notes HF/JW, 1.
48. Hans Frei, *Types of Christian Theology*, ed. George Hunsinger and William C. Placher (New Haven and London: Yale University Press, 1992), 137–8.
49. Frei, *Eclipse,* 21.
50. Ibid.
51. Ibid. H.-J. Kraus, "Calvins exegetische Prinzipien," *Zeitschrift fur Kirchengeschichte,* 79–80, 1968–9, 331; Calvin's *Institutes of the Christian Religion,* 1.7.4, 5.
52. Ibid., 22.
53. Ibid., 22–3.
54. Hans Frei to the author, September 21, 1978.
55. Frei, "History, Church and Nation," 18.
56. David E. Laurence, "Religious Experience in the Biblical World of Jonathan Edwards: A Study in Eighteenth-Century Supernaturalism" (Unpublished PhD. dissertation, Yale University, 1976), passim.
57. Harry S. Stout, *The New England Soul: Preaching and Religious Culture in Colonial New England* (New York: Oxford University Press, 1986).
58. Notes HF/JW.

59. Ibid.
60. As told to the author by Geraldine Frei, November 1992.
61. Notes HF/JW, 3.
62. Frei did not, however, try to emulate Barth's theology even while Barth was one of the two theologians from whom he learned the most. As Garrett Green has written, "like Barth, he [Frei] has remained committed through thick and thin to what Barth would have called *die Sache*, and this *Sachlichkeit,* this stubborn refusal to be seduced by current trends or other people's programs—even if called narrative theology—is what gives his work integrity" ("Editor's Introduction," *Scriptural Authority and Narrative Interpretation,* xi).
63. Notes HF/JW, 4.
64. Ibid.
65. Ibid.
66. Ibid; cf. Frei, *The Identity of Jesus Christ,* xi.
67. Ibid.
68. Ibid., 5.
69. Ibid.
70. Ibid., 3.
71. For further discussion see Frei, *Types of Christian Theology,* 51.
72. Erich Auerbach, *Mimesis: The Representation of Reality in Western Literature,* trans. Willard R. Trask (Princeton: Princeton University Press, 1953), 15.
73. See David H. Kelsey, *The Uses of Scripture in Recent Theology* (Philadelphia: Fortress, 1975), 39 f.
74. Auerbach, *Mimesis,* 41–5.
75. Hans Frei, "Theological Reflections on the Accounts of Jesus' Death and Resurrection," *The Christian Scholar* XLIX, no. 4 (Winter 1966): 292–7; cf. Frei, *Identity,* 126–38.
76. Charles M. Wood, "Hermeneutics and the Authority of Scripture," in *Scriptural Authority and Narrative Tradition*, ed. Garrett Green (Philadelphia: Fortress Press, 1987): 14. Wood is worth quoting in full: "The task of interpretation is to learn the sense of scripture undertaking whatever development of one's own capacities is requisite to that end, rather than to submit scripture to explanation in terms of one's present knowledge and capacities ('making sense of it') on the assumption that the latter are essentially adequate to whatever scripture may contain. To recognize the authority of scripture is, among other things, to submit one's understanding to it: to be willing to be guided by it and to allow one's previous understandings to be challenged, extended, and transformed by it."
77. Kathryn E. Tanner, "Theology and the Plain Sense," 59–78; Gene Outka, "Following at a Distance: Ethics and the Identity of Jesus," 144–60; George Lindbeck, "The Story-Shaped Church: Critical Exegesis and Theological Interpretation," 161–78 in *Scriptural Authority and Narrative Interpretation.*
78. Charles P. Price, review of Frei's *Identity of Jesus Christ, The Virginia Seminary Journal,* March 1978, 41.

79. Hans Frei to the author, April 26, 1978.
80. Ibid.
81. Ibid.
82. Price, review, 42.
83. Frei letter, April 26, 1978. Later he wrote, "... I'm not a story theologian and antimetaphysical enthusiast; for it must be evident that I identified pretty strongly with the theology of Barth I described in the 3d part of the review. And surely Barth, while thinking of the world of Christian discourse as narrative in the first instance, never thought of narrative as a substitute for *theological* truth affirmations or for analytical procedures by which to get at affirmations of meaning and truth" (Hans Frei to the author, September 21, 1978).
84. The review appeared in *The Virginia Seminary Journal,* Vol. xxx, no. 2, July 1978, 42–6; the book under review was Eberhard Busch, *Karl Barth: His Life from Letters and Autobiographical Texts,* trans. John Bowden (Philadelphia: Fortress, 1975).
85. Frei letter, April 26, 1978.
86. Office memorandum from William A. Clebsch to the author, 21 August 1978. Frei's review appeared in *The Virginia Seminary Journal,* July 1978, 42–6.
87. Conversation with Geoffrey Bromiley, University of Southern California, Los Angeles, June 20, 1990.
88. Hans Frei to the author, January 17, 1979.
89. Notes HF/JW, 2.
90. Frei, "History, Church and Nation," 15.
91. Ibid., 18.
92. Ibid., 19.
93. George Lindbeck to the author, March 19, 1994.
94. As George Hunsinger has pointed out perceptively, "Regardless of the subject matter he was discussing, it was as though he possessed a strong, immediate intuition of various complex interrelations between the whole and the parts, as well as among the various parts themselves. The agony [of writing] seemed to arise from trying to describe some particular part without losing its concrete and complex embeddedness in the matrix of the whole, with all the subtle interrelations and contrasts which that embeddedness seemed to entail." "Hans Frei as Theologian: The Quest for a Generous Orthodoxy," *Modern Theology*: 8, April 2, 1992, 104.

    There is some tendency to overstate Frei's difficulty or at least over-conscientiousness in writing. It may be worth recording that when he took on the Busch biography of Barth, Frei wrote: "I most certainly will send you the review of the Barth biography by March 15, but I hope you won't mind if it arrives just before the deadline. I have to give two talks on the west coast in early March ... and they are going to be like pulling teeth. I'll do the review immediately on getting back, and since by now I know the book inside out, it should take no time at all! It is certainly an astonishing piece of work from which Barth emerges as a rather overwhelming person, brilliant, courageous but also rather enigmatic. Well, I'll see what I can do" (Hans Frei to the author, January 26, 1978). And he did it—meeting the deadline.

95. One suspects that Frei, who read widely in current events, would have modified his emphasis on the nation in such a way as to include the new, nongovernmental organizations so compellingly described by Jessica T. Matthews in her "Power Shift," *Foreign Affairs* 76, no. 1 (January/February 1997): 50–66.
96. Hans W. Frei, "Conflicts in Interpretation," *Theology Today,* October 1992, 356.
97. See for instance, Frei, *Identity of Jesus Christ,* 152.
98. Hans Frei, "Saint, Sinner and Pilgrim: Three Paths in quest of Christ's Presence," uncompleted ms, 3f, Frei Papers, Yale University.
99. In a recent study by David E. Demson, *Hans Frei & Karl Barth: Different Ways of Reading Scripture* (Grand Rapids and Cambridge: Wm. B. Eerdmans Publishing Co., 1997), Frei's "lack" of treatment of Jesus' relationship with his disciples is a recurring theme: 11, 22, 30, 41, 48, 60, 94, and so forth.
100. Frei, "The Encounter of Jesus with the German Academy," *Types of Christian Theology,* 136.
101. Ibid.
102. Ibid., 137.
103. Ibid., 140.

PART THREE

Theological Themes in Frei's Work

CHAPTER FOUR

Frei's Early Christology: The Book of Detours

GEORGE HUNSINGER

When I first read Hans Frei's book *The Identity of Jesus Christ*,[1] shortly after it was published in 1975, I was still a graduate student. I can remember how frustrated I felt about the opening chapters that were captioned "The Problem of Presence." Why focus so abstractly on the term *presence*, I wondered, and why problematize it at such length? Wasn't this an artificial place to start? If the goal was to discuss Jesus Christ's identity, why not just get on with it and come straight to the point? Beginning with "presence" as a way of getting to "identity" struck me as tedious and unnecessary, especially because Frei as much as conceded, for about thirty-five belabored pages, that there was in fact no viable way from the presence of Jesus Christ to his identity. Had anyone ever supposed otherwise?, I wondered. Had anyone argued that Christ's identity *could* be derived from his presence? Wasn't Frei tilting at a problem where none existed in the first place? As I reread these chapters nearly forty years later, I must confess to a remembrance of things past. My old feelings of frustration and perplexity resurfaced as I encountered Frei's decision to fret at such length over the so-called "problem of presence."

I can also remember a corresponding sense of relief when I later turned to Frei's companion piece entitled "Theological Reflections on the Accounts of Jesus' Death and Resurrection." This essay, appearing in the *Christian*

Scholar in 1966,[2] apparently predated a much longer article called "The Mystery of the Presence of Jesus Christ," which was published in *Crossroads* in 1967.[3] It was this latter work that was then eventually reprinted between two covers as Frei's *Identity* book. The *Christian Scholar* article managed to make Frei's central points without sinking into the quagmire of "presence," and indeed without mentioning the term, at least with respect to the idea of "self-presence." Starting immediately with the Gospel accounts of Jesus' death and resurrection, it goes straight to Frei's two proposed modes of identity-depiction: the intention/action scheme and the self-manifestation scheme, to which we will return at a later point. The *Christian Scholar* article makes Frei's foregrounding of the category of "presence" in his *Identity* book all the more perplexing. Nevertheless, I can think of three reasons why he may have done so.

The first is the idea of what Frei dubbed "coinherence." This term had been central to his 1956 Yale dissertation on "The Nature of Barth's Break with Liberalism."[4] Barth's break with liberalism, Frei argued, was carried out largely as a break with coinherence. Coinherence was, by this account, the secret premise of modern liberal theology. It posited that the reality of God was somehow interior to and given with universal human self-consciousness. (Although Frei does not say so, it is possible that for this idea Calvin's "seed of religion" stands somewhere remotely in the background.) An immediate relationship with God was seen as constitutive of human nature (*BBL*, 137). The objective content of revelation was then posited in and with its subjective apprehension in human self-consciousness. In principle, the result was a relationship of coinherence or *Ineinanderstellung* "in which Jesus Christ, the Word of God, or even history is immediately present in ... faith" (*BBL*, 119).

This coinherence of revelation's subjective apprehension with its objective content meant two things. Not only was God not radically an object over against present experience, but at the same time a kind of "relationalism" resulted in which the two—God and religious self-consciousness—were seen as innate aspects of one and the same subjective reality. Furthermore, because the relationship between the two was posited as symmetrical, it was also in principle reversible. The logic of relationalism thereby made it vulnerable to reductionism. It allowed God to be unmasked as nothing but an illusory projection of religious self-consciousness. Feuerbach's smile was waiting in the wings. Frei's worry about "presence" in his *Identity* book owes something to this worry about the logic of relationalism and the corresponding danger of reductionism (*IJC*, 149).

Second, in the new preface added in 1975 when the *Crossroads* essay was published as a book, Frei tells us that through the concept of "presence" he was trying to capture a broad phenomenon in modernity with a single term. He writes, "This notion of 'presence' seemed to me to be the distillate of the philosophical conceptuality under which such otherwise very different people as Hegel, Schleiermacher, Kierkegaard, and the dialectical theologians of the 1920s [like Bultmann and Gogarten] set forth their religious and theological proposals" (*IJC*, ix).

Although Frei is sweeping and elusive here, it seems that he is thinking once again, only this time more obliquely, about what his dissertation had called "coinherence" and "relationalism." Once again, an innate relation to God— which was supposedly constitutive of the self—set the terms for Christian revelation. Jesus Christ's presence to the self was somehow implicated in the self's presence to itself. Christological presence and self-presence were very much entangled.

Whether or not this is the difficulty that Frei had in mind, he immediately saddled himself with a liability. Contrary to what he intended, the concept of "presence," at the outset of his argument, tended to overpower his discourse about Jesus Christ. At least rhetorically, it seemed that Christ was being explained with reference to "presence" rather than the other way around. If instead the accent had fallen on the living Christ, Frei's portrayal of "presence" might have seemed very different. The living Christ in his concrete presence to faith might have been set forth as a presence that was active and self-communicating. Christ's presence would then have been differentiated more sharply from human self-presence. That is clearly where Frei wanted to go. Nevertheless, he was hamstrung by his philosophical starting point. He unwittingly instantiated, even if only indirectly, the difficulty he intended to remove.

A third reason why Frei may have chosen to foreground the problem of presence perhaps lay closer to home. In H. Richard Niebuhr's posthumously published volume of lectures from the 1950s, entitled *Faith on Earth: An Inquiry into the Structure of Human Faith*,[5] a number of remarks appear that are strikingly reminiscent of the issues Frei was struggling with in his early Christology. "We cannot proceed from a pre-existent Christ to an incarnate Christ," wrote Niebuhr, "we can only move *backward* from the contemporary Christ to the historical, from the historical to the pre-existent" (*FE*, 88, italics added). This remark is followed by a footnote in which the present tense is described as "the Locus of Reality" (*FE*, 88n.). The proper procedure, Niebuhr continued, is to move *"backward from the present givenness of Jesus Christ* in whom we trust and to whom we want to be loyal" in order to find the proximate ground of this presence in the community that mediates him, but ultimately in Jesus' own self-consciousness relative to God (*FE*, 89, italics added). "The *present* Jesus

Christ of faith is the companion who reconstructs the faith by which we have lived in the past" (*FE,* 89n., italics original).

Our confidence in the Christ who is present to us is not based on "confidence in those who reported his deeds" (*FE,* 90). It is rather based on our encounter with him here and now. We encounter him "as a person who accompanies *in unseen presence* those who believe in him" (*FE,* 91, italics added). "He has," Niebuhr explains, "all the characteristics of a mythological figure" (*FE,* 92). Christ is present to us in mythological form as "the personification of ... faithfulness" (*FE,* 92). He is present to faith "not as a remembered figure," but as "a living being present with his past" (*FE,* 94). Christ's resurrection is not something we recollect, according to Niebuhr, but something we experience in the present (*FE,* 97), *"He is built into the structure of our conscience"* (*FE,* 98, italics added). He functions to turn "our distrust of God ... somewhat in the direction of trust" (*FE,* 99). The spiritual transition from disloyalty to loyalty is the saving significance that Niebuhr ascribes to the mystery of the presence of Christ.

I have slightly oversimplified what Niebuhr says in these lectures in order to highlight their evident points of contact with what was worrying Frei at about the same time. Was Frei consciously but covertly contradicting some key views of his mentor? Whether he may have read or heard the Niebuhr lectures collected in *Faith on Earth* is by now impossible to determine. As Niebuhr's prize student and Yale colleague, however, it does not seem far-fetched to suppose that Frei may have encountered these Niebuhrian themes in some form. The "common conceptuality" (*IJC,* ix) that troubled Frei about modem academic Christology may also have been something that he perceived in his mentor.

To sum up: whether in his dissertation, in his *Identity* book, or perhaps also in his teacher, Frei regarded the concept of "presence" as the Achilles' heel of modern Christology. Having lost confidence in the historical veracity of the Gospel narratives, modern Christology had relocated itself firmly in the domain of religious self-consciousness. Christology was no longer grounded in history so much as in religious experience. The identity of Jesus as a particular person was less important than his function as a religious symbol. However, if the source and ground of the Christ symbol were ascribed to religious self-consciousness, then the mystery of his presence and the mystery of self-consciousness were ultimately one and the same. The reduction of Christ's presence to consciousness could not be far behind. Anthropology had asserted itself as the meaning of Christ.

Where was saving significance to be found? That was the question—in Christ as a particular person or in Christ as a religious symbol? To explain Frei's solution to this dilemma, let me summarize the main argument of his *Identity* book. Over against what he discerned in modern Christology, and perhaps even in H. Richard Niebuhr, Frei contended that Christ's identity and saving significance could not be grounded in his presence. On the contrary, the reverse was true: his saving presence was a function of his prior identity as a particular person. In short, we cannot proceed from Christ's presence to his identity, but only from his identity to his presence. It helps to see that the terms *identity* and *presence* can be correlated with those of *witness* and *mediation,* although Frei did not make this move. We can then say that for Frei "witness" gives us the identity of Jesus Christ, while "mediation" gives us his presence.

For Frei, the saving identity of Jesus Christ was grounded in the Gospel narratives. These narratives, as he understood them, belonged more nearly to the genre of "legendary witness" than to that of "historical report." The stories were stylized portraits more than literal accounts. Nevertheless, although it was not their primary purpose to report historical facts, neither were they entirely devoid of such facts.[6] It followed that the stories could not be relegated merely to the category of "myth" or "symbol." Any mythological elements that may have been employed were in fact "demythologized," Frei argued, by their being subsumed into Jesus Christ's identity as a particular person. The meaning or claim of the narratives was that these mythological or universal elements had been entirely co-opted by the particularity of Jesus. It was finally he who gave content to them, not they to him.

Jesus was an unsubstitutable person in his saving significance. He did not illustrate or symbolize anything other than himself. He was of universal significance precisely in his radical particularity. The depiction of his unsubstitutable identity was grounded most especially in the Gospel stories surrounding his resurrection. Regardless of whether their claim to universal significance was true, that was the meaning of the stories when read in their own terms. It was in this sense that the stories served to attest the saving identity of Jesus. He was an irreducibly particular person for whom none other could be substituted. As someone irreducibly particular, he enjoyed universal saving significance.

If witness gives us Jesus Christ's saving identity, then mediation gives us his saving presence. The very narratives by which his identity is depicted are also the means by which his presence is made available to faith here and now. As Frei states more broadly, the Word of Scripture is the temporal basis of Christ's presence while the church's Sacraments are its spatial basis (*IJC*, 17–18, 156, 158–9, 165). In other words, the mystery of Christ's presence to faith is not only grounded in his resurrection as attested by the Gospel stories. At the same time his presence is also mediated into the present by Word and Sacrament.

Frei could perhaps have made this point more clearly if he had spoken more directly about the risen Christ as a living and active Subject. He could then have said that the risen Christ is our Contemporary who attests himself whenever he is spoken of in accord with the Gospel witness, and that he also mediates himself and his presence to faith by means of Word and Sacrament. If the risen

Christ had been explained not just as a "presence," but as the living Subject who at once attests and yet also mediates himself through Word and Sacrament, he might have emerged more distinctly as a reality over against religious self-consciousness. Christ's sovereign presence as an acting Subject would not have remained so occluded by German Idealist conceptions. The idea of union and communion with Christ (*Christus praesens*), which Frei mentions only sparingly, might also have been etched more sharply.

Unfortunately, in his *Identity* book Frei does not immediately explain why Christ's identity cannot be grounded in his presence. Before arriving at his announced destination—namely, a narrative account of Christ's saving identity as a particular person—Frei allows his argument to travel down many unexpected byways. No clear map for this itinerary is provided. Only in retrospect can the reader perhaps grasp why these detours were taken. One's bafflement—having been first elicited by the abstract discussion of presence—only intensifies as Frei's next stop turns out to be not the Gospel narratives, but formal patterns of identity depiction, with special reference to Gilbert Ryle. One then has to pick up again almost immediately for an excursion into Gnosticism and dying-and-rising savior myths. Like a child on a long road trip, one may begin to ask oneself, are we there yet? Regrettably, as so often happens, the answer is still no. The reader is next led on a guided tour through several twentieth-century novels to see how unsuccessfully they depict their heroes as Christ-figures. Only after that does light start to appear at the end of the tunnel, or perhaps better, at the end of the warren. Just as a sinking feeling may set in that the argument has gone hopelessly astray, Frei arrives, as promised, at "The New Testament Depiction of Jesus Christ." Nevertheless, even the most indefatigable traveler cannot help wondering, why so many detours along the way?

Why did Frei turn his *Identity* book into a book of detours? Although no definitive answer can be given, at least two possible factors may be relevant. First, Frei seemed to have possessed a mind like a highly sensitive photographic plate. He took in everything all at once, and he did so in fine-grained detail.[7] When he tried to articulate his perceptions, he sometimes had difficulty in sorting out the forest from the trees. He would no sooner take up one topic than it led him to think immediately of another. His inherent sense of subtleties and complexities could outstrip his capacity to express them. Consequently, he often seemed more profound than clear.

Moreover, a fine line exists between subtlety and obscurity, and Frei was not unknown to cross the line. He once confided to me that one of his philosophical colleagues at Yale regarded him as a fuzzy thinker. Even when he may have been fuzzy, however, he was never superficial. In the midst of any possible fuzziness, important insights were struggling to get out.

Aspects of Frei's early Christology have been subjected to a thoughtful critique in a book by David Lee called *Luke's Stories of Jesus: Theological*

Reading of Gospel Narrative and the Legacy of Hans Frei.[8] Although I cannot do full justice to Lee's rich and fair-minded discussion, I want to lift up three of his most telling concerns.

First, I think he is right to point out that in the *Identity* book, Frei works only with a generalized version of the Gospel story. This is ironic given Frei's plea that the whole text should be respected in its final form. It raises questions about how much his Christology is really derived from the Gospel narratives (*LHF,* 60n., 66–7).

Second, Lee questions Frei's intention-action scheme of identity depiction. Is it truly as formal and descriptive as Frei claims? The identity of Jesus in the Gospel narratives, Frei argues, emerges through the interaction of character and circumstance, more or less as characters emerge in a realistic novel. As the Gospels proceed, according to Frei, Jesus is increasingly identified by what he does and what he undergoes. From a strictly literary standpoint, however, as Lee points out, the intention-action scheme emphasizes narrative events at the expense of other narrative elements, especially Jesus' narrated teachings, which are not much engaged. In Frei's interpretation, too much of the narrative is simply bracketed out (*LHF,* 64). I will return to this point later, because it has significant Christological implications.

Finally, Lee also questions Frei's other scheme of identity depiction, involving what Frei calls a person's self-manifestation. A person's identity, Frei argues, is manifested by events or activities that display what a person is like when he is most fully himself. Jesus is then claimed to be most fully himself in the resurrection stories, because they most clearly depict him in his oneness with God. I think Lee is right to argue that here Frei's point is not convincingly made. It is not clear that the Gospel stories must lead inexorably to his resurrection. From a literary standpoint, as George Steiner has argued, they might have ended otherwise (*LHF,* 74, n. 67). Nor, as I will argue more fully later, is Frei's "Anselmian" argument convincing that Jesus cannot *not* be conceived as raised, and that to know his identity is to have him be present (*LHF,* 70–5).

Lee concludes that in his *Identity* book Frei's reading of the Gospel narratives is governed by theological or dogmatic interests. I think this judgment is correct, but it is again ironic, because the subtitle of the book states the relation in reverse. Frei claims to be elucidating "the hermeneutical bases of dogmatic theology" when what he actually develops, in practice, I think, are more nearly the theological or dogmatic bases of scriptural hermeneutics. I want to suggest that this is one of those fuzzy areas in Frei where something profound is struggling to get out. Furthermore, what I think is struggling to get out is something that Frei himself calls a "high christology" (*TN,* 32, 37).

For the remainder of this paper I want to do three things. I want to show first, that Frei thinks his *Identity* book offers a high Christology; second, that he does not succeed in this project; and finally, that at the end of his career he does succeed in showing how a high Christology can be based on an interpretative scheme that avoids his earlier deficiencies.

First, in his *Identity* book Frei thinks he is offering a high Christology. For our purposes a high Christology may be defined as one in which the death of Jesus as a particular person has universal saving significance. Frei supposes that he has assembled the elements of a high Christology through his critical analysis of Christ-figures as they are depicted in modern novels. The novelistic Christ-figures fail, he argues, because they cannot hold together the defining elements that allow a Christ-figure to emerge as the Savior. Novelistic Christ-figures are indeed invested with an irreducible particular identity, but they cannot carry universal saving significance. This makes them the diametrical opposite of dying-and-rising savior figures as found in mythology. They are indeed of universal saving significance, but devoid of all particular personal identity. Only Jesus as depicted in the Gospels, Frei maintains, can hold particularity and universality together in a single person. The particular and universal elements as depicted in the stories also force us to raise the question of factuality, according to Frei, because of how the narratives climax in the events of Jesus' death and resurrection.

Along with particularity and universality, a high Christology needs one more element. It needs what Frei calls the pattern of exchange. According to this pattern in its simplest form, Jesus dies so that others might live. Furthermore, although he is innocent, he dies for the guilty. The guilt of the guilty is laid on him so that through him their guilt might be exchanged for his innocence. Although Frei's account of this pattern remains terribly sketchy, I think he is right as far as he goes.[9] That is, I think a high Christology does entail a pattern of exchange. Frei argues that novelistic Christ-figures cannot pull it off, but that the Gospel stories succeed in ascribing this pattern to Jesus. Frei also thinks he has succeeded in showing that this is the case.

Second, in his *Identity* book Frei does not succeed in his project of developing a high Christology. He handles only one of its elements successfully. His analysis of how the Gospel stories depict Jesus as a particular person who as the Savior cannot be substituted for anyone or anything else is reasonably convincing. Frei does not succeed, however, in explaining how Jesus can have universal saving significance. His two schemes of identity depiction—the intention/action scheme and the self-manifestation scheme—both tend to militate against it. They give us only a Jesus who is fully human but not one who is fully divine. In a high Christology, however, it is ordinarily the deity of Jesus that makes his saving significance to be of universal scope. By his own admission, the identity-depiction schemes that Frei uses function only to describe Jesus as a "full human being" (*IJC*, 137). They are ill-equipped to portray him as anything more.

In the Gospel stories, Jesus' deity is depicted, if at all, in two main ways: first, through what he says and does; and second, through his resurrection appearances. When the narrated Jesus speaks of himself as the Son of Man, when he forgives sins, when he performs miracles of healing, when he stills the storm at sea or walks on water, when he is accused of blasphemy, an implicit claim is arguably being made that he is more than merely human. By factoring out this kind of material, which he approaches with a moderate skepticism, Frei deprives his argument of one possible narrative source for ascribing deity to the identity of Jesus Christ and therefore universal significance to him.

Perhaps the most obvious way in which the Gospel stories of Jesus' resurrection appearances might seem to invest him with deity would be through their depiction of the risen Jesus as the object of worship. Leaving aside the Gospel of Mark, whose oldest manuscripts notoriously include no appearance stories, all three other Gospels, each in its own way, depict Jesus as someone who is now worshipped as God (Matt. 28:9, 17; Luke 24:52; John 20:28). These stories are certainly suggestive, though perhaps not devoid of ambiguity. In any case, Frei does not avail himself of this narrative element.

Instead he takes another tack. On the one hand, Frei claims that in the resurrection appearances Jesus is "most fully himself," while on the other hand, he also plays his "Anselmian" card. Neither move is successful. The self-manifestation claim seems unconvincing, because the idea of Jesus being "most fully himself" is not a clear and distinct idea. Not only is it a subjective and perhaps slightly whimsical judgment, but it is also not obviously a narrative element in the appearance stories.[10] If Jesus is fully but merely human—and Frei's identity-depiction schemes offer nothing more—then it is hard to see how the appearance stories manifest Jesus as "one with God," as Frei claims. We would need to know in what sense Jesus is thought to be one with God, and in any case why he is not still merely human. For someone to be raised from the dead entails no logical implication, by itself, that he is thereby not just human but truly God. If the appearance stories somehow depict him as being truly God, as for example when he is worshipped, that is another matter entirely. The bare fact of his being raised would not be enough to make him more than human, even if his comings and goings were portrayed as mysterious.

Unfortunately, neither will Frei's "Anselmian" argument for Christ's resurrection hold up to scrutiny. Disbelief in Christ's resurrection is said to be "rationally impossible" (*IJC*, 151). Frei asks: "How can he who constitutes the very definition of life be conceived of as the opposite of what he defines? To think of him as dead is the equivalent of not thinking of him at all" (*IJC*, 148). To grasp who Jesus Christ is is to see that his nonresurrection is inconceivable (*IJC*, 145). His identity "is such that he cannot be conceived as not present" (*IJC*, 155).

This line of argument fails to distinguish between two types of necessity, the one strict and the other conditional. In his famous (and famously vexing) ontological argument, Anselm relies on the idea of strict necessity. The formulation "that than which no greater can be conceived" cannot be denied to the definition of "God," he argues, without lapsing into logical incoherence. The conclusion (that "therefore God necessarily exists") takes the form of strict necessity (regardless of whether one decides the inference is valid or not).

The same cannot be said of Frei's proposal, which might be rephrased as follows: "If the identity of Jesus Christ is what the Gospel narratives depict it to be, then he cannot be conceived as not risen from the dead." In this case the conditional clause can be denied without incoherence. Hence while the conclusion follows logically from the premise (supposing that Frei is correct about how the narratives depict Jesus), its necessity is still conditional, because the premise is merely conditional. A careful reading suggests that Frei saw the difference between these two types of necessity without ever making it clear. His point was more limited than may have appeared at first glance. Anyone who had accepted the conditional clause, he wanted to say, was logically committed to the stated conclusion—a point of some pastoral (and perhaps polemical) significance (*IJC*, 152).[11]

The third element in a high Christology is the "pattern of exchange." In order for this pattern to be sustained, Jesus must be truly God as well as truly human. If he were not truly human, he could not take sin and death upon himself in order to bear them away for the good of others. If he were not truly God, on the other hand, he would lack the power to overcome the terrible destruction he freely embraced, again for the good of others.[12] Because Frei fails to establish the deity of Jesus Christ, he fails to establish his universal significance, and without his universal significance the pattern of exchange cannot be sustained.

A further problem may be noted in passing. Frei does not succeed in deriving the pattern of exchange from the Gospel stories. He can only import it by drawing on other scriptural texts, like Isa 53 (the Suffering Servant passage) and Phil 2:6–11 (the Pauline hymn about Jesus' humiliation, obedience unto death, and subsequent exaltation). Frei's reading of the Gospel stories at this important juncture in his argument suggests that his narrative interpretation is again being driven by larger dogmatic considerations.

To sum up: Frei offers a convincing account of Jesus' irreducible particularity, but fails to establish Jesus' universal saving significance, because he fails to establish that Jesus is truly God. Consequently, he cannot sustain his account of the pattern of exchange, which requires that Jesus have universal significance for the good of others. Therefore, although in his *Identity* book Frei wishes to propound a high Christology, he succeeds in establishing only one of its three defining elements by means of a narrative analysis.

In an essay written prior to his *Identity* book, Frei discusses the Christology of H. Richard Niebuhr in light of the Chalcedonian formula. He notes with approval that in the book *Christ and Culture*,[13] Niebuhr propounded a "moral analysis" of the Incarnation as opposed to a "metaphysical analysis." Rather than focusing on Jesus' divine and human "natures" in their mysterious unity-in-distinction, Niebuhr sought to find Jesus' divine-human union in his "moral, historical acts." The result, Frei suggested, pointed toward a unique "moral Sonship" in which Jesus was completely one with God's will while also being completely one with human beings. This oneness was moral and volitional as opposed to metaphysical or ontological. Frei described Niebuhr's approach as "an important and fruitful new suggestion in modern theology" which held "every promise of being useful."[14]

It is intriguing to think that Frei might have conceived his *Identity* book as an attempt to expound upon Niebuhr's suggestion. Like Niebuhr, he seemed to think that Christology should focus on Jesus' deeds as opposed to his natures. Frei would thus be drawing positively upon his teacher, not just possibly attempting to correct him. It is instructive, however, that in pursuing such a program Frei was unable to provide a convincing account of a high or Chalcedonian Christology. Rather than being alternatives, it seems that a "moral Christology" could not be successfully worked out in accord with Chalcedon without being developed as a "metaphysical Christology" at the same time.

In his 1986 Princeton lectures, shortly before the end of his life, Frei returned to the problem of a high Christology in accord with Chalcedon. Although he had long since left his earlier Christological project behind, he had not lost his interest in the Christological significance of the Gospel stories. Although they no longer served as the basis for deriving a high Christology, he believed that they could be interpreted through the lens of the Chalcedonian formula. It would be an ecclesial, committed interpretation, informed at once by both dogmatic and exegetical reflection. It would presuppose, in effect, a complex and subtle feedback loop that moved dialectically from exegesis to dogmatics and back again, in a continual process of dynamic interaction.

Frei's insight into how the Chalcedonian formula functions is the most brilliant suggestion for its use that I have seen. "The formula," he writes, "is a conceptual redescription of a synthesis of the gospel stories understood as narratives identifying Jesus Christ."[15] The Gospel stories, Frei now suggests, are to be read through Chalcedon as a hermeneutical lens or an interpretive rule. Just because some episodes depict Jesus in his humanity (e.g., John 19:28), that does not mean that he is not truly God. Conversely, just because others depict him in his deity (e.g., Mark 4:39, 6:49), that does not mean he is not truly human. When the human predication is in the forefront, the divine is always presupposed, and vice versa. Faithful or ecclesial reading moves back and forth between these predications.

As Karl Barth points out, the true deity and true humanity of Jesus can neither be simultaneously depicted nor inclusively apprehended. "When the one is heard, the other can be heard only indirectly, in faith. ... Faith is the perception either way of what is not said."[16] In this way the two predications are held together by Jesus as the single subject of the Gospel stories as confessed by faith. The unity of these divergent predications in the narrated figure of Jesus must be accorded priority, states Frei, over "their abiding logical distinctness" (*TCT*, 126). "What is at stake," he concludes, "is the proper identification of the agent under a categorical scheme ... [T]he meaning of the doctrine is the story rather than the meaning of the story being the doctrine" (*TCT*, 126). The meaning of Chalcedon, in other words, is the story rather than the reverse.

What we encounter here is the maturation of Frei's hermeneutical thought. He still proposes to read the Gospel stories identifying Jesus through a hermeneutical scheme. The scheme is no longer regarded merely as a formal device, however, because Chalcedon is at one level a first-order statement that summarizes and asserts the mystery of Jesus' divine-human identity (*TCT*, 124). Nor is this interpretive scheme derived merely from the Gospel stories. It is derived from the New Testament witness taken as a whole. From the standpoint of faith, it was formulated by an ecumenical council of the ancient church under the guidance of the Holy Spirit. It serves as an authoritative device that establishes the "literal sense" of the New Testament witness to Jesus as confessed by the faithful community. The Chalcedonian formula thus authorizes and ensures the kind of high Christology with a narrative orientation that the early Frei had sought but never found. Although he took many detours to get there, he arrived at Chalcedon as his hermeneutical home.[17]

NOTES

1. Hans W. Frei, *The Identity of Jesus Christ: The Hermeneutical Bases of Dogmatic Theology* (Philadelphia: Fortress Press, 1975). Hereafter cited in the text as *IJC*.

2. Frei, "Theological Reflections on the Accounts of Jesus' Death and Resurrection," *Christian Scholar* 49 (1966): 263–306. Reprinted in Frei, *Theology and Narrative: Selected Essays*, ed. George Hunsinger and William C. Placher (New York: Oxford University Press, 1993), 45–91. Material from this volume is hereafter cited in the text as *TN*.

3. Frei, "The Mystery of the Presence of Jesus Christ," in *Crossroads* 17 (January–March 1967): 69–96 and (April–June 1967): 69–96.

4. Frei, "The Doctrine of Revelation in the Thought of Karl Barth, 1909 to 1922: The Nature of Barth's Break with Liberalism," unpublished dissertation, Yale University, 1956. Hereafter cited in the text as *BBL*.

5. H. Richard Niebuhr, *Faith on Fourth: An Inquiry into the Structure of Human Faith* (New Haven: Yale University Press, 1989). Hereafter cited in the text as *FE*.

6. For a discussion of how Frei deals with the factuality question, see George Hunsinger, "The Daybreak of the New Creation: Christ's Resurrection in Recent Theology," *Scottish Journal of Theology* 57 (2004): 163–81; on pp. 176–7.

7. I have also used this image to describe Frei in an earlier essay: George Hunsinger, "Hans Frei as Theologian: The Quest for a Generous Orthodoxy," *Modern Theology* 8 (1992): 103–28; on p. 104.
8. David Lee, *Luke's Stories of Jesus: Theological Reading of Gospel Narrative and the Legacy of Hans Frei* (Sheffield, England: Sheffield Academic Press, 1999). Hereafter cited in the text as *LHF*. (I should mention that Lee also delves deeply into Frei's later work.)
9. "Luther," Frei told John Woolverton in an interview, "was an early influence on me at Yale Divinity School." Martin Luther seems to be in the background when Frei refers to "The Pattern of Exchange" (*IJC*, 74–84, 160). In *The Freedom of a Christian* Luther wrote, "[Faith] ... unites the soul with Christ as a bride is united with her bridegroom ... Christ is full of grace, life, and salvation. The soul is full of sins, death, and damnation. Now let faith come between them and sin, death, and damnation will be Christ's, while grace, life, and salvation will be the soul's. For if Christ is the bridegroom, he must take upon himself the things which belong to his bride and bestow upon her the things that are his. If he gives her his body and very self, how shall he not give her all that is his? And if he takes the body of the bride, how shall he not take all that is hers?" (*Luther's Works* [American edition, Augsburg-Fortress, 1955] 31:351). Frei offers nothing this detailed and specific. For Karl Barth on the pattern of exchange, see Barth, *Church Dogmatics*, Vol. IV, part 1 (Edinburgh: T&T Clark, 1957), 75–7. For Frei's personal reference to Luther, see John F. Woolverton, "Hans W. Frei in Context: A Theological and Historical Memoir," *Anglican Theological Review* 79 (1997): 369–93; on p. 378.
10. As Lee observes about the Emmaus Road story in Luke 24: "Jesus is concerned not to assure the disciples that he is risen, but rather that it was necessary that he should suffer" (*LHF*, 292). This is said over against Frei, who wrongly seems to suppose that the story serves mainly to identify Jesus as risen. The Emmaus story also seems to imply that the true identity of Jesus is made known through the Scriptures (Luke 24:27) and the breaking of bread (Luke 24:30) (not narrowly through the Gospel stories themselves).
11. I have drawn here upon an argument I made in Hunsinger, "Christ's Resurrection in Recent Theology," 177–8. (*Infra*, n. 6.) (George Hunsinger, "The Daybreak of the New Creation: Christ's Resurrection in Recent Theology," *Scottish Journal of Theology* 57, no. 2 [May 2004]: 163–81.)
12. In the *Christian Scholar* article, Frei wrote about Jesus' "omnipotence" (*TN*, 49), but in his *Identity* book he dropped the term, in favor of a contrast simply between "power and powerlessness."
13. H. Richard Niebuhr, *Christ and Culture* (New York: Harper & Brothers, 1951).
14. Hans W. Frei, "The Theology of H. Richard Niebuhr," in *Faith and Ethics: The Theology of H. Richard Niebuhr*, ed. Paul Ramsey (New York: Harper & Brothers, Publishers, 1957): 65–116, especially the section entitled "Christology" (104–16). I have quoted from pp. 110, 114, and 116. Note that Troeltsch, however, had already formulated the relationship of God and Christ as "a unity of will, not as an essential unity in substance." See Ernst Troeltsch, *The Christian Faith* (Minneapolis: Fortress Press, 1991), 90; cf. 100.

15. Hans W. Frei, *Types of Christian Theology*, ed. George Hunsinger and William C. Placher (New Haven: Yale University Press, 1992): 125. Hereafter cited in the text as *TCT*.
16. Karl Barth, *Church Dogmatics*, Vol. I, part 1 (Edinburgh: T&T Clark, 1975), 180.
17. Perhaps the major question that Frei left open regarding the identity of Jesus Christ pertained to whether he thought God suffered and died in the Incarnation to save us from sin and death. In his early Christology, with its rather Niebuhrian and Troeltschian undertones, he seemed to lean in a somewhat "dualist" direction. In that case he might most consistently have held that God did not suffer in the Incarnation. With his later espousal of Chalcedon, however, Frei might have been open to a more "unitary" and theopaschite interpretation.

CHAPTER FIVE

Frei's Later Christology: Radiance and Obscurity

JASON A. SPRINGS

Hans Frei died much too young, leaving behind him a body of published work as compelling in its content as it was slender in its magnitude. Even more so, he bequeathed a trove of materials at least as rich to be worked through, made sense of, and grappled with in their details and implications. The twenty-five years since Frei's passing has inspired numerous attempts to sift and clarify, explicate and extrapolate, expand upon it, and of course, to critically assess its strengths and weaknesses. Frei's work evokes interest from so many different directions—theological and hermeneutical, of course, but also sociological, philosophical, literary, and historical. In my judgment, this is one of the reasons that Frei's work has remained so compelling for several generations of students in the twenty-five years since his death.

The title of my essay gestures toward both the radiance and obscurity of the role of Christology in Frei's later work. The role of Christology in Frei's later work has been rightly characterized as its most pivotal dimension. In an article that perhaps most precisely differentiates Frei's later work from that of his friend and colleague, George Lindbeck, Mike Higton pinpoints the force of Frei's Christological focus and objectives as one of the points at which Frei and Lindbeck most starkly diverge.[1] As Higton has stated it, in Frei's later work, the Church's taking the narrative reading of the Bible as primary is not to say that "the Church mastered the Bible, but rather, precisely by taking a narrative reading as primary rather than an allegorical or purely symbolic one, the Church allowed the Bible to stand over against it as an independent norm which it could not control."[2] Higton continues:

> This isn't just a contingent fact of history, said Frei. It came about precisely because Christians looked to the unsubstitutable man Jesus of Nazareth as their source and norm, and so learned to read their scriptures in such a way as to take them to be about that historically specific man. ... [Moreover] ... this narrative reading is coherent with, informed by, and ultimately only intelligible on the assumption of, an incarnational theology.[3]

This passage sketches well the central Christological orientation in Frei's later work.[4] And yet, it is precisely this orientation that is, at times, obscured by the multidimensionality that so fully comes to the fore in the final decade of Frei's life and work.

Arguably, it is the multidimensionality of Frei's work during the 1980s that makes it tantalizing to a wide-ranging array of readers. The interest generated by Frei's engagement with literary theorists, his wrestling with the concept of "narrative," his increasingly explicit—but intrinsically ad hoc—uses of Wittgenstein and Clifford Geertz that have drawn the largest share of attention. Even those who have broached the significance of the role of Christ in Frei's later work have done so in a quite condensed fashion.[5]

In what follows, then, I aim to deliberately hold open the question of the extent to which there is development in Frei's Christological orientation that occurs as an accumulative effect emerging across several of his latest occasional writings. I propose to do this by way of close exposition and commentary upon these arguably least-attended-to essays and lectures. I aim, moreover, to expand and unpack the multiple senses in which, as Higton rightly puts it, the emergence of the orientational role of the literal sense was not the Church's "mastering the Bible," nor simply a felicitous accident of history. I propose to elucidate the Christological bases upon which Frei's account articulated and justified the Bible's orientation "as an independent norm which [the Church] could not control."

Frei's Alexander Thompson Memorial lecture delivered at Princeton Seminary in 1986, "Conflict in Interpretation," exemplifies the kind of complex integration of interests characteristic of Frei's work throughout his career. There he devotes extensive attention to the lessons to be gleaned from literary critics who have come to attend to biblical narratives, among whom British literary theorist Frank Kermode is an exemplar. Kermode arrived at the categorical claim that the relationship between text and truth is irreducibly variegated, that the meaning of the text is ultimately indeterminate—it yields multiple, indeed irreducibly diverse, interpretations. This, according to Kermode, makes "outsiders" of even those who take themselves to be "insiders" to a particular interpretive community. For Christian reading communities, this would mean that the separateness of what is written and what is written about positions Christian readers, those following Jesus, as merely a different variation of outsiders. "World and book are hopelessly plural, endlessly disappointing," Kermode writes. "[O]ur sole hope and pleasure is in the perception of a momentary radiance, before the door of disappointment is finally shut on us."[6] The ultimate indeterminacy of interpretations, the narrative's multiplicity of potential implications for ways of being in the world, results finally in Hegel's "night when all cows are black," and in the final analysis, the text makes outsiders of us all.

The position is a bracing one, and in many ways it captivated Frei—enough so, at least, that Frei engaged Kermode's position in detail, meticulously unpacking and commenting upon several lengthy passages from *The Genesis of Secrecy*.[7] And while Frei finally parts company with such claims about the interpretive indeterminacy, and thus, ultimate obscurity of the biblical narratives, he pauses to derive an important cautionary insight here for Christian readers. The history of biblical interpretation in the modern era is littered with an array of efforts all too eager to move "from text to truth or from language to reality." Such efforts either conceptualize the adequacy of the text in terms of how it is taken to simply point to what it implies, whether that be the spiritualized sense of what "is hidden within" it, or the literalism of ostensive reference that slides down the slope of either historical-critical skepticism or the infallible certainties of fundamentalism.[8]

How does Frei respond? Frei casts his lot with the Protestant Reformers in identifying the biblical text as "the Word of God," on one hand, and thus "sufficient," but simultaneously warning against an overdetermination of the biblical text as capturing without remainder that to which it refers, that which it portrays (either through the kind of ostensive reference in which the sentences putatively "mean" in virtue of referring to their subject matter or by providing a linguistic point of departure from which to "thrust ... beyond the literal shape" to "language transcending reality," for instance, by way of their metaphorical extravagance to "a mode of being in the world"). In short, the text is sufficient, but we dare not make an idol of it.[9]

To expand this point Frei invokes the concept of "witness"—the text is adequate in its witnessing to the Word of God. In fact, he says, the text's *authority* derives from its witness to the Word of God, "rather than from," he clarifies, "any inherent divinized quality."[10] This witness occurs in and through the literal sense of the text, which Christian traditions of scriptural reading and interpretation (at least, Frei says, through the end of so-called precritical interpretation) recognized as authoritative, and indeed, orientational for their interpretive practices.

What is the warrant for this authority of the literal sense? That the emergent tradition took it to be authoritative? That the literal sense happened to find common use, and eventually authoritative influence, in the Christian community? Is common use in the Christian communal tradition of reading what makes the ascriptive mode authoritative—"that it is *this* story about *this* person as agent and patient"; "that 'Jesus'—not someone else or nobody in particular—is the subject, the agent, and patient of these stories is ... their crucial point, and the descriptions of events, sayings, personal qualities, and so forth, become literal by being firmly predicated of him"?[11]

On one hand, Frei points out that the Reformers differ from the early church in that they consider the literal sense to be sufficiently "perspicuous" in itself to conduct agreement, and thus not in need of "authorization from the interpretive tradition."[12] And while Frei clearly understands himself to be following the Reformers, it is the multiple ways that he finds Karl Barth carrying forward the legacies of the Reformation that lead Frei to historically situate and sociologically contextualize the interwoven relationship of text and tradition—to reconceptualize them together (text and tradition in the sense of sociocultural object-directed practice that extends historically over time). Frei seeks to relate the two seamlessly, yet not without distinction (without, that is, collapsing one into the other or synthesizing the two). Coming to this position occurs as a lengthy even leisurely development over the course of Frei's thinking and writing, markedly between his overreliance upon the literary genre of "realistic narrative" in the *Identity of Jesus Christ* and the work in the final decade of his life in which he turned to the practices of "literal reading."[13]

So, for instance, while Frei says that it was not "logically necessary" that the literal sense became the plain sense (the orientational or primary sense) of Scripture for the tradition, at the same point he indicates how the "rule of faith" or "rule of truth" emerged among early followers of Christ (albeit informally) not as framework imposed externally, but derived from the emergent formation of tradition. This appears in passages of Frei's "Literal Reading" essay that are easy to pass over as insignificant. Indeed, compared to the extensively rigorous attention received by Frei's consistently ad hoc appropriation of tools and insights from nonreductionist social science, or his references to narrative and engagement with literary theory, comparatively, these passages of the essay (and comparable passages that have the appearance of interrelation when Frei's latest writings are viewed in intertextual perspective) remain in obscurity.[14]

Nicholas Wolterstorff claims that Frei was not concerned with how or why the literal sense became the plain sense for the Christian tradition. Frei's concern, as he sees it, is with the sense that happened to become authoritative for the tradition. The literal sense, according to Wolterstorff, was the sense that the Christian community found most beneficial.[15] And yet there is far more at stake than the ostensive starting point that happened to accrue in the Christian tradition of reading and interpretation. "Ruled reading"—what comes to be formally articulated in the "rule of faith" or "rule of truth" by the end of the second century—appears in Frei's account of how the literal sense became plain (authoritative, traditional) for the early Christian community. He demonstrates how such reading would retain central significance (although its significance was conceptualized differently at different points in time) into the contemporary era of the Christian church (even, that is, through the period at which the narrative surface of the texts about Jesus was considered to be reports or evidence which referred to purported ancient events).

Frei seeks to hold together the Christian tradition of scriptural reading and interpretation, what the text portrays of Jesus, and how it portrays that. Informal rules which prefigured the formal articulation of the "rule of truth" are central to Frei's conception of how ruled reading came to be central to that authority of the literal sense. He points out that it did this "right from the beginning," and again, in what he calls the ascriptive (as opposed to descriptive) mode—"That 'Jesus'—not someone else or nobody in particular—is the subject, the agent and patient of these stories is said to be their crucial point, and the descriptions of events, sayings, personal qualities, and so forth, become literal by being firmly predicated of him."[16] This is the sense in which the text witnesses to the Word in a way that makes—or ought to make—the literal sense orientational for whatever other interpretive approaches or readings are addressed to the witness of Scripture. Yet Frei is not content to descriptively explicate this process as it likely unfolded, and does not belabor his exposition of that process. In fact, he is as vexingly sparse in his treatment of the details of this emergent unity of text and tradition in the early church as he is provocatively suggestive in his passing comment that while the literal reading became the plain reading for the Christian tradition, it was not "logically necessary" that it did so.[17] This is significant because it aids in illuminating the role, albeit understated in Frei's work, of what Katherine Greene-McCreight identifies as the "verbal sense."[18]

Frei sketched an analogue to the verbal sense in the terms of attending to both the literary-literal and grammatical/syntactical features of the text, *as well as* the use of the text in context. In fact, Frei describes and endorses an account of the literal sense that entails both the grammatical/syntactical (traditionally referred to as the "verbal sense") and the literary-literal ("not only as use-in-context but as unity of grammatical/syntactical sense and signified subject").[19] Note how this characterization integrates constraints upon the literal sense exerted by the "grammatical/syntactical relation between the narrative sequence and what it renders descriptively" (i.e., what Frei much earlier in his career had mistakenly assimilated reductively to the general category of "realistic narrative") along with concerns about "use-in-context." In short, the text does not mean whatever the community takes it to mean (e.g., whatever uses the community makes of the text vis-à-vis its interests and purposes, or sense of its "mission"). In other words, in no way does Frei's account grant the community "the role of the ultimate arbiter of the meaning of any and all biblical texts."[20] While the literal sense did not emerge as the plain sense for the early church as a matter of "logical necessity," it emerged nonetheless as that reading from which the rule of faith/rule of truth derived, and which the rule of faith/rule of truth further exerted constraints upon in framing what could count as truthful interpretations of Scripture. The literal sense became plain (e.g., authoritative, the traditional sense) because of what the literal sense ascribes to Jesus—what it claims in witnessing to the lordship of Jesus Christ. In fact, on Frei's account, the literal sense became authoritative as plain (i.e., as the entry level to which the other senses of the text and unavoidable external categories are accountable) insofar as it was recognized as true. As Frei put it, "The singular agent enacting the unity of human finitude and divine infinity, Jesus of Nazareth, is taken to be itself the ground, guarantee, and conveyance of the truth of the depicted enactment."[21]

Note that Frei's description of the literal sense does not preclude asking and exploring, as possible, the factuality or the character of the truth-claims. Indeed, here we see the significance of Frei's retention of "historical reference" in that conclusive evidence against the resurrection could prove to be decisive. On this point, William Placher is especially helpful in his exposition of Frei's approach:

> The stories capture through narrative a person's identity. Reading these stories, one learns who Jesus is—that is, one learns both the characteristics of his human life and the fact that that human life was somehow the self-revelation of God. Many of the episodes serve as biographical anecdotes, "true" if they illustrate his character authentically even though the particular incident they narrate never happened, and the overall shape of the narrative portrays something of Jesus' identity .... Historical evidence, on this account, can *refute* faith. Theological reflection on the logic of the narratives as identity descriptions works out what themes or particulars of the story are crucial to Jesus' identity and, if historical evidence persuasively refuted the relevant claims, one would have to give them up—either give up this sort of theological project or give up being a Christian.[22]

In principle, then, the claims of Scripture are falsifiable. However, if they are true, then they witness to events that defy exhaustive explanation or speculation (i.e., the miracle of Christ's resurrection).

Of course, Frei goes further to identify the text as an object around which Christian communities' scriptural practices cohere. This is the basis on which

Christian communities' scriptural practices are answerable to the features of the text. The text, Frei says, "is not inert but exerts a pressure of its own on the inquiring reader." In other words, its uses in the sociolinguistic community of the Christian church are accountable to what the text portrays (i.e., most centrally and nonnegotiably, its witness to the life, death, and resurrection of the Jesus Christ). This adds a further dimension to Frei's account of why and how it was the literal sense that came to be taken as orientationally authoritative (i.e., "plain"). To recognize this text as Scripture is to recognize the condition of subordinating oneself to that to which the text witnesses (i.e., what it literally ascribed to this particular person Jesus—"occurrences, teaching, personal qualities and religious attributes"[23]).

Now, within the parameters provided by Scripture's orientational witness, there was sometimes wide-ranging disagreement about how to understand and interpret this text. But notice that, on Frei's account, these disagreements emerged precisely because scriptural text "resisted" any reading by Christian communities that purported to exhaustively interpret it ("there can be no non-residual reading, no complete interpretation" because a "good enough text has the power to resist," Frei puts the point[24]). For this reason, when such readings conflict and inspire controversy, the task of reading and consulting Scripture is not one where the readers take a vote to determine which account they agree to be authoritative. Rather, Frei describes this process as sitting down and holding each other accountable to "the features of the text." The features of the text are part and parcel to the practices of reading, consulting, and understanding Scripture. Moreover, understandings and interpretations are accountable to those features. Thus, Frei explains, "When we disagree in our interpretations of a text, it is well to check on what each of us is doing, but it would be silly to do that and not pay attention to the features of the text or act as though it had none or as though they varied simply as our reading of them varied."[25]

Given these constraints, as well as the normative constraints constitutive of the practices of reading and sense-making ("when we disagree ... it is well to check on what each of us is doing"), the text does not say whatever some reader or community of readers takes it to say; its features do not simply vary as readings, or uses, of them vary. In other words, whatever some community of readers takes to be an authoritative reading of the text is accountable to the features of the text, as well as the norms constitutive of the practices in which reading and consulting this text occur. Textual meaning is not determined simply by what some reader or community takes them to say, or however a community decides to use them. In fact, on this view, in virtue of the resistance of the textual features and normative constraints that are constitutive of practices of reading and consulting texts—and to which, Frei says, readers and interpreters hold one another accountable—the individual reader or community of readers may be wrong in how it uses Scripture; she or they may be wrong on the meaning that emerges as a result of their uses of the text. And this objective dimension of the scriptural practice and use means that one may be wrong *not* simply in virtue of disagreeing with the community's agreement upon the text's significance and beneficial or "useful" use.

On the bases of the complex warrants above, what Frei identified as the minimal agreement about reading the Scriptures in the Christian tradition framed wide-ranging diversity of interpretations and disagreements, and facilitated multiple approaches. Frei wrote,

> First, Christian reading of Christian Scriptures must not deny the literal ascription to Jesus and not to any other person, event, time or idea, of those occurrences, teachings, personal qualities and religious attributes associated with him in the stories in which he plays a part, as well as in the other New Testament writings in which his name is invoked. ... Second, no Christian reading may deny either the unity of Old and New Testaments or the congruence (which is not by any means the same as literal identity) of that unity with the ascriptive literalism of the Gospel narratives. Third, any readings not in principle in contradiction with these two rules are permissible, and two of the obvious candidates would be the various sorts of historical-critical and literary readings.[26]

As we saw above, Frei identified the distinction between, yet interdependence of, the dual warrant of text and tradition for the authority of the literal sense in the early church. He had pointed, further, to the sufficient "perspicuousness" by which the Reformers thought "what the text says" through its literal rendering is adequate and authoritative in virtue of its mode of witness to the Word. Here I would like to return for a moment to the point at which I left off my explication of Frei's Princeton Seminary lecture of 1986. For Frei comes to the crux of the 1986 lecture by holding forth this question: "And is that Word which is witnessed to, is that not the truth, at once ontologically transcendent and historically incarnate?"[27] He then gestures to Barth, in succession to the Reformers, as one who most insisted on this dual claim about Scripture. Frei continues with some of the most decisive lines in his later writings:

> What is written is the Word of God. The divine touch on it is not that extravagance by means of which what is written, the word, might be transformed into that about which it is written. Christians do have to speak of the referent of the text. They have to speak historically and ontologically, but in each case, it must be the notion of truth or reference that must be re-shaped extravagantly, not the reading of the literal text. Any notion of truth such that that concept disallows the condescension of truth to the

depiction in the text—[any notion of truth that disallows the truth's] own self-identification with, let us say, the fourfold story of Jesus of Nazareth taken as an ordinary story—has itself to be viewed with profound skepticism by a Christian interpreter. The textual world as witness to the Word of God is not identical with the latter, and yet, by the Spirit's grace, it is "sufficient" for the witnessing.[28]

On one hand, this paragraph comes as a burst of radiance in the wake of Frei's meticulous engagement with Frank Kermode's claim about the ultimate obscurity of the Gospel narratives in the pages that precede it. Here we catch a full glimpse of how concentrated Frei's account is: reference, history, ontology—each of which must be reshaped by the literary-literal reading of the text, and even more basically, "the condescension of truth to the depiction in the text." And yet, at the same time, this passage confronts readers with a brevity and density that cry out for further illumination. These lines come across provocatively freighted with background that remains to be elucidated and unpacked. What is clear is that Frei takes himself to have gestured toward his own account of the literal sense in which the technical and conceptual implements that readers bring to their readings of the text—as indeed they must—are nonetheless bent toward, conformed to, and oriented by the witness of the text to which the literal sense makes a primary contribution. What of "truth"? Truth does—indeed, must—condescend to the depiction of the text. And yet, at the same time, these words are fit for witnessing to the Word. What does this reflect of Frei's later Christology?

Frei gives his readers little else to go beyond the above passage from "Conflicts in Interpretation." And so it is with the above remarks in view that I turn to Frei's remarks in response to the evangelical theologian Carl F. H. Henry for some intertextual illumination. Indeed, at several points in the secondary literature on Frei's work, these remarks have been cited as perhaps his clearest on these topics in his later work.[29]

Frei's claim about "the condescension of truth to the depiction in the text" echoes in his response to Henry's critique of what he called "narrative theology" in a series of 1985 lectures at Yale. So Frei:

The truth to which we refer we cannot state apart from the biblical language which we employ to do so. And belief in the divine authority of Scripture is for me simply that we do not need more ... Even if I say that history is first of all the facts—and I do have a healthy respect for evidence—I come across something else. Is Jesus Christ (and here I come across the problem of miracle) a "fact" like other historical facts? Should I really say that the eternal word made flesh, that is, made fact indeed, is a fact like any other?... [Y]es, "Jesus" refers, as does any ordinary name, but "Jesus Christ" in scriptural witness does not refer ordinarily; or rather, it refers ordinarily only by the miracle of grace. And that means that I do not know the manner in which it refers, only that the ordinary language in which it is cast will miraculously suffice.[30]

Frei's explicit concern in such passages is his conception of how the biblical text refers beyond itself, and in rebutting Henry's notorious charge that, for Frei, the world of the biblical text is discrete and self-contained, putatively referring to nothing beyond itself.

And yet his response to Carl Henry parallels closely Frei's description "the condescension of truth to the text." For even as the text refers to the earthly Jesus (either as history-like "identity descriptions" testifying to who Jesus is,[31] or referring to specific occurrences that happened in some form or fashion along the lines of what the biblical text portrays[32]) the very notion of reference is conformed to, and oriented by, the textual witness by which the risen Lord encounters and makes himself plain to us here and now, and this, Frei says, "by the miracle of grace."[33] We have here a claim, tentatively stated, admittedly unsystematic, still somewhat inchoate, that Scripture gives us not just any witness, or a witness among other possible witnesses, but "the witness without parallel." It is the indispensable means by which Jesus encounters us in the mystery of the resurrection. In this we find further illumination of "the condescension of truth to the depiction in the text."[34]

And yet even these remarks call for further elucidation. In fact, the degree to which these lines illuminate what I describe as the orientational— and, indeed, high—Christology in Frei's latest writings is further illuminated by a little article written just before Frei's death. This is an article far less attended to in the literature. The article was published the year following Frei's death in the *Journal of Anglican and Episcopal History* under the title "How It All Began: On the Resurrection of Christ."[35] There, Frei has this to say (I will quote these all-too-frequently unattended-to passages at length):

> The mystery to which the New Testament accounts testify—or which they render for us as texts inadequate yet adequate—is the continuity of the identity of Jesus through the real, complete disruption of death. He is the same before and after death. We know nothing of a reversal of the physical conditions of full death once it has set in; moreover, we also know nothing of a human identity that is not physical. The New Testament accounts do not invite us to speculate on a specific solution to the quandary of a live physical presence after death, nor do they answer the question of how the person raised can be one with the One who raised him from the dead. The point of the stories is simply to bear witness to the fact that Jesus, raised from the dead, was the same person, the same identity as before. That is

the central Christian affirmation, vigorously reaffirmed both in the Creeds and in this article with its stress on the physical nature of the risen Jesus—a physicality that is indispensable if he is to be efficacious on our behalf. The great Patristic saying, "What he did not assume [i.e., anything less than full humanity], that he could not save" is as true of him in the resurrection as in his life before death. That, stated straightforwardly, is what affirmation that the resurrection happened in the first place to Jesus, not to the Christian community, is all about. It is Jesus Christ who remains capable of saving us in our mortal condition, who continues to be efficacious on our behalf. In his full and constant identity as Jesus of Nazareth, he is God's Word in our midst. He remains himself .... Even more startling than the continuity of the identity of Jesus through death and resurrection is the affirmation associated with it in Christian faith: his identity as this singular, continuing individual, Jesus of Nazareth, includes humankind in its singularity. He is the representative and inclusive person .... The miraculous rise [of faith out of unfaith] ... is accounted for by the miraculous inclusion of us all vicariously in the singular identity of Jesus, the fact that it was his very identity, his being, to give himself efficaciously on our behalf. He enacted his identity on the cross and it was confirmed in his resurrection. He was and is what he did for us. Because we are comprehended in his self-identifying action ("we were there") and his resurrection includes us, he is the ground of our faith and the source of its arising in us through the New Testament message, as it did in the early Christian community— [T]he message and miracle of faith are accounted for by the very character, and are therefore a function of Jesus' being and his resurrection from the dead; and so Jesus and faith, as well as reality and text, belong together as the miracle of resurrection.

(204–5)

While avoiding the temptation to overread this passage, I find it to shed further light on the more obscure passages from writings and lectures that I sifted above. Does Frei here demonstrate any further development toward the kind of "high Christology" that he took himself to be articulating as far back as his "Remarks on a Theological Proposal"?[36] To put the questions differently: in what sense do his remarks here move beyond the Christological account that Frei set forth in *The Identity of Jesus Christ*?

What are the crucial differences and points of expansion? Notice the difference in the "pattern of exchange." Here Professor Hunsinger has meticulously unpacked the ways that what Frei took to be a "high Christological" account in *Identity* left many things unspoken, and perhaps altogether unattended to—at least insofar as Frei took himself to be articulating a "high Christology." For instance, in *Identity* the "pattern of exchange" is "unidirectional." In other words, while Frei persistently says that Jesus takes on the guilt of others in exchange for his own purity, Frei does not explicitly say anything regarding the opposite direction—in which Jesus' purity becomes the purity of others before God. "Yet without such a movement in the opposite direction, how can Jesus' self-sacrificing purity ... have universal meaning and saving power, not symbolically but realistically, and therefore as a finished, unrepeatable, and vicarious work?"[37] Do we get a sense from Frei's exposition of the fourth article above of how Frei's thinking came to respond to such a concern?

We have here the emphasis upon Jesus as a particular and unsubstitutable human being, and fully human identity, that Frei emphasizes time and again throughout *The Identity of Jesus Christ*. Frei's language about Jesus "enacting his identity" I take to be consistent with Frei's claim that "individual, specific, unsubstitutable identity of Jesus" is available in what Jesus did (i.e., who he is, is in what he did; "the person is in the work, and the work is in the person"). We also have a distinct statement about the inclusion of humanity in Christ's humanity, and thus in his crucifixion and resurrection as well (as Frei puts it, "we were there"). Clearly, Frei does not go so far as to state anything close to the claim that in Christ's "exchanging his purity for our guilt, his purity becomes ours before God."[38] What he does say is that

> [Christ's] full self-identification with us is perpetual and not temporary .... [which] entails the consequence that we are judged and are to be judged by none other than the one who is our saving representative .... [O]ur common Judge is no ruthless stranger appearing suddenly out of an eternal nowhere but the one who bore the universal burden on our behalf, both when we were victimized and when we were victimizers.[39]

Second, what he says follows the Creeds in affirming, as Frei puts it, "the eternal identity of Christ and God" (205). Does this evince some identifiable motion away from the distant echoes of adoptionism that haunted Frei's use of intention-action description in *The Identity of Jesus Christ*—particularly the impression created there that it is not until Christ's resurrection that God's presence fully coincides with that of Jesus?[40]

If we identify some significant difference on these points between Frei's account in *The Identity of Jesus Christ* and passages such as these, it must be admitted that here Frei is explicitly incorporating attention to the Creeds and the Thirty-Nine Articles of the Church of England as the bases for these claims. And that contrasts with the restrained hermeneutical basis that he focuses upon in *The Identity of Jesus Christ*.

In fact, some might raise the concern that the article that I am belaboring here (aside from being a mere five pages, and again, a condensed series of paragraphs) is, fundamentally, Frei's exposition and elucidation of Article 4 of the Thirty-Nine Articles of the Church of England—the article on the resurrection of Jesus. That being the case, we should not be surprised that Frei writes here of the resurrection with a pointedness perhaps not paralleled anywhere else in his writings. However, an inquirer might press, do we really have grounds to take this as Frei's articulation of his own position? Could such a concern be one of the reasons that this piece of Frei's has received relatively so little attention by those who have worked either to charitably explicate, or to finally set aside, Frei's work in the intervening twenty-five years?

In my view, the passage above is exemplary of the recurring patterns in Frei's scholarship, and nicely models Frei's thinking in microcosm. In this passage— and throughout the piece itself—Frei explicates the fourth article by way of an ad hoc methodological formation of types—of four different kinds of views of the resurrection of Christ. The first view Frei identifies as "mythological," in which resurrection symbolically reflects the rise of faith in the followers of Jesus, whatever Jesus' own personal fate. There was despair, and now there is faith. Frei's second view is a kind which posits the New Testament accounts as "an absolutely accurate record of the things that actually happened when Jesus was raised from the dead."[41] The third view Frei describes "spiritualizes" the New Testament accounts as so-called resurrection appearances. In short, these accounts are not to be taken literally. Whether the reports are true or false (e.g., Was the tomb physically empty? Were the physical details of the resurrection as the text depicts?) are not matters of importance. Of this type, Frei says, the reality is more important than the text, and the two are not that closely related.

Frei's articulation of the fourth view is saturated with the language and phrasing that run throughout his own writings in the final two years of his work. Here the texts are taken to "mean what they say, so that their subject is indeed the bodily resurrected Jesus." Here "the miracle of the resurrection ... is [taken to be] a real event. ... [Though] human depiction and conception are [ultimately] inadequate [to depict and account for it] ... the literal description is the best that can be offered. ... Text and reality are adequate, indeed, indispensable to each other but not identical ..." and again, "[T]he literal account of the text is adequate to the reality of the events by divine grace."[42] In short, Frei's characterization of the fourth type is less Frei tipping his hand than it is Frei laying his cards out on the table. In other words, this is Frei's view, articulated far more clearly and succinctly than in his response to Carl Henry, or in the dense passages in the final paragraphs of his Princeton Seminary lecture of 1986. And while Frei does not explicitly endorse it in first-person terms here, the pattern of exposition apparent here recurs strategically throughout his work.

Clearly, Frei's stated purpose is to elucidate the key claims, points of contrast, and similarities of each type vis-à-vis the others. And yet by virtue of the ad hoc typological exercise, Frei simultaneously, and subtly, executes a polemic. In other words, Frei is not merely laying out an array of views for the reader to survey, and perhaps be edified by this exercise in explication and elucidation. Frei takes pains to demonstrate how the view that may bear closest affinities with his preferred view on crucial points has its ostensive strengths accounted for and its terminal deficiencies overcome by his own. The first view—the mythological view or a Bultmann—is both "embraced" and then "reversed" by the fourth view. Both view a "vital connection (though not identity) between texts and reality of the resurrection"; and for both, the "miracle of the resurrection is the miraculous rise of faith out of unfaith" in the present and future, as we see it in the past in virtue of the text's testimony. And yet, in the first view, Jesus and the rise of faith are represented as a function of the message. In the fourth view, faith arises from Jesus' being and his resurrection from the dead—and so, says Frei, "Jesus and faith, as well as reality and text, belong together as the miracle of resurrection."[43] It is in the subtlety of this polemic that Frei's own position finds succinct and powerful articulation in a roundabout way. Here we have a somewhat clearer characterization of what Frei means when he invokes the notion of "Christology" in his writings at the time of his death.

Clearly, it is safe to say that these passages (along with those collected and posthumously set forth in *Types of Christian Theology*) are "of a piece" with Frei's earlier claims. Do we not see here some evidence of a more developed, more robust Christology? Admittedly, Frei gives us very little to go on in these writings and lectures at the time leading up to his untimely passing. And I do not aim to press such a case too far on the basis of such slender passages, albeit passages freighted with content to be unpacked and explicated at the point that Frei died. Nonetheless, such passages—especially when read across Frei's late writings and lectures, and in light of their cumulative effect—evince important development and enrichment of Frei's Christology—Christology which was a motivation, and which he labored to maintain as an orientational concern from his earliest essays until the time of his death.

NOTES

1. Mike Higton, "Frei's Christology and Lindbeck's Cultural-Linguistic Theory," *Scottish Journal of Theology* 50(1) (1997): 83–95.
2. Ibid., 92.
3. Ibid.
4. Other treatments of Frei's work in which the priority of his Christological concerns feature prominently include Charles Campbell's *Preaching Jesus* (Grand Rapids: Wm. B. Eerdmans Publishing Co., 1997); Ben Fulford foregrounds Frei's Christology in the constructive engagement he stages between Frei and Gregory of Nazianzus in *Divine Eloquence and Human Transformation* (Minneapolis: Fortress, 2013); see also my *Toward a Generous Orthodoxy* (Oxford: Oxford University Press, 2010). For a recent effort to expand Frei's thinking and work in

the direction of scriptural reasoning, see Jacob Goodson, *Nanative Theology and the Hermeneutical Virtues: Humility, Patience, Prudence* (Lanham, MD: Lexington Books, 2015).

5. Higton constrains his treatment of Christology in Frei's later work to all of a page and half (91–2) in the essay above. George Hunsinger's exposition of the later work, and Frei's account of Christ therein, appears as an epilogue to the otherwise meticulous critical exposition of Frei's Christology in *The Identity of Jesus Christ*. See his "Afterword: Hans Frei as Theologian," in *Theology and Narrative* (Oxford: Oxford University Press, 1993): 257–64. Material from this volume is hereafter cited in the text as *TN*.

6. Frank Kermode, *The Genesis of Secrecy: On the Interpretation of Narrative* (Cambridge, MA: Harvard University Press, 1979), 144.

7. Frei, "Conflict in Interpretation," *TN*, 157–62.

8. Ibid., 164.

9. Ibid., 163.

10. Ibid.

11. Frei, "Theology and the Interpretation of Narrative," *TN*, 113, 122.

12. Frei, "The 'Literal Reading' of Biblical Narrative," *TN*, 122–3.

13. Elsewhere I have made the case that this process did not occur (as has often been portrayed) as a sudden break between his early and later work, or a "turn away" from his earlier work, but is better characterized as a shift of focus that takes the form of an expansion "from Word alone to Word and Spirit." See Springs, *Toward a Generous Orthodoxy*, chapters 2, 7–8.

14. Frei, "The 'Literal Reading' of Biblical Narrative," *TN*, 121–4, at which point Frank Kermode again appears as one of Frei's key interlocutors.

15. Wolterstorff, *Divine Discourse*, 219–20. Having ascribed the norm of "beneficial" to Frei, Wolterstorff then puzzles over what "beneficial" might mean. Frei nowhere uses the word "beneficial," nor makes the claim that the "beneficiality" of a particular textual sense provides the warrant for the Christian community's taking the literal sense to be authoritative. Wolterstorff's characterization on this point finds an echo in the work of John Allan Knight, who ascribes to Frei the position that "literal reading is the proper one because it is the one the church has found useful in pursuing its form of life." See Knight's *Liberalism vs. Postliberalism* (Oxford: Oxford University Press, 2012), 281–2. In effect, Knight follows Wolterstorff on this point, though admittedly, Knight's criticisms diverge widely from Wolterstorff's in that he sees this claim as the result of what he argues is Frei's status as a "full blown follower of the later Wittgensteinian" (and this in terms of the deeply problematical reading of the later Wittgenstein found in Scott Soames's *Philosophical Analysis and the Age of Meaning, Vol. II*, Princeton: Princeton University Press, 2003). On this basis Knight concludes that that "Frei's ... commitment to a Wittgensteinian understanding of meaning ... gives to the community the role of the ultimate arbiter of the meaning of any and all biblical texts." While addressing the full depth of the problems with this reading would take me too far afield from my present objective, suffice it to say I find myself fully persuaded by the reservations about Knight's reading of Frei gently raised by Ben Fulford in his "Review of Liberalism vs. Postliberalism: The

Great Divide in Twentieth-Century Theology," *Journal of Theological Studies* 65, no. 1 (2014): 363–7. For entrée into the controversies surrounding Scott Soames's treatment of Ryle and Wittgenstein (among others) upon which Knight predicates his critical strategy, see Michael Kremer's review of Scott Soames in *Philosophical Analysis in the Twentieth Century, vol. 1: The Dawn of Analysis* (Princeton: Princeton University Press, 2003) and *Philosophical Analysis in the Twentieth Century, vol. 2: The Age of Meaning* (Princeton: Princeton University Press, 2003), *Notre Dame Philosophical Reviews* (September 19, 2005): https://ndpr.nd.edu/news/24868-book-l-philosophical-analysis-in-the-twentieth-century-vol-l-the-dawn-of-analysis-book-2-philosophical-analysis-in-the-twentieth-century-vol-2-the-age-of-meaning/, accessed March 11, 2014. See also Michael Beaney, "Critical Notice: Soames on Philosophical Analysis," *Philosophical Books* 75, no. 3 (2006): 255–71 (esp. 262–3).

16. Frei, "The 'Literal Reading' of Biblical Narrative," *TN*, 122–3.
17. Katherine Greene-McCreight has done work in accounting for the processes by which the literal sense of Scripture came to have the authoritative influence that it did in the early Christian community, how that opened up space for considerable flexibility and creativity within the encompassing normative framework in the church's interpretive practices. See her *Ad Litteram: How Augustine, Calvin, and Barth Read the Plain Sense of Genesis 1–3* (New York: Peter Verlag, 1999).
18. Greene-McCreight glosses the verbal sense by likening it to Michael Fishbane's description of peshat as focusing upon "the givenness and autonomy of the text, on its independence from the words of interpretation." See Fishbane, "The Teacher and the Hermeneutical Task: A Reinterpretation of Medieval Exegesis," *Journal of the American Academy of Religion* 43 (1975): 712–13.
19. Frei, "Theology and the Interpretation of Narrative," *TN*, p. 110 (italics added).
20. John Allan Knight, *Liberalism Versus Postliberalism* (NY: Oxford University Press, 2013): 209.
21. Frei, "The 'Literal Reading' of Biblical Narrative," *TN*, 143.
22. William Placher, *Narratives of a Vulnerable God* (Louisville: Westminster/John Knox, 1994), 92–7 (here 92, 93).
23. Frei, "Theology and the Interpretation of Narrative," 145.
24. Frei, *Types of Christian Theology* (New Haven: Yale University Press, 1992), 86–7.
25. Frei, *Types*, 86–7.
26. Frei, "The 'Literal Reading' of Biblical Narrative," *TN*, 145–6.
27. Frei, "Conflicts in Interpretation," *TN*, 163.
28. Ibid., 163–4.
29. For a particularly lucid engagement, see Kevin Hector, "Postliberal Hermeneutics: Narrative, Community, and the Meaning of Scripture," *Expository Times* 122(3): 105–16.
30. Frei, "Response to 'Narrative Theology'," *TN*, 210, 212.
31. Again, see, Placher as quoted above, *Narratives of a Vulnerable God,* 92–97 (here 92, 93).

32. As Frei insisted that the resurrection accounts, at a minimum, must. See *The Identity of Jesus Christ: The Hermeneutical Bases of Dogmatic Theology, Expanded and Updated Edition* (Eugene, OR: Cascade, 2013), chapter 13.
33. Ibid. Cf. George Hunsinger, "What Can Evangelicals and Postliberals Learn from Each Other," *The Nature of Confession*, 176. Timothy Phillips and Dennis Okholm eds., *The Nature of Confession* (Dowers Grove, IL: Intervarsity, 1996).
34. Frei, "Response to 'Narrative Theology'," 212.
35. *Anglican and Episcopal History*, 139–45 *(TN*, 200–6).
36. Frei, "Remarks in Connection with a Theological Proposal," *TN*, 26–44.
37. Hunsinger, "Afterword," *TN*, 248–9.
38. This concern is raised by Hunsinger, *TN*, 248.
39. Frei, "Of the Resurrection of Christ," *TN*, 206.
40. Hunsinger, *TN*, 249–50.
41. Frei, "Of the Resurrection of Christ," *TN*, 202.
42. Ibid., 203.
43. Ibid., 205.

CHAPTER SIX

The Barthian Heritage of Hans W. Frei

JOHN ALLAN KNIGHT

ABSTRACT

Hans Frei and the "Yale School" of narrative theology are often understood to be Barthian in orientation, but only rarely have the origins and contours of Frei's engagement with Barth been treated in the secondary literature. Frei's dissertation itself remains unpublished, with the exception of an oddly edited abridgment that appeared ten years after Frei's untimely death. This lacuna is unfortunate, because Frei's dissertation on Barth, and especially his treatment of Barth's method, is of signal importance in that they set the agenda and orientation for much, if not all, of Frei's later work. Consequently, in this article I analyze Frei's dissertation on Barth, focusing primarily on his treatment of Barth's protest against "relationalism." On Frei's reading, three moves constitute Barth's break with relationalism: the primacy of ontology over epistemology, the subordination of method to positive affirmations about God, and the conformance of interpretative method both to Barth's methodological commitments and to his affirmations about God. In his dissertation, Frei argues that Barth believed that, without these moves, theology would be vulnerable to Feuerbach's critique. Frei's construal of Barth's break with relationalism sets the agenda for Frei's own later work, in which he appropriates these Barthian moves by insisting on the primacy of biblical narratives in theological method. Similar to Barth, Frei takes twentieth-century hermeneutic theology to be vulnerable to deconstructionist critique. His insistence on the primacy of a literal reading of the biblical narratives is his attempt to rectify this vulnerability.

I wish to thank Cass Fisher, Melody Knowles, Kathryn Tanner, and Bill Wright for reviewing and commenting on an earlier version of this article. I would also like to thank my former colleagues at Nazarene Theological Seminary, who provided insightful discussion of the article at a faculty forum. All errors, omissions, and misreadings, of course, remain my own responsibility, but the article has been greatly improved by their thoughtful comments.

Hans Frei and the "Yale School" of narrative theology he inaugurated are often understood to be Barthian in orientation. Although this appellation should be nuanced in the case of some of Frei's followers, one need not hesitate about using it to describe Frei, at least if the appellation refers to Frei's self-conscious and intentional alignment with Barth's project. When writers describe Frei as "Barthian," typically what they seem to mean is that Frei shares Barth's dislike of apologetics. If Barth argued that the best apologetics is a good dogmatics, Frei argues that Christian theology should eschew apologetics and limit itself to Christian self-description.[1] At various points in his career, Frei himself has tried to explicate this stance and to provide arguments in support of it. Many have found these explications dense or obtuse, and only rarely have the origins and contours of Frei's engagement with Barth been treated in the secondary literature.[2] Although several very good biographical sketches have been published,[3] so far as I am aware, only two pieces have been published that address Frei's dissertation on Barth. The first did not undertake any substantive analysis of Barth's theological method. Instead, it provides a very fine treatment of the form and structure of the dissertation.[4] The second, by the same author, Mike Higton, contains a much more substantive analysis of Barth's dissertation, although its focus is quite different from mine. Higton highlights, as I do here, the importance to Frei of Barth's protest against "relationalism." But Higton also brings out Frei's objection to Barth's "epistemological monophysitism," which indicates the direction of Higton's analysis. Higton's excellent treatment of Frei's early work seeks to show Frei's early orientation as a theologian primarily concerned to develop a theology which can do justice to concrete historical life. As such, Higton argues, in Frei's hands (*pace* some of Frei's critics) theology is truly public.[5]

Frei's dissertation itself remains unpublished, with the exception of an oddly edited abridgment that appeared ten years after Frei's untimely death.[6] In my view, however, Frei's dissertation on Barth, and especially his treatment of Barth's method, is of signal importance in that it sets the agenda and orientation for much, if not all, of Frei's later work. Consequently, rather than integrating a discussion of Frei's dissertation into a larger treatment of Frei's early work, as Higton's very fine book does, what I hope to do in this paper is to analyze Frei's dissertation on Barth. Furthermore, I shall largely ignore Frei's criticism of Barth's "epistemological monophysitism" and focus on his treatment of Barth's protest against relationalism, picking out three themes that in my view were most important to Frei's own theological project. These themes—the primacy of ontology over epistemology, the subordination of method to positive affirmations about God and the conformance of interpretative method both to Barth's methodological commitments and to his affirmations about God—are the subject of separate sections. After discussing Frei's dissertation on Barth, I shall conclude by making a few comments about the way these themes inform Frei's later work.

THE INFLUENCE OF FREI'S DISSERTATION ON BARTH

Frei wrote his doctoral dissertation, "The Doctrine of Revelation in the Thought of Karl Barth, 1909–1922: The Nature of Barth's Break with Liberalism," under H. Richard Niebuhr.[7] It was completed in 1956, and it concerned the changes that Barth's theological method underwent as a result of his break with liberalism. As he wrote his dissertation, Frei became convinced that Barth's break with liberalism was the most important event in Protestant theology in the modern period.[8] Fundamentally, on Frei's reading, Barth believed that theology must move away from an anthropological starting point if it is to avoid Feuerbach's critique. To escape from Feuerbach, Barth sought to subordinate not only theological anthropology, but also theological method, to positive ontological affirmations about God. Writing a half century later, Frei takes a similar "neo-Barthian" move to be theology's best defense against deconstructionist critics. Frei's fear of deconstruction and his belief that the kind of hermeneutic method practiced by David Tracy and Paul Ricoeur is vulnerable to it bear remarkable resemblances to Barth's fear of Feuerbach and Barth's belief that nineteenth-century liberal theology was vulnerable to Feuerbach's argument that theological claims about God were merely projections of anthropological beliefs about human beings. Frei believes that deconstructionist critique of hermeneutic theory (whose instantiation in theology Frei sees as the most prominent heir of modern liberal theology) is structurally very similar to that of Feuerbach. Consequently, he sees his own project as a continuation of Barth's.[9]

To summarize briefly, in his dissertation Frei elucidates three themes in Barth, all of which are designed to move Barth's theological thinking away from its anthropological starting point. First, as he makes his break from liberalism, Barth begins to emphasize the priority of ontology over epistemology.[10] In Barth's view, one of the things that made liberal theology subject to Feuerbach's critique was that it began with epistemological considerations and then refused to make claims that could not meet its epistemic criteria. After the break, Barth insists that theology must begin with ontological affirmations about God, and these affirmations are given in the incarnation and the testimony to it in the Bible. Frei makes a very similar move in insisting on the priority of the biblical narrative in theology. The second theme is closely related to the first and concerns theological method. After the break, Barth insists that theological method must be subordinate to, and be governed by, positive ontological statements about God, a position derived from Barth's prioritizing of ontology over epistemology. It implies that theology cannot be truly systematic, because Barth believes that all true systematizing will be anthropologically and epistemologically driven. Frei likewise insists that theological method must be governed by the revelation of God given in the biblical narratives. The third theme is interpretation of the biblical texts. Barth insists that interpretative method must be governed by his methodological commitments and his ontological affirmations about God. In the next three sections I shall address these themes in more detail from Frei's dissertation on Barth.

THE PRIMACY OF ONTOLOGY OVER EPISTEMOLOGY

First, Barth's break with liberalism reversed the relation of ontology to epistemology. Before the break (i.e., prior to 1915), epistemology not only determined the agenda of theology, but was conceptually prior as well. During his liberal phase, Barth understood one of the theologian's most important tasks to be that of finding normative conceptions to express the experience of Christ. In his dissertation, Frei views this task as fundamentally epistemological: it is concerned with "the possibility of knowing God and saying something significant about that 'knowledge'."[11] Barth is not as concerned, that is, with the fact or notion of revelation in itself as with the rational explication of revelatory experience.[12] This epistemological concern marks Barth as a liberal during this period, as does his basic "relational" approach to the problem (an approach or method of *Ineinanderstellung*). There must be some mode or capacity in human beings, on this approach, that permits them to receive God's revelation.[13]

When Barth came to consider the question of God, however, Barth was haunted from the beginning by the ghost of Feuerbach. There is an obvious antinomy in the particular concrete encounter with God, which is an experience of positive or particular revelation, and the universal or transcendent nature of God. Even in his liberal period, or at least the latter part of it, Barth refuses to resolve this antinomy, because, among other things, he wants to resist Feuerbach's charge that God is nothing more than human wishes projected onto a transcendent plane. This refusal leaves Barth with a dialectic in thought form that provides a continuity with his post-liberal dialectical method.[14] In Frei's view, what is novel in Barth's break with liberalism is not, therefore, his dialectical method, but his "rejection of immediate experience as the source of faith."[15] Barth was also concerned, during the liberal period, with the primacy of God, and he rejects any notion of cooperation in which divine and human work constitute cooperating means toward grace. Before the break, he sees the method of *Ineinanderstellung* as preventing such cooperation. After the break, however, he comes to regard this method as a conceptualization of divine–human cooperation and therefore rejects it.[16]

Even after the break with liberalism, epistemology continued to have a strong influence on the direction of Barth's theology, in Frei's view, but its relation to ontology changes. During the most strongly dialectical period, ontology and epistemology seem to be collapsed into one another.[17] After the second edition of *Der Römerbrief*, however, ontology begins to assume a conceptual primacy. By the time of Barth's book on Anselm, the conceptual primacy of ontology is largely accomplished. After the break, in other words, the basis of the knowledge of God does not lie in any immanent relation between human existence and God, nor in immediate experience or *Ineinanderstellung*. Instead, "The ground and possibility of knowledge of God lies within the nature of God as he reveals himself of his own free grace. Hence, the epistemological judgement of faith is *in ordo essendi* (which is also normative for the *ordo cognoscendi*) preceded by, and based on a judgement of objective, ontic reality—the reality of God."[18]

According to Frei, the priority of ontology is the result of Barth's engagement with the biblical realists.[19] For them, the activity of the Holy Spirit and scripture is correlated in the Word of God.[20] This is what enables Barth to assert the primacy of God's revealing activity even in the area of the knowledge of God.[21] This correlation of Spirit and scripture in the Word of God, a correlation that is carried out wholly by divine action, is the ground not only of our relationship with God, but also of our knowledge of God.[22] Barth's basic dogmatic plan, then, is as follows: "the content of revelation is the Word of God; the objective ground and possibility of revelation is the Incarnation of the Word of God; the subjective actuality and possibility of revelation lies in the outpouring of the Holy Spirit."[23] This is what Frei calls Barth's radical realism, and it is characteristic of his break with liberalism. It is the avenue through which Barth attempts to avoid relationalism, on the one hand, and fundamentalism, on the other. For his part, Frei will also attempt to navigate between two shoals: on the one hand, a liberal scheme of understanding into which biblical texts must fit, and a fundamentalist literalism on the other. In the later 1920s and 1930s, however, Barth argues that, in this correlating act of God, God becomes analogous to "that which it creates in the recipient: faith as obedience—including rational obedience."[24]

Even this analogy, however, is grounded in the free activity of God, and it is this grounding in which Barth's assertion of the primacy of ontology over epistemology consists.[25]

THE SUBORDINATION OF METHOD TO POSITIVE AFFIRMATIONS ABOUT GOD

The second theme that is important to Frei is that of theological method, and this theme has three thematic submoments. The first is closely related to the primacy of ontology over epistemology. Despite this primacy of ontology, on Frei's reading, Barth's basic concern remains epistemological: how are we to understand (or come to rational belief about) the relation of humanity to God? Throughout his career, both before and after the break with liberalism, the relation of humanity to God has primacy—indeed, a kind of transcendental primacy— over all other human relations.[26] But the way Barth comes to understand this relation changes after the break. In the liberal period, the relation itself was primary; it could be extrapolated from anthropology. After the break, however, the relation can no longer be understood "from below." Humanity can never make its way to God. Knowledge of God can no longer come by inferring a relation to our creator on the basis of an understanding of creation or of human experience. That is, our epistemic access to God must be construed in light of the primacy of Barth's ontological affirmations about God. Methodologically, this means that the doctrine of revelation must move into the foreground and become asymmetrical.[27] As it does, the objective content of revelation becomes conceptually independent of and prior to understanding.[28] Searching for God along the path from the finite to the infinite is impossible, for all one sees is the "constantly receding limits of finitude." On the other hand, "if one sees the path from the infinite to the finite, one sees God in his relation to his creature .... But this path, this view of God in his relation to his creature is possible only for God himself."[29] Thus relationalism is impossible, because "there is no synthesis between the endeavor of man seeking to relate himself to God, and God's relating of himself to man."[30] In Frei's view, this constitutes Barth's break with liberalism: Barth no longer construes human experience as constituted by a relation between faith and its object such that an analysis of human experience as such can yield any knowledge of God.[31] So construed, this break means that the relation of humanity to God must be a derivative from the doctrine of God.[32]

Barth's problem, then, his "enduring concern" after the liberal phase, is, as Frei puts it, to find "a proper understanding of the relation of God to man within a proper *doctrine of God*."[33] This will give him the clue to the proper theological method. The starting point for finding this understanding of God's relation to us is Jesus Christ. Thus Barth's Christocentricity carries forward from the liberal period throughout Barth's career. After the break, though, Christ is no longer conceptually a step along a path from humanity to God. Instead, the doctrine of the incarnation is also a derivative from the doctrine of God, and this, Frei argues, accounts for the growing importance of the doctrine of predestination in Barth's thought. Theology must be Christocentric simply because of God's act of predestination.[34] According to Frei, "The question about Jesus Christ is no longer, why is he and not someone else the actualiser of our religious experience? The issue instead is to find the eternal ground for Jesus Christ's incarnation within the objective ground of the relation of God to man."[35]

Frei's reading of Barth's writings on christology outlined the following problem: "is the relation in faith to Jesus Christ the clue to the understanding of faith, history and revelation? Or, is it conversely true that Jesus Christ is a fact understood from the prior perspective of a theological and/or philosophical system?"[36] After the break, Barth insists that any resolution of this issue must sharply distinguish between the divine and human dimensions. Frei asserts that one can do this in three ways: "by sheer proclamation, i.e., by the refusal to allow methodology to predominate; by 'dialectic' or by analogy."[37] Barth tried all these ways. The writing of the second edition of *Der Römerbrief* was a strongly dialectical effort, and by the time of the book on Anselm he was using a doctrine of analogy. But throughout all his post-break changes, he sought to have his positive affirmations about God govern not only the content of his thought, but his method as well.

This refusal of primacy to method is the second thematic submoment of Frei's concern with theological method in Barth. Even during his liberal period Barth had stressed the primacy of God. He followed Schleiermacher during this period in refusing to see faith as independent of revelation. Thus, when Barth attempts to stress the "absolute priority, independence, and sovereignty" of God's grace, for Frei this means pre-eminently to work out both a theological method and an understanding of our knowledge of God in terms of God's priority, independence, and sovereignty.[38] After the break, this emphasis on the methodological priority of God eventually developed into a consistent doctrine of predestination.[39] There were other continuities as well, including Barth's Christocentricity. During the liberal period, Barth saw christology as the only content of theology, which must be expressed in a relational form. After the break, christology remains the only content of theology, but it now becomes an eschatological notion giving content to the proper object of theology, the Word of God.[40]

On Frei's view, Barth walks a fine line between two opposing dangers.[41] On the one hand, he could capitulate to the liberals by translating (or transliterating) the Word of God into his own conceptual forms. On the other, he could remain purely critical, making only dialectical statements, thus consigning theology to prolegomena that could never get beyond method to substantive content.[42] If he wanted to move past criticism to a constructive phase—i.e., positive knowledge of God—Frei poses his problem thus: how can we have any knowledge of God at all without, on the one hand, positing some immediate divine–human complementarity within human nature that survives the fall, or, on the other, relying on a supernatural revelation that sunders faith and reason?[43] To achieve positive knowledge of God while avoiding these twin sirens, Barth needs to subordinate theological method to the substantive content of his doctrine of God. But the problem is how to effect this subordination without falling back on a pre-rational (or suprarational) supernatural revelation. It was his study of Anselm that provided Barth with the breakthrough that helped him address this question. For Barth, Anselm regards faith as a call to cognitive understanding, through which we participate (in a limited way) in God's mode of being. Faith is not faith, therefore, unless it involves right belief. "Faith, he insists after Anselm, is relative to the 'Word of Christ', and is reception, knowledge, affirmation of this Word."[44]

An important ingredient in Barth's methodological breakthrough, and one that exercises a pervasive influence on Frei, is that there can be no separation of form from content.[45] Thus, not only the content of theology, but the form as well must be brought under the lordship of Christ. Theological method cannot be prolegomena, but must be consistent with its substantive claims, especially its claims about God. In order to fulfil this intention, in Frei's view, Barth gave a leading role to the content of revelation and sought to have this content determine his method.[46] The content of revelation is concrete, undialectical and prior to dialectic. Thus, dialectic cannot synthesize its formal and material elements.[47] Barth's breakthrough consists in the fact that "content, or rather the object, constantly dominates the thought-form in Barth's understanding. Hence, thought-form and the meaning of its content are never properly and systematically balanced in his thought."[48]

Finally (the third thematic submoment of Barth's method), Frei is particularly interested in Barth's opposition to systematizing. Indeed, the place of his principal critique is in this area. After the break with liberalism, Barth continued to maintain some form of the continuing immediate presence of God to creation. Yet without some kind of relational complementarity—i.e., in denying that anything about God can be read off creation—it is difficult to conceive God's immediate presence. So relationalism continued to influence Barth in that it kept epistemological concerns within Barth's field of concern. In addition, it kept Barth concerned with theological method. Barth insists that the objective content of revelation cannot be limited by predetermined epistemological limits. Thus, Frei argues that the task that preoccupies Barth after the break is how to articulate "the manner in which the complete primacy, uniqueness, and subjecthood of God conditions from the very outset the manner in which we may know him."[49] Barth tries to accomplish this task by insisting that the Word of God is both the content of theology and the basis of theological method. But this insistence presents Barth with a problem: how can this insistence be made to cohere with the freedom, spontaneity, and subjectivity of human beings? Ultimately, Barth finds the answer to this question in the doctrine of double predestination. Through this doctrine, the free grace of God can be the basis of the freedom, spontaneity, and subjecthood of human beings.[50] Thus, our freedom is not grounded in any "given" relational complementarity through which God's freedom can be understood. Instead, it is the free act of God in speaking God's Word to us that funds both human subjectivity and our knowledge of the freedom and sovereignty of God. Revelation is therefore based on the doctrine of God alone (through the doctrine of the Word of God), and natural theology is ruled out. In this way, Barth was able to assert the sovereignty of God not only over our destiny, but over our epistemic access to God as well. At the same time, if God is known only through God's freely spoken Word, theological method must be founded on this same doctrine of the Word of God, and in doing so Barth is able to assert the absolute primacy and sovereignty of God over theological method as well.[51]

Frei takes this move to have radical implications for theological method. It means, first, that there can be no independent or objective standpoint from which to view the relation of Creator and creature. Second, any method that takes the free and sovereign grace of God as its sole focus cannot produce any theological system.[52] Theology must therefore remain critical, and cannot take a constructive turn.[53] "For dialectic is incapable of providing positive theological content."[54] This is why, in Frei's view, Barth finally made the turn to the *analogia fidei*, and it is this analogy that enables him to defend his positive, constructive claims, as well as to provide more coherence to his thought. But it is precisely here that Frei believes he runs the greatest risk of betraying his insight that systematizing must be resisted. And it is here that Frei's appraisal of Barth takes its most critical turn:

> Under these circumstances Barth's protest—the only genuinely consistent and completely consequential protest in academic theological circles—against liberal relationalism was entirely justified. But it is not nearly as evident that Barth did not then stand in danger—a danger apparently not completely overcome—of systematizing in the opposite direction. Is it really possible to understand the knowledge of revelation, the correlation (if the negativity of dialectic can be called a correlation) of revelation and faith—solely on the ground of the doctrine of God or of revelation? Is this assertion not already too "systematic"?[55]

THE CONFORMANCE OF INTERPRETATIVE METHOD TO BARTH'S METHODOLOGICAL COMMITMENTS AND AFFIRMATIONS ABOUT GOD

The first two themes, then, that Frei takes from Barth are that epistemology must be subordinate to ontology, and that this priority of ontology has implications for theological method. That is, method must be subordinate to a doctrine of God (i.e., our epistemic access to God can only be ascertained on the basis of our positive ontological affirmations about God), and any systematizing must be ruled out. The third theme I wish to highlight from Frei's initial work on Barth is that of interpretation. On Frei's reading, Barth works hard to make interpretative method consistent with his substantive claims. That is, interpretative method must be governed by the methodological commitments discussed above: the primacy and priority of God's free, initiating gracious act, the impossibility of any knowledge of God in the absence of such a divine act, and the resistance to systematizing. These commitments imply that the reader of scripture is dependent on the guidance of the Spirit as the author of scripture in order to understand the revelation that occurs through scripture. This implies, importantly, that the meaning of the scriptural texts cannot consist in their referential function. If it did, in Frei's view, the reader would have to have some knowledge of the referent to which the text refers, as well as the referential intent of the author. But this kind of knowledge is precisely what the methodological commitment to the priority of the free, initiating divine act rules out.[56] And this just means that any correlation between the "word"—the scriptural text—and the Word of God that the scriptural text reveals cannot be systematic, but must remain ad hoc.[57]

Barth's method has its price, though, in Frei's view, and the price is paid in the areas of theological anthropology and human understanding. As the doctrine of revelation gradually evolves, after the second edition of *Der Römerbrief*, any understanding of human nature in Barth becomes derivative from Barth's christology.[58] Frei expresses the problem thus: "The inability to grant, unsystematically but concretely, positive content to human nature derives in large part from the fact that revelation and the doctrine of God form the ground of all doctrine, and that Jesus Christ is the sole content of that doctrine, so that everything beside him, especially in separation and 'over against' him, appears to be abstract."[59] Frei himself attempts to avoid this problem through his articulation of narrative identity. This understanding of identity allows him to retain the methodological primacy of ontological affirmations about God while giving concrete, unsystematic content to human nature. Divine revelation, theology's starting point, is given primarily through a narrative depiction of Jesus' identity, and any understanding of human nature must also derive from the concrete narrative identity of particular human beings.

HOW THESE THEMES APPEAR IN FREI'S OWN WORK

I have tried to identify three themes in Barth's work that remained important guiding insights for Frei throughout his career: the subordination of epistemology to ontology, theological method, and interpretation. Let me now simply mention a couple of examples of the appearance of these themes in Frei's own work, beginning with his magnum opus, *The Eclipse of Biblical Narrative*. If Barth's own project in theology, and in particular his turn away from liberalism, is a project worth continuing, then there must be some way of describing just what was theologically wrong with the modern or liberal turn in Protestant theology. In Frei's view, behind the liberal turn lay two mistaken assumptions. First, modern liberal theologians were in large part motivated by an apologetic impulse to justify or defend the claims of Christian theology to Western intellectuals who were increasingly skeptical of these claims. One of the reasons this apologetic effort or impulse was mistaken was that it does not do justice to the nature of the biblical stories on which such claims are based. The apologetic impulse, that is, ignores the "tyrannical" nature of the biblical stories. Second, modern liberal theologians assumed a referential theory of meaning by which not only words, but sentences and indeed the stories themselves have meaning only insofar as they are able to "refer" or point to entities outside the text itself. Frei takes this understanding of meaning to be contrary to the nature of the biblical stories themselves, as well as being indefensible in its own terms.

Frei tells this story in the justly famous book *The Eclipse of Biblical Narrative*.[60] Frei's historical sketch of eighteenth- and nineteenth- (really, early nineteenth-) century hermeneutics proceeds under the following thesis:

> a realistic or history-like (though not necessarily historical) element is a feature, as obvious as it is important, of many of the biblical narratives that went into the making of Christian belief. It is a feature that can be highlighted by the appropriate analytical procedure and by no other, even if it may be difficult to describe the procedure—in contrast to the element itself.[61]

Prior to the modern period, Christian preachers and theologians had envisioned the world as "formed by the sequence told by the biblical stories."[62] On Frei's analysis, three features of this kind of reading were most important. First, if a biblical story were to be read literally, then it must have "referred to and described actual historical occurrences."[63] Second, if the world described by the biblical stories is one single world (i.e., one single temporal flow), then the stories must themselves tell one cumulative story. And the way the stories were joined together into a single cumulative story was by making the earlier stories figures or types of the later stories. In Frei's view, this kind of figural reading does not conflict with the literal sense, but is a natural extension of it. Third, since the biblical stories tell one cumulative story of the only real world, then these stories must also tell the story of each present age and the individuals in it. A Christian was to understand and to conduct his own life so that it made sense as a part of the single cumulative biblical story.[64]

This method of biblical interpretation was thus primarily a matter of the interpreter interpreting her own life and the world around her as a part of the world made accessible by the biblical narratives. During the eighteenth century, however, Frei argues that this mode of interpretation increasingly broke down, among both radical thinkers like Spinoza and conservatives like Johannes Cocceius and Johann Albrecht Bengel. For these thinkers, the "actual" historical world became detached from the world depicted in the Bible. Instead of making the world accessible, the biblical stories simply "verify" or provide evidence for these independently accessible events.[65]

As Frei puts it, the direction of interpretation now reversed itself. The principal interpretative question was no longer how to make my own life and experience of the world intelligible in terms of the biblical narratives. Instead, the primary question was whether the biblical texts (and whatever concepts may be derived from them) depict the "real" world as I otherwise apprehend it.[66] A crucial implication of this new direction was that "whether or not the story is true history, its *meaning* is detachable from the specific story that sets it forth."[67] This detachability of meaning resulted in the literal reading of the stories being divided from and opposed to the figural reading, with the latter becoming increasingly "discredited both as a literary device and as a historical argument."[68] In its isolation from figural reading, the literal reading of a story now came to mean two things: first, grammatical and lexical precision in estimating what a text meant to its original audience, which in turn implied a single meaning of statements; and, second, the coincidence of the description with the historical facts.[69]

The *Eclipse*, then, is "an investigation of the breakdown of realistic and figural interpretation of the biblical stories, and the reversal in the direction of interpretation."[70] In Frei's telling, interpreters even after the reversal continued to attend to the literal sense of the stories. But the literal sense came to mean the single meaning of a text, which was given by the event or reality to which the text referred. Nonetheless, all agreed that something more was necessary for interpretation, and that was "ideational meaning or religious significance."[71]

When modern interpreters turned away from figural interpretation, the crucial point was not that they denied any nonliteral meaning to the texts, but that their understanding of the literal meaning changed. Instead of being the literal depictions themselves, the meaning of the narrative was "located" in some extra-textual event or idea to which the text referred. In Frei's view, this occurred because biblical scholars had available to them a method of investigating any historical reference contained in a text, but no literary method by which realistic narratives could be understood. Thus, the separation of story from its meaning occurred because scholars confused history-likeness (literal meaning) with historical likelihood (ostensive reference). As the story was separated from its meaning, the narrative itself went into "eclipse."[72]

When one considers the three themes in Barth's work that most impressed Frei in his formative dissertation, one can see why it was so important for Frei's own project to chart this understanding of the meaning of the biblical texts. On my reading, Frei takes all the three Barthian themes that come through in his work on Barth to be undermined by the referential understanding of meaning that he analyzes in the *Eclipse*. When meaning is located outside the texts themselves, Frei argues that the conditions and criteria of the meaning of such texts must be given by independently established epistemological principles. This is precisely what happens in the work of Anthony Collins, for whom the criteria and possibilities of the meaning of biblical texts are given by Lockean epistemological principles. The work of Collins figures so prominently in the narrative Frei tells in the *Eclipse* because it established that epistemology must be prior to ontology in theological method—the establishment of a mistake as far as Barth and Frei are concerned.

Second, this priority of epistemology transformed all debate about the meaning of biblical texts into debates about their reference. This transformation was motivated by an apologetic impulse, beginning with referents that all should consider plausible, then arguing that such reasonable referents (whether historical, ideal or located in Jesus' consciousness) are the real referents of the biblical stories. The meanings of such stories were articulated so as to make them amenable to apologetic argument, creating an ordered pair of meaning and understanding that were complementary and universally accessible. On Frei's telling, whether in an earlier Lockean form (such as that of Collins), or in a more sophisticated hermeneutic form (such as that of Schleiermacher), the fundamental duality of this ordered pair persisted. Such a systematic ordering gives priority to method over any positive affirmations about God. That is, whatever the biblical texts may say about God, in Frei's view the meaning of such statements must be construed in conformity with this independently established ordered pair.

Finally, any interpretative method that has a referential understanding of meaning as a constituent part cannot be governed by the primacy and priority of God's free and initiating grace, because in Frei's view such a method assumes, rather than denies, epistemic access to God in the absence of such an initiating act. When the meaning of the biblical texts is held to consist in their reference to some extra-textual reality, and when the conditions and criteria of that meaning are given in advance by a prior theory of understanding, it follows, on Frei's view, that the reader must already have some independent understanding of the reference of the texts if she is to understand their meaning. Interpretative method is therefore governed not by the priority of God's free and initiating grace, but rather by an independent theory of understanding. All of this overturns the primacy of ontological affirmations about God given in the biblical narratives and makes them subordinate to the epistemological needs of apologetic argument.

Frei's creative and interesting book, *The Identity of Jesus Christ*,[73] published almost contemporaneously with the *Eclipse*, also evidences Frei's construal of Barth's project. This book, which Frei considers to be his own articulation of the essence of Christianity, begins not with any kind of epistemological prolegomena, but instead with an articulation of the category of identity and an extended reading of Jesus' identity as it is depicted in the gospels. Instead of presenting an argument for belief in Christ's resurrection and presence that would be available to an unbeliever, he leaves intact the gap between faith and unfaith. Again following Barth, he prioritizes ontology over epistemology, arguing for a biblical literary kind of quasi-ontological argument for Jesus' continuing presence rather than beginning with epistemological conditions and arguing that they are fulfilled. This argument itself borrows Auerbach's understanding that the biblical texts are "tyrannical" in that they seek to overcome our reality with their own. This is precisely what happens in Frei's quasi-ontological argument. The overall movement of Frei's thought in the *Identity* is (1) to begin with the narrative structure of the gospels, (2) to provide a narratively structured description of the identity of Jesus, (3) to provide an argument from that very narrative structure for the truth of the central gospel claims about God's own presence in Christ, and (4) to spin out nutshell accounts of the Word of God, the sacraments, the Holy Spirit, and the church and its mission and ethical obligation. The book is a remarkably creative attempt to accomplish these objectives in a way that is faithful to the Barthian project described above.

To recapitulate, Barth's insistence on the primacy of ontology over epistemology can be seen clearly in Frei's work, in both the *Eclipse* and the *Identity*, as well as in his later essays.[74] One can also see Frei's commitment to the primacy of ontology in his extended criticisms of apologetics precisely because he takes apologetics to be grounded in epistemology.[75] Furthermore, Frei advances Barth's agenda regarding the second theme, theological method. He argues for the subordination of theological method to a doctrine of God by giving primacy to the narrative form of the gospels (in his earlier work) or their literal sense (later). Theological method, he insists, must derive from a reading of the gospels, and its subordinate nature prevents both the determination of method by epistemology and any true systematizing.[76] Thus, he will argue that the adequacy of any theological method must be judged by how well it is able to take account of either the narrative structure of the gospels (earlier in his career) or the literal sense of the narratives (in his later years). The third theme, the subordination of interpretation to these methodological commitments (and thereby to positive affirmations about God), can also be seen in Frei's work. Because the incarnation is the source of our affirmations about God, and because any knowledge of the incarnation must come through the narrative depiction of Jesus' identity in the gospels, any interpretation of their meaning as consisting in their referential function is ruled out. Frei's use of Auerbach's notion of the "tyrannical" nature of the biblical texts is part of his attempt to make his own theological method derivative from the narrative structure (earlier) or the literal sense (later) of the biblical texts. In my judgment, these three Barthian themes animate all of Frei's work.[77]

NOTES

1. See, for example, Frei's discussion of Barth and the limitation of the task of theology to Christian self-description in Hans W. Frei, *Types of Christian Theology*, ed. George Hunsinger and William C. Placher (New Haven, CT: Yale University Press, 1992). Whether Frei's interpretation of Barth's various polemical statements against apologetics is the best interpretation of Barth is a question worthy of consideration, but one I cannot engage here. For my purposes, it is enough that Frei himself takes his proposal for limiting theology to Christian self-description to be a faithful continuation of Barth's project.

2. One widely read book, David E. Demson, *Hans Frei and Karl Barth: Different Ways of Reading Scripture* (Grand Rapids, MI: Wm. B. Eerdmans Publishing Co., 1997), limits its treatment of Frei to Hans W. Frei, *The Identity of Jesus Christ: The Hermeneutical Bases of Dogmatic Theology* (Philadelphia: Fortress Press, 1975; repr. Eugene, OR: Wipf & Stock, 1997) and Hans W. Frei, *The Eclipse of Biblical Narrative: A Study in Eighteenth and Nineteenth Century Hermeneutics* (New Haven, CT: Yale University Press, 1974).

3. For a brief biographical sketch, see Placher, "Introduction," in Hans W. Frei, *Theology and Narrative: Selected Essays*, ed. George Hunsinger and William C. Placher (New York: Oxford University Press, 1993), 3–25, esp. 4–5. For a fine account relating Frei's personal journey (based not only on Frei's publications, but also on extensive interviews and conversations) to his public theological proposals, see John F. Woolverton, "Hans W. Frei in Context: A Theological and Historical Memoir," *Anglican Theological Review* 79 (Summer 1997): 369–93. Mike Higton has provided a more detailed sketch, drawing on Placher and Woolverton, as well as other unpublished sources. Mike Higton, *Christ, Providence and History: Hans W. Frei's Public Theology* (London: T&T Clark International, 2004), 15–20.

4. Mike Higton, "An American Theologian of History: Hans W. Frei in 1956," *Anglican and Episcopal History* 71, no. 1 (March 2002): 61–84.

5. Higton, *Christ, Providence and History*.

6. Hans Frei, "The Doctrine of Revelation in Karl Barth," in *Ten Year Commemoration of the Life of Hans Frei (1922–1988)*, ed. Giorgy Olegovich (New York: Semenenko Foundation, 1999): 103–87. The excerpt of Frei's

dissertation appeared along with several other papers that were presented at a conference celebrating Frei's life and work.

7. Hans Wilhelm Frei, "The Doctrine of Revelation in the Thought of Karl Barth, 1909–1922: The Nature of Barth's Break with Liberalism" (PhD. dissertation, Yale University, 1956).

8. "No more crucial event has taken place in modern Protestant theology than Karl Barth's break with liberalism," ibid., iii.

9. Given the scope of Frei's dissertation, one might expect Barth's earlier work to have influenced Frei more substantially than the later work. And indeed, one could argue that Barth's work during 1915–31 exerted substantially more influence on Frei's view of theological method than the later volumes of the *Church Dogmatics*. On the other hand, Frei himself states that it was Barth's figural exegesis of various Old Testament passages in the later volumes of the *Dogmatics* that provided Frei with his characteristic constructive response to what he took to be the principle errors of modern liberal theology. Frei, *Eclipse of Biblical Narrative*, viii. The examples Frei cites as paradigmatic are *Church Dogmatics*, II/2, 340–409, and IV/1, 224–8. Higton notes this influence as well: *Christ, Providence and History*, 12.

10. "Among other things, this [Barth's break with liberalism] means a total reversal of his understanding of theological epistemology." Frei, "Doctrine of Revelation," 118.

11. Ibid., 26, 30.

12. Ibid., 31.

13. Ibid., 42–8.

14. A related form of this dialectic can be seen in Barth's attempt to be Christocentric in the early period: "To Barth's thinking, the endeavor to be totally Christocentric and yet to think completely as a 'man of culture' is bound to result in a clash." Ibid., 69.

15. Ibid., 63.

16. The method of *Ineinanderstellung* involves an attempt to depict the nature of God and God's redemptive activity toward humanity via an articulation of human capacity. It involves, that is, an anthropological orientation to theology in general and the doctrine of God in particular.

17. Ibid., 199.

18. Ibid., 119 (citations omitted).

19. The most important of these seem to be J. C. Blumhardt and Hermann Kutter. It was biblical realism that allowed Barth to express his belief in the objective, literal truth of the events narrated in scripture, "without being tied thereby to a fundamentalist, literalist interpretation of these events." Ibid., 150–1. Also ibid., 148–67, 434–8.

20. In Frei's view, "the fundamental conviction in regard to theological theory of knowledge on the part of Biblical realists is the correlation of the Holy Spirit and Scripture in the Word of God." Ibid., 502.

21. "This, then, is the first and most important lesson which Barth learned from Biblical realism: in order to assert as normative (not only negatively but positively

in dialectical fashion) that the concrete content of the limit placed on man, history, and nature is the self-revealing God, one must begin with God whose revelation is altogether founded in his freedom. Thus our relation to him is founded solely on his freedom to be for us in grace and revelation. To know this is to discover it in one source only—in Scripture." Ibid., 504.

22. "Here, then, is Barth's typical affirmation during this period, that the ground of the relationship with God and of the knowledge of this relationship is the correlation which lies totally within the action of God, in the correlation of Spirit and Scripture which is the Word of God." Ibid., 510.

23. Ibid., 119 n. 161.

24. Ibid., 121.

25. Ibid., 120–3.

26. "At all times Barth has firmly held to the conviction that we are always in the presence of something or someone not created, and that this relationship between creature or finite man and the infinite is the prime relation in and through which all other relations take place." Ibid., 108–9.

27. "In revelation, he comes to see, there is a priority of ontic affirmation over epistemological or noetic affirmation." Ibid., 565.

28. The issue with which theology must come to terms is "to see the originality of the infinite as the origin and goal of the finite, to see the path from the infinite to the finite, rather than the path from the finite to the infinite." Ibid., 111.

29. Ibid., 111 (citation omitted).

30. Ibid., 112.

31. "Barth breaks radically with his liberal past, because he refuses to acknowledge a relational nexus in which faith and its historical content meet in experience." Ibid., 113.

32. "Positively expressed, this means that the relationship of God to man is wholly grounded in God." Ibid., 115.

33. Ibid., 126 (emphasis in original).

34. Ibid., 128–9. "Double predestination is the unique act of God in Jesus Christ alone ..." Ibid., 129.

35. Ibid., 127. When Barth broke with liberalism, what he opposed most fundamentally was liberalism's "confusion or synthesis of Christocentric revelation with religion." Ibid., iv. To resist this, Barth attempted "to express the sovereignty of God in his self-revelation over the very means and the mode of reception of revelation." Ibid. Frei argues that Barth had no choice but to try to express this notion of sovereignty through the available traditions, which were academic liberalism, biblical realism, and skepticism. Ibid., iv–vii. Through these conceptual traditions, or some combination of them, Barth sought "to found the doctrine of revelation solely upon the doctrine of God, and to do so without violating the freedom and subjectivity and spontaneity of man." Ibid., vii.

36. Ibid., 65–6. "Barth in his early days equates Christ with history and faith with experience ..." Ibid., 72. The question formulated by Frei and quoted in the text, it seems to me, anticipates Frei's understanding of the central problem not only of christology, but of theological method.

37. Ibid., 554–5.
38. Ibid., 439.
39. Ibid., 431–2. Furthermore, on Frei's reading, Barth incorporates to a large degree the thought forms of German idealism, particularly as used by Hegel and Schleiermacher.
40. This does not change even after 1931, though at that point Barth no longer understood the Word of God dialectically, but through an analogy between grace and nature that "is based solely on the congruence of grace and nature given uniquely and miraculously in the Incarnation." Ibid., 433.
41. Barth faced "diametrically opposed dangers at the same time in his radical realism." Ibid., 187.
42. Ibid., 188.
43. Ibid., 193.
44. Ibid., 194.
45. Frei states that "content torn from its form is no longer the same." Ibid., 546.
46. "But one must go further and state that no conceptual content is 'given' in itself. Its meaning, on the contrary, consists in its relation to other judgements and (in principle) to the totality of thought content." Ibid., 109.
47. "There is thus a constant choice, an inconclusive dialogue between one type of language which, however inadequately, represents its object, and another type which is only a negative pointer to its object or subject and is more interested in indicating the distance between itself and its object." Ibid., 537.
48. Ibid., 539.
49. Ibid., 443.
50. Ibid., 455.
51. Ibid., 452–8. This dual foundation in the Word of God can tend to collapse ontology and epistemology, and in Frei's view this is what happens in the 2nd edn of *Der Römerbrief*: the Word of God remains both the object and the means of knowledge. Ibid., 460–1. It is not until Barth turns to a positive doctrine of analogy that he is able to prevent the collapse of epistemology and ontology and reassert the primacy of ontology.
52. "He wanted to emphasize the primacy of objective intention and norms over methodological considerations without committing himself thereby to a system; for he thought, then as well as subsequently, that a theological 'system' is a contradiction in terms." Ibid., 547.
53. Ibid., 462–3.
54. Ibid., 499.
55. Ibid., 566–7.
56. Frei states this insight as follows: "Barth discovered that the object, revelation or the Word in the Scripture, is never understood except through the guidance of the author. In fact one must put the matter more strongly than that: the Word is not understood except through the author's letter. To assume that for an understanding of the author's objective intention, his words or concepts have but 'symbolic' meaning, that they are as remote from the object as they are near to it, that they

deflect to the same extent that they reflect meaning, is to assume an independent position from that of the author toward the object of his own intention. One assumes then that he has prior knowledge of that which is also the author's objective intention. But just this is impossible, especially in the case of Scripture: it is simply true that we do need the letter of Scripture to tell us of revelation. We have no independent information of this normative object." Ibid., 542.

57. "But the relation between the 'word' and the Word of God is paradoxical. It goes without saying that there is no *systematic* coincidence between them. The fact that they do become correlated is due to the non-dialectical, free activity of God in his Word." Ibid., 543. This failure of systematization also means that there is no direct or immediate presence of the Spirit to the reader, and possibly not to Paul, either: "The Spirit is not then directly or immediately present to both Paul and commentator, nor do the thoughts of Paul and of the commentator merge into each other in a timeless dimension of truth above history. There is no 'merging,' there is only pointing from each to the other, from Paul to the Spirit to the commentator; from the Spirit to Paul to the commentator." Ibid., 545.

58. "The doctrine of revelation gradually evolves after the second edition of *Der Römerbrief*, and true to indications already present in that period it has positive content even though that content must be dialectically presented for the most part. But there is no such positive content as a counter-part in a doctrine of man. With regard to the doctrine of God and of revelation (the two tend to merge in the dialectical period) systematization and abstractness are guarded against successfully, and the positive, purely objective intention shines through with eminent success. This is not nearly so true of the doctrine of man and of human understanding, which tend to be sublated." Ibid., 568. Consequently, in Frei's view, "even though he later denies, in his understanding of the doctrine of man, any coalescence between Christology and anthropology, it is only in the light of Christology that any and all content of anthropology may be understood." Ibid., 569–70 (citations omitted).

59. Ibid., 571.

60. Frei, *Eclipse of Biblical Narrative*.

61. Ibid., 10.

62. Ibid., 1.

63. Ibid., 2.

64. Ibid., 2–3.

65. Ibid., 3–4.

66. Ibid., 5.

67. Ibid., 6 (emphasis in original).

68. Ibid., 6.

69. Ibid., 7. Under this new separation of literal and figural reading, the closest successor to literal reading became historical reconstruction, while the closest successor to figural reading became biblical theology. Ibid., 8.

70. Ibid., 9.

71. Ibid., 10. "Attention continued to be paid to the verbal sense of the stories. In the course of the eighteenth century it came to signify not so much a literary depiction

which was literal rather than metaphorical, allegorical, or symbolic, but rather the single meaning of a grammatically and logically sound propositional statement." Ibid., 9.

72. Ibid., 10–12, 16, 27. Frei's thesis about the causes of the eclipse (as distinct from the eclipse itself) has not gone unchallenged. Nicholas Wolterstorff, for example, thinks it more likely that alternatives to realistic interpretation were sought because of rising skepticism about the propositional content of the literal sense of an increasing number of parts of the biblical narratives. Nicholas Wolterstorff, "Will Narrativity Work as Linchpin? Reflections on the Hermeneutic of Hans Frei," in *Relativism and Religion,* ed. Charles M. Lewis (London: Macmillan Press, 1995): 71–107, esp. pp. 92–3.

73. Frei, *Identity of Jesus Christ*.

74. I have not discussed these essays in the interest of space, but it is important to note that Frei's view of the meaning of the biblical texts underwent a shift after the publication of the *Identity*. In the later essays, the "literal sense" of the biblical texts replaces the narrative form as the primary determinant of their meaning. Nonetheless, Frei remains committed to the Barthian themes discussed herein. Indeed, his shift to the literal sense was motivated by his conclusion that it served his construal of Barth's agenda better than the narrative structure.

75. These criticisms are prominent both in *Eclipse* and in the essays collected in Frei, *Theology and Narrative,* ed. Hunsinger and Placher.

76. See esp. Frei, *Types of Christian Theology,* ed. Hunsinger and Placher.

77. Frei's formative influences include not only Barth, but also Gilbert Ryle and Erich Auerbach. Considerations of these influences exceed the scope of this paper. Barth, however, was fundamental in this sense: what Frei gained from Ryle and Auerbach were additional argumentative or conceptual tools for advancing his Barthian agenda.

CHAPTER SEVEN

Hans Frei and Anselmian Theology

JEFFREY STOUT

The following paper, which is a review of a *Festschrift* for Hans Frei, was written at the invitation of the American Academy of Religion's "Narrative Theology" group, and circulated to members of that group before the annual meeting of the Academy in November 1987. The group's program, which was meant to celebrate Frei's contributions to theology and religious studies, included my oral delivery of a shortened version of the paper, formal responses from Charles Wood and Kathryn Tanner, and questions and comments from the audience, which included Frei himself. None of us realized at the time that Hans would no longer be with us when the group next met, a year later. So in retrospect, the event acquired more importance than anyone had intended it to have. I will always consider myself privileged to have had the chance to honor Hans personally and in a festive, public setting.

The paper reconstructs and applies the typology of Christian theology that Frei was still working on at the time of his death. I had heard him deliver lectures on this topic under the auspices of the Humanities Council at Princeton University in the spring of 1987. The content of those lectures was essentially identical to the material included in appendices A and B in the posthumously published volume entitled *Types of Christian Theology*.[1] He had also shared with me the grant proposal in which he had originally summarized his typology, reprinted in the same volume under the heading, "Proposal for a Project." I had also read his review of Eberhard Busch's Barth biography, reprinted as appendix C of *Types,* and most of the material later collected in another posthumous volume, *Theology and Narrative: Selected Essays.*[2] As a result of this reading, the experience of teaching much of the same material in my graduate seminar on "The Fate of Academic Theology" in the spring of 1987, and various conversations with Frei himself, I felt I had a reasonably firm grasp on what he was trying to do. But in presenting a version of his typology to an audience largely unfamiliar with either his Princeton lectures, the Shaffer Lectures he had delivered at Yale Divinity School in 1983, or the Cadbury Lectures he had delivered at the University of Birmingham in 1987, I was anxious to avoid hemming him in. His version of the typology and mine were different. I didn't want to saddle him with an interpretation of his typology that he would subsequently have to distinguish from his own preferred version. The paper therefore refers to my version, modestly and gingerly, as "something like" the one he had been developing in his lectures.

When Frei died, I deliberately refrained from publishing the paper, so that *Types of Christian Theology* would be free to present the typology to the reading public in his own words. I have never regretted that decision, but in fact the paper probably found its way into the hands of nearly as many readers as it would have reached if it had been published in an academic journal. The reason for this is that more than four years passed between my public presentation of "something like" Frei's typology and the publication of *Types.* During that period, my paper was the only version of the typology most students of theology could get their hands on. Demand was high. Now that a full decade has elapsed since Frei's death, it occurs to me that there might be some slight historical value in allowing the paper to appear in print, if only to allow scholars who haven't had access to it to take note of its differences from Frei's version. And if it is to appear, where better than in a collection of essays intended to honor Frei's career, which was the paper's original intent.

How does my version of the typology differ from Frei's. The paper refers to mine as "more streamlined" than his. Frei seems to have arrived at his version inductively. He conceptualized each type with a few paradigmatic figures in mind, isolating and then generalizing the most important features they had in common. When he came across a prominent modern theologian who seemed not to approximate a type he had already conceptualized, he began the process of defining a new type. The typology assigns top priority to one variable, namely, interpretations of the person of Jesus, the topic of Frei's never-completed account of Christology in England and Germany, but it also attempts to factor in certain other variables, such as: whether theology is defined as an activity that could, in principle, be practiced outside the semiotic system of Christianity; whether theology's cognate discipline, if it has one, is taken to be philosophy or interpretive social-science; whether theology is taken to have priority over Christian communal self-description or vice versa; whether the traditional doctrine of the *sensus literalis* of the biblical text is accorded primacy over allegorical interpretation of some kind; and so forth. It is clear that these variables all pertain to a cluster of closely related topics, but Frei did not design his version of the typology in a way that made their relation structurally evident. In Frei's version, the connections among the various traits associated with a given type of theology remain rather loose. As a result of this looseness, Frei himself had trouble resolving borderline cases when assigning theologians to types. And given that the typology does not claim to be exhaustive, he left open the question of why he delineated only five types, why, for example, he did not construct a type for thinkers (like Emerson and Santayana) who take poetry as theology's cognate discipline.

I do not mean to imply that Frei's version of the typology was ill-suited to his historiographical purposes. There is nothing wrong with formulating a typology inductively with the heuristic aim of sorting out the various kinds of things one wants to write about as a historian. Nor is there anything wrong with leaving those "kinds" as vague as the historical agents one is writing about would themselves take them to be. Too much clarity of the wrong kind in a typology designed to serve historiographical purposes like Frei's would simply distort the historical record. For this reason, Frei was suspicious of typologies that had defined "theological types by their outlook toward science, culture, or some other reified totality." He complained that such typologies "have often been oversimplified and not sufficiently encompassing."[3] An oversimplified typology makes things too clear by eliminating consideration of too many of the variables that modern theologians themselves have cared about when picking fights and choosing allies. What such a typology fails to encompass is the full range of traits that a theology would have to possess to count as satisfying to a practitioner of the relevant type. So in the inductive process of typology construction, there is a trade-off between structural clarity and historical adequacy. The purpose of introducing distinctions among types in the first place is to clarify the options a bit. The means of achieving this purpose is simplification. But there is also a point of diminishing returns beyond which more clarity counts as "oversimplification." Furthermore, the vagueness of his types actually served Frei's rhetorical purposes, because it allowed him to present Schleiermacher and Barth as very close theological relatives—with the latter's theology counting as a relatively clear case of type 4 and the former's counting as an anything-but-clear case of type 3. Frei wanted Schleiermacher and Barth to be classified in such a way that they would have to stand cheek-by-jowl. He enjoyed the irony involved in tweaking Barth's inflated sense of the importance of choosing between himself and his predecessor, but Frei was also concerned to demonstrate that Barth's proximity to Schleiermacher on a whole range of issues had tended to be obscured by the received distinction between liberal and neo-orthodox theology. At the same time, he wanted to differentiate theologians like Gordon Kaufman and David Tracy pretty clearly from both of them. This judgment reflected his historian's sense of the terrain he had spent his whole adult life exploring, but it also reflected his theologian's sense of where the real clarities and vagaries lie. In any event, he didn't want to adopt definitions of types that made the terrain seem clearer than it was.

The purpose of my version of the typology was quite different. I was using it to make a few points about how Frei's own theology should be interpreted, while also making a general point about the confusions involved in using "narrative theology" as a category. For this purpose, especially in a paper meant for oral delivery, I needed a streamlined version. Because I wanted to put distance between Frei and various other theologians who had shown interest in narrative, I was perfectly content to define my categories in a way that would heighten clarity *on that issue* while accepting the cost of making the categories less adequate for the purposes of writing a full-scale history of modern theology. Since I wasn't writing such a history, this cost was painless. With only one issue in view, I was able to reconstruct the typology around one key theme, namely, the nature of the relationship theologians seek to establish between what the paper called "biblical language" and the "nonbiblical language" in which they purport to be writing. My emphasis on this one theme made my version of the typology seem clearer than Frei's, a difference Frei himself seems to have noted.[4] Because the logical structure of my version is relatively perspicuous, there is no need for me to speak weakly of "elective affinities" among the traits associated with each type, and the vagaries that would otherwise create borderline cases are eliminated.

One worry expressed, as I recall, in Charles Wood's response to my paper, was that I had apparently overestimated the significance of language as an issue in Christian theology. But this worry missed the point of the exercise. I wasn't saying that the theme highlighted in my version of the typology was the most important variable on which modern Christian theologies had differed. I was happy to grant that it was one variable among many others. Suppose we generated a typology of boats based on their color. This might be the right typology to employ when judging a race of a certain kind, where all the red boats, let's say, are competing for one cup and all the blue boats are competing for another. On another day with different ends in view, one might have reason to prefer a typology that partitions boats according to the number of masts they carry (when organizing the bicentennial celebration) or the volume of water they displace (when policing passage through the Panama Canal). And if one is writing a history of boating (analogous to Frei's projected history of modern Christology), one will need to construct another sort of typology altogether, one that clarifies the differences among the kinds of boats there have been without departing too much from the distinctions that have mattered to boat builders and seafarers. In any event, to make the points I wanted to make about

Frei and "narrative theology," I needed to highlight precisely the variable I had placed my finger on. If there were other purposes, like Frei's historiographical ones, for which some other typology would be needed, I was not troubled in the least. Two versions of a typology designed for somewhat different purposes need not be in competition with one another.

A question that gave me more pause was the one Nicholas Wolterstorff raised shortly after the session ended. He asked what I had meant by a language. To this question it must be said that I didn't have a very clear notion of "language" in mind at all. What I had in mind, I guess, was no more than a metaphor, that of theology as a process of translation, moving from one language to another—and I wanted to use that metaphor to cash out what Frei was saying about the various kinds of relationships theologians had established between scripture as something linguistic that theologians are in the business of interpreting and whatever they proposed as the discursive practice in terms of which the interpretation should be given. If pressed for further specification of my own views in the philosophy of language, I would want to speak in detail about the notion of discursive practices, more or less along the lines suggested by Wilfrid Sellars in "Some Reflections on Language Games" and recently restated with great sophistication by Robert Brandom.[5] But I doubt that this paper would be improved any by the addition of such detail. For one thing, I didn't want to ascribe my philosophy of language to the theologians I was discussing. Their conceptions of language are quite various and in many cases quite unlike my own. But whatever a theologian's own conception of language might be, he or she can still be described as establishing a relationship of some sort between scripture as one linguistic domain and whatever discursive practice provides the conceptual wherewithal for his or her interpretations of everything belonging to that domain. The real issue raised by Wolterstorff's question is whether the translation metaphor is good enough, without further unpacking, to assist me in making my points about Frei and "narrative theology." I have come, on reflection, to believe it is.[6] What follows, then, is the paper pretty much as it was circulated in 1987; I have updated the notes, and deleted one sentence from the text that seemed misleading in retrospect, but otherwise left the text in its original form.

1. TWO *FESTSCHRIFTEN*

Consider these words from a certain *Festschrift,* and ask yourself whose Christology is being explicated:

> The being of the person Jesus Christ is not, as it is for the psychologizing school—an ineffable state of awareness behind act and teachings; nor is the

full personal being inaccessible to us, as it is for the theologians influenced by form criticism. The unity of the person of Jesus Christ is embedded in and immediately present to his teaching and practice. It is the focus of unity in the teaching and acts of the Lord. In one sense, no series of acts or moral virtues in teaching and active exemplification exhausts the significance of a person's being. Nevertheless, one can say that the being does not stand ineffably behind the series or the essence behind the phenomena, distinguished from them and only inferentially to be interpreted: rather, the being is concretely exhibited, embodied in the series of phenomena.

You may think that I have just quoted one of the essays in *Scriptural Authority and Narrative Interpretation*,[7] that the Christology being explicated is Hans Frei's, but you would be wrong. For the *Festschrift* I have just quoted was one I found in a used bookstore as a college sophomore in the year 1970, back when I didn't know what a *Festschrift* or a Christology was, let alone the identity of Hans Frei. The book was already a dozen years old by then and it had the ugliest cover I had ever seen on a book in my life. Its title: *Faith and Ethics: The Theology of H. Richard Niebuhr*.[8] So it was Niebuhr's Christology, not Frei's, being explicated in the passage I quoted. But it was Frei doing the explicating. And it was in reading Frei's two long essays at the front of *Faith and Ethics* that I first felt I understood something about modern theology.

What struck and instructed me most, at the time, about Frei's essays was not their account of Niebuhr in particular but rather their ability to make sense of the entire theological landscape in terms of the problems theological authors were responding to and the assumptions that compelled them to say the strange things they said. I felt that I could begin to see the more or less determinate range of possibilities for solving such problems so long as one made this or that assumption, and I could sense the power an author can exercise over the rest of the landscape simply by calling into question an assumption long taken for granted.

Frei did not persuade me to ascribe much significance to Niebuhr's Christology. If anything, Niebuhr fell in my estimation as I read Frei's essays in his honor. He seemed increasingly to be absorbed into the landscape in which Frei placed him, dwarfed by predecessors named Barth, Schleiermacher, and Troltsch. Rereading those essays now, however, Frei's discussion of Niebuhr's Christology takes on new significance. For nothing brings home more forcibly how thoroughly Frei has himself transformed the context within which his predecessors must be read. Subtract Frei's subsequent redescriptions of the problems and possibilities of modern theology, take away his probing questioning of Christological and hermeneutical assumptions, and it is hard to imagine seeing the brief section of *Christ and*

Culture Frei was explicating back in the mid-1950s as worthy of the attention he lavished on it. If Professor Frei has since vindicated his original judgment of that section, he has done so mainly by conferring upon it a significance it did not used to have. For now we are bound to read it as a partial and incomplete anticipation of Frei's own mature Christology. Thus, according to Nietzsche and Bloom, does a strong writer create his own past, through backward causation.

Scholars strong enough to reconfigure the past dramatically in the eyes of their readers and students deserve the high honor a *Festschrift* aims to confer. What do we want from their *Festschriften*. First, that such books themselves be good enough to bestow the honor they intend. Hans Frei has no reason to be embarrassed by this volume, for there is much in it to confirm the quality as well as the extent of his influence—too much, alas, for me to talk about in detail in the limited time at my disposal. What else do we want. Ideally, that the *Festschrift* begins to draw the lines along which the next generation will come to terms with the accomplishment of the scholar it honors. Toward this end, *Scriptural Authority and Narrative Interpretation* makes only a very modest and sketchy start.

Nobody in this volume even begins to do for Frei what Frei once did for Niebuhr. That is, nobody ventures an interpretation of his place in the unfolding history of recent theology. Surely, however, this would have been a lot to expect. Not only has Frei been a reluctant author, whose only published books burst suddenly on the scene a scant thirteen years ago, but he has also been, at best, an enigmatic one, not given to complete and clear systematic statement of his views. Moreover, many of us who have heard the lectures he has given in the last several years at Yale, Princeton, or Birmingham are bound to feel that the typology of modern theology he has been working on will require yet another radical rethinking of the tradition and his place in it. We have good reason to conclude, then, that it may simply be too early to do for Frei what he did for Niebuhr, that the best is yet to come.

In this paper I shall set such daunting thoughts aside and endeavor to show how something like the typology he has been developing in his lectures might help us come to grips with Frei's accomplishment while also providing a framework for interpreting and quarrelling with his various admirers and critics, including the contributors to his *Festschrift*. I refer to the typology I shall be employing as "something like" his, rather than simply "his," for two reasons: first, because the version I will employ here, while similar in some respects to a version I have heard him present, also consciously differs from it in others (I need a streamlined, more strictly formal version for my purposes); and second, because Professor Frei should remain free to draw and redraw his distinctions as he sees fit without feeling that he needs to disown anybody's premature interpretations of his admittedly tentative drafts.

2. FIVE TYPES OF THEOLOGY

Assume, for present purposes, that all Christian theology needs to establish some sort of relationship between biblical language and nonbiblical language. Given that assumption, we can distinguish types of theology according to the kind of nonbiblical language they deem relevant to the theological task and the kind of relationship they seek to establish. Many types are logically possible. At least five are needed to account for theological controversy in the. modern period.

The first type seeks to translate scripture into another language (call it Esperanto) which is treated as *the* language within which the deep structure of all intelligibility and truth can be laid bare. Practitioners of type 1 (call them Esperantists) do not aim for translations that preserve everything from scripture. They are content to preserve only what would seem intelligible and true to the ideally rational speaker of Esperanto.

The second type seeks to translate scripture into another language (call it Presentese) which, though not necessarily the sole language in which intelligibility and truth could conceivably be discerned, is nonetheless thought to represent the distinctive mode of rationality of *our* age and thus the only language *we* might reasonably use in interpreting and appraising scripture. Practitioners of type 2 (call them Presentists) require a privileged language for their mapping of scripture but it needn't be one whose right to privileged status can be shown to be permanent and necessary. Aside from this difference, however, Presentist theology resembles Esperantist theology. Both aim to separate the wheat of scripture from its chaff, and only what survives the process of translation into the privileged language counts as wheat. In each case, this often involves supposedly charitable reinterpretation of scripture so that many of its sentences can be construed as elliptical statements of truths capable of straightforward statement in the privileged language.

The third type of theology (call it Dialogical) seeks to correlate scripture with the languages of our own age, though without according either side of the correlation privileged status and without supposing that it will be possible to arrive at an integrated theory for determining such matters. The Dialogical theologian moves back and forth between scripture and other languages, hoping to bring them into deeper and more meaningful conversation, all the while treating them (in Frei's words) as "heterogenous equals." He or she may introduce theory or utter hermeneutical generalizations, so long as such remarks do not themselves take on the character of a privileged language. "Theory" and "hermeneutics" here remain parasitical upon the process of conversation itself. They are merely the conversation in its moments of reflective self-inventory. They do not replace it with a free-standing linguistic system into which the conversation must be translated in order to be meaningful.

I call the fourth type of theology Anselmian, for its practitioners often take Anselm's phrase, "faith seeking understanding," as their motto.[9] The understanding they seek is, as they see it, wholly achievable within scripture but not wholly exhausted by the know-how involved in using scripture in such activities as prayer, worship, preaching, and practical deliberation within the community. The central task of theology, on this view, is precisely to elucidate the use of scripture by describing, more or less as an ethnographer would, the characteristic patterns of attitude-acquisition, inference, and action scripture makes possible. As reflexive ethnographers, such theologians are not condemned merely to repeat sentences from the scripture or liturgy of the Christian community, but neither are they engaged in an effort to translate scripture into a linguistic framework alien to it. Rather, convinced that scripture is not a static system, they are fully prepared to develop conceptual resources within scripture that will assist in the task of Christian self-description. Because they stand fully and self-consciously within scripture, according to it whatever privileged status it implicitly or explicitly claims for itself, they are hesitant to treat *any* other language as its equal in conversation, let alone as a privileged source of intelligibility and truth. This does not, however, reduce them to silence concerning the relation between scripture and other languages, as one might be tempted to suppose. For it remains possible to describe other languages from within scripture, thereby helping achieve such "intratextual" ends as these: (a) improving one's understanding of scripture by displaying its similarities to and differences from the rest; (b) acquiring used parts and fresh insights from other languages in hope of enriching scripture's theological metalanguage; and (c) engaging in what Frei calls "ad hoc apologetics," a form of intellectual guerrilla warfare in which one attempts to inflict devastating polemical effects on the opposition without incurring the theoretical costs of systematic defense.[10]

The fifth type of theology is Segregationist. Like type 4, it takes its stand wholly within scripture, but unlike type 4, it avoids both the development of a metalanguage within scripture and any attempt to relate scripture to other languages "intratextually." A theological metalanguage can be dispensed with, on this view, because the only understanding faith can seek is already there in the actual skills and habits one acquires when learning scripture. As for relating scripture to other languages "intratextually," there is no point in it. The following reasons, associated with "vulgar Wittgensteinianism," are sometimes given in defense of this conclusion: (a) scripture is already understood perfectly well by those who actually use it, so knowledge of its similarities to and differences from other languages would serve no real religious purpose; (b) spare parts imported from other languages are more likely to distort than to enrich scripture; and (c) even ad hoc apologetics fails to take full cognizance of the "fact" that no language-in-use or form of life can be criticized from the outside.[11]

3. TWENTY-ONE THESES

So we have five types: Esperantist, Presentist, Dialogical, Anselmian, and Segregationist. I am now in a position to advance the following twenty-one theses:

1. Hans Frei is best viewed as the leading Anselmian theologian of his generation. All of his primary contributions to theology fall into place if seen in relation to his commitment to the Anselmian model.

2. The central importance of Frei's essays for the Niebuhr *Festschrift* had little to do with Niebuhr. It consisted rather in a reading of Barth which, though not entirely novel, secured a hearing for him as the great Anselmian theologian of our time. According to this reading, it was no accident that Barth's book on Anselm was the crucial turning point in his authorship. Once this reading had been fully articulated, interpretations like Brunner's could no longer be taken seriously. It became impossible to read him, and thus dismiss him, as an especially odd or paradoxical advocate of some other theological type.

3. *The Eclipse of Biblical Narrative*[12] is an instance of Anselmian ad hoc apologetics carried out by historiographical means. Its main targets are Esperantist and Presentist modes of translating scripture into supposedly privileged languages. One ironic effect of the story told in this book was a portrait of various dialects of Enlightenment and post-Enlightenment Esperanto as parochial languages that arose under quite particular historical circumstances. Another was a portrait of various dialects of Presentese as well-suited only for an age already rapidly receding into the past.

4. *The Identity of Jesus Christ*[13] is Frei's one extended attempt to elucidate, in accordance with the Anselmian program, what he takes to be the most central fragments of scripture, as its canonical stories about Jesus Christ. The theological metalanguage he has worked out is intended to display how the stories work, thus aiding in their understanding, without in any way presuming to take their place. Two concepts in particular became crucial to this metalanguage as he originally developed it, namely, identity and presence, but by the time he wrote the preface of *Identity* he was concerned that the latter concept had acquired a life of its own and threatened, in practice, to push his interpretations away from type 4 in the direction of type 1 or 2. The chapter on "Jesus Christ and Modern Christ Figures" is an Anselmian attempt to deepen understanding of scripture by means of comparative literary analysis. It also functions as an instance of ad hoc apologetics designed

to undermine the notion that there can be a genuine Christ figure aside from the actual Christ.

5. Frei's recent paper, "The 'Literal Reading' of Biblical Narrative in the Christian Tradition: Does It Stretch or Will It Break,"[14] includes another example of Anselmian ad hoc apologetics, this time carried out largely by means of arguments borrowed from deconstructionists and directed against David Tracy and Paul Ricoeur. It is also meant to vindicate the idea that a kind of biblical interpretation essentially continuous with Anselmian theology constitutes the mainstream of interpretive practice in the Christian tradition.

6. Gary Comstock's interpretation of Frei as the confused and self-contradictory leader of the "pure narrativists" is the contemporary analogue of Brunner's interpretation of Barth.[15] All narrativists, according to Comstock, insist "that stories are primary in the order of human knowing and acting" and are committed to the notion that narratives are not reducible to other linguistic forms. What makes Frei a pure narrativist, as Comstock sees it, is his refusal to defend the very claims that make him a narrativist. But describing Frei as a narrativist, thus defined, makes him seem like an advocate of a form of Esperanto or Presentese in which narratives play roles that used to be played by such notions as "clear and distinct ideas." Describing him as a pure narrativist simply makes him seem like an especially pig-headed and unforthcoming theologian of type 1 or 2, one who, when defending his refusal to argue, sounds suspiciously like the vulgar Wittgensteinians of type 5, thus raising basic questions about the consistency of his position.

7. Frei is not a narrativist in this sense at all. His position does not rely on the claim "that stories are primary in the order of human knowing." If he isn't a narrativist, it follows that he isn't a pure one either. He is an Anselmian theologian whose theological metalanguage includes the term "narrative," as well as such other expressions as "the literal sense," "meaning," and "reference." At his best, Frei uses these expressions without relying upon or committing himself to any particular philosophical theory in which they play a part. He abandoned the term "presence" when he sensed he could not go on using it without implicitly buying into such a theory. And he seems now to be worried that his use of the term "narrative" will be assimilated, in the minds of many readers, to what Comstock calls narrativism or to what David Kelsey describes as the "celebration of the importance of narrative for Christian theology" (p. 121).

8. Kelsey distinguishes between "foundationalist" and "nonfoundationalist" celebrators of narrative, grouping Stephen Crites among the former and Frei among the latter. He is right to see a difference between them, but his distinction hardly does justice to the variety of claims nowadays being made on behalf of narrative's importance. Any of the first four types of theology can make the concept of narrative central to its account of scripture. So it is not enough to distinguish Frei's view from an approach that sees narrativity as a "universal characteristic of human consciousness" delineated by transcendental analysis. For on Frei's view, as I understand it, even a nonfoundationalist epistemology that stresses the importance of narrative can acquire the status of a privileged interpretive language over against scripture. To see what kind of significance he places on narrative, one needs to take full account of his Anselmian program, which Kelsey does not do in his essay.

9. Kelsey goes on to argue that the "nonfoundationalist" approach is, ironically, incapable of producing a theological anthropology. He thinks that the essence of this approach has to do with claims about the capacity of narrative to display an individual's unique personal identity, whereas theological anthropology is essentially a set of answers to highly general questions about human beings, questions of a sort that simply couldn't be answered (directly) in reference to a narrative's uniquely individuating description of a person. But, as Kelsey himself seems to concede, this feature of the New Testament stories about Jesus, the feature most clearly relevant to Frei's Christology, need not be the feature an Anselmian would want to emphasize when turning to theological anthropology. Frei might argue, for example, that the stories are structured so as to give a uniquely individuating description of the identity of Jesus Christ and, simultaneously, so as to place clear constraints on how the questions of theological anthropology should be answered. Nothing requires him to emphasize the same feature of scriptural narratives, or even the same type of scriptural narratives, in responding to all theological questions.[16] Moreover, nothing in his Anselmian program *requires* him to "celebrate narrative's importance" for theological anthropology.

10. It would be interesting to hear what Kelsey would have to say about Gene Outka's "Following at a Distance," which artfully draws out the significance of Frei's *Identity of Jesus Christ* for Christian ethics, a branch of theology that seeks answers to general questions not entirely unlike those of theological anthropology. It is, I think, Outka's best

published essay to date. He draws attention, as Kelsey does not, to Frei's view that each reader of Christian scripture is invited to see within the text not only a uniquely individuating description of the identity of Jesus Christ but also the shape of his or her own life and the shape of our own era's events as "figures of that storied world" (p. 145).[17] Outka also brings out the critical implications of Frei's work for any theological anthropology "heavily freighted" with such philosophical categories as alienation (p. 151). Working this closely with Frei keeps Outka clear of the characteristic temptation of his earlier interpretive writings in Christian ethics, which tended to translate biblical concepts all too easily (and without a sense of loss) into the contemporary Kantian and analytic dialects of moral Esperanto. Even here one would like to see Outka work harder to justify his reliance on the concept of respect (p. 156).

11. Stephen Crites, in his contribution to the *Festschrift*, undertakes an analysis of "The Spatial Dimensions of Narrative Truthtelling." It is a marvelous essay in its own right, but it does tend to confirm Kelsey's judgment that Crites and Frei have different ends in view. When Crites says that "storytelling is one of the primary means by which we human beings establish a homology between our own inner space and the multidimensional space outside and between, above and below, us in which we are psychically as well as physically located," he is right to add: "I think I already see Professor Frei beginning to frown" (p. 99).

12. Stanley Hauerwas, in his contribution, directly addresses the question of why "Professor Frei has begun to feel uneasy with some aspects of the upsurge of interest in narrative for theology" (p. 188). Hauerwas gets off to an excellent start in trying to answer this question when he says: Frei "rightly fears that the theological construal of scripture as a narrative of God's work in behalf of his creation might be qualified by claims of the narrative quality of existence or the self" (p. 189). Frei, as I would put it, is a theologian of type 4 hoping to avoid being confused (in this case) with theologians of types 1–3. But Hauerwas seems less concerned with following up on this point than with trying to dodge a charge once made by Ronald Thiemann, roughly, that Hauerwas tends to waver between the Anselmian position and a position of type 2 or 3 in which a philosophical idiolect derived from Alasdair MacIntyre either acquires a privileged status or becomes one pole in a Dialogical theology of correlation. Unfortunately, much of what Hauerwas proceeds to say in the remainder of his essay reinforces my impression that Thiemann was probably right.[18]

13. Outka's is only one of several essays in *Scriptural Authority and Narrative Interpretation* that can be read as attempts to follow through

on details of the Anselmian program. The interesting contributions of Thiemann, Lindbeck, and Wood can be read in this way as well. Maurice Wiles, in an essay which adds the strongest note of dissent to the volume, takes this very trio to task for writing books that make excessive claims on behalf of narrative interpretation. Wiles is to be thanked for relieving the monotony of unrelenting praise the authors of this volume tend to direct toward each other's work, but his essay consistently fails to anticipate plausible responses open to his opponents, and his reasons for concern seem to derive as much from his own excessively rigid conception of narrative as from anything they actually intend to say.[19]

14. Kathryn Tanner's essay, which to my mind stands with Outka's as one of the most important in the book, aims (at the most general level) to clarify the sense in which what I have called Anselmian reflexive ethnography resembles "nonreductive social science." Why would such an endeavor be important? Because Anselmian theology is often regarded as intrinsically incapable of fruitful conversation of the sort Dialogical theology prizes so highly, whereas Tanner's essay (like recent books by Thiemann, Lindbeck, and Wood) demonstrates that such conversation may now be possible for Anselmians, provided they choose their principal conversation partners well. If so-called interpretive social science and antifoundationalist philosophy prove hospitable to this apparent opportunity, and a rich conversation develops between them and theologians of the fourth type, a central charge against the Anselmian camp will have been rebutted. Furthermore, while there are some points at which I would want to quarrel with Tanner over details, I believe her paper is quite successful in achieving its specific purpose, which is to explicate the notion of "the plain sense of scripture" without appealing to "any general hermeneutic or epistemological treatment of the relation between text and interpreter but by an analysis of what follows from a particular convention in community practice as that becomes clear against the background of logically possible alternatives" (p. 75). In fact, for reasons that will be clarified somewhat in a moment, I believe her explication is superior to Frei's in one crucial respect: it does not rely on the concept of the meaning of a text.

15. Garrett Green speaks for many of Frei's admirers when he says that "Of particular importance for both constructive theology and biblical studies is the distinction that Frei draws between literal meaning and historical reference" (p. 79). Frei has invited this reading of his accomplishment by claiming in various writings that his opponents are just plain wrong about something called *the meaning* of realistic

narratives, that the actual meaning of such narratives is nothing other than the story they tell. This way of putting his point seems to beg for defense in terms of a general theory of meaning, or at least a theory of what realistic narratives mean. When Frei resists giving such a theory, he seems to beg the question at issue and opens himself to criticisms like those leveled against him by Comstock. As I have argued at length on another occasion,[20] theoretical assertions about *the meaning* of a text nearly always beg the question and rarely lead to fruitful debate. On this point, I would refer Frei and Green to *The Formation of Christian Understanding*, where Wood argues that the term "meaning" should "drop out of prominence and assume a less conspicuous and more modest function in the discussion of interpretation."[21]

16. If we eliminate or reformulate Frei's flat assertions about the meaning of texts, don't we threaten to destroy or diminish Frei's main claim to fame as a student of biblical interpretation? I think not. In the first place, we can preserve his readings of biblical texts, defending their adequacy relative to Anselmian purposes. Second, it remains possible to reformulate and extend Frei's negative criticisms of the readings he was struggling against in *Eclipse* and *Identity*. For we can say that such readings, far from capturing anything worth calling *the meaning* of biblical texts, simply translated those texts into a dialect of Esperanto or Presentese *assumed* to have hermeneutical and epistemological privilege. They were, despite their pretensions, no more than readings in the service of Esperantist or Presentist purposes. But the privilege these languages claimed for themselves is itself highly susceptible to immanent criticism. So Frei is free to attack Esperantist and Presentist readings by attacking assumptions and purposes underlying them. And here he is able to make ad hoc use of antifoundationalist, pragmatic, and deconstructionist arguments without presupposing a general theory.

17. He is also free, by the way, to use arguments from the real Wittgenstein, Charles Taylor, Richard Rorty, and others in an ad hoc fashion to undermine the vulgar Wittgensteinianism most commonly used to defend Segregationism. It is by strengthening the contrast between types 4 and 5 that Frei can most plausibly respond to some of Comstock's complaints about irrationalism and fideism, as well as the following remark by Hauerwas:

> the difficulty with the suggestion that theology's task is largely one of conceptual redescription is that one is unsure how the question of truth can ever be raised. As long as one remains in the 'language

game' what one says may seem intelligible and even significant, but by the very nature of the 'game' one will not be permitted to ask questions external to the narrative.

(p. 191)[22]

18. What Hauerwas here calls "the question of truth" is raised repeatedly throughout *Scriptural Authority and Narrative Interpretation* but never treated rigorously or persuasively. Comstock thinks, wrongly, that Frei's theology eschews truth-claims altogether and that it does this for vulgar Wittgensteinian reasons. Nothing could be farther from Frei's Anselmian intentions, which are deeply shaped by Barth's ontological realism. Like Barth, Frei is utterly unabashed about making strong theological truth-claims. The point of distinguishing meaning from truth or reference, as I see it, was to argue that it is possible to understand a realistic biblical narrative (by Anselmian lights) without having independent epistemic access to whatever historical referents it might have. The point was not to *avoid* the "question of truth" but rather to distinguish it from the "question of interpretation," the better to answer the latter properly, thereby improving one's chances of understanding whatever theological truth-claims one wishes to make.

19. What Frei does intend to avoid, however, is the task of supplying systematic justification of his position, especially if that means adopting a language alien to scripture as the ultimate source of epistemic authority. Frei is convinced that truth-claims, for example, about the identity of Jesus Christ, are essential to Christian theology rightly understood, and as a Christian theologian he is perfectly prepared to make them.[23] But systematically justifying such truth-claims, in the sense of offering compelling reasons within some other language (like Esperanto or Presentese) for accepting the vocabulary and ontology one would presuppose in using scripture, is: (a) in all likelihood impossible, (b) in tension with characteristically Christian conceptions of faith, and (c) obviously antithetical to Anselmian theology. One cannot defend Anselmian theology by such means without falling into contradiction. So Frei does not try. This does not make him an irrationalist, for he can still claim that he is justified in accepting the truth-claims he makes as a Christian, and he can still engage in a kind of reasoned argument against his opponents. Being justified in believing something and being able to justify it *to* someone else, especially in a language of *that* person's choosing, are not the same thing. And it is possible to make reasonable arguments against one's opponents by restricting oneself to ad hoc apologetics, exhibiting what Kelsey calls

"the partial inadequacy of the available alternatives" (p. 123) and showing that the Anselmian program can succeed on its own terms.[24]

20. Esperantists, Presentists, and Segregationists all typically incur heavy philosophical debts. Esperantists and Presentists borrow from philosophy in order to confer privileged status on a language of rational commensuration. Segregationists borrow from philosophy in order to protect scripture from external interference or internal development. But to a secular philosopher like myself, these borrowing habits betray a certain irony. For it is precisely where its philosophical debts have been highest that modern theology has proved most susceptible to immanent criticism. Anselmian ad hoc apologetics has been able to exploit this irony to great advantage in an attempt to narrow the competition within contemporary theology. Frei is at his polemical best, it seems to me, when he employs immanent criticism to show that his opponents' philosophical proposals are bound to fail on their own terms.

21. What, then, does he see as the strongest alternative to his own Anselmian program. Frei is Barthian even in his temptations (I refer here only to *theological* temptations, mind you). Like Barth before him, he thinks that it must be Schleiermacher who is right if he is wrong. Schieiermacher, as Frei reads him, is a Dialogical theologian, not a Presentist. And the Dialogical effort at correlation seems to attract him for two reasons: first, because of the modesty of its philosophical ambitions, and second, because it at least aims to do full justice to both sides of the academic theologian's identity—the side bound up with the academy as well as the side bound up with the church. Whether full justice can be done to both sides without finally calling the authority of one or the other radically into question, thus precipitating movement either in the direction of Presentism or in the direction of Anselmian theology, is, of course, the crucial question. While Frei remains inclined to answer it in the negative, even he must admit that his ad hoc apologetics have thus far been least effective at just this point. The new typology is designed to portray Dialogical and Anselmian positions as the principal contenders for theological attention. What those of us following Professor Frei at a distance eagerly await, however, is a detailed account, from his point of view, of their respective strengths and weaknesses. In the meantime, more power, and all due honor, to him.[25]

NOTES

1. Hans W. Frei, *Types of Christian Theology* (New Haven: Yale University Press, 1992).

2. Hans W. Frei, *Theology and Narrative: Selected Essays* (New York: Oxford University Press, 1993).

3. Frei, *Types*, 1.

4. "Jeffrey Stout has redescribed the types in a way that Frei once told me orally he found clearer than his own," writes Eugene Rogers in "Schleiermacher as an Anselmian Theologian: Aesthetics, Dogmatics, Apologetics and Proof," forthcoming in *The Scottish Journal of Theology*. It was just like Frei to praise others for their clarity at his own expense. I am saying that in this case he was right, modesty notwithstanding, to find my version of the typology clearer than his but that the clarity was more suited to my purposes in discussing him and the narrativists than to his purposes in discussing Barth, Schleiermacher, et al.

5. Wilfrid Sellars, "Some Reflections on Language Games," in *Science, Perception, and Reality* (London: Routledge and Kegan Paul, 1963): 321–58; Robert B. Brandom, *Making It Explicit: Reasoning, Representing, and Discursive Commitment* (Cambridge: Harvard University Press, 1994).

6. I am aware, of course, that Wolterstorff has another concern in mind that relates directly to the question of how language should be defined—namely, the complaint that modern theology has generally neglected the claim that God speaks, that the discourse found in the Bible is God's discourse. The significance he ascribes to this claim leads him to construct an account of "divine discourse" in terms drawn mainly from speech-act theory. See Nicholas Wolterstorff, *Divine Discourse* (Cambridge: Cambridge University Press, 1995).

7. *Scriptural Authority and Narrative Interpretation*, ed. Garrett Green (Philadelphia: Fortress Press, 1987). Page references to this book will appear in parentheses in the text.

8. *Faith and Ethics: The Theology of H. Richard Niebuhr*, ed. Paul Ramsey (New York: Harper and Row, 1957). Frei's essays are entitled "Niebuhr's Theological Background," 9–64, and "The Theology of H. Richard Niebuhr," 65–116. The quoted passage appears on p. 115.

9. The analogue of this motto in Dialogical theology could be "conversation seeking understanding."

10. I don't mean to make ad hoc apologetics sound overly bent on destruction. Ad hoc apologetics can have its aggressive side, but it also favors unusually intimate forms of argumentative encounter, and it therefore constantly risks learning from, and possibly even converting to, the very opposition it sets out to convert or defeat.

11. It is possible, however, to be a Segregationist without being a vulgar Wittgensteinian. All it takes to be a Segregationist is commitment to the idea that scripture is an autonomous linguistic system which one inevitably distorts by relating it to other such systems or by developing a metalanguage within it for the purpose of enhancing its practitioners' self-understanding.

12. Hans W. Frei, *The Eclipse of Biblical Narrative* (New Haven and London: Yale University Press, 1974).
13. Hans W. Frei, *The Identity of Jesus Christ* (Philadelphia: Fortress Press, 1974).
14. Frei in *The Bible and the Narrative Tradition*, ed. Frank McConnell (New York and Oxford: Oxford University Press, 1986), 36–77. Reprinted in *Theology and Narrative*, 117–52.
15. Gary Comstock, "Truth or Meaning: Ricoeur versus Frei on Biblical Narrative," *Journal of Religion* 66, no. 2 (April 1986): 117–40.
16. One point where Frei does emphasize a feature of scriptural narratives distinct from the one Kelsey singles out is the section of *Identity* (pp. 161–4) that begins with this sentence: "In our endeavor to narrate the as-yet-unfinished pattern of history, we reach for parables that might serve to set forth a kind of pattern, though not to confine history and the mysterious providence of God to these symbolic meanings." It is most important to see that when Frei discusses a scriptural narrative, the *sensus literalis* is primary, not solitary.
17. The quoted phrase comes from *Eclipse*, 3. For another discussion relevant to this issue, see Thiemann's comments on the closing of Matthew (p. 37).
18. I am especially confused by two charges he makes against Frei on p. 196. This first is this: "What is frustrating about Frei's (and Wood's) position is the failure to specify the liturgical context through which such consensus is formed" (n. 11). I wonder what Hauerwas thought Frei was doing when he closed off *Identity* with "A Meditation for the Week of Good Friday and Easter," and emphasized the importance of "ritual performance" (*Identity*, p. 169). I also wonder what he thought Wood was doing in the penultimate paragraph of *Formation* (pp. 119–20). Here is the second charge: "While Frei is certainly right to emphasize the 'plain sense' as primary, 1 think that he does not sufficiently note that the 'plain sense' is that determined through the corporate life of the Christian community" (n. 12). *Pace* Hauerwas, Frei gives great prominence to precisely this theme throughout "The 'Literal Reading.'"
19. See especially pp. 47–8, where Wiles writes: "Almost any combination of things can be read as one story, given sufficient ingenuity ... But where twists of fortune and shifts of character in some proffered narration become excessive, we would say to anyone who still wanted to call it one story, that in that case it was a very bad story." To make this argument tell against his opponents, Wiles would have to come to grips not only with the history of the modern novel (including Nabokov, Proust, and Joyce) but also with literary analysis of the sort Robert Alter has brought to bear on biblical materials (see Thiemann's essay, 29–39).
20. Jeffrey Stout, "What Is the Meaning of a Text?" *New Literary History* 14 (1982): 1–12. See also another essay of mine, "The Relativity of Interpretation," *Monist* 69, no. 1 (1986): 103–18.
21. Charles M. Wood, *The Formation of Christian Understanding* (Philadelphia: Westminster, 1981), pp. 22–3.
22. Whether Hauerwas considers this difficulty a real or merely apparent one for Frei's theology, I'm not sure.
23. Comstock takes Frei to be saying that "members of the Christian religion are entitled simply to claim that when we talk about Jesus' identity we are not making

rational, 'true' claims" ("Truth or Meaning," 128). If I am right, Comstock isn't. To adjudicate the issue, we might well begin by debating the upshot of what Frei says in the following passages from *Identity*: "... since the narrative involves truth-claims concerning facts and salvation as well as some lifelike and also some stylized religious elements ..." (p. 125). "But at one point a judgment of faith concerning the inspiration of the descriptive contents and a judgment of faith affirming their central factual claim would have to coincide for the believer" (p. 150). "... because it is more nearly factlike than not, reliable historical evidence *against* the resurrection would be decisive" (p. 151, his italics). See also the passage beginning at the bottom of p. 145.

24. Comstock seems to assume that because "rational conversations by definition are open to all reasonable persons," Frei must either couch his arguments in Esperanto or abandon rational argument altogether ("Truth or Meaning," 128). Frei's response ought to be that the hope for a neutral and universal language of rational commensuration has never been fulfilled, that all rational conversations must be couched in some particular language or other, and that preferring some other language to scripture without defending one's preference begs the question against Anselmic theology. From Comstock's point of view, this response will smack of vulgar Wittgensteinianism. But unlike the Segregationists, Frei does not treat scripture as a closed system incapable of engaging outsiders in rational argument. Hence the importance of ad hoc apologetics.

25. I wish to thank John Bowlin and Paul Ramsey for making helpful comments on the first draft of this paper.

CHAPTER EIGHT

Frei and the Project of Christological Reflection

DAVID H. KELSEY

THE PROJECT OF CHRISTOLOGICAL REFLECTION

It is a commonplace that Christology underwent deep changes in theology's transition into the culture of modernity. To identify what drove those changes and suggest an alternative possibility, it will be useful to compare briefly two overlapping but importantly different diagnoses of the transition, one by Schubert Ogden, *The Point of Christology* (1982), and the other by Hans Frei, *The Identity of Jesus Christ* (1975).

Ogden centers on the following change: traditionally theologians' christological reflections had focused on God, or more exactly, on God the Second Person, relating to Jesus by "taking on flesh," assuming human nature, in Jesus' conception and birth and, in relating to Jesus, on God also relating to humankind (we might call this the "metaphysical Jesus"). This approach has often been characterized as "Christology from above." According to Ogden, behind this focus lay the New Testament's basic christological assertions, which, for all of their diversity of expression, address the same complex of three interrelated questions: "Who is Jesus?" "Who is God?" "Who are we?" (27–28). By contrast, Christology in the modern period tends to focus on the historical Jesus considered apart from his meaning for us (15–16). Ogden calls this Jesus the "empirical-historical Jesus." It is a methodological axiom of such revisionist Christology that only when a picture of the historical Jesus is secured can christological claims about how Jesus makes a "saving" difference for humankind have any basis. This approach has often been characterized as "Christology from below."

Ogden holds both traditional and revisionist Christologies to be problematic. Traditional Christologies are held to be problematic for several reasons. Scientific developments in early modernity appeared to make incredible the picture of the world that traditional Christology took for granted. Therewith they seemed to make the metaphysical conceptuality that traditional Christologies employed at best irrelevant, at worst just wrong. Advances in historical-critical study of the Bible made a naive reading of the Gospels as accurate historical reports impossible, focusing attention on the question of what, if anything, could be affirmed about who Jesus historically had really been. Traditional explanations of what it means to say that, while "truly God," Jesus was also "truly human" became unpersuasive in the light of modern notions of what it is to be a human being. In some ways this last issue was the most important for Christology: in the context of modernity and its regnant anthropologies, traditional Christologies seemed more and more clearly to tend toward docetism. Although the allegations about the metaphysical implications of the modern scientific world picture in relation to Christology require a very great deal of refinement and nuancing to have any force, I am content here to let stand these reasons for finding traditional Christologies conceptually problematic. The strong tendency to docetism in traditional Christologies is by itself sufficient grounds for finding them conceptually problematic.

Christologies revised to speak to modernity focused on the human Jesus in order to secure the claim about his true humanity, and only as a second move focused on what and how God has to do with Jesus and, in him, with us. The human Jesus was assumed, almost as a matter of definition, to be the historical Jesus—i.e., the Jesus historians could reconstruct on the basis of available evidence, almost all of which had to be sifted out of New Testament texts by means of the disciplines of the academic historian. Ogden's own judgment, which I share, is that the revisionist christological tradition has been as problematic as was traditional Christology. This is true for two reasons (1982, 14, 55–60). First, the quest for the historical Jesus as a basis for Christology turns out to be impossible. There is insufficient evidence to warrant confidence in the results of the inquiry as the basis of theological remarks—i.e., as the basis of Christology. For another, the project is theologically unnecessary. Granted, christological remarks make empirical-historical assumptions. Therefore, in principle they can be disconfirmed by historical research that makes those assumptions improbable. That christological remarks have this logical status relative to historical research is a good thing, for particular fact claims that cannot in principle be challenged risk being contentless (61). Historical claims about Jesus are a necessary but not sufficient basis of christological claims. However, Ogden argues, christological claims are above all theological claims, claims about God and God's relation to Jesus and God's relation to us, and historical research is incompetent to confirm or disconfirm claims about God and God relating. So the revisionist christological project of grounding Christology in the historical Jesus is theologically unfruitful and unnecessary.

For his part, Ogden's constructive proposal retrieves some elements of both traditional and revisionist Christologies. With traditional Christologies and against revisionist ones, he insists that an adequate Christology must address all three of the interrelated questions addressed by the New Testaments basic christological assertions, "Who is Jesus?" "Who is God?" "Who are we?" Thus, the point of Christology is an existential point. That is, to make an assertion about who Jesus is, is even more fundamentally to make an assertion about who we are. In Ogden's formulation, the basic christological assertion is, "Jesus is the decisive representation of [the meaning of] God for us" (1982, 59; cf. 77–8, 80). Hence the subject of christological assertions is not, as it has been for revisionist Christologies, the "empirical-historical Jesus" considered apart from what he means for us, but what Ogden calls the "existential-historical Jesus."

Nonetheless, the form of such a Christology must be (with revisionist Christologies and against traditional ones) truly critical. It must test both the meaning and the truth of christological assertions. The meaning of christological assertions must be exhibited by showing how they express adequately the christological assertions of the earliest Christian witness. That witness is identified by historical-critical study of the New Testament. Ogden calls it the "Apostolic witness" (cf. 1982, 101, 103, 113, 121). The substance of the apostolic witness is that Jesus is the decisive representation of the meaning of God for us—unbounded and unconditioned love. To live in faith in that love is to be liberated to live in freedom (cf. 120–3). Here "love" is not a metaphysical description of God but an expression of the meaning of being for us (144). Christological predicates asserted of the existential-historical subject of christological assertions are to be tested as to their Christian appropriateness by their coherence with this basic christological assertion of the apostolic witness. New Testament documents formulate this witness in different ways. However, their formulations are functionally interchangeable, even when they are metaphysically conflicting. They are all expressions of witness that Jesus is the decisive representation of God (76, cf. 38). Thus, the apostolic witness addresses, not a metaphysical question about God *in se,* but a religious (i.e., existential) question about the meaning of God for us (36–7).

On the other hand, the truth of christological assertions is to be assessed both ethically and metaphysically. Insofar as christological assertions are assertions about who we are, their truth is tested ethically by how far we in fact love all who are embraced by God's love,[1] for the freedom that comes in faith is faith working through love (157–8). It includes the freedom to take personal responsibility for otherwise purely secular political decisions in concrete situations aimed at increasing our neighbors' liberty (157, 159). The truth of christological assertions is tested metaphysically by metaphysical arguments showing that the meaning of ultimate reality for us (viz., that it is boundless love) is always and universally implicitly presented to us in our own existence (80, 82; also Ogden 1966). With revisionist Christologies and against traditional ones, a Christology with this form and substance is a "Christology from below." It is grounded in the historically earliest Christian witness to the existential-historical Jesus as the decisive representation of the meaning of God for us, not in the descent of the Second Person of the Trinity. While unlike revisionist and like traditional Christologies, it has a metaphysical as well as an existential dimension, the metaphysics have to do not with the relation between divine and human natures of a single divine *hypostasis* but with the relation between ultimate reality and every human being here below. Nonetheless, for all of its being a Christology from below rather than from above, Ogden's Christology retrieves the New Testament's focus on the question of the identity of Jesus as the subject of christological inquiry.

Furthermore, if I may formulate Ogden's point in a way in which he does not, in his Christology the identity of Jesus is understood from the outset in explicitly theological categories. If Jesus is the decisive representation to us of the meaning of God for us, then not only is the answer to the question of "Who is Jesus?" also an answer to the question, "Who are we?" but neither question can be answered except in terms of an answer to the question, "Who is God?" Namely, God is boundless love. Unlike modernity's revisionist Christologies and like traditional Christologies, Ogden's Christology does not presume to infer from a historical reconstruction of the identity of Jesus to claims about whether and how God relates to Jesus and, in him, to us. Rather, it begins with an identity description of Jesus that is defined in terms of God relating to him.

In *The Identity of Jesus Christ* (1975), Hans Frei offers a different diagnosis of what has happened to Christology in the modern period. So far as I know, neither Frei nor Ogden ever engaged the other's Christology in print. What follows here by way of comparison and contrast rests entirely on inferences I draw from Frei's 1975 essay. In general, I suggest, Frei's analysis of Christology in the modern period is for the most part compatible with Ogden's diagnosis. It differs chiefly in what it emphasizes and in the theological significance of what it sees to emphasize. That difference points to a constructive alternative to both traditional and revisionist Christologies that seeks to avoid both the problematic features of revisionist Christologies that Ogden notes and one that he does not identify. I have taken the space to contrast Ogden and Frei because doing so brings into clear relief what I see as the theological advantages of the approach to Christology I believe is suggested by the sketches of the narrative logics of the Gospels.

Like Ogden, Frei holds that the subject of christological assertions is the identity of the one witnessed in New Testament texts. Furthermore, for Frei as for Ogden, the answer to "Who is Jesus?" is inseparable from the answer to the questions, "Who are we?" and "Who is God?" For Frei as for Ogden, the subject of christological claims is the existential-historical Jesus, not the empirical-historical Jesus. Hence, for Frei as for Ogden, christological claims are in principle vulnerable to disconfirmation by historical research; but since christological claims are theological claims from start to finish, historical claims cannot provide their basis. Correlatively, for Frei as for Ogden, christological questions, christological claims, and the arguments in their support are all framed in theological terms from the outset. There is no point of transition from claims about Jesus based on historical research to theological claims about Jesus. Finally, it is a fair surmise, it seems to me, that Frei recognizes as clearly as does Ogden the ways in which traditional christological claims are now problematic. So, too, it is clear that Frei shares Ogden's judgment that revisionist Christologies are also problematic.

However, Frei's diagnosis of why revisionist Christologies are problematic stresses a point that Ogden does not make. I suggest that despite Ogden's penetrating critique of typically modern Christologies, given the analysis Frei offers of revisionist Christologies, Ogden's own constructive christological proposal is subject to the same internal problem they all share. At issue is the subject of christological claims: the identity of Jesus Christ, the answer to the question, "Who is he?"

We can locate the problem Frei wants to underscore in revisionist modern Christologies at the intersection of two passages in his Preface to *The Identity of Jesus Christ,* a retraction and a throwaway remark. Frei notes that the book had begun as a piece written for a church adult education magazine as a theological experiment testing out "the basic conviction" that "Christian faith involves a unique affirmation about Jesus Christ—namely, not only that he is the presence of God but also that knowing his identity is identical with having him present or being in his presence" (1975, vii). However, eight years later, at the time of writing this Preface, Frei "would not now put nearly the same stress on 'presence' as a category" (vii).

Why this retraction? The answer, I suggest, is entailed in a throwaway remark Frei makes later in the Preface distinguishing between two different types of theological inquiry. It is a throwaway remark in the sense that, having introduced it, he makes no further explicit systematic use of it in the book (although, I am suggesting, the distinction is part of the web of convictions that make up the book's background beliefs). Frei distinguishes between theology as inquiry into the "logic of belief" (1975, xii) and the "logic of coming to belief."

The former explores the logic by which the entire set of Christian beliefs about various topics are more or less systematically interrelated such that changes in one of them ramifies in changes in all the others. An example would be the elaboration of an account of the identity of Jesus that explores its ramifications for Christian beliefs about who God is and who we human beings are. Frei names this inquiry "dogmatic theology" (1975, xi), apparently in a broad Anselmian fashion as "faith seeking understanding." It is a "clarifying operation that may well bring in its train a sense of Christian life and a vision of the enormous outreach of Christian faith" (xiii).

By contrast, inquiry into the logic of coming to believe seeks a universal pattern of argument or curriculum of life stages through which human beings move from unbelief to belief. The patterns of argument in relation to christological claims may be evidentialist, based, for example, on data established in faith-neutral ways that cumulatively demonstrate the veracity of Gospel narratives about Jesus or the veracity of certain persons' visions or other experiences of Jesus. Or they may be speculative arguments in relation to christological claims, exhibiting in rationally irrefutable ways the reality, say, of a cosmic Logos that is unmistakably exemplified in the person of Jesus, or the reality of the cosmic process of the self-actualization of Absolute Spirit, the decisive moment of which simply is the Spirit's self-alienation and subsequent self-reconciliation in the person of Jesus. Alternatively, inquiry into the logic of coming to belief in relation to christological claims may take the form of analysis of the distinctively Christian life-stance of faith as existential response to Jesus and analysis of the stages persons must move through from a life-stance of nonfaith to faith.

Frei names this inquiry "apologetics." He does so without prejudice and not as part of an "in principle" rejection of the project of apologetics. He acknowledges his own skepticism about the project of identifying some one universal curriculum for movement to belief: "For myself, I am quite persuaded that there is no single road to Christianity, either as a matter of universal principle or in practice" (1975, xii). And as for the project of identifying evidentialist or speculative epistemic foundations for belief, Frei himself works as a nonfoundationalist (cf. 4). However, Frei does acknowledge a role for some sorts of apologetics in Christian theology, "as an ad hoc and highly various exercise" (xii).

Frei probably uses "apologetics" too narrowly here. Theories about the logic of coming to faith constitute one type of apologetics. However, another apologetic project is to exhibit the compatibility of the broadly theological beliefs whose internal logic is exhibited by dogmatics with other beliefs, mostly about how the world goes and warranted by any of a large array of self-critically disciplined inquiries. The latter apologetic task may be undertaken in the service of maintaining theological beliefs in the face of apparent conflict with other and well-grounded beliefs, but it is not necessarily an exercise in theorizing the logic of coming to belief. The questions addressed by this second type of apologetic enterprise create one kind of conceptual space for the ad hoc apologetics Frei acknowledges.

Frei's formal point is not, Barth-like, to denounce inquiry into the logic of coming to believe (i.e., his narrow sense of apologetics), but to insist on the importance of the *distinction* between it and inquiry into the logic of beliefs.

> The order of belief is logically a totally different matter from that of coming to believe or the apologetic justification of Christianity. Suppose—quite theoretically—that someone believed that the theological explanation of his own and other peoples' faith is God's predestinating grace. It really would matter little to the logical or dogmatic status of the belief whether the way one came to have faith was gradual nurture, a religious experience, the exercise of neighborly affection, the upheaval of finding oneself in despair over humanly irreparable guilt, or even reflection on an argument. ... In this arena an ounce of living is usually worth a pound of talk, and especially of writing.
>
> (1975, xii)

This formal point is crucial to a fresh diagnosis of why revisionist Christologies are problematic: they are part of distinctively modern, largely academic- or university-based *Wissenschaftliche* Christian theology, one of whose hallmarks is that it conflates inquiry into the logic of beliefs with inquiry into the logic of coming to believe. The result is that, in them, "the rationale of how one comes to believe comes to control, indeed to be virtually identical with the logic of belief, *i.e.*, the meaning and interconnection of dogmatic statements" (Frei 1975, xii). What christological claims such as "Jesus is Lord," "Jesus is Savior," "Jesus is the Word of God," and "Jesus is Son of God" are said to mean is that "Jesus," whether the human person, as biblically pictured, as religious symbol, or as kerygmatically proclaimed, fills a specifiable function or role in the process of persons' coming to faith.

Frei can agree with Ogden that the subject of christological claims is the unsubstitutable personal identity of the one witnessed to by the New Testament. He can agree with Ogden that revisionist Christologies, in contrast to traditional Christologies, err in initially framing their inquiry in historical rather than in theological terms when they address the question, "Who is Jesus?" He can agree that revisionist Christologies shift the subject of christological claims from the existentialist historical Jesus to the empirical historical Jesus. He can agree that the consequence is Christologies in which the systematic connections among the questions "Who is Jesus? "Who is God?" and "Who are we" are severed and that the moves they make from the first question to the other two questions are profoundly problematic. However, Frei would have to insist that these features of revisionist Christologies are but symptoms of a more basic methodological problem: because they confuse what they say is the logic of coming to believe christological claims with the logic of christological beliefs themselves, they systematically subvert the putative subject of their christological claims—namely, the identity of Jesus. They systematically dissolve Jesus' unsubstitutable personal identity into a role or function, or a set of roles or functions, in the process of our coming to faith.

We are now in a position to return to the question of what was at stake in Frei's retraction of his own use in Christology of the category of presence. Frei does not elaborate his reasons. It is unfair to attribute to him views he never explicitly affirmed. So it must be understood in what follows that in drawing the connections I make among themes in Freis thought I construct an argument that is suggested but never formulated by what he explicitly wrote. Verdict first; trial later: The final judgment is that revisionist Christologies (and given Freis analysis of them, Ogden's proposal in 1982 itself falls into the revisionist camp) are problematic because they construe Jesus' identity in terms of his mode of presence now, with the result that the very way in which they address the core christological question, "Who is Jesus in his unsubstitutable personal identity?" ends up undermining the very notion of Jesus as an unsubstitutable personal identity. Hence, to avoid replicating this pattern of reflection it would be better to avoid technical systematic use of "presence" in Christology. (One may nonetheless end up with a problematic Christology, but at least it will not be problematic in the ways typically modern revisionist Christologies are!)

The argument leading to this conclusion goes something like this:

Begin with a descriptive observation. Modern Christologies tend to focus on explaining in what way Jesus may be said to be present now. Theological addresses to the question of "Who is Jesus?" tend to take the explicit form, "Where is Jesus?" That transformation of the core christological question is a sign of the apologetic thrust of such Christologies. The apologetic challenge to Christology takes both a general and a specific form.

Generally, the apologetic challenge is the same as the challenge to all Christian beliefs: What is the rationale of persons' moves from disbelief to belief? The christologically specific challenge is: what can it mean to affirm that Jesus was raised from the dead? In nineteenth-century and twentieth-century theology, that apologetic challenge has typically been met in terms of some theory of universal human nature that has two aspects: (1) a theory of specifically human being as constituted by some sort of dynamic that drives toward human fulfillment or full human actualization and resists frustration, incompletion, or repression of full human actualization, where the state of human fulfillment just is beatitude or the ideal religious state of faith, and the overcoming of its frustration, incompletion, or repression is called "salvation"; (2) some concrete trigger of persons' movement away from frustration, incompletion, or repression of their full self-actualization toward their human fulfillment, which is always religion-specific. In the case of Christianity, that concrete trigger in some way is Jesus, and the way in which he triggers off or occasions the movement to faith just is the mode in which he is present in their lives—whether it be construed as the influence of the historical Jesus, of Jesus' religious experience (e.g., W. Hermann), of the biblical picture of Jesus (e.g., F. Schleiermacher, P. Tillich), of the struggle for liberation exemplified by the historical Jesus (e.g., some liberationist and feminist theologians), of kerygmatic proclamation about Jesus (e.g., Ebeling, Kasemann), or of apostolic witness to Jesus (e.g., Ogden).

What is problematic about all this is not the notion of Jesus' presence. Traditional Christologies also make claims about Jesus' presence now, especially in, perhaps *as,* the church, in the sacraments, in the word. Frei also develops just those themes, if very briefly (1975, 154–68). In Frei's view, as I understand it, what is problematic is not revisionist Christologies' attention to the material topic of Jesus' presence now, but a formal issue about the conceptual relationship between descriptions of Jesus' identity and Jesus' presence. Where traditional Christologies typically developed descriptions of the modes of Jesus' presence framed in terms provided by a logically prior and independently formulated description of Jesus' unsubstitutable personal identity, revisionist Christologies typically do the reverse. They develop descriptions of Jesus' identity framed in terms provided by a logically prior and independently formulated description of the mode of Jesus' presence now, a description shaped as part of an apologetic designed to show how and why people move from disbelief to faith. *This reversal has at least two important and, in Frei's view, problematic consequences for Christology.*

One is that the logic of christological beliefs is conflated with (some particular proposal about) the logic of coming to believe. For example, the claim "Jesus is God-with-us" is explicated, in one way or another, as meaning (inquiry into the logic of the belief) "God's action to fulfill human life is mediated in some way by Jesus [e.g., by the influence of the historical Jesus; by the biblical picture of Jesus; by proclamation of the Jesus kerygma; by the apostolic witness to Jesus; by participation in liberation struggle exemplified by Jesus; etc.]" (inquiry into the logic of coming to believe). More particularly, "Jesus is risen from the dead" is explicated as meaning (inquiry into the logic of the belief) that "Jesus is present to you now insofar as, in some sort of relation to Jesus, you undergo deliverance from whatever frustrates, keeps incomplete, or represses your human fulfillment" (inquiry into the logic of coming to believe). Frei objects that this move in effect identifies the meaning of such christological claims with the (reader's, hearer's) personal or existential appropriation of the claims. But surely that conflation is a confusion. Surely a christological claim's meaning and its appropriation are quite different things.

The second problem concerns what happens to affirmation of Jesus' full humanity. The core christological question, Frei and Ogden agree, is "Who is Jesus?" in its complex conceptual interrelations with two other questions, "Who is God?" and "Who are we?" The core question asks for a description of Jesus' personal identity. A deep and long-lasting intuition, shared by Christians and many others, is that human beings are unsubstitutable in their personal identities. They are obviously substitutable for one another in many of the roles they fill in their social worlds. However, no matter how interdependent or how deeply relational human persons may be in their sociality and historicity, they each are nonetheless deemed unsubstitutable, as each person is, for or by anybody else. Revisionist Christologies, we just saw, typically describe Jesus' identity in terms provided by a description of the mode of his presence now; and they explicate the mode of his presence now in terms of a functional role filled now in persons' lives—namely, the role of occasioning (or "triggering") those persons' movement away from frustrated, diminished, or repressed humanity toward full self-actualization in the state of religious faith. The meaning of christological claims, especially high christological claims such as "Jesus is the Son of God," "Jesus is the Word of God," "Jesus is God Incarnate," is explained in terms of their being expressions of persons' experience of Jesus functioning in that role, a function that only the power of the Creator—the divine power—can fill. This holds true also for Ogden's proposal that the basic christological affirmation is "Jesus is the decisive representation of the meaning of God for us." For all of the overlaps between Frei's project and Ogden's, on Frei's analysis Ogden's proposal exhibits the pattern of thought that defines revisionist Christologies. *In short, revisionist Christologies typically dissolve Jesus' humanity into a divine function*, perhaps associated with a historian's artifact (if the Christology begins with claims about the historical Jesus, or with the apostolic witness, or with the earliest faith community). However, that undercuts our intuition that human beings' humanity cannot be reduced to the functional roles they fill in the food chain, in society, or in other people's lives. It seems that *subtle docetism of a sort* persists, even in Christologies done from below. A description of Jesus in his unsubstitutable personal identity cast in terms of the functional roles he fills simply fails to render Jesus the human person.

Frei suggests that both of these problematic features of revisionist Christologies arise from the systematic use in Christology of a particular technical concept of presence:

> It was Kant's transcendental ego, transformed into Idealist subjectivity or romantic consciousness, and heightened to the point of a unique perspective on self, others, and the universe at large. The present was the crystallization of this self-positioning in time and history which, far from being merely an aspect of human experience, actually constituted the self. It could therefore be known only by the performance of the original self-positioning moment itself and never at second hand.
>
> (1975, viii)

That concept of presence suffered "too heavy an infestation of the vagaries and dogmas of its Idealist parentage" (x). However, in Frei's view, no technical concept of presence, no matter from what intellectual tradition it is borrowed, should be used in a systematic way in Christology. That comes clear as he qualifies his retraction of his own use of the concept. He distinguishes between informal religious uses of the concept and technical and systematic uses and is retracting only the latter (viii).

> If I were writing the essay over again, ... and if I found in the process of theological reflection about Jesus Christ that I had to refer to "presence" as a technical category, I would confine myself to saying that *if* one thinks of him under this rubric one cannot conceive of him as *not* being present. Further than that I would not go.
>
> (ix)

That last comment signals an important hermeneutical upshot of this excursus into method in Christology.

SCRIPTURAL NARRATIVE AND CHRISTOLOGICAL CLAIMS

Given Frei's analysis of what is problematic about revisionist Christologies, and why, the following picture of the christological project emerges: christology is an exploration of the logic of Christian beliefs about the unsubstitutable personal identity of Jesus in which a description of his personal identity is logically prior to, is formulated independently of, and provides the terms on which it also offers a description of his presence. Recall Frei: "*if* one thinks of him [Jesus] under this rubric [presence] one cannot conceive of him as *not* present." It is *he* who is present. An identity description of him in his unsubstitutable personal identity defines who it is that is present and how he is present. The description of Jesus' mode of presence does not describe how he constitutes himself to be who he is. To proceed as though it did would be, on Frei's analysis, to replicate the most problematic move of revisionist Christologies. Given this analysis of the fundamental change Christology has undergone in the modern period, Frei contended that it has an important hermeneutical implication regarding construal of the Gospels.

In brief, the hermeneutical upshot is this: any christological project seeking to give an identity description of Jesus in his unsubstitutable personal identity, seeking to trace out the logic of Christian beliefs that answer the question of "Who is he?" must be guided and normed by the narrative structure (or "plots") of the Gospels construed as having the force of offering identity descriptions of Jesus. It is possible, of course, to construe those very same texts in other ways, as having other sorts of force. When one does so, one is led to privilege other features of the Gospels than their narrativity.

Revisionist Christologies, for example, typically construe the Gospels in either or both of two ways. They typically construe the Gospels as having expressive force. They take the literary units assembled into narratives by the editors of the Gospels to be expressive of a movement from unbelief to faith on the part of the person, persons, or communities of persons who first formulated them, and they take the use of those same units in the common life of communities of Christian faith to be the occasion (the "trigger") for other persons to make the same move to faith. That is, whether construed as religious symbols, or religious myths, or religious images, these units are interpreted in terms of their function in some analysis of the "logic of coming to belief" (cf. Kelsey 1977/99 56–89). The norm by which the Christian adequacy of any christological proposal is assessed consists of the specific expressive and occasioning role these units play in Gospel texts construed, in George Lindbeck's phrase, to have this "emotive-expressive" force. Second, revisionist Christologies typically construe the Gospels as a set of ancient texts that provide almost all of the available evidence on the basis of which to construct either (or both) an account of the historical Jesus or an account of the earliest communities of Christian faith, their witness to the meaning of Jesus for them, and a phenomenology of their move from unbelief to faith. Many liberationist Christologies seek to be warranted by a picture of the historical Jesus. Other revisionist Christologies, like Ogden's, judge that search is problematic and limit themselves to the latter. In either case, it is the historical reconstruction, whether of Jesus or of the phenomenon of the earliest instance of the movement from unbelief to Christian faith and the witness in which it expressed itself, that directly norms the Christian adequacy of christological claims; the Gospels do so only indirectly, by providing the data on which historical reconstruction is based.

When construed as expressivist texts, the Gospels are interpreted as collections of somewhat disparate individual literary units (pericopes), like so many beads on a string. Form-critical and redaction-critical studies have developed subtle analytical techniques for distinguishing and classifying such units. The meaning of each unit lies in the mode of personal existence (e.g., "life in faith") that their authors had appropriated, a mode of personal existence that each textual unit now presents to a reader as the meaning she may herself appropriate, thereby recapitulating in her own life the authors own movement from unbelief to faith. This is entirely appropriate if the point of Christology is to exhibit the logic of coming to faith by specifying just how Jesus is so present now as to occasion just that move. However, if the point of Christology is to describe who Jesus is, offering an identity description of him precisely in his unsubstitutable personal identity, and not in terms of his mode of presence and role in triggering persons' move to faith, then such a construal of the Gospels is no help. A series of separable literary units, each of which has basically the same logical force (expressive) and existential function (occasioning a move to faith), cannot individually or collectively convey an agent's personal identity.

Nor can any person be described in his unsubstitutable personal identity by using a body of theory about what persons are, whether it is theory in one of the human sciences or a philosophical theory, neither continental phenomenological philosophy nor Anglo-American analytic philosophy. That is not because theory in the nature of the case generalizes whereas human individuals are unique. Indeed, they are; so are grains of sand. "Unique" is too abstract to index the difficulty with trying to use some body of theory about persons to describe someone in his unsubstitutable personal identity. Rather, it is because human beings are construed as persons in the modern sense of the term. The methods and conceptualities of the human sciences and all kinds of philosophical anthropology are designed to be appropriate to persons. Nonetheless, any given person can never serve as more than an instance of a type of person defined by the conceptual grid of one of the human sciences, an instance interchangeable with and thus substitutable for other instances of the same type. Any given person can serve as no more than an instance of the phenomena of self-constituting, self-manifesting subjects identified by a philosophical phenomenological analysis of the transcendental conditions of the possibility of subjects constituting and manifesting themselves, an instance interchangeable with and substitutable by any other person understood as a self-constituting center of consciousness. Any given person can serve as no more than an instance of the type of intentional agency or free agency, whether understood in compatibalist or incompatibalist ways, whose metaphysics is outlined in an analytic philosophical anthropology, an instance interchangeable with and substitutable by any other such agent. The systematic conceptual schemes on offer in such theories do not necessarily fail to describe how a given individual human being may be unique in certain respects, nor how it is personal. But his personal identity in its unsubstitutability just slips through the conceptual mesh of all such theories. They are unable to render it (cf. Kelsey 1987, 122–31).

Nor, theoretical technical terms aside, can someone's personal identity be adequately conveyed to somebody simply by attributing a list of properties to a logical subject who is given that person's proper name, using terms current in some informal ordinary language. When that is done it is assumed that the subject to whom the attributions are made (the reality of the person whose unsubstitutable identity is in question) is an otherwise featureless subsistent individual entity that somehow exists behind or below the properties ascribed to it. The effort to describe the personal unsubstitutable identity of "Maria" by the successive predication of "her" of such attributes as "female primate," "species *Homo sapiens*," "five feet three inches tall," "120 pounds," "French speaking," "married," "mother of two daughters and a son," "highly educated," "a research microbiologist," "present queen of Prussia," and so on, no matter how precise and nuanced the list of attributes became, would fail to render her in her unsubstitutability. It may identify her in the sense of making it possible for us to pick her out of a crowd of people. However, it would fail to convey her unsubstitutable identity. It would not fail because the terms used were technical, defined by their place in the rigorously defined conceptual scheme of a body of systematic theory, for the terms are routinely used in unsystematic and nonrigorous ways. It would fail because her unsubstitutable personal identity is not an otherwise featureless individual entity lying somehow behind or underneath the sum total of all the attributes that may truly be ascribed of her. Nor does it consist of the sum total of those attributes, for there is no such sum total. The list of attributes that could possibly be ascribed to her is indefinitely long. It would be more nearly correct to say that her unsubstitutable personal identity lies just in the unsubstitutable way in which she concretely exemplifies them across time in changing circumstances. Her personal identity defines what each of those attributes concretely is in her case. So, too, the unsubstitutable personal identity of Jesus cannot be conveyed by a list of attributes collected out of the Gospels: "Word of God," "Son of God," "Messiah," "Son of Man," "Savior," and so on. These titles also are terms used informally in an ordinary, if ancient, language, and not technical terms defined by their systematic use in a rigorously formulated body of theory.

What can describe persons' unsubstitutable personal identity literarily is more or less realistic narrative. Such narrative can describe it by rendering it. That is, a description can be accomplished by narrative that simultaneously describes the continuity of a "person who acts and is acted upon through a stretch of time" and describes "the genuine changes, sometimes to the very core of a persons being, that occur both in that person's character and in the circumstances of the story" (Frei 1975, 88). Frei liked to quote Henry James' deceptively simple explanation of how a good storyteller manages to accomplish both without any apparent rifts in the seamless flow of the telling: "What is character but the determination of incident? What is an incident but the illustration of character?" (88). Such narrative need not be realistic in the sense of being naturalistic. On the contrary, for example, narrative in the mode of magical realism that contains all kind of unnaturalistic occurrences and characters may nonetheless convey a character's personal identity in all its unsubstitutability.

If, as I believe is correct, the task of Christology in secondary theology is to explore the logic of Christian beliefs about who Jesus is, and not the logic of coming to those beliefs, then its initial task is to offer a description of Jesus in his unsubstitutable personal identity. Granted, it is only the initial task of a fully developed Christology. Christology has other tasks: for example, to explore the logical relations between that description of Jesus' unsubstitutable personal identity and theological proposals made in regard to other theological loci; to explore the logical relations between that description of Jesus' unsubstitutable personal identity and other apparently related beliefs that are well-warranted by various types of critically disciplined inquiries in history and relevant human and physical sciences; to propose modifications of received formulations of christological claims (i.e., traditional christological claims) that may be required by new knowledge yielded by those critically disciplined inquiries; and to test critically the truth of the claim that a man fitting the description of Jesus' unsubstitutable personal identity lived in first-century Galilee and Judea. Although conclusively demonstrating the nonexistence of a person or an event is perhaps even more difficult than proving its existence, it is nonetheless possible in principle that historical evidence could surface that would tend strongly to disconfirm the claim that a man fitting a description of Jesus' unsubstitutable personal identity normed by the Synoptic Gospels' narratives lived in first-century Galilee and Judea. Whether someone lived in first-century Galilee and Judea who fits that identity description is a different question than the one raised here. Why some people have come to believe that such a person did live then is yet another question. The point being made here is that the initial task of secondary theology's christological proposals is to offer a description of Jesus in his unsubstitutable personal identity.

Furthermore, if execution of that task ought to be normed by Christian canonical Scripture, and especially by the Gospels, as I believe it should, then, I suggest, the character of the christological task itself dictates a hermeneutical judgment about the Gospels: insofar as they are normative for the Christian adequacy of christological proposals, they are to be construed as having the force of rendering Jesus' personal identity. Construing them that way entails a hermeneutical judgment: the Gospel's narrativity is of utmost christological importance because it is by their narrativity that they render an identity description of Jesus precisely in his unsubstitutable personal identity. Consequently, insofar as the Gospels norm the Christian adequacy of christological remarks, their interpretation ought to focus on their pattern of narrative movement, their plotting, their narrative logic. That is what I have attempted to do in this chapter.

One important difference that focuses on the Gospels' narrative logics makes for the christological claims they norm is something that concerns the status of the crucified Jesus' resurrection from the dead. If the Gospels are read as sequences of literary units each of which is construed to have the force of expressing the experience or event of its author(s) coming to faith, then the units telling of the discovery that Jesus' tomb was empty and the units telling of disciples' encounters with the Jesus known to have been crucified to death are each treated as independent attributes that may or may not be truly ascribed to a logical subject whose reality is already known independently of them and thus stands somehow behind them. In that case this judgment is invited: "Was he or was he not raised from the dead?" That judgment belongs to the same logical class as judgments about such questions as "Did he or did he not in fact tell parable x, teach moral commandment y, heal disease z, and so on?" The claims about Jesus' resurrection are construed as claims about a particular, very odd historical fact claim. Like all the other apparent historical fact claims made in the Synoptic Gospels' narratives, in any search for the historical Jesus it must be critically assessed in its own right and independently of all other particular fact claims about things Jesus did or said. In order to do that one would need to have some idea what sort of a historical event Jesus' resurrection was, just as, in order to know how to go about assessing critically whether it is historically probable that Jesus told parable x, one has to have some idea what it is for someone to tell a story and some idea of whether Jesus is likely to tell the kind of story x is. However, if the Gospels are construed to have the force, not of uniquely individuating identity descriptions that pick Jesus out from all other human beings, but the force of renderings of Jesus' unsubstitutable personal identity, then "Jesus rising from the dead" turns out to be inherent in that description of his unsubstitutable personal identity. It is definitive of who he is—i.e., of who it is that did or did not tell parable x, teach moral commandment y, heal disease z, and so on. At any rate, the reflections on the narrative logics of the Synoptics in the first parts of this chapter come to just this conclusion about the way those narratives render Jesus' unsubstitutable personal identity: his mode of presence is inherent in and defined by his identity, rather than his identity being defined by his mode of presence, the latter being established on independent grounds. Read that way, they norm the christological remark that inherent in descriptions of Jesus' identity is that he is alive now.

NOTE

1. Schubert Ogden, *The Point of Christology* (San Francisco: Harper & Row, *1982*), 130.

PART FOUR

Postliberal Hermeneutics

CHAPTER NINE

Hans Frei and the Hermeneutics of the Second Naïveté

GARRETT GREEN

One brief incident during my graduate studies at Yale stands out in my memory: it must have occurred on December 11, 1968. Three of us grad students, teaching assistants in Mr. Frei's undergraduate course, were walking with him along College Street in New Haven, returning from class to his office in Silliman College. The three of us were laughing and joking about who knows what when he suddenly stopped in his tracks, turned, and rebuked us for our jollity—something so utterly out of character that I have never forgotten it. "Don't you know," he admonished us, "that yesterday Karl Barth died in Basel?"

We knew, of course, that Barth was the theologian Frei took most seriously. He made frequent reference to him in his teaching and in the few published writings he had produced at that time, and he assigned passages from the *Church Dogmatics* for us to read in his graduate courses. I had come to Yale fresh from a divinity degree at Union Theological Seminary, where I had heard about (but never read) Barth, known there as the leading theologian of "neo-orthodoxy," a movement in which many of my teachers at Union had been educated, but which, they believed, was now (thankfully!) fading into obscurity as theology sought to recover its bearings amidst the intellectual and cultural turmoil of the 1960s. I recall one prominent theologian at Union telling us that, since the "great parenthesis" of neo-orthodoxy was now safely behind us, theology could get back to the real questions facing modern Christianity.

When I reflect today on the legacy of Hans W. Frei, what first comes to mind is his teaching rather than his published theology: he was the one who taught us how to read Karl Barth. Frei was the most astute reader of Barth in our time, teaching us as much by example as by anything he said or wrote about Barth's theology. Barth's reception in the English-speaking world was badly distorted from the outset, especially by the misconception that he was a neo-orthodox thinker, one who wanted to repeal modernity in order to reinstate the old orthodoxy. In 1968, and for a long time thereafter, Frei was a voice crying in the wilderness. Almost singlehandedly he reoriented and revivified Barth studies in the United States and Great Britain. And for the most part, he did so unintentionally, not by giving lectures and writing books about Karl Barth, but by employing what he had learned from Barth to tackle the theological tasks that he himself found so pressing. Others have excelled as Barth scholars (one thinks of George Hunsinger, Bruce McCormack, and John Webster), but Frei's contribution has been different, less comprehensive but more focused. From the outset, as his doctoral dissertation on Barth's dogmatics shows, he was never an uncritical reader, even of Karl Barth—i.e., he was never a Barthian. One might say that he was not so much an interpreter of Barth's theology as one who learned from Barth how to read scripture and the theological tradition and then spent his career doing it. In this way, he exemplified one of Barth's most cherished virtues: he always kept his sights firmly on *die Sache*, on the real subject matter of theology.

Frei's lectures reflected his way of thinking. He once made a revealing comment to an audience at the beginning of a formal lecture: "... no matter how well I prepare," he told them, "I don't like to read from a manuscript; I have to work it out from the notes." Fortunately for us, the lecture was being recorded and is now available to a much wider audience.[1] It turned out to be one of the clearest accounts he ever gave of his theological project, quite likely for the reason that he was speaking freely from notes. As he once admitted in a letter, "I can write decent prose for about three pages, and then complexities inevitably get the better of me."[2] He used the same method when lecturing to classes at Yale. Those of us who served as his teaching assistants can remember arriving at his office just as his undergraduate class was about to begin, only to find him scribbling furiously on a legal-sized yellow pad. This way of working may explain why he published so few books and articles but left behind a treasure trove of notes and works in progress, and it testifies to his integrity and humility as a theologian. It also helps to explain why he was such a revered and effective teacher: he continually presented not finished products of his research and scholarship, but rather his active, ongoing struggle to articulate the theological issues that were driving him at the time. By so doing, he modeled the vocation of the theologian.

At the time of his death in 1988, it was easy to think that Frei, having finally published his long-awaited historical work *The Eclipse of Biblical Narrative* as well as an original and suggestive theological essay *The Identity of Jesus Christ*, had been tragically prevented from carrying out the promising task that these works seemed to presage. (I still recall my immediate reaction upon hearing of his death. "But he still had so much more to do!" I blurted out at the time.) Now, however, three decades later, Frei's true accomplishments are coming into focus, thanks in large part to the painstaking work of Mike Higton, who has made available unpublished lectures and papers, as well as some revealing letters written to friends and colleagues.[3] Higton's report on his archival research in his book *Christ, Providence and History* includes a kind of intellectual biography of the man, revealing a career spent in pursuit of answers to theological problems that was more focused and sustained than most of us who were his students and friends realized at the time. In what follows I would like to show that Hans Frei did more than merely prepare the way for a theological project he did not live to accomplish. On the contrary, he pursued throughout his entire career a most original historical and theological thesis, one that goes a long way toward resolving the greatest dilemma facing Christian theology in the modern era—namely, the problem of faith and history.

Frei worked throughout his whole career as both a historian and a theologian, but it is clear, especially in retrospect, that the two were complementary. In the Department of Religious Studies at Yale he oversaw the program in Historical Theology (as distinguished from two other kinds of theology, systematic and philosophical). Frei's work as a historical theologian can be seen as an effort to explicate and defend the orthodox Christian use of the Bible against various voices of modernity that claim to have shown the fallacy or impossibility of such a reading of scripture. Moreover, Frei endeavored to refute those *Christian theologians* who accepted these flawed critiques and wanted to reconstruct Christian teaching in order to accommodate them. He carried out this program not by polemical attacks on the modernizers, but rather by careful, persistent intellectual labor, especially through detailed historical analysis of modern Christian thought since 1700. His stubborn adherence to this task without regard to the prevailing winds of the theological academy is evidence of a kind of faithful Christian integrity that attracted like-minded supporters to his side. To this day those who studied with Mr. Frei (as we always knew him) share a fraternal bond—even when our various theological careers have carried us in quite divergent directions.[4]

Some years ago the philosopher Paul Ricoeur captured the pathos of modern religious thought in an arresting image. He takes note of the impact of modern criticism, which has called into question our inherited faith through the "dissolution of the myth as explanation." While affirming criticism and insisting that "we are in every way children of criticism," Ricoeur nevertheless says that "we seek to go beyond criticism by means of criticism, by a criticism that is no longer reductive but restorative."[5] His solution invokes imagery that has resonated with many of his, and our, contemporaries:

> Does that mean that we could go back to a primitive naïveté? Not at all. In every way, something has been lost, irremediably lost: immediacy of belief. But if we can no longer live the great symbolisms of the sacred in accordance with the original belief in them, we can ... aim at a second naïveté in and through criticism. In short, it is by *interpreting* that we can *hear* again. Thus it is in hermeneutics that the symbol's gift of meaning and the endeavor to understand by deciphering are knotted together.[6]

If we take with a grain of salt the Hegelian overtones of Ricoeur's triadic schema (virtually inevitable in a modern European thinker), it is hard to deny the appeal of his vision of a "second naïveté": a way to overcome the challenges to traditional Christian belief by various forms of secular critique since the Enlightenment. It epitomizes a goal that so many Christian thinkers over the past three centuries have wanted to achieve.

I want to suggest that we can understand Hans Frei's achievement as a theologian in terms of Ricoeur's vision of a second naïveté. I am speaking metaphorically, for Frei most surely does not seek a second naïveté as Ricoeur does, by means of a "restorative" philosophical "revivification" of traditional symbols. Frei, in fact, explicitly takes exception to Ricoeur's view, which, he writes "tends to force realistic description to become metaphor." He calls Ricoeur's philosophical system "dangerous" because it "does not allow realistic narrative a genuinely realistic status."[7] Frei does, however, agree with Ricoeur that the way to a second naïveté involves a *hermeneutical* task. For Frei, the modern critique that presents the greatest challenge to Christian faith is the problem of faith and history, the alleged conflict between the historical claims Christians make about the gospel story of Jesus Christ and the results of modern historical-critical interpretation of the New Testament. Frei's hermeneutical attempt to answer that critique, I am arguing, though different in nearly every way from Ricoeur's own, succeeds in pointing the way to a renewed "naive" reading of the gospel accounts of Jesus in spite of the challenges made by historical criticism. One might even describe Frei's approach as "neo-orthodox" in a strictly hermeneutical sense, for his proposal seeks to justify the straightforwardly realistic way that Christians, including premodern Christians, have always read scripture, modern historical-critical scruples notwithstanding.

THE HISTORICAL CHALLENGE: FAITH AND HISTORY

Among the many things Frei learned from Karl Barth and then developed in his own work as historical theologian is the importance of David Friedrich Strauss, whose monumental *Life of Jesus* (1835) came to epitomize the problem of faith and history. Though not the first to employ the concept of myth to interpret the New Testament, Strauss was the one who first applied it consistently to the gospel accounts of Jesus' life from beginning to end. In the words of James Livingston, Strauss was the one "who first raised, in such a radical way, the question of the historical accessibility of Jesus. His importance as a theologian is assured if for no other reason than for posing this historical question, for it has remained at the center of theological discussion to the present day."[8] Barth had called Strauss, along with Ludwig Feuerbach, the "bad conscience" of modern theology.[9] Although later scholars have criticized Strauss for overemphasizing the extent of mythology in the gospel texts, he never intended simply to reduce the story of Jesus to myth. Rather, his method was "to test *the historical claims* of the New Testament concerning Jesus"[10] by separating out the historical events from their mythological elaboration. While not denying that there were elements of genuine historical recollection in the narratives, he argued that they were overlaid and supplemented by the mythological imagination that was the characteristic way of thinking for the premodern mind. Strauss believed myth to be "the natural language of religion."[11] Strauss's importance for later theology, however, does not depend on the particulars of his methodology or his conclusions but rather on the fact that he called into question the historical reliability of the New Testament writings by introducing a distinction between the scriptural narrative and actual historical events. It would not be long before theologians were wrestling with the relation between the "Jesus of history" and the "Christ of faith."[12]

Barth underscored the importance of Strauss's challenge to later theologians. "One must love the question Strauss raised, in order to understand it"; but most people, he added, "have feared it." Most theologians, Barth claims, instead of facing the issue, have ignored it or tried to find a way around it. And that is why Strauss remains the "bad conscience" of theology. But a final comment in Barth's chapter on Strauss contains an odd twist. "Proper theology," he writes, "begins just at the point where the difficulties disclosed by Strauss and Feuerbach are seen"—and here comes the surprise—"and then laughed at."[13] Frei agrees that proper theology should begin with Strauss's challenge. And there are indications that he also shares Barth's desire, in the end, to laugh at Strauss nevertheless.[14] But how can these two responses coexist?

Many of Barth's critics are convinced that they cannot. Livingston is typical, agreeing with Barth that "too many theologians have avoided and bypassed"

Strauss's challenge, and he adds that "chief among these 'avoiders' ... are Karl Barth himself" and his dialectical followers.[15] There is strong evidence, however, that Hans Frei took both of Barth's responses to Strauss with equal seriousness. To start with, he followed Barth's suggestion and began his theological endeavors by confronting the problem exposed by Strauss, and then he struggled for many years to find a way that theologians might read the gospel narrative of Jesus realistically without becoming either skeptics or fundamentalists. Higton argues that "Frei's work can be seen, without too much distortion, as one long attempt to laugh at Strauss—not because he has found a way of ignoring him, but because he has learnt to defeat Strauss with Strauss's own tools."[16] I am not sure whether Frei used Strauss's own tools, but I do believe that he found a way to overcome the Straussian impasse by developing a hermeneutic of realistic narrative that allowed him to read the gospel narrative of Jesus Christ and to affirm its truth without ignoring or bypassing the results of historical criticism.

Frei employs a two-pronged strategy—one that, not surprisingly, is both historical and theological. He is best remembered for the historical side. Those of us who studied with him and followed his career before the publication of *The Eclipse of Biblical Narrative* in 1974 had sometimes doubted that the project would ever be completed. When I visited Yale in 1967 as a prospective graduate student, I remember his teaching assistants at the time telling me in hushed tones about the groundbreaking book Frei had long been working on. It was going to electrify the theological world, they said—if only he could ever admit that it was finished and allow it to be published! His perfectionism was legendary. The closer he got to the end, the more he worried that critics would discover some error or omission; and so he continued scribbling on his yellow legal pads. When *The Eclipse of Biblical Narrative* at last appeared in print, it quickly became a major focus of theological discussion. Not least among its attributes was the title, which provided a metaphor to describe how a way of reading the Bible that had long been practiced by Christians up to and including the Protestant Reformers had seemingly vanished in the following two or three centuries—while at the same time hinting that, like the moon, it might eventually reemerge. In an effort to show how the eclipse had come about, Frei included detailed accounts of both hermeneutical theory and literary developments in Europe, primarily in Germany and England. By the time Schleiermacher developed his "hermeneutics of understanding" in the early nineteenth century, Frei concludes, the possibility of reading narrative realistically had been thoroughly eclipsed:

> At that time the search for the subject matter beyond the text had obscured narrative meaning. Now it was the quest for narrative unity or continuity in the consciousness of the author, or in the inner form as represented by

the characters' consciousness, which prevented the descriptive or narrative shape from assuming its rightful place.[17]

Left hanging in the air at the end of this groundbreaking book is a question that readers were bound to ask: Will the eclipse come to an end at last? Can realistic narrative meaning be rediscovered? And if so, how?

THE THEOLOGICAL RESPONSE: THE IDENTITY AND PRESENCE OF JESUS

In retrospect we can now see that the historical side of Frei's work was never the main point. He was, after all, an historical *theologian*. And for the remainder of his life it was the theological solution to the problem of faith and history that consumed his energies.

It must have come as a surprise to many of Frei's readers, after the long wait for *Eclipse*, that a second book appeared in print just a year later.[18] *The Identity of Jesus Christ*, it is now clear, represented the other prong of Frei's program, the theological complement to *The Eclipse of Biblical Narrative*. In fact, however, it had been written nearly a decade earlier and published in two parts in an obscure periodical for adult education under the auspices of the Presbyterian Church. For reasons that remain puzzling even today, the second book—despite its importance in Frei's larger project—was not received with the interest one might have expected. It appeared, in the words of one observer, "to a tepid reception, and has been overshadowed since."[19] One reason for its disappointing impact at the time may be the odd process by which it had come into being. Higton, in briefly reviewing its circuitous route to publication as a book in 1975, calls it "this strange project ... [the] strange accompaniment ... to the massive and groundbreaking *Eclipse*."[20] Another reason for its failure to capture the imagination of readers could be Frei's own ambivalence. He himself later expressed doubts about the book, and rather than revising his argument and defending its main thesis, he turned to other projects, some of which involved further historical work on nineteenth-century thinkers. Perhaps the very success of *Eclipse* and the continuing attention it received from others diverted his attention from the theological project that was its natural complement. Higton suggests other private and personal issues that consumed his energies,[21] but none of these speculations (however interesting they may be biographically) contribute to an understanding of Frei's eventual theological accomplishments.

With the help of the considerable evidence now available, but not published during his lifetime, we are now in a position to gain a clearer picture of Frei's *theological* response to the problem of faith and history—the demon with which he had been wrestling since the start of his career. Yet the key to its resolution has all along been hiding in plain sight, we could say, in the concluding chapters of *The Identity of Jesus Christ*. I recall a conversation with him in his office in which he was describing the argument that subsequently appeared in Chapter 13 of *Identity*. The heart of matter is a claim he makes about the relation of Jesus' identity and presence: "To know *who* he is in connection with what took place is to know *that* he is."[22] At the time, I commented to him that it sounded to me like an ontological argument for the presence of Jesus Christ—to which he replied, "Precisely!"[23] This Anselmian insight into the gospel narrative of Jesus' resurrection, he says in *Identity*, "is the climax of the story and its claim. What the accounts are saying, in effect, is that the being and identity of Jesus in the resurrection are such that his non-resurrection becomes inconceivable."[24] What makes this interpretation of the narrative so intriguing and yet so puzzling is Frei's apparent ambivalence about its fictional or historical status. Recall that much of his attention in *Eclipse* was devoted to developments in fictional writing during the eighteenth and nineteenth centuries. He now brings this same attention to realistic fictional narrative to bear on his reading of the gospel account of Jesus: "The realistic or history-like quality of the narrative," he writes, "whether historical or not, prevents even the person who regards the account as implausible from regarding it as mere myth. Rather, it is to him a kind of hyperfiction claiming to be self-warranting fact."[25] For a few brief paragraphs, Frei wrestles with this fiction/fact duality. He asks, tantalizingly, "Of what other fact can we say that complete commitment is a way of taking note of it?" And then he adds what I can only describe as the seed of a theological answer to Strauss's challenge:

> But grateful love of God and neighbor is the proper manner of appropriating the presence, based on the resurrection of Jesus, who in perfect obedience to God enacted men's good in their behalf on the cross. That this act is the only manner of appropriating the resurrection we cannot doubt. In this instance—and in this instance alone—commitment in faith and assent by the mind constrained by the imagination are one and the same.[26]

Then he drops the subject, saying only that "we cannot dwell here on the manner of appropriation." Nevertheless, he does further comment about "the issue of where to make the transition from literary description to factual, historical, and theological judgment."[27] He sees no way to argue from actual historical occurrence to the truth of the biblical narrative, nor any way to argue against it on historical or factual grounds. All we can conclude is that "there is a kind of logic in a Christian's faith that forces him to say that disbelief in the resurrection of Jesus is rationally impossible." Frei's last word is agnostic: we have no way of knowing why some readers of the Gospel narrative believe and others do not. But either way, we can be sure that it is "a matter of faith and not of arguments from possibility or evidence."[28]

For whatever reasons, readers of *The Identity of Jesus Christ* failed to recognize in it Frei's theological response to the historical problem posed in *The Eclipse of Biblical Narrative*. Perhaps they failed to see the importance of the concluding interpretation of Jesus' resurrection because it followed upon a long and rather tedious treatment of the various ways of describing a person's identity. The unclarity may also be due to the fact that *Identity*, though published in book form in 1975, had been composed much earlier, and before completion of *Eclipse*. One can only wonder how differently Frei might have presented his theological response to Strauss had he waited to write it until after working through the historical process by which a realistic narrative reading of the Bible had ceased to be a live alternative. With the aid of archival materials, unpublished at the time of their composition but now available to us, we are able to gain a clearer picture of Frei's proposed resolution of the problem of faith and history.

Two lectures that Frei delivered in the mid-1970s help us to flesh out his theological response to Strauss and his present-day representatives, the historical-critical interpreters of the Bible. Both lectures were delivered from notes, but both were recorded on tape and have now been transcribed and published. The first one, delivered in Toronto in 1974, is not about Frei's own project (at least not directly) but rather about Karl Barth.[29] As Frei describes Barth's hermeneutical convictions and practices, it becomes evident that he sees his own project as an application of Barth's method. Frei has learned from Barth how to read the Bible realistically and then put that hermeneutical approach to work in his own interpretation of the passion-resurrection narratives in the New Testament. He begins by recalling Barth's well-known claim in the first edition of his Romans commentary that (in Frei's paraphrase) "he was happy that he did not have to choose between historical criticism and the old doctrine of inspiration, but that if he did he would choose the old doctrine of inspiration."[30] The virtue of the "old doctrine" is its insistence that "the subject matter of the Bible [is] in the text, rather than ... [in] the peripheries that were behind the text, which was what historical criticism did." Frei further highlights the way Barth uses historical criticism. According to Barth—and Frei clearly agrees— "you look steadily at the text and what the text says, and then you utilize, on an *ad hoc* basis, what the historical scholars offer you" (55). Frei stresses that the use of historical-critical material cannot be systematically described; there can be no general theory of the relationship of theological interpretation and historical criticism. Frei also makes clear that he learned from Barth to see the similarity between fictional writing, such as the modern realistic novel, and the New Testament narrative of Jesus' passion and resurrection. Not that Barth ever spoke explicitly about the Bible and the modern novel, but he "wanted the text always to be literal in that same fashion: it means what it says. It is to be taken literally *whether or not* something happened" (57, emphasis original). It is characteristic of Frei's modesty that he does not claim to be the originator of this insight into the "history-like" quality of biblical narrative but says he learned it by observing how Karl Barth interprets the Bible.

Having clarified and endorsed Barth's way of reading scripture realistically while making ad hoc use of historical criticism, Frei concludes the Toronto lecture by explicitly connecting this insight to the possibility of a second naïveté. And he does so not simply in reference to the passion-resurrection narratives in the New Testament but to the Bible as a whole. Barth's realistic hermeneutic, Frei claims, puts him "in the position to suggest that we must be as naïve as our forebears were before the rise of criticism in the interpretation of the Bible and as naïve as the Bible itself" (57). But this naïveté, just as in Ricoeur's schema, is not precritical—it's not your grandfather's naïveté, we might say today. No, Barth is now in a position "to suggest that in a certain way we *can be critical. We are no longer at the same stage as the naïve precritical forebears*" (57, emphasis original). The example Frei calls upon is not about Jesus' resurrection but about how we read the creation stories in Genesis. Barth, he says, "did not deny the truth or (in a peculiar, hard-to-get-at sense) the *historicity* of Genesis." He always "insisted that the creation accounts are *Geschichte* but ... not *historische-Geschichte*." That hard-to-get-at sense is (to use Frei's own terminology) *literary*, like a novel, but is at the same time *true*, and true in a way that cannot be verified or falsified by historical (*historisch*) research. "The Bible," Frei says (without limiting its scope to the gospel narratives of Jesus' passion and resurrection), "is largely and centrally realistic narrative." Although the question of its narrative realism is a separate issue from its truth, the distinction does not matter for Barth. Frei explains it this way: "Remember that, for Barth, [the Bible] depicts the one real world in which we all live so that to understand the meaning of it is the same as understanding the truth of it. If you understand it rightly you cannot *not* think of it as real." Here Frei once again appeals to his Anselmian argument, but this time in relation not just to the resurrection of Jesus but to the Bible as a whole. "That strange, marvelous little book on Anselm's proof for the existence of God is in a peculiar sense also applicable to Barth as an interpreter of the Bible as realistic narrative." In summary, Barth's ambition—and, Frei's—is "to be a *direct* reader of the text, and not of some hypothetical subject matter behind the text." And one reads this way "not as an uncritically naïve reader but as a critically naïve reader"(59). Frei concludes his lecture with a reminder that historical-critical exegesis must always be at the service of theological exegesis: "as a handmaid rather than either a mistress or a mother."

The other newly available essay from the 1970s is the tenth annual Greenhoe Lecture that Frei delivered at Louisville Seminary in 1976, entitled "On

Interpreting the Christian Story."[31] It contains an especially clear and accessible summary of Frei's overall program in both its historical and theological aspects. But it then goes on to draw out some surprising theological implications that clarify and extend Frei's thinking in ways that do not appear elsewhere in his published or unpublished writings. These latter reflections are more personal, even autobiographical, than his usual way of expressing himself. More than any of his other writings, this lecture not only allows us to see the overall scope of Frei's thesis but also to learn why he thought it to be so important and what difference it ought to make in how contemporary Christians understand their faith and practice.

Frei begins his deliberations as before with Strauss's *Life of Jesus*, but this time he points out that the issue—"the problem of historical revelation and the reliability of the Bible"—had already been raised in the eighteenth century (74). The various attempts to solve it led to "an enormous shift" in how the Bible was interpreted, including loss of the literal sense. When the Reformers talked about the literal sense, they had meant what Frei calls the "*literary*-literal"; that is, the Bible gives us "the right description, not a symbol, not an allegory ... it meant exactly what it said" (75). This way of reading the Bible included figural interpretation—something that Frei had long emphasized in his teaching and writing. Figuration means that "there are certain things, or certain occurrences, or concepts ... in the Old Testament (say the law, or Noah's ark) that are what they are; they mean in their own right—and yet ... they are also figures that will be fulfilled in what they prefigure." Frei stresses that in precritical exegesis "the literal sense actually went hand in hand with the figural sense"; in fact, figural interpretation is more closely allied with the literal sense than with allegory. The text still means what it says even if it sometimes points ahead to other events in the narrative. But when the change came in the eighteenth century, "story began to mean something else," because "the narratives and that which they are about began to separate" (76). As a result, the very meaning of *literal* changed: to this day when people talk about taking the Bible literally they mean that it corresponds to historical events beyond the text. "The literal sense now," Frei writes, "... refers us to something 'out there,' which is literally represented by the story." This kind of story can be tested, verified to see if it actually corresponds to external events. One needs to search for evidence in order to confirm its accuracy. "And from this notion," Frei concludes, "historical criticism springs"(76). People tried to bridge the gap between the text and its meaning in various ways (e.g., by naturalist, supernaturalist, or mythical interpretation), but in each case "the representation and that which it represents have a gap between them" (77).

Against this background (which amounts to a concise summary of *Eclipse*) Frei offers his audience an equally concise account of what it means to read the text as realistic narrative. The gap that led to the eclipse of biblical narrative disappears when we read the text realistically. A realistic story, he says, "is like any realistic historical narrative, in that it does not have a subject matter that you can state apart from the narrative itself" (78). In the case of the Gospel story of Jesus, he is precisely the one who is portrayed, through the interaction of character and circumstance, in the story itself. Expressed theologically, "Jesus Christ the person is nothing other than the enactment of his person in his work" (79). If one wants to know what the facts are to which the story refers, one can only respond that they "are facts that we *cannot* have apart from the story." Up to this point the Gospel story is just like a fictional narrative. But what about its *truth*? Frei acknowledges that Christians rightly consider the biblical narrative to be true fact, but "in a way that, although it may bear a family resemblance to the set of empirical facts we call history, is not identical with it." What's more, this fact is "rendered effective to us through the story and we cannot have it without the story in which it is given to us" (79–80). Here Frei makes an unexpected move, one that some might want to call mystical. Recalling Austin Farrer's characterization of scripture as "God's self-enacted parable," Frei suggests that a kind of figural reversal occurs when we read the Bible:

> It is as though we, ordinary human beings, were living in a world in which the true reality is one that we only grasp in this life as if it were for us a figure. Yes—but it is *we* who are the figures and it is that reality embodied by the resurrection that is the true reality of which we were only figures. It is as though our sense of reality were to be turned about; it is what is depicted... which is real, and it is ordinary world history that is a parable, a figure of that reality. And that is the mystery, it seems to me, of our life into which the story and the facts fit together.[32]

FREI'S SOLUTION: ON LEAVING THINGS THE WAY THEY ARE

In the second half of the Greenhoe lecture, Frei's solution to the problem posed by Strauss, the problem of faith and history, comes most clearly into view. Perhaps *solution* is not the right word (*resolution* might be a better choice), because what he finally concludes is that the problem has all along been based on a misunderstanding—a *hermeneutical* misunderstanding. Ever since about 1700, theologians and biblical scholars have been trying to read the Bible the wrong way. They have been barking up the wrong tree, trying to take a speck out of believers' eyes without noticing the log in their own. Frei titles this part of his lecture "Interpretation and Devotion: God's Presence for Us in Jesus Christ."[33] But in his very first sentence he suggests an alternative title: "Notes on Leaving Things the Way They Are." It is significant, I believe, that just at this point Frei adopts a more personal tone and begins speaking in the first person.

He wants to talk about a problem that affects him not only in his academic studies but also personally. Unlike so many other theologians, he has no wish to make the ancient message of the Bible "meaningful" for our secular world today. By "meaningful," he says, "they usually mean how does one allow it to be a *possibility*" for people today. While admitting some sympathy for that desire, he says that "there always seemed to me something callow and shallow about it that bothered me." As an example, he takes the death-of-God theology of the 1960s. He never took it seriously, he says, although he believed that it "did bespeak a certain problem," most likely the fact that "some ministers, theological students, and theologians found it difficult to pray, and [therefore] … said that God was dead." His response contains one of his best one-liners. He said to himself: "Well, all right, if Christianity is going to go out (let us assume for a moment that it depends on what *we* do and not on the grace of God!) it's had a magnificent history and I'd rather see it go out with an orthodox bang than a liberal whimper." For himself, however, "the great problem was always this: How does one express, grasp, and speak— … articulate the sense of Christianity? What is its *essence*?" The way he set about solving this problem was to look for "a certain center" of the Bible, in which the gospel message appears most clearly, and then to articulate it as best he could. Acknowledging that others have found that center elsewhere in the Bible, for himself "it is in the Synoptic Gospels" that we find "the identity of the account with what the account is about." Christology is therefore "the center of the New Testament," and it's a high Christology "focused on Jesus Christ as not simply the unique revealer but also the atonement through whose death and resurrection we and the whole world have life." Here "we have in the form of a realistic story the rendering of our salvation." That story obviously claims to be a true story, "but [even] if it is not true *that is still what it means*."[34] On no account is he willing to reopen a gap between the biblical text and its meaning.

Then he turns from Christology to the other great issue of modern theology: "*the presence of God in Christ now*." Once again he returns to his "ontological argument," which he describes as follows:

> I put it to myself in a very simple, perhaps rather naïve way, which ultimately derives from the ontological argument of Anselm of Canterbury. I want to tell you how that came about, but let me simply state it: if Jesus is really who the Bible says he is; if that is his identity; then he *cannot not be present*. If he is who the Bible says he is then, having died once, he lives; he is in some manner present, here to us—to be sure in a very unique and unrepeatable manner, and yet he is.

(83)

Frei has now given us his own interpretation of "the two things that the history of modern theology has been all about".[35] If he is right, he has achieved the goal that Ricoeur taught us to call "a second naïveté." And he has done so in a far more convincing way than Ricoeur himself ever managed to do. Ricoeur's path to a second naïveté exemplifies the erroneous way of dealing with these twin issues that Frei finds typical of modern theology. That erroneous way "has been to think that human beings are consciousnesses" who can encounter God through limit experiences, and that these experiences are ultimately what the Bible means, although it expresses its message indirectly through symbols, myths, and stories. Frei is characterizing here what his colleague George Lindbeck, writing a few years later, would label "experiential-expressivism."[36] The example Frei uses in the Greenhoe lecture is not Ricoeur but Kierkegaard and Tillich, but he might have picked from any number of others in the past two centuries. He locates the problem at one particular point ("where everything seemed wrong to me"): in order to close the gap between the text and its real meaning, these thinkers must first explain the problem and then its solution by using some kind of technical language. They must supply "a certain technical or theological language" in order to explain what happens in solving this problem (85).

At this point Frei's alternative title comes into play: "Notes on Leaving Things the Way They Are." He takes his cue not from a theologian but a philosopher—one who is not even a Christian. We learn from Ludwig Wittgenstein, Frei tells us, "that language doesn't often work in technical concepts." The mistake that so many modern theologians have made is to think that in order to affirm that Jesus Christ is somehow present to us now they must "*explain* [it] by translating the notion of presence into some explanatory concepts. That is precisely what I think cannot be done, and which I think need not be done. There is, it seems to me, a very ordinary way of talking about the presence of Christ." The job of Christian theology "is simply to talk about the way Christian language is used by Christians, and to ask if it is being used faithfully"— in other words, whether it is faithful to biblical language and the tradition that flows from the Bible. (Although he doesn't point it out here, this too is something he learned from Karl Barth.) This task does *not* require us "to *translate* Christian language into a language that will be relevant to our situation." In fact "the whole metaphor of translation there is misleading." After all, Frei has demonstrated that at its very heart the Bible *"means what it says*—so there is no need to translate it; no need to reconceptualize it. There may be a need to *redescribe* it, but that's a very different thing."[37]

This realization was a great relief to Frei, as it should be to us, for it liberates Christian theology from so much tedious and misleading conceptualizing and theorizing. Frei puts it this way: "One of the marvelous and—to my mind—startling and liberating little sentences that Ludwig Wittgenstein wrote was when he said, 'Don't ask for meaning, ask for use'" (87). Frei calls it getting rid of "a verbal cramp" (91). One can sense his relief as he approaches the end of his 1976 lecture:

> I am suggesting there is no need for an explanation. I am suggesting there *is* no explanation. I am suggesting that *there is no problem*. I am suggesting that this is precisely the function of Christian language; this is its character, its ordinary use, and, if you will, at the same time its uniqueness: it is both these things .... To try to go to a level underneath them, you see, is precisely what I am saying is wrong, and is precisely where the technical theologians have been wrong. And we need to be released from that verbal and conceptual cramp.
>
> (92, emphasis original)

What Hans Frei has bequeathed to us is a theological hermeneutic that does not set us another theoretical or conceptual task but rather sets us free to do the real work of theology.

One more point needs to be made. In Frei's official title for part two of the Greenhoe lecture, he speaks of *devotion*, an uncommon word in his theological vocabulary. After his plea to turn away from technical language to ordinary Christian language, he explains why he has included the term in his title. "I use 'devotion,'" he says, "simply to circumscribe, to have a term for, *Christian language in use*. Christian language in meditation, in public worship, private prayer, in the obedience of the moral life: Christian language in the public and private use of faith" (86, emphasis original). He may have been influenced here too by his reading of Wittgenstein, who reminds us that "to imagine a language means to imagine a form of life"; that "the *speaking* of language is part of an activity, or of a form of life."[38] Once Frei has liberated Christian language from the prison house of theory, we are able to see it (*hear* it!) in its proper context—in the everyday life of Christian men and women in the world. The most important legacy of Hans Frei is his call for an end to the academic captivity of Christian theology. At the end of the Greenhoe lecture he provides a one-sentence summary of his thesis that includes a small but significant emendation: "What I am saying," he tells them, "is that I don't need to think about *how* he can be present; his identity and his presence are given together in the ordinary usage of *Christian practice* and Christian language."[39] Here he takes the step that he had hesitated to take in *Identity* when he hinted that the way to "take note" of the story of Jesus' resurrection is by means of a "total commitment."[40] At the crucial Anselmian point in Frei's argument, when it dawns on the reader of the Gospel story that Jesus cannot *not* be present here and now—at just this point, where "commitment in faith and assent by the mind constrained by the imagination are one and the same"—interpretation merges into appropriation so that we can no longer tell them apart. The Christian life is not something we first come to grasp intellectually and then go on to practice; rather, one discovers the truth of the gospel when one hears the call of God and obeys. Knowing Jesus and following Jesus are two sides of one reality.

A PERSONAL EPILOGUE: READING THE BIBLE WITH PRISONERS

I no longer live in the academic world. Although I still make occasional forays into its conferences and annual meetings and try to keep up on my theological reading, for the past several years I've spent far more time in prison than in lecture halls. How I ended up as a volunteer prison minister is as much a mystery to me as why I believe the Bible is the Word of God. (Come to think of it, they are probably the same mystery.) For some time now I've felt that the two poles of my present life—working with prisoners and doing academic theology—are about as far from one another as the East is from the West, even though I value them both. Writing this essay has taught me that they may be more closely akin than I thought.

Studying the Bible with Christian inmates has taught me is that precritical naïveté is to be found not only in our historical past but also among our fellow believers today. I didn't know that before, because I seldom associated with Christians who didn't have a college degree, if not a PhD. Now I spend most of my time with men who may have finished high school or may still be working on their GED in prison. In theory, of course, I always knew that a person's standing before the Lord had nothing to do with their formal education, but I still found it hard to believe. Now I know it is true because I see the faith of Christian prisoners every time we read scripture together, pray together, and worship together. One of the qualities of the second naïveté is that it doesn't need to force criticism upon those who haven't encountered it. Since the Bible "means what it says," we can read scripture together naively and hear the same Word of God. I've become more tolerant of fundamentalists (the real ones, who generally refer to themselves not as fundamentalists but as "fundamental Christians"). I've finally outgrown the fundamentalist-bashing that I learned growing up in mainline churches and heard throughout my career in academia.

One of my biggest surprises in prison has been discovering that theological discussions with inmates are often better—more animated and also more insightful—than class discussions in my college courses. One reason is that many of the inmates know their Bible much better than my college students did (they frequently admonish one another to "stay in the Word"). In fact, some of them know their Bible better than I do. I hear it in conversations with them and also in their prayers, which are often filled with biblical language and allusion. But there's a deeper reason, too: prisoners understand that what we are doing when we study Bible and theology is a matter of life and death. That's why it's easier to teach and preach the Christian gospel in the prison than in the university. I would not have believed it if I did not hear it so often from inmates: "I'm so glad God sent me to prison!" One of the first inmates I worked with (I thought of him as "my Colombian drug dealer" ... because he was) told us one evening at Bible study that he had just heard from his family and had learned that all of his former friends and associates back home were dead. Prison had quite literally saved his life.

The opportunity to ponder the legacy of my old *Doktorvater* has been a blessing—almost like being back in graduate school with Mr. Frei. Best of all, I think I finally understand what he was trying to teach us. Part of the reason is that I've learned more about what he was saying then by reading his newly published *Nachlass*. But the other reason has to do with my change of venue from classroom to prison. As I was working on this essay, I kept wishing that I could talk things over with Mr. Frei now—now that I'm in a context where I can finally understand what he has been saying all along. I think I know what his response would be. I think he would not be at all surprised at what I've learned in prison. And I'd like to think that he'd be pleased.

NOTES

1. Hans W. Frei, "On Interpreting the Christian Story," in *Reading Faithfully: Writings from the Archives*, 2 vols., ed. Mike Higton and Mark Alan Bowald (Eugene, OR: Cascade Books, 2015): 1:69.
2. Letter to Dennis Nineham, July 1, 1976, in *Reading Faithfully*, 1:27.
3. Mike Higton, *Christ, Providence and History: Hans W. Frei's Public Theology* (London: T&T Clark International, 2004).
4. For a fuller account of this sense of familial commonalty among Frei's students, see the lovely description of Frei as teacher in George Hunsinger's brief forward to the first volume of *Reading Faithfully*. Hunsinger notes how Frei "managed to make each of his doctoral students feel affirmed and encouraged without provoking a sense of rivalry among them" (vii).
5. Paul Ricoeur, *The Symbolism of Evil*, trans. Emerson Buchanan (New York: Harper & Row, 1967), 350.
6. Ricoeur, *Symbolism of Evil*, 351 (emphasis in original).
7. Letter to Gary Comstock, November 5, 1984, in *Reading Faithfully*, 1:37.
8. James C. Livingston, *Modern Christian Thought*, 2nd ed. (Minneapolis: Fortress, 2006), 1:220.
9. Karl Barth, *Protestant Thought: From Rousseau to Ritschl* (New York: Simon & Schuster, 1959), 389.

10. Livingston, *Modern Christian Thought*, 1:216 (emphasis original).
11. Livingston, *Modern Christian Thought*, 1:217, paraphrasing Strauss.
12. In a letter to Julian Hartt in 1981, Frei refers to "the seemingly everlasting Jesus of history / Christ of faith juxtaposition." *Reading Faithfully*, 1:33.
13. Barth, *Protestant Thought*, 389.
14. Higton entitles his first chapter on Frei's theology "Laughing at Strauss."
15. Livingston, *Modern Christian Thought*, 1:220.
16. Higton, *Christ, Providence and History*, 35.
17. Frei, *The Eclipse of Biblical Narrative: A Study in Eighteenth and Nineteenth Century Hermeneutics* (New Haven: Yale University Press, 1974), 312–13.
18. Frei, *The Identity of Jesus Christ: The Hermeneutical Bases of Dogmatic Theology* (Philadelphia: Fortress Press, 1975). A new edition, including a foreword by Mike Higton and an introduction by Joshua B. Davis, was published by Cascade Books in 2013. Page numbers are accurate to both editions, unless otherwise indicated.
19. Joshua B. Davis, Introduction to Hans W. Frei, *The Identity of Jesus Christ: The Hermeneutical Bases of Dogmatic Theology* (Eugene, OR: Cascade Books, 2013), xxii.
20. Higton, *Christ, Providence and History*, 18–19.
21. Although Frei, by his own account, "felt that he had 'found his voice,'" Higton describes his work in the 1970s as "a strange mixture of confidence and anxiety," including a sense of isolation from his roots in the church. Higton, *Christ, Providence and History*, 19.
22. Frei, *Identity of Jesus Christ*, 145 (emphasis original).
23. The term *ontological* could introduce confusion unless it is made clear (as it was to Frei) that it simply refers to the famous argument of Anselm of Canterbury in his *Proslogion* (ca. 1077), which has been dubbed the "ontological argument" by later interpreters.
24. Frei, *Identity of Jesus Christ*, 145.
25. Ibid., 143.
26. Ibid., 146.
27. Ibid., 150 (2013 ed., 149).
28. Ibid., 151, 152 (2013 ed., 150).
29. Frei, "Scripture as Realistic Narrative: Karl Barth as Critic of Historical Criticism," in *Reading Faithfully*, 1:49-63.
30. Frei, *Reading Faithfully*, 1:53. Barth's statement is found in *The Epistle to the Romans*, trans. Edwin C. Hoskyns (New York: Oxford University Press, 1933), 1. Subsequent references to *Reading Faithfully*, Vol. 1, will be given parenthetically in the text.
31. Frei, "On Interpreting the Christian Story," in *Reading Faithfully*, 1:68-93.
32. Frei, *Reading Faithfully*, 1:80. I have slightly emended the text and supplied some punctuation in order to make clearer what I believe Frei actually said.
33. Frei, *Reading Faithfully*, 1:80-93.
34. Ibid., 1:83 (emphasis original).

35. Frei, *Reading Faithfully*, 1:83.
36. George Lindbeck, *The Nature of Doctrine: Religion and Theology in a Postliberal Age* (Philadelphia: Westminster Press, 1984). See especially chaps. 2 and 3.
37. Frei, *Reading Faithfully*, 1:85–86 (emphasis original).
38. Ludwig Wittgenstein, *Philosophical Investigations*, 2nd ed., trans. G. E. M. Anscombe (New York: Macmillan Co., 1958), §19 and §23.
39. Frei, *Reading Faithfully*, 1:92 (emphasis added).
40. Frei, *Identity of Jesus Christ*, 146.

CHAPTER TEN

The Gospel of Jesus Christ as a Story to Be Told: Eberhard Jüngel and Hans Frei on "Narrative" in Christian Theology

R. DAVID NELSON

Eberhard Jüngel and Hans Frei continue to garner recognition as ranking among the most significant Christian theologians of the period "after Barth." Both worked, as it were, beneath Barth's long shadow, and occupied themselves addressing issues and extending conversations that emerged earlier in Barth's writings. Neither Jüngel nor Frei simply reiterates or paraphrases Barth, of course. Rather, in their respective programs, they demonstrate the liveliness of theology done in a Barthian key by taking dogmatics stimulated by Barth's thought into new and unexpected directions.

To be sure, both Jüngel and Frei are interesting by their own rights, and not just in light of Barth's influence and *his* ongoing significance for Christian theology. Indeed, among those theologians working within the post-war era and in veins struck during the preceding generation, Jüngel and Frei stand out for their own originality and creativity. It is no wonder that the works of Jüngel and Frei continue to draw critical attention from theologians today. Interest in

Jüngel's thought recently has undergone a revival of sorts among Anglophone scholars, with a number of dissertations passing muster before committees in recent years, other secondary studies appearing in books and peer-reviewed journals, and some new translations of key German texts written by Jüngel on the horizon. Frei's work has never fallen out of fashion in North America, not least because of the efforts of erstwhile students who have continued to wrestle with his legacy. Among twentieth-century North American theologians, Frei and his Yale colleague George Lindbeck together stand out as perhaps the only ones who might qualify as doyens of a school of thought—the Yale School, also known as post-liberalism. As long as former students remain active (and there are many active former students of Frei and Lindbeck), and critical engagement with post-liberalism thrives, Frei's influence will stay in ascendency.

In the remarks that follow, I bring Jüngel and Frei into a dialogue of sorts. I am particularly concerned here in what Jüngel and Frei have to say about the significance for Christian theology of categories associated with the phenomenon of language. In the late 1960s and 1970s, during which time the problem of language and theology was very much *en vogue* both in Europe and in North America, Jüngel and Frei commenced separate but surprisingly similar research trajectories on this constellation of issues. On the continent, Jüngel, first in his doctoral dissertation on Paul and Jesus[1] and with his inaugural lecture as full professor at Zürich, which was later expanded and rendered into English as "God—As a Word of Our Language,"[2] had set out on a course of research and writing that concluded with his signature study, *God as the Mystery of the World*, first published in German in 1977.[3] At the same time and in North America, Frei was deeply immersed in the "analysis of analyses of the Bible"[4] which would yield a number of lectures and essays and, eventually, *The Eclipse of Biblical Narrative*. He also was following leads in modern Christology breaking off from the main branch of his research into the history of interpretation and biblical criticism, and in 1975, the year after *Eclipse* appeared, published his important little book *The Identity of Jesus Christ*.[5] Demonstrably, all of the signal publications generated by Jüngel and Frei during this period zero in on the intersection of the theology of language and the Christian confession of the person and work of Jesus Christ. Even though, by all accounts, Jüngel and Frei never met nor corresponded during this period, nor do they engage each other's work, the texts at hand, particularly *Paulus und Jesus*, *God as the Mystery of the World*, *The Eclipse of Biblical Narrative*, and Frei's Greenhoe Lecture, "On Interpreting the Christian Story,"[6] reveal some common theological commitments.

Here we will consider Jüngel and Frei in turn, concentrating on how these two theologians employ the category of "narrative" in Christian theology. While they draw inspiration for their particular uses of narrative from different quarters (Jüngel from Heidegger's later philosophy and from the hermeneutical theology flourishing in Germany in the 1950s and 1960s; Frei especially from Erich Auerbach and also from other trendsetters in American and English literary criticism in the 1960s and 1970s), they end up drawing some similar conclusions. At the same time, their approaches to narrative theology reveal deep and striking differences between their programs for theology after Barth. If there is a leitmotif in the comments that follow, it is the problem of language's referential character, that is, the capacity of words and discourses to signify external objects and states of affairs. As I demonstrate, both Jüngel and Frei seize upon the "problem" (as they both deem it) of the *structure* of referential language. And yet, how Jüngel and Frei frame this issue and what they do in order to resolve it are conspicuously different in the arguments they unfurl. And this difference, I show, folds back upon their distinct agendas for recovering narrative in theological discourse.

I. Jesus' Parables and Jesus as the Parable of God—Eberhard Jüngel on Narrative as Interruptive Word-Event: Jüngel's claim that the coming of God to the world is a narrative, or, as Darrell Guder's English translation sometimes renders the German word *Erzählung*, a "story to be told," is ingredient to his overarching argument in *God as the Mystery of the World*, his best-known and most challenging work. An important clue for understanding Jüngel's use of the idea of narrative in *God as the Mystery of the World* is found in the book's opening section, "The Definition of the Problem."[7] Jüngel's remarks here on what he calls the "traditional hermeneutics of signification" tidily encapsulate his approach to the problem of God's relation to human language. His analysis runs more-or-less as follows: the Latin theological tradition, following Augustine's reception of a basic Aristotelian hermeneutical principle—the distinction between form and content—[8] supposes that reality consists of signs and things signified. Human languages exhibit this structure, since a language is a system of signs—words—organized according to flexible syntactical and grammatical rules such that the speaker is able to apprehend things which exist, as it were, extrinsically to speech. Jüngel raises no quarrel with this as a structural description of the denominative and indicative modes of human language. But there are uses of language, he observes, where the structure of form and content, of sign and thing, breaks down. For instance, in ordinary language, invectives and imperatives are "acts of inclusion," insofar as "the person addressed ... is included in the word event."[9] Poetry, too, resists the partition of sign and thing, since "in a poem it is possible that the thing talked about is actually taking place."[10] Jüngel acknowledges that the words of an invective or a poem retain their signifying functions when deployed in these contexts, otherwise an epithet or a curse or a sonnet would have no discernable meaning. For Jüngel, though, what is truly interesting about such modes of language is that they exhibit new possibilities for conceiving how the words of a language present what they signify.

Jüngel proposes in *God as the Mystery of the World* that theological speech fits the bill as an *extraordinary* mode of language in the speaking of which the distinction between form and content breaks down. He suggests, however, that the Latin theological tradition, which has never quite emerged from under the spell of at least latent (and sometimes overt) Augustinism, has assumed that the linguistic mode of signification is at work in words about God. In his reading, that is, the tradition speaks *about* God in theological language; God is theological language's object. Accordingly, God, as the thing signified (the *res significata*) by the sign (the *signum*) of the theological word, remains remote from that word, absent to the speech that signifies God. We thus observe the horns of the dilemma Jüngel endeavors to address in the book: in his assessment of the tradition, so described, (1) God is assumed to be the object of theological speech and thought, but (2) God cannot truly be encountered in speech and thought, since God remains, as it were, beyond the signs that make up human language. Jüngel goes on in the book to develop what he calls a "theological countermovement"[11] to this troubled hermeneutical tradition.

The approach to this problem that unfolds in *God as the Mystery of the World* displays Jüngel's commitment to the so-called "New Hermeneutic," sometimes otherwise labeled the "new" or "second quest for the historical Jesus." A few comments on this strange and now obsolete trend in mid-twentieth-century interpretation are in order as they help shed light on the connection Jüngel draws between, on one hand, the problem of signification and, on the other, the Christian gospel as a "story to be told." Briefly then: the origin of the New Hermeneutic is the presumed problem of the relationship between the man Jesus of Nazareth and the Christ of Christian faith, a point of neuralgia which had dominated German discussions in theology and biblical studies from the middle of the nineteenth century up to the Great War. In the background here is the rise to prominence of the organizing principle of "historical consciousness" in the nineteenth-century German university, which would eventually give way to an obsession among scholars in the historical origins of the Christian religion. With the emergence of dialectical theology and, later, neo-orthodoxy after the War, the quest for the so-called historical Jesus and the supposition that the Jesus of history is distinct from the Christ of faith—and that all of this is, in fact, a problem—receded into the background. To risk a gross generalization, Barth, Bultmann, Brunner, and others were not interested nor were they particularly confident in employing the tools of critical historical research to find the real Jesus of history. However, beginning with Ernst Käsemann in a famous essay from 1953,[12] a small group of Bultmann's former students renewed the quest for the historical Jesus. With Bultmann and Barth, these scholars contended that faith in no way has its ground in history, such that faith can be proven or disproven through the means of historical inquiry. But, against Bultmann and Barth, they argued that faith indeed should be interested in its historical origins. After all, Christians across the ages have confessed that Jesus of Nazareth was a real man who, upon his resurrection from the dead, was declared the Lord Christ. Faith, that is, assumes continuity between the Christ it confesses and the Nazarene. To ignore the Jesus of history is to neglect this continuity, and risks unmooring Christianity from its historical origins.

The New Hermeneutic was carried to its zenith in the late 1950s by two theologians, both of whom played formative roles in Jüngel's theological development—systematic theologian Gerhard Ebeling, who taught Jüngel during a study-abroad fellowship undertaken in Zürich in 1957; and New Testament theologian Ernst Fuchs, who served as Jüngel's *Doktorvater* at the turn of the decade.[13] Heidegger's late-career musings on the ontological entailments of language were in the air at the time, and it should come as no surprise that Ebeling and Fuchs borrow liberally from Heidegger in addressing theological questions. In their hands, the problem of continuity and discontinuity between the historical Jesus and the exalted Christ gets resolved by way of an oddly Heideggerian theology of language. In his public ministry, the man Jesus preached interruptive speech-events (*Sprachereignisse*—Fuchs's term for it[14]); in Christian proclamation, preaching about Jesus too is an interruptive speech-event. Here, speech is conceived as no mere signifier, but the presentation or enactment in language of that which is spoken.

At the outset of this chapter I counted Jüngel as a theologian "after Barth." I certainly think that designation is accurate and have written about Jüngel's relationship to Barth in several locations.[15] For now, however, it is necessary to stress that Jüngel cut his theological teeth on the New Hermeneutic. In fact, Jüngel's doctoral dissertation *Paulus und Jesus*, which was supervised by Fuchs in Berlin, is, in many ways, the quintessential statement of the New Hermeneutic. There is, moreover, a thread running from *Paulus und Jesus*, published in 1962, to *God as the Mystery of the World* fifteen years later; a thread that helps us better understand the topic at hand; namely, Jüngel's idiosyncratic approach to theological narrative.

The sustained thesis of *Paulus und Jesus* is that the new hermeneutical concept of "speech-event" identifies the connective tissue between Jesus of Nazareth and the Christ proclaimed by faith. Jüngel argues that Jesus' parabolic discourses and the "Son of Man" statements from the synoptic tradition, and then later Paul's proclamation of the gospel of justification by faith, are speech-events in the occurrences of which what was spoken (the kingdom of God and God's justifying righteousness) *came* to the hearer *as* the event of speech. "The Kingdom comes in parable as parable (comes) to speech," he writes in *Paulus und Jesus*. "The parables of Jesus bring to speech the Kingdom as parable."[16] Likewise, Christian proclamation, as it were, presents or enacts the gospel. Salvation comes to the hearer as the word of Christ is proclaimed.

Note that the distinction between form and content is not in play here. Defined as "speech events"—i.e., the coming to speech of the kingdom—the parables are hardly mere signifiers. For Jüngel, the parables of Jesus cannot be construed as linguistic *signa* that point beyond themselves to some things external to the event of language. He argues that to understand the parables this way (i.e., as stories that signify) is to see them as "literary constructions."[17] In sharp contrast to this way of reading the parables, Jüngel argues in *Paulus und Jesus* that, in the event of Jesus' proclamation of the parables, the kingdom of God arrives. Jüngel thus refuses "from the very beginning to separate the 'content' of Jesus' proclamation from ... the bare 'form' of it."[18] Consequently, as John Webster puts it, for Jüngel "the relationship between the parables and the kingdom is quasi-sacramental: Jesus' parables are the real presence of the kingdom."[19]

In *God as the Mystery of the World* a decade and a half later, we discover Jüngel continuing to develop this approach to the parables. Here he revisits the line of argument from *Paulus und Jesus* precisely in order to explain the sense in which the gospel must be narrated. The parables, he insists, are narrated events of the word of God. If the point of the parable is communicated in parabolic language only in such a way that it becomes concrete through the event of speech, then it becomes impossible to abstract the point from the words used to communicate it. "A parable is not a thesis and has no theme at all," he explains. "Rather, it is an event which then makes something else happen."[20] In just this way, he observes, the parable is like a successful joke that evokes a response—laughter—in the event of its telling. Earlier in *God as the Mystery of the World* he colorfully illustrates this event character of language by pointing to the use of the invective: "If one Swabian says to another 'Halbdackel' ('half a dachshund' or 'stupider than a dog'), then he is impugning the being of that individual ... If the word were only a sign, a denominating, then the person who was cursed could respond 'Wrong signification!'"[21] In a successful joke and an invective barb, and thus especially in the extraordinary speech events of Jesus' parables, the point of speech is inextricably tied to the capacity of the language used to bring the hearer into the event of speech. "While (the parable) is being told," Jüngel asserts, "the listener is being focused on its point ... And with the point, the kingdom of God itself in the parable arrives in the hearer."[22]

While there is much more that can be said here, the preceding comments should suffice to show some of the problems that manifest themselves in Jüngel's approach to this nest of issues. In Jüngel's work from this early period, the categories of the New Hermeneutic are employed liberally and in such a way that various theological topics get shoehorned into the rather narrow space contoured by the dilemma of the relationship between theology and language. At all points, the ordinary referential function of language—i.e., language as signifying—is construed as something that must be overcome in events of the word of God and, likewise, by a phenomenology of theological language. Parable, proclamation, revelation, and even the general theological use of words are mapped out according to the assumed distinction between signification and speech event.

I suggest that all of this works against any conception of the parables as *stories*,[23] which, in turn, problematizes Jüngel's appeal to the idea of narrative as a theological category. We have seen that, for Jüngel, the point of one of Jesus' parables is not that it actually narrates anything, but that it is an interruptive event in which the kingdom comes to speech. Upon reading the entire trajectory of Jüngel's works from *Paulus und Jesus* to *God as the Mystery of the World*, we discover that, even though he mentions the parables in nearly every text from the period, he says nothing about the plots of the parabolic stories. When he introduces *Erzählung*—narrative—in *God as the Mystery of the World*, this pattern obtains. The narrative of the gospel, he proposes, is "the retelling of the past." But what must be told, we discover, is not the whole story of Jesus Christ, but only the interruptive episode of the cross, the significance of which is confirmed in the interruptive episode of the resurrection.[24]

So what, then, is "narrative" for Jüngel? Stepping back, we see that he is not interested in the, as it were, *literary* aspects of narrative. Plot, structure, setting, dramatic action and conflict, characterization, and so on receive almost no attention from him. Likewise, it does not seem significant for Jüngel that a story *unfolds* as it is told. Rather, theological narrative *just is* the interruptive, extraordinary word of the speech-event, in the eschatological occurrence of which God comes to the world.

II. The Unity of Figuration and the sensus literalis—*Hans Frei on the Recovery of Realistic Biblical Narrative*: Frei's contribution to the recovery of narrative in Christian theology emerges in his work on the fate of biblical interpretation in modernity. He traces the decline of biblical narrative to a paradigm shift in hermeneutics that unfolded over the course of the eighteenth and nineteenth centuries and in the context of the "enlightened" universities of Western Europe (particularly those in Germany). Frei notes that, prior to the Enlightenment, as a rule exegetes approached the Bible attuned to the "narrative structure" encompassing reality and text.[25] In his reading of the history of interpretation, the magisterial Protestant Reformers soar as the great harmonizers of the insights of the "pre-critical" period of biblical exegesis. For Luther and Calvin, Frei asserts, the narrative of Scripture is *realistic*; that is, as he puts it at the outset of *The Eclipse of Biblical Narrative*: according to the Reformers, "the words and sentences [of Scripture] meant what they said, and because they did so they accurately described real events and real truths that were rightly put only in those terms and no others."[26]

The pre-critical exegetes, especially the Reformers, took for granted that both the literal and figural senses of Scripture depicted or described the reality of the world. The *sensus literalis*, which in his Greenhoe Lecture Frei qualifies, again with reference to Luther and Calvin, as "*literary*-literal not *grammatical*-literal,"[27] accurately depicts or describes *as narrative* the historical events being narrated. As such, "the literal sense and the historical sense meant exactly the same thing"[28] in pre-critical exegesis. This identification of the *sensus literalis* and the history it narrates lead us around the question of the historical reliability of the text, a post-Enlightenment area of critical inquiry that was, by and large, not investigated prior to the eighteenth century. Rather, as Frei shows, Christian exegetes from the pre-critical period assumed that the Bible's "cumulative story" corresponded to "the real historical world."[29] This correspondence between the entire narrative arc of Scripture and the whole of reality sheds light upon the pre-critical exegetical strategy of figuration, at least as Frei paraphrases it:

> The several biblical stories narrating sequential segments in time must fit together into one narrative. The interpretive means for joining them was to make earlier biblical stories figures or types of later stories and of their events and patterns of meaning. Without loss to its own literal meaning or specific temporal reference, an earlier story (or occurrence) was a figure of a later one.[30]

We see then that, for Frei, the brilliance of pre-critical exegesis lies in its presupposition of the *unity* of figuration and the *sensus literalis*. "In figural interpretation," he writes, "the figure itself is real in its own place, time, and right, and, without any detraction from that reality, it prefigures the reality that will fulfill it." As such, "each person, each occurrence is a figure of that providential narrative in which it is also an ingredient."[31] This conception is significant not least of all for the Christian interpretation of the Old Testament: "There are certain things, or certain occurrences, or whatever, in the Old Testament (say the law, or Noah's ark) that are what they are; they mean in their own right—and yet, even though they mean in their own right they are also figures that will be fulfilled in what they prefigure."[32] What this indicates is that Christian reading of the Old Testament need not require a choice between figuration and "literal" exegesis. On the contrary, as Frei puts it, for the Reformers "you could read the Old Testament in such a way that you saw Christ prefigured in it and yet could at the same time also affirm that you believed in the literal sense and not in anything else."[33]

Frei demonstrates that nineteenth-century critical scholarship on the Bible shattered confidence in both figural exegesis and the *sensus literalis*, not to mention in attempts to coordinate the two. Interestingly, his insight into how this loss of confidence ensued trades upon the issue we encountered earlier at the heart of Jüngel's argument in *God as the Mystery of the World*, namely, the hermeneutical dilemma of referential theories of meaning. Here, though, it is not Augustine's semiotics in *De Doctrina Christiana* which draws Frei's critical ire, but some assumptions embedded in eighteenth-century approaches to the intersection of history, texts, and meaning which eventuated in the historicist hermeneutics of the mid-to-late nineteenth century. With Jüngel, Frei worries about the gap between word and object, sign and thing signified, that obtains in referential modes of language and meaning. However, in his reading of the history of interpretation, Frei is particularly concerned with how the gap between word and object opens up when, with the rise of empiricism, the literal sense of the text becomes tethered to the senses, installing a hiatus between, on one hand, the story of Scripture and, on the other, the reality "out there" to which the story refers.[34] As Frei sees it, the referential structure of knowledge that develops with empiricism becomes, when applied to hermeneutics and biblical interpretation, the genesis of historical criticism. Under the spell of empiricism:

> The literal sense now is that sense that refers us to something "out there," which is literally represented by the story ... The story refers to something outside itself, and that subject matter outside itself now is not only the meaning, but that subject matter if it is history can also be verified in various ways, or it can be disconfirmed by evidence. And from this notion historical criticism springs.[35]

Significantly, though, and in contrast to Jüngel, Frei is wary of proposing a *new* hermeneutic demanding a radical reconceiving of the structure of language for the sake of avoiding the gap between reference and object. Indeed, for Frei it is the recovery from the pre-critical exegetes of an *old* hermeneutic, with its marriage of *sensus plenior* and *sensus literalis*, that resolves the dilemma. Frei has read Ebeling and Fuchs, familiarizing himself with the alternative approach to this problem emerging contemporaneously in German theology. But he swiftly dismisses the New Hermeneutic idea of "speech events" as the conflation of meaning to, as he puts it, "Aha! events"—"a kind of momentary analogy, simile, perhaps a metaphor for something that happens; a kind of mental event."[36] Frei grants that such events of language strike parallels with ordinary modes of understanding, and may in this sense be useful for theology and hermeneutics. But he regards the clumsy and indiscriminate deployment of the idea of "speech event" as a first principle as something of a sophistry. "To make *something* [of the idea of 'speech event'] is at once very important and rather platitudinous," he writes. "To make an enormous amount of it is something that always puzzles me."[37] In his review of the New Hermeneutic in *The Two Horizons*, Anthony Thiselton dubs this "Aha!" character of *Sprachereignisse* as "word magic."[38] We catch a whiff of the same concern in Frei's comments. It is fair enough for theology to acknowledge that words—not least, *God's* words—can and do behave *extraordinarily*, transcending their capacity as mere signifiers. But to erect an entire theology of theological language on the premise of the ecstatic, interruptive character of the word of God is to risk dislodging or alienating the word from ordinary human words and, indeed, from the world.[39]

As I have already indicated, Frei intends to close the "gap" of referential language via a different approach; one which, at least so he thinks, establishes sublime connections between theological language and language's ordinary usages. In a passage ghosted by Wittgenstein's famous remarks on the relation between meaning and use,[40] Frei suggests that Christian language constitutes "a very specific ordinary language."[41] The church's language, he says later on, "is a language in use"[42]; language which takes syntactical and grammatical and lexical shape according to the beliefs and practices of the Christian community. Frei's reading of this issue points back to his understanding of the structure of biblical narrative. We have seen that, for Frei, the narrative arc of Scripture corresponds to a reality; we might dare say that the text and the reality it describes or depicts interpenetrate one another. Likewise, language of faith is the church's means of describing or depicting the reality to which it corresponds and the beliefs and practices according to which it orients its life and mission.

A related and significant issue that emerges in the bevy of Frei's texts from the first half of the 1970s, and which receives extensive treatment in the 1975 monograph on the topic, is Frei's interest in the question of the *identity* of Jesus Christ. The connection of theological language and Christology—which, as we have seen, is a key theme in Jüngel's argument in *God as the Mystery of the World*—stimulates a number of Frei's insights here, and once again we find him resisting the circumscription of meaning (here, the meaning of the story of Jesus Christ) to language's referential capacities. For Frei, the identity of Jesus Christ is "rendered through the story of his life."[43] While he takes seriously enough the modern enterprise of "historical Jesus" research,[44] he views the "quests" for the Jesus of history as something of a red herring. Regarding the pursuit of an objective, historical Christ who putatively existed, as it were, *apart from* or *behind* the Gospel narrative, Frei comments:

> At best, it would involve endless and inconclusive arguments about the relation of the description of the 'Jesus of history' to that of the 'Christ of faith,' in the vain hope that adding these two abstractions together would somehow provide us with the description of one concrete person. At worst, we could expect to end up with the discovery that the endeavor to understand Christ's presence to ourselves is a projection of our own presence.[45]

The better course, Frei argues, is to recognize that the aim of the New Testament, especially of the Evangelists, is to communicate the identity of Jesus Christ through the gospel's narrative.

All of this demonstrates, again, that Frei's inquiry into the identity of Jesus Christ folds back upon his ambition to revive the category of narrative for the interpretation of Scripture. Indeed, as I have shown, these two trajectories of research intertwine around each other in Frei's work from the period. All of which exhibits striking parallels to what Jüngel was working on in the German scene at around the same time; namely, a program for dogmatics springing up from the crossroads of hermeneutics and Christology. But Frei is more interested than Jüngel in the "literary-literal" aspects of narrative, or in the *realism* of the Christian story. Frei's narrative approach to this nest of issues utilizes those, as it were, *ordinary* aspects of human storytelling—plot, dramatic structure, character, tension, and so on—to establish profound connections between, on one hand, Christian experience and practice and, on the other, the unfolding story of Christian Scripture.

III. Time and Narrative—Jüngel and Frei on How the Gospel Story Gets Told: By way of conclusion, let me draw together a few salient points that emerged in the foregoing readings of Jüngel and Frei. Some comments by French philosopher Paul Ricœur written contemporaneously to the texts we have examined here come to our aid. In the preface to his treatise *Time and Narrative*,[46] Ricœur reflects for a moment on the developmental relationship between the project at hand and his seminal work *The Rule of Metaphor*, the first edition of which had appeared eight years prior.[47] The two books "form a pair," Ricœur writes, and "were conceived together." He explains that he endeavored over the course of the two studies to investigate a "basic phenomenon of semantic innovation" occurring commonly in metaphor and narrative. At stake in both modes of discourse is the relationship between language, apprehension, and time. "With metaphor," he observes, "the innovation lies in the producing of a new semantic pertinence by means of an impertinent attribution." That is, a metaphor succeeds when we are able to perceive meaning in a discourse in spite of the fact that the words employed do not literally correspond to the things or states of affairs they signify. As such, "the metaphor is alive as long as we can perceive, through the new semantic pertinence ... the *resistance* of the words in their ordinary use and therefore their *incompatibility* at the level of a literal interpretation of the sentence." On the other hand, Ricœur argues, "with narrative, the semantic innovation lies in the inventing of another work of synthesis—a plot. By means of the plot, goals, causes, and chance are brought together with the temporary unity of a whole and complete action."[48] And later: "The plot of a narrative is comparable to ... predicative assimilation. It 'grasps together' and integrates into one whole and complete story multiple and scattered events, thereby schematizing the intelligible signification attached to the narrative taken as a whole."[49] Again, for Ricœur in both metaphor and narrative "the new thing—the as yet unsaid, the unwritten—springs up in language."[50] Metaphor expresses the new in surprising, extraordinary ways by exploiting the tension between language and referent. By contrast, narrative expresses the new by assimilating, integrating, and schematizing what is signified within the discursive pattern of "one whole and complete story."

Ricœur's distinction between metaphor and narrative is helpful, I think, for grasping the differences we have discovered between Jüngel and Frei on the structure of theological language. When Jüngel invokes the concept of *Erzählung* in *God as the Mystery of the World*, what he has in mind, I propose, is more akin to Ricœur's phenomenology of metaphor than it is to Frei's robustly literary understanding of narrative. Not incidentally, three years prior to the publication of *God as the Mystery of the World*, Jüngel co-authored with Ricœur a short volume on metaphor, which the two dedicated to Heidegger.[51] In *God as the Mystery of the World*, Jüngel uses "metaphor" and "narrative" (*Metapher* and *Erzählung*) interchangeably to describe Jesus' parables, eventually offering the qualification that "the parable is regarded as an extended metaphor, or the metaphor can be called an abbreviated parable. The difference consists of the fact that a parable narrates while a metaphor coalesces the narrative in a single word."[52] At all points here, Jüngel stresses the basic semantic character of what, as we have seen, Ricœur identifies as metaphor; namely, that a metaphor is an event of language marked by "the resistance of the words in their ordinary use and therefore their incompatibility at the level of a literal interpretation of the sentence." Frei, on the other hand, is not nearly as confident as Jüngel that the literary device of metaphor aptly describes the parables.[53] Rather, the force of his entire reading of the problem of biblical and theological language brings him close to Ricœur's phenomenology of narrative, namely, to the story as an assimilating, integrating, and schematizing nexus of meaning.

Jüngel's pathway into such issues as revelation, parable, and narrative stresses the *extraordinary* character of theological language; Frei's the *ordinary*. We observed that both theologians are concerned with the putative "gap" between language and object that obtains in referential or signifying language. In step with the New Hermeneutic, Jüngel counters the hermeneutics of signification by arguing that evangelical language about God—i.e., the proclamation of the gospel—is extraordinary speech in the speaking of which the one who is spoken comes to the world *in* language. Frei, too, is concerned to counter the reduction of theological language to sheer signification. But his tack involves bringing together evangelical language about God—for him, the testimony of the entire witness of Scripture—and the singular reality in which God and creatures participate. The result is Frei's refusal to drive a wedge between words about God and ordinary modes of language; indeed, as we have seen, for Frei theology *just is* a specific kind of ordinary language. If anything is lost here, it is the sense in which theological language can provoke or illuminate. In addition, we noted that Jüngel deploys the New Hermeneutic idea of *Sprachereignisse* to solve a host of diverse theological problems. When he employs *Erzählung*—narrative, story, account—in *God as the Mystery of the World* the discussion folds back upon the idea of interruptive, alien speech. By contrast, Frei's use of narrative capitalizes on literary features of storytelling such as plot, character and characterization, action, and so on.

Ricœur managed to do justice to both metaphor and narrative in the course of his investigation into the phenomenology of human language. It is demonstrable that Jüngel never moved from a metaphorical account of narrative (as it were), which owed much to the origins of his theology in the New Hermeneutic, to a nuanced appreciation of the literary aspects of narrative. For this reason, and oddly enough, his theology of narrative calls for the recovery of the gospel's story, but not that story's plot. Frei, on the other hand, pursued those literary aspects of narrative for which Jüngel had little use. But, demonstrably so, and perhaps as a result of his wariness of theology's use of metaphor, his narrative theology subdues the interruptive, surprising character of the gospel's story. All as such, contemporary efforts to retrieve the idea of narrative for Christian theology would do well to take heed of *both* of these bygone voices.

NOTES

1. Eberhard Jüngel, *Paulus und Jesus – Eine Untersuchung zur Präzisierung der Frage nach dem Ursprung der Christologie*, 7. unveränderte Auflage, Hermeneutische Untersuchungen zur Theologie 2, hgs. Gerhard Ebeling, Ernst Fuchs, and Manfred Mezger (Tübingen: J.C.B. Mohr [Paul Siebeck], 2004).
2. Eberhard Jüngel, "God – as a Word of Our Language: For Helmut Gollwitzer on His Sixtieth Birthday," in *Theology of the Liberating Word*, ed. Fredrick Herzog (Nashville: Abingdon Press, 1971): 25–45.
3. Eberhard Jüngel, *God as the Mystery of the World: On the Foundation of the Theology of the Crucified One in the Dispute between Theism and Atheism*, trans. Darrell L. Guder (London: Bloomsbury T&T Clark, 2014).
4. Hans W. Frei, *The Eclipse of Biblical Narrative: A Study in Eighteenth and Nineteenth Century Hermeneutics* (New Haven and London: Yale University Press, 1974), vii.
5. Hans W. Frei, *The Identity of Jesus Christ: The Hermeneutical Bases of Dogmatic Theology*, Updated and expanded edition (Eugene, OR: Cascade, 2013).
6. Hans W. Frei, "On Interpreting the Christian Story," in *Reading Faithfully*, Vol. I, *Writings from the Archives: Theology and Hermeneutics*, ed. Mike Higton and Mark Alan Bowald (Eugene, OR: Cascade, 2015): 68–93. Frei delivered the lecture at Louisville Seminary in 1976. The published text was prepared from an audio recording made during Frei's presentation. The lecture consists of a clear, concise summary of the main concerns animating *The Eclipse of Biblical Narrative*

and *The Identity of Jesus Christ*. As such, it stands as a nifty synopsis of Frei's work during this critical period.

7. Jüngel, *God as the Mystery of the World*, 3–14. See especially pages 4–9.

8. Our passage from *God as the Mystery of the World* consists of a brief engagement with *De Doctrina Christiana*. Jüngel does not mention Aristotle here, but introduces him into the book's analysis later on. See particularly his comments on Aristotle's approach to analogy on pages 266–72. An extensive engagement with the Aristotelian distinction of form and content in light of the problem of theological language (specifically, theological interpretation of Jesus' parables) is found in idem, *Paulus und Jesus*, 87–139 and 92–8.

9. Jüngel, *God as the Mystery of the World*, 10.

10. Ibid.

11. Ibid., 9.

12. Ernst Käsemann, "The Problem of the Historical Jesus," in *Essays on New Testament Themes*, trans. W. J. Montague, Studies in Biblical Theology 41 (London: SCM Press, 1964): 15–47.

13. The key texts of the New Hermeneutic from Ebeling and Fuchs are: Gerhard Ebeling, *Word and Faith*, trans. James W. Leitch (Philadelphia: Fortress, 1963); and idem, *Introduction to a Theological Theory of Language*, trans. R. A. Wilson (Philadelphia: Fortress Press, 1976); Ernst Fuchs, *Studies of the Historical Jesus*, trans. Andrew Scobie, Studies in Biblical Theology 42 (London: SCM Press, 1964); idem, *Zur Frage nach dem historischen Jesus* (Tübingen: J.C.B. Mohr, 1960); and idem, *Hermeneutik*, 4. Auflage (Tübingen: J.C.B. Mohr [Paul Siebeck], 1960). See also James M. Robinson, *A New Quest for the Historical Jesus*, Studies in Biblical Theology 25 (London: SCM, 1959); Günther Bornkamm, *Jesus of Nazareth*, trans. Irene and Fraser McLuskey (New York: Harper & Row, 1960); and Ethelbert Stauffer, *Jesus and His Story*, trans. Richard and Clara Winston (New York: Knopf, 1960). An outstanding, sympathetic but critical summary of the period can be found in James M. Robinson, *Language, Hermeneutic, and History: Theology after Barth and Bultmann* (Eugene, OR: Cascade, 2008), especially pages 69–146.

14. See especially Ernst Fuchs, *Zur Frage nach dem historischen Jesus*, 424–30; and idem, *Jesus: Wort und Tat* (Tübingen: J.C.B. Mohr [Paul Siebeck], 1971), 88–91.

15. Notably in R. David Nelson, *The Interruptive Word: Eberhard Jüngel on the Sacramental Structure of God's Relation to the World*, T&T Clark Studies in Systematic Theology 24, ed. John Webster, Ian A. McFarland, and Ivor Davidson (London: Bloomsbury T&T Clark, 2013), 2–10, 179–96. I also address the relationship between Jüngel and Barth in the forthcoming volume, John Webster, *Jüngel: A Guide for the Perplexed* (London: Bloomsbury T&T Clark, 2019).

16. Jüngel, *Paulus und Jesus*, 135.

17. Ibid., 136.

18. Ibid., 135.

19. John Webster, "Eberhard Jüngel on the Language of Faith," *Modern Theology* 1 (1985): 257.

20. Jüngel, *God as the Mystery of the World*, 294.

21. Ibid., 10.
22. Ibid., 294.
23. I am not the first interpreter of Jüngel's theology to express this concern. See the entirety of E. Lohse's reading of Jüngel's approach to the exegesis of the parables in *Gottersherrschaft als Gleichnis? Eine Untersuchung zur Auslegung der Gleichnisse Jesu nach Eberhard Jüngel*, Europäische Hochschulschriften 403 (Frankfurt: Peter Lang, 1990); Eta Linnemann, *Parables of Jesus: Introduction and Exposition* (London: S.P.C.K., 1966), 154, ft. 26; and John Webster, "Jesus in Modernity: Reflections on Jüngel's Christology," in Webster, *Word and Church: Essays in Christian Dogmatics* (Edinburgh and New York: T&T Clark, 2001): 157–9.
24. For sake of space I will leave aside the significant christological problem encapsulated in this statement; namely, that Jüngel offers a rather compressed account of the person and work of Christ, fixating on the prophetic office instead of unpacking a comprehensive treatment of the *munus triplex*, and limiting talk of the salvific actions of Christ to the crucifixion and resurrection. On such problems in Jüngel's Christology, see Webster, "Jesus in Modernity"; and Nelson, *The Interruptive Word*, 87–111.
25. Frei, *The Eclipse of Biblical Narrative*, 31.
26. Ibid., 1.
27. Frei, "On Interpreting the Christian Story," 75.
28. Ibid.
29. Frei, *The Eclipse of Biblical Narrative*, 2.
30. Ibid., 2. Note the past tenses in this citation. Here Frei is describing, still early on in *The Eclipse of Biblical Narrative*, how pre-critical exegetes *back then* approached the text realistically and literalistically.
31. Ibid., 153.
32. Frei, "On Interpreting the Christian Story," 75.
33. Ibid.
34. Ibid., 76.
35. Ibid.
36. Ibid., 89.
37. Ibid., 90.
38. Anthony Thiselton, *The Two Horizons: New Testament Hermeneutics and Philosophical Description* (Grand Rapids: Wm. B. Eerdmans Publishing Co., 1980), 337.
39. See the entirety of Thiselton's argument in *The Two Horizons*, 335–47. See also the full scope of Nelson, *The Interruptive Word*.
40. Frei, "On Interpreting the Christian Story," 86–8. The Wittgenstein reference is to *Philosophical Investigations*, 3rd ed., trans. G. E. M. Anscombe (Oxford: Blackwell, 2001), §43, p. 18.
41. Frei, "On Interpreting the Christian Story," 86.
42. Ibid., 87.
43. Ibid., 83.

44. See, for instance, Frei's comments on the first quest for the historical Jesus in *The Eclipse of Biblical Narrative*, 224–32.
45. Frei, *The Identity of Jesus Christ*, 95.
46. Paul Ricoeur, *Time and Narrative*, Vol. I, trans. Kathleen McLaughlin and David Pellauer (Chicago and London: The University of Chicago Press, 1984), ix–xii.
47. Paul Ricœur, *The Rule of Metaphor: The Creation of Meaning in Language*, trans. Robert Czerny with Kathleen McLaughlin and John Costello, S. J. (London and New York: Routledge, 2003).
48. Ricœur, *Time and Narrative*, ix. Emphasis added.
49. Ibid., x.
50. Ibid., ix.
51. Paul Ricoeur und Eberhard Jüngel, *Metapher. Zur Hermeneutik religiöser Sprache* (München: Kaiser Verlag, 1974). Jüngel's chapter from the volume is available in English as "Metaphorical Truth: Reflections on the theological relevance of metaphor as a contribution to the hermeneutics of narrative theology," in *Theological Essays I*, ed. and trans. J. B. Webster, 16–71.
52. Jüngel, *God as the Mystery of the World*, 289.
53. See Frei, "On Interpreting the Christian Story," 88–93.

CHAPTER ELEVEN

The Eclipse of Biblical Narrative: Analysis and Critique

GEORGE P. SCHNER

To offer an analysis and critique of so complex and difficult a text as *The Eclipse of Biblical Narrative* requires not only the technical skills of careful reading but also insightful extrapolation in dealing with what is at times impenetrably turgid prose. Moreover, given the sweep of authors and topics which *Eclipse* discusses and the complexity of its argument, judicious choices must be made as to what can and cannot be dealt with. To accomplish the former task, I have devoted the initial parts of this essay to an analysis of the contents of *Eclipse*, basing my extrapolations on a winnowing of other writings by Frei for passages which seem to illuminate the meaning and purpose of *Eclipse*. The second task is carried out in accord with my own area of expertise, philosophical theology, by furthering Frei's treatment of Kant and Hegel so as to aid the argument he wishes to make. The entr'acte will be an aside about how Frei's work has been of help to some Catholic theologians, and I shall conclude with a short epilogue.

    I found it helpful to keep in mind two images as I worked with *Eclipse*, the first being a view of the Calder mobile which hangs in the National Gallery in Washington. Frei's text is like an immense set of brightly colored counterbalancing weights suspended ultimately from one pivot and in constant motion, often passing through the same trajectory, the whole not being available to appreciation unless one considers the skill it takes to keep the parts in balance and motion. The second image is a memory of Hans Frei in motion himself, walking down Wall Street in New Haven, between the Religious Studies Department and Ezra Stiles College. It is a peculiarity of his gait which stands out in my memory. He always walked slightly quickly, especially when alone, leaning slightly forward, as if walking into a stiff wind which no one else could detect. I have often wondered if that invisible wind was the theological stream which he sensed himself to be going against, and that what seemed like a tilting forward to us seemed to be quite upright to him. I would like to imagine that it is this theological wind which is the invisible something that he is struggling with in *The Eclipse of Biblical Narrative.*

I

My analysis will consist of seven views of *Eclipse* beginning with remarks about (1) its style and structure; and (2) the scope and flow of its chapters; followed by attention to (3) its own stated purpose and its perceived effects; (4) the characterization of the seventeenth to twentieth centuries which it offers; (5) the range of types of theology which it diagnoses; (6) its definitions of realistic narrative at the heart of the work; and (7) some essential presuppositions which are grounding for the work. Using the image of the mobile, one might say that many views of *Eclipse* are necessary to experience it fully, since the text's contents shift place and relation as the mobile itself moves about.

What is the surface of the text of *Eclipse* like? Many of its sentences are complex arrangements of sets of oppositions posed in combinations of either/or's, or both/and's, with parenthetical remarks, additional cautionary remarks, and historical and evaluative remarks combined. They present the care and cautious scholarship of their author. They also present the complexity and perplexity of their subject matter. When combined into paragraphs and chapters, they occasionally present repetitive material, with frequent summary statements determining the character of a century or a part of it, and sometimes material which seems difficult to relate to the title of chapter or section. More importantly, the subtlety of the text is due to the mixing of diachronic with synchronic analysis, such that one is constantly immersed in particular persons and theories in their historical context but simultaneously related to other figures, theories, or consequences throughout the span of five or more centuries which Frei considers. As well, the text constantly moves between England and Germany, not only because of the intellectual commerce between them, but for the purpose of comparing authors in light of the thesis governing the exposition. Finally, there is the presence of an analysis of three strands of theory: apologetic and biblical theology, historical criticism, and biblical hermeneutics proper. What are the flow and structure of chapters in which all this is accomplished?

I suggest *Eclipse* divides into three sections with two introductory chapters. This division reflects the announcement in the "Introduction" of the "three elements in traditional realistic interpretation of the biblical stories, which also served as the foci for the rebellion against it."[1] These elements are: (1) the relation of the biblical story to historical occurrences; (2) the function of figuration in forming the biblical books into a single, unitary canon; and (3) the ability of the world rendered by the biblical narratives to embrace the experience of any present age and reader. The "Introduction" establishes the parameters, intent, and focus of the work, and there follows a chapter on precritical interpretation, chiefly about Calvin, with some remarks on Luther, Spinoza, and Cocceius which establish the agenda and background for the remaining chapters. All three elements are discussed throughout, though there is a general progression from concern with reference, to unity, to efficacy.

The first major section of *Eclipse* deals principally with English authors and the issues of historical criticism and meaning-as-reference, although the issues of apologetics and religious application are also treated, principally through discussion of German authors. There is an important summary of positions in the course of this section, to which I will return, and this part ends as it began with a discussion of the English situation, attention now being given to the English novel. The second section begins with a brief chapter on the German situation in the late eighteenth century and continues with a chapter on three varieties of biblical theology, the issue under discussion being the quest for unity in the biblical text. The third and final section consists of a discussion of the contributions of Herder, Strauss, and Schleiermacher primarily on the third issue announced in the "Introduction," namely the reverse in the direction of interpretation, the biblical world now having to fit into the present age rather than the reverse. The next question to pose is, to what purpose this complex structure?

In the "Introduction" Frei offers a straightforward description of *Eclipse* as being "about one segment of the history of the theory of biblical interpretation" (10), principally in the eighteenth and early nineteenth centuries, not a full history but "a historical study under a thesis" (10). That thesis is a complex one asserting the following points: (1) "a realistic or history-like element" (10) is a feature of biblical texts important for the making of Christian belief; (2) this feature "can be highlighted by the appropriate analytic procedure and by no other, even if it may be difficult to describe the procedure—in contrast to the element itself" (10); (3) this feature was "acknowledged and agreed upon" (10) by eighteenth-century commentators; (4) the "procedure for isolating it had irretrievably broken down in the opinion of most commentators" (10); (5) the feature "finally came to be ignored, or—even more fascinating—its presence or distinctiveness came to be denied for lack of a 'method'" (10) despite the initial agreement about its presence in the biblical text. My third view of the text begins with the question, what does this historical analysis accomplish?

The result of applying this thesis in the historical study is the discovery of new ways to understand and evaluate the use of the biblical text and theories about that usage before and since the Reformation. First, as to the period prior to the eighteenth century, Frei's colleague, George Lindbeck, puts it succinctly. For many readers this historical study under a thesis

> has shown how the confusion in the last two centuries of biblical studies, between the narrative and historical (i.e., "factual") senses, has resulted in gross misunderstandings of premodern interpretation as this was generally practised up through the Reformation.[2]

Second, as to the eighteenth, nineteenth, and twentieth centuries, the search to explain what happened to realistic narrative uncovers a complex of dynamics which have persisted to our own time, and which large parts of Christian theology have taken as common sense. In a passage that adverts to the title of the book, Frei gives one of many summations of the eighteenth century generally:

> The apologetic urge from left to right, for which explication and application had to walk in harmony, was only one reason for the strange eclipse of the realistic narrative option in a situation in which many observers actually paid heed to that feature. Hermeneutics stood between religious apologetics and historical criticism, and these two worked against the narrative option.
> (134)

Summing up the end of the period and listing what has perdured to the present, Frei observes:

> One comes closer to the heart of the problem if one recalls that the mythical school, together with practically everybody else, affirmed that understanding the text's subject matter (*Sache*) has priority over understanding its words, indeed that the text's words have to be interpreted through the subject. Once this point has been made, it is quite secondary whether the subject is historical events, the general consciousness or form of life of an era, a system of ideas, the author's intention, the inward moral experience of individuals, the structure of human existence, or some combination of them; in any case, the meaning of the text is not identical with the text.
> (278)

What the historical study under a thesis uncovers functions as an agenda for both a refusal and a retrieval within Christian theology. The retrieval is for something we used to do as Christians, and the refusal is of things we tend to prefer to do with the biblical text but we ought not to. Lindbeck neatly summarizes the retrieval for us:

> For many of Hans Frei's readers, his greatest contribution has been to make possible the restoration of the christologically centered narrative sense of scripture to its traditional primacy.[3]

It is not the retrieval of a proper understanding and use of realistic narrative for its own sake, but for a theological and pastoral purpose. Similarly, the refusal to appeal to any one of that long list of "behind-the-scenes projections" (281), which theorists of the past three centuries have increasingly preferred, is ultimately for the same theological and pastoral purpose, namely to allow to happen what is essential for Christian theology but which can only happen through an act of mimesis construing appropriate parts of the biblical text as a realistic narrative. Only in that way can we come to a knowledge of Jesus as Lord and Saviour into whose world we are all to be taken up.

These first three views of *Eclipse* can now be more sharply focused by attending to Frei's summary remarks about each of the five centuries he explores, his various definitions of what realistic narrative is and does, and the two typologies he offers of positions taken in the eighteenth and nineteenth centuries (which still dominate, he contends, the twentieth century).

Beginning with the sixteenth century and generally the entire period prior to it, Frei in part presumes and in part argues that the Reformers and their predecessors read biblical narratives as both literal and historical, read the whole Bible as "preaching Christ" (40) particularly through the use of figural reading, and read for a comprehension of "the way things really are" (36), that is, submitting their present world to the world of the biblical narrative. Summations about the seventeenth century begin to contain phrases and words like "subtle transformation" (4), "split" (41, 42), and "first uncertain steps" (156) to name the origins—chiefly discussed in the works of Spinoza and Cocceius—of historical criticism and of the separation of two pairs of notions: explicative sense from historical reference, and narrative depiction from meaning or subject matter. Summations of the sixteenth and seventeenth centuries are relatively few, however, by comparison to the next three centuries. Frei is constantly offering synopses or recapitulations of these centuries throughout the text, with the chapters on Herder, Strauss, and Schleiermacher being the general exceptions. When combined into subsidiary mobiles within the larger balancing of parts these summations are quite illuminating.

As to the eighteenth century generally, Frei argues that if one looks for the change in outlook and argument about narrative biblical texts, one finds that "the strange eclipse of the realistic narrative option" (134) was due to the rise of historical criticism abetted by rationalistic interpretation on the one hand and religious apologetics on the other. The former unity of literal and historical in the treatment of realistic narrative breaks up and a reintegration of the two begins. Over all, the "fact issue," as Frei calls it, dominated the hermeneutical discussions in an age in which "realism was not simply a literary movement but a broad apprehension of the world and man's place in it" (136–7). In the only lengthy italicized part of *Eclipse,* Frei notes the asymmetry of realistic narrative literature and its criticism flourishing in England while absent in Germany, and the reverse—lack of critical analysis of biblical writings absent in England but flourishing in Germany. And all this occurred when the "realistic character of the crucial biblical stories was actually acknowledged and agreed upon by most of the significant eighteenth century commentators" (10).

Concerning the late eighteenth century Frei offers even more summary remarks, perhaps because the situation, to his eye, has become even more complex. Historical criticism had begun to develop its own oral and literary tradition with a growing confidence in Enlightenment rational investigation free from authoritarianism, in the autonomy and integrity of historical inquiry, and in the general hermeneutics which had set aside mystical, allegorical and spiritual readings (although certain reactions against all three of these did occur). General biblical hermeneutics as exegesis employs a distinction between *Worterklärung* and *Sacherklärung,* with subject-matter interpretation "regarding the *Sache* of a biblical narrative as either space-time event (meaning as ostensive reference) or as teaching, which could in turn be either dogma or general religious ideas (meaning as ideal reference)" (101). Thus the explicative sense of the narrative text was its ostensive or ideal reference; and its applicative meaning was a truth revealed historically, or a universal spiritual truth, or the former dependent ultimately on the latter. Frei notes, however, that "almost everyone, a few of the Deists and Reimarus excepted, affirmed that explication harmonized with application" (124), although the options of the acceptance of revelation as a unique, salvific, and miraculous occurrence or the rejection of positive revelation in favor of natural religion were to persist into the nineteenth century in the arguments about the relation of faith and history.

Turning to the nineteenth century, Frei's summary remarks can be gathered under the umbrella of a thoroughly synoptic comment: "all commentators are agreed that biblical hermeneutics underwent a sea change in the early 19th century" (282). That change saw, first, the development of a hermeneutics based upon theories of understanding, in which a free and self-conscious self-positioning toward the world is an independent and indispensable factor in shaping the depiction of that world with its bearing on the self.

(200–01)

Second, historical criticism now dominated both the "theological-apologetical and antitheological endeavours" which originated among other things the variety of accounts of the life of the historical Jesus. Both factors reinforced the determinative character of the results of exegesis over the work of dogmatic theology, resulting in the extremes of someone like Strauss who

> had demonstrated to the satisfaction of young radicals that historical exegesis of the gospels does not justify basing the dogma of divine-human reconciliation on the historical factuality of Jesus' story.
>
> (224)

The alternatives of mythical or ostensive meaning—which Frei claims to be symptomatic of the deeper issue quoted above—serve as a summary of the early nineteenth century, namely the priority of understanding a text's subject matter over understanding its words.

When it comes to remarks about the twentieth century, the purpose and importance of *Eclipse* become evident. Frei considers that most of the major problems and positions taken in the late eighteenth and early nineteenth centuries concerning the three basic elements of reference, unity, and efficacy and the three major positions of apologetics, historical criticism, and biblical hermeneutics persist to the present. One quotation will do to summarize:

> How to relate or correlate the two things, denotative or connotative verbal sense and historical reference on the one hand, and inner understanding seeking its mental or spiritual counterpart in the text on the other hand, was to become a monumental preoccupation among Idealist and post-Idealist interpreters for the next two centuries, long after the demise of Pietism as a major intellectual and cultural (though not religious) force.
>
> (219)

Issues of the positivity of Christianity, of the priority of self-understanding as the source of unity for the text, of ostensive reference, and of reconstruction of the historical context of the text are other ways of naming the persistent problems. They are all concerned with questions of the origin, reliability, and abiding meaning and value of the texts, and for Frei they are all pursued without taking realistic narrative for what it is.

Frei holds together this plethora of theories and figures in several typologies, and in my fifth view of *Eclipse* I wish to present a combination of the two major typologies he presents first in Chapters 6 and 7, and again in Chapter 13.[4] The former presentation is highly nuanced with relations among all the types being adverted to.[5] The latter presentation is more schematic with a helpful summary at the end of Chapter 13. The focus of the two typologies is also different: the earlier one primarily uses the fact issue, and matters of reference, religious significance, and the relation of explication and application; whereas the later one, as the title of the section indicates, is explicitly concerned with "The Range of Subject Matter Proposals" (255). Only Ernesti seems to escape the typology, though not entirely since he is understood precisely in opposition to but in contradictory allegiance with all the other positions. Finally, we might ask where, if at all, realistic narrative and its ghostly supporters *might* find themselves and where Schleiermacher and Hegel might be placed. Answers are possibly given in a typology Frei developed more recently and which can be profitably compared to the present ones.[6]

Using a remark this later piece on typology ends with,[7] I would range Reimarus and the Pietists as the two extremes on a continuum of positions. Deist, mythophiles, and rationalists (Kant in particular), and allegorists range in that order from the Reimarian extreme toward the center. On the other end Orthodox traditionalists, actually, vie with Pietists for the extreme position, with Supernaturalists, Naturalists, and the mediating positions of Neologians and Latitudinarians (also called in part the Apologetic position) filling out the continuum toward the center, in that order. I wonder if the various positions in the later typology Frei developed, which move from the submission of theology to philosophical requirements (in rationalist and correlationist theologies, Kant and David Tracy, for example) to Wittgensteinian fideism (in D. Z. Phillips, for example), with Schleiermacher and Barth as positions in between, may not help us to locate supporters of realistic narrative as somewhere in the middle of *Eclipse's* typologies (with Herder almost representing them). If, of course, we recall that recognition of realistic narrative was made difficult by the double pressure of historical criticism on one side and apologetic hermeneutics on the other, then we cannot place it easily within the continuum, but rather must range it along side all of the positions mentioned, since they constitute, as it were, the eclipsing agent.[8]

To construct as my sixth view an answer to the question of what realistic narrative actually is, I have gathered together direct and indirect references to it throughout *Eclipse*. If grasping Frei's judgment about each of the centuries is difficult because of his careful cross-referencing of movements and individuals for the sake of the subtlety and complexity of history, grasping what realistic narrative is poses yet another sort of difficulty. What do we know of that which is eclipsed? What we see throughout *Eclipse* are the theories comprising the somewhat smaller moon causing the eclipse. What we know of it is the heuristic halo of light, as it were, which is somewhat limned in the discussion of Calvin, but cannot be considered to have been fully presented. So the notion remains heuristic in two senses, the something hidden by the very wealth of historical detail and analysis, and the something whose recognition and use presumably have its own history and exemplars.

What realistic narrative is *not,* is a text which has a "more profound stratum" (318) to which it refers and in terms of which its "use" can be determined. That reference might be to external sets of affairs, to internal states of the human person, or to metaphysical or cosmic realities. When external, these sets of affairs require the reconstitution of the historical or cultural context through factual description, with judgments about the reliability of those facts in terms of historical veracity. When internal, one searches for consciousness in general, or the particulars of inward moral experience, the author's intention, or the general spirit or outlook which generated the text. When metaphysical or cosmic, the more profound stratum consists of abiding religious meaning or some such system of ideas. In all these efforts the mistaken conviction is that

> the narrative is neither logically (or essentially) identical with the subject matter depicted, nor does it render directly accessible the temporal sequence talked about. The cohesion of depiction with subject matter on the one hand, and of subject matter with its accessibility to present understanding on the other, requires something more than the narrative account itself.
>
> (189)

Put positively,

> ... the location of meaning in narrative of the realistic sort is the text, the narrative structure or sequence itself. If one asks if it is the subject matter or the verbal sense that ought to have priority in the quest for understanding, the answer would be that the question is illegitimate or redundant.
>
> (280)

It is this identity of form and content, of the text and its proper "reality" (if I may put it that way), which forms that particular *Gestalt* which is realistic narrative. Frei variously calls the form or shape a bond, a web, a pattern, a story; an identity; an interaction; and, as above, a cohesion. What is held together or present in and through the text alone are: a person, agents, speech, verbal communications, circumstances, social context, character, incident, and continuity. This last content, continuity, is expressed in several ways as temporal framework, chronological continuity, occurrence pattern, and temporal sequence, and by the adverbs "cumulatively" and "accretively." Five verbs are used principally to indicate the motion or operation by which form and content as one indissoluble whole are activated, as it were, in and through the text: articulating, rendering, deploying, depicting, and instantiating. I think these verbs and others like them are an essential part of an appreciation of what realistic narrative is, how it is used, and perhaps even as to how it can be retrieved. I will return to this at the conclusion of the second part of this paper.

My seventh and final view of *Eclipse* consists in locating two passages which point to what might be considered the larger theological and philosophical agenda and purpose of *Eclipse*. I have chosen only two among several evident foundational items, the choice being governed by my own concern with philosophical theological matters.[9] Perhaps most important for understanding the force and significance of the historical analysis, the thesis, and the deeper theological purpose of *Eclipse* is the Epilogue to Chapter 11, which might well have been the epilogue to the entire book. It begins with another of Frei's summations gathering up the last three centuries:

> While the complex of technical issues in the relation of hermeneutics, biblical criticism, and theology have remained much the same since the late 18th century, the cultural significance of post-narrative, post-figural interpretation, especially in connection with the question of Jesus and revelation, remains in doubt.
>
> (224)

What is not in doubt for Frei is the basic insight of Marx's view of the criticism of religion, for it confirms the basic insight of *Eclipse*, namely:

> the very development of historical-critical investigation into the gospels, whether in support or denial of Christian belief in Jesus Christ, was itself already one of the signs that the christological belief or doctrine under investigation had ceased to be of historic significance.
>
> (227)

And again Frei observes:

> ... the historical-critical investigation of the gospels is an admission of the fundamental cultural uninterest of the notion of christological salvation in history and of the notion of a relation between history and faith.
>
> (227)

Thus he is able to show the irony of Schweitzer's praise of German theology for its invention of the critical investigation of the life of Jesus, and his colleague Lindbeck seemingly in reference to the same section of *Eclipse* notes:

> They (many of Frei's readers) are inclined to think that Frei's work marks the beginning of a change in biblical interpretation as decisive—though in a different direction—as that occasioned by Albert Schweitzer's *Quest of the Historical Jesus*.

A second hint at a philosophically important presupposition of the text, already mentioned in the "Preface," is the brief passage at the end of Chapter 14 concerning Gilbert Ryle. The immediate context is a repudiation of the search for the "mind of the author" as distinct from or accessible in isolation from the text itself of the author. But the sort of philosophy which Ryle represents generally is an important clue to the agenda of *Eclipse*. Those who question the entire turn to the subject of modern philosophy, its resultant dichotomy of mind and matter, and who subsequently take language itself as the proper focus of philosophical investigation are judged by Frei to be

> a marvellous antidote to the contorted and to my mind unsuccessful efforts of certain phenomenologists and philosophers of "Existence" or "Being" to tackle a similar dualism.
>
> (viii)

My proposal for a rereading of Kant and Hegel will suggest how they both recognize the importance of these two presuppositions and offer clues for understanding realistic narrative.

Other texts than the *Eclipse* are exceptionally helpful in sorting out the intellectual mathematics of the mechanics which makes Frei's great mobile such a feat of balance and motion, despite its unwieldy collection of multiple parts. I have chosen a few quotations with the intent of showing in part the interconnection of realistic narrative with christological concerns and philosophical preferences. In a recorded account of lectures and discussion at Yale Divinity School in 1969,[10] speaking of Barth, Frei observes:

> No theologian ever saw these two aspects of Christology, the being and the activity of Jesus Christ, in closer integration: They are but two differing descriptions, where we have no single description, of the one 'self-enacted parable,' to use Austin Farrer's eloquent phrase.[11]

Furthermore, the divine-human unity that is Christ is both actually and logically grounded in God's own act; this is to be understood not only as the correct expression of the reality of the reconciliation in Christ, but also as the correct understanding of how it is we come to know this truth. It is the same source, then, for a critique of the search for anthropological need or possibility (a la Tillich or Schleiermacher) within human nature, or within the striving of human society and history as a whole. This unity will also be an issue of importance to Kant and Hegel, as we will see.

Although the text consists of a transcript of a conversation, it continues with a number of passages which confirm the general preoccupation of the *Eclipse*. They are about Barth principally, but Frei often enough indicates that the comments reflect his own thinking about theological construction. The priority is given to the "story," sometimes called the "narrative"; that story, both New and Old Testaments, is about Jesus Christ; any metaphysical issue is read "in the light of the narrative of the Gospel" and cannot contradict it; reading the text is not "doing historical criticism"; but "we have a hard time describing how we do that," that is, "read a story"; "the meaning is the story, and the doctrines are kind of secondary repetitions"; and at one point Frei comments, "I must confess I'm a little uneasy, because I don't know at that point how much I'm reading myself into Barth." Summing up the core of the story, Frei observes about Barth:

> Jesus is not the incarnate Lord who, as a separable or added action, performs and undergoes reconciliation of God and man. No, he is what he does: the reconciliation. No theologian ever saw these two aspects of Christology, the being and the activity of Jesus Christ, in closer integration. ...[12]

It is striking to read this remark in juxtaposition with the following remark made twenty years later, in the essay "Barth and Schleiermacher: Divergence and Convergence." The vocabulary is somewhat changed, but the insight is identical:

> In that sense and that alone, one can say that Barth became a "narrative" theologian: Jesus was what he did and underwent, and not simply his understanding or self-understanding. He was an agent in a narrative plot, in his particular narratable plot, that is, the restoration of the broken covenant which is also the realization of the aim of divine creation. It is more accurate to say that the meaning of the theological doctrines or conceptual redescriptions is the *story* of which they are (partial) redescriptions, rather than conversely, that the meaning of the story is the doctrines.[13]

Could the search for realistic narrative be a question of rediscovering or restating the problem of the place of the "scandal of particularity" in Christian theology in contrast to the hermeneutical priority of the "meaning context" requisite for the epistemological and religious significance of Christology? From the essay "Theology and the Interpretation of Narrative: Some Hermeneutical Considerations," I note the following:

> The linguistic account, i.e. the narrative is itself the reality narratively rendered. We have the reality only under the depiction and not in a language-neutral or language-transcending way. Nor are we barred from the reality by language. No further knowledge is needed, none is available. The narrated world is as such the real world and not a linguistic launching pad to language-transcending reality, whether ideal essence or self-contained empirical occurrence.[14]

Is realistic narrative, then, a way of naming the uniqueness of Christianity, its own particular distinguishing mark, and possibly its very particular scandal? In the same text, Frei sums up for us what cannot be a substitute for the text itself:

> Neither objective reality, whether historical occurrence or eternal metaphysical essence, nor transcendentally grounded understanding or mode-of-being-in-the-world-in-a-limit-way is the referent of narrative.[15]

These clarifications in other works of what realistic narrative is, and its relation to the christological and philosophical issues confirm, and perhaps even intensify, the argument and import of *Eclipse*. They point out to me, however, the usefulness of a rereading of Kant and Hegel to supplement the reading of them which Frei provides, for the purpose of aiding his argument not contradicting it. Questions of unity of content and manner of knowing that content, of particularity in relation to universality, and of the role of language in these matters are clearly of concern to Hegel, perhaps less so, but not less importantly so, to Kant. A fear of falling into the mode of rationalist, correlationist, or fideist theology does not seem a sufficient warrant for not engaging in this rereading. In addition, if the basic insight which Frei proposes throughout his works is to be in conversation with theologians for whom Kant and Hegel, and philosophy in general, have been essentially positive ingredients in theological construction, then the rereading is doubly important.

Having taken seven views of the text, I will now pass to some general remarks of criticism of the text preparatory to the entr'acte and the discussion of Kant and Hegel in the second part.

Criticism of *Eclipse* could proceed in several directions, depending upon one's choice of aspect in the text. There are questions to ask about the historical work done in it, about the thesis concerning realistic narrative, and about the theological and philosophical impact of the text. I will comment briefly about all three by posing a variety of questions for further study, which are intended to wonder about ways in which what is actually done in the text may or may not be conducive to the prosecution of Frei's purposes or the illumination of the material under consideration.

Concerning the historical work of *Eclipse,* the first question is about its starting point. Reventlow,[16] in a study which parallels the first part of *Eclipse* sharing much of the same subject matter, makes clear that the eclipse has its roots well before the post-Reformation era, in Spiritualist, Erasmian, and leftwing Reformation movements. It would be enlightening to see the eclipse as part of the longstanding tendencies in the spirituality of the Christian Church, evidenced dramatically in the fourteenth and fifteenth centuries, which begin from a high estimation of the individual or the group filled with the spirit, on whom possession of the spirit bestows a higher form of knowledge which makes superfluous both the letters of Holy Scripture and all external forms of the communication of salvation.[17]

This broadening of the search for the origins of the eclipse could include, for instance, investigation of the parallels between the developments in the theology and practice of the Eucharist and the alterations of liturgical practice and ecclesiastical politics of the period, in order to confirm but also situate the fate of a realistic reading of biblical narratives. The use of the biblical text in the theory and practice of liturgy, morality, and Church polity is an important parallel to what Frei himself observes becomes a rather confined discussion among academics (however much it becomes Christian common sense for many by the twentieth century).

This leads me to a corollary remark about the concentration on Protestant sources and situations, on Calvin as the prime example of former "correct" usage. In effect, the absence of discussion about Roman Catholic and Orthodox developments throughout this period (though Catholics are included in remarks about the twentieth-century results) does not so much call into question the scholarship as hamper it. If, however, thorough and subtle research on Catholic and Orthodox sources were brought to bear on the same issues, and if the context of liturgical and pastoral practice were explored, the question remains as to how complete the eclipse of realistic narrative was, and what additional clues might be found to its retrieval.[18]

The same sort of remark can be made about Frei's philosophic preferences in *Eclipse*. In this case the work of Buckley[19] on the origins of modern atheism is a helpful parallel study whose conclusions are remarkably similar to Frei's. The cast of characters investigated begins earlier and follows a quite different path, but a few remarks from his conclusion will show the convergence of discovery:

> In an effort to avoid a developing fideism, associated either with Montaigne or with Calvin, and to lay a common basis for rational discussion, any appeal to the witness of a person—which is fundamental to Christianity—became inadmissible. The theologians followed the Thomistic lead, or what they understood as the Thomistic lead, and consigned Christology with its endless refinements to a more remote phase of theology. It is not without some sense of wonder that one records that the theologians bracketed religion in order to defend religion.[20]

Christology and its endless refinements were no doubt in need of a dose of realistic narrative. Bracketing religion for apologetics and theological foundations is bracketing Christ, and it seems that bracketing Christ results from (or at least involves) bracketing realistic narrative. What Herder is for Frei, Malebranche is for Buckley, both being characters who almost but not entirely saw the eclipse occurring. However, not unlike Reventlow in historical matters, Buckley in philosophical matters begins in the fifteenth century and traces the story through French and Belgian as well as English and German sources. As well, Buckley sees the importance of expanding beyond Christology, of including the communal context, and of relating to metaphysical issues:

> The Christian god cannot have a more fundamental witness than Jesus Christ, even antecedent to the commitments of faith; Christian theology cannot abstract from Christology in order to shift the challenge for this foundational warrant onto philosophy. Within the context of a Christology and a Pneumatology of both communal and personal religious experience, one can locate and give its own philosophical integrity to metaphysics, but Christology and Pneumatology are fundamental.[21]

These criticisms, then, tend to confirm the history and thesis of *Eclipse* by expanding its base of analysis in multiple ways, but also requiring it to accept potential emendation.

Frei's preference for philosophers like Ryle, for movements like the language philosophies of the middle twentieth century, undoubtedly aids in understanding the eclipse, and more particularly in providing clues to the retrieval by countering the contorted and (to Frei's mind) unsuccessful efforts of idealist, neo-idealist, existentialist, Heideggerian, phenomenologist—ultimately any philosophy other than language philosophy. The minimalist intrusion (i.e., non-foundationalist possibilities) of the use of language philosophy in theology and its minimalist claim, both metaphysically and epistemologically, are of significant value for present-day theology. However, a rereading of Kant and Hegel, without a drastic reversal of Frei's judgments about them, can provide clues not only to the occurrence of the eclipse but also to the subtle presence of realistic narrative and means for its retrieval which Frei seems to overlook. In the years following the publication of the *Eclipse* Frei continued to reconsider his reading of Schleiermacher—if not directly concerning hermeneutics, then at least concerning other theological issues. I take this instance of rereading as an encouragement for my suggestions about a rereading of Kant and Hegel.

II

My concern to reread Kant and Hegel is also a strategic matter. For some Roman Catholic scholars, Frei's efforts to uncover the historical origins and internal agenda of Protestant treatments of the biblical text and its implications for Christology and other doctrinal areas, and for theological methodology, have been exceptionally enlightening. Though Barth may still remain foreign to Catholic scholars, the impact of Frei's teaching and writing has provided an avenue of discovery and invention which is an important alternative to the inherited patterns of treating the challenges of eighteenth- and nineteenth-century German thought.[22] However, it has been the epistemological and ontological claims of Kant and Hegel which have been the focus of the conversation engaged in by Catholics such as Karl Rahner and other transcendental theologians who have increasingly become the new textbook figures of late twentieth-century Roman Catholic theological teaching. This focus is presumably what Frei considers

> the idealist conviction that the knowledge of every spiritual, cultural object, (if not all data) has to be analyzed under the scheme of a subject-object, self-other or spirit-world correlation.
>
> (201)

It was in reaction to the kind of theology which dealt with the modern philosophical tradition as adversarial, and out of a situation in which even ordinary historical-critical exegesis had only begun to make an impact in doctrinal theology, that the preferred agenda of revisioning Catholic theologians was conversation with Kant and Hegel for apologetic, even accommodationist, purposes, by adopting them systematically and foundationally. My remarks will suggest that there are sources within both authors that might forward an expanded maintenance of Frei's valuable insights in *Eclipse,* and offer theologians uses for Kant and Hegel beyond those currently preferred.

III

Proposing a rereading of Kant and Hegel is not to suggest that Frei's discussion of either author is unsatisfactory, but rather that, given the reliance of *Eclipse* on the two presuppositions I have suggested, his treatment of Kant and Hegel (both in *Eclipse* and elsewhere) tends to systematically ignore those hints at or even points of explicit agreement with, the theological agenda of *Eclipse.* I am looking for material to further the discussion of those philosophic categories associated with the priority of realistic narrative, namely: person, particularity, temporal sequence, unity of content and manner of coming to know, symbolism, and language.[23]

Frei's concise remarks in *Eclipse* concerning Kant's philosophic position are a model of clarity and nuance. In his designation of Kant as an allegorist in the typology in Chapter 13, Frei relates Kant's sense of the unity of the canon to Kant's recovery of the significance of narrative shape.

> This stress on the narrative feature and its mirroring of an actual moral process makes Kant's 'subject matter' in the New Testament far more than a simple, abstractly statable moral idea.
>
> (264)

And in an endnote, Frei qualifies the placement of Kant in "subject-matter" hermeneutics by observing that:

> though he (Kant) allegorized scripture, his use of it tended toward symbolism, if by symbolizing we mean that certain fact-like descriptions, while not making literal sense, nevertheless are indispensable in the representation of a complex of meaning known apart from them.
>
> (340)

The passages on Kant in *Eclipse* can be supplemented with remarks in the chapter on Niebuhr's theological background[24] where Kant's status is that of the *pons asinorum* for those "still desirous of explicating their faith in God in terms positively related to the cultural thought of the day."[25] As well, there are the several remarks in the essay on Strauss[26] which confirm the general assessment of Kant's dichotomy of real and ideal, and his radical reinterpretation of Christology.

A rereading of Kant might begin with the rule-like passage contained in the introduction to the discussion of the "Ideal in General" found in Chapter 3 of Book 2 of the transcendental dialectic, where he defines the role of the archetype,[27] and with the immediately following caution:

> But to attempt to realize the ideal in an example, that is in the field of appearance, as, for instance, to depict the character of the perfectly wise man in a romance, is impracticable. There is indeed something absurd, and far from edifying, in such an attempt, inasmuch as the natural limitations, which are constantly doing violence to the completeness of the idea, make the illusion that is aimed at altogether impossible, and so cast suspicion on the good itself—the good that has its source in the idea—by giving it the air of being a mere fiction.[28]

This ideal is not, of course, extra-mentally real, but neither is it a "figment of the brain." Just what existence it has is a perplexing question. How can one have an ideal whose conduct we are to emulate if that ideal and conduct have no content, content being of necessity for Kant a matter of the manifold? Is the ideal purely formal, and if so, of what use is it?

These passages from the *Critique of Pure Reason* have their succinct companions in *Religion within the Limits of Reason Alone*.[29] As with the categories of understanding, so also with this archetype, a rudimentary question concerns what warrant Kant has for simply asserting their existence as part of the human constitution. Kant's refusal of a romance-like fiction might be enlisted as a covert appeal for realistic narrative, but less far fetched would be attention to his insistence on the edifying and complete character of the ideal in its presentation of the "good itself." Returning to the first critique, before even reaching the question of the particularities of the instantiation of the ideal of pure reason, the question of its existence is dealt with in terms of the necessity for having a presupposition of "the sum of all empirical reality as the condition of its possibility" and "owing to a natural illusion" the regarding of that principle as valid for things in general, such that an empirical principle becomes a transcendental one. In what follows, the mere representation passes into being the source and supplier of the empirical, so that there is a passage from realization, to hypostatization, and finally to personification. Kant calls it a "natural procedure of human reason" but lays the motive power for the passage on the need to come to a decision:

> ... if, that is to say, the existence of some sort of necessary being is taken as granted, and if it be agreed further that we must come to a decision as to what it is—then the foregoing way of thinking must be allowed to have a certain cogency.[30]

In the Appendix to this section of the *Critique* Kant begins and ends his discussion of the regulative usage of the ideas of pure reason with a metaphor which furthers his exposition of the tendency of human nature to function with the ideal of reason, in a regulative manner which he finds altogether salutary. The ideas direct us toward

> a certain goal upon which the routes marked out by all its rules converge, as upon their point of intersection. This point is indeed a mere idea, a *focus imaginarius,* from which, since it lies quite outside the bounds of possible experience, the concepts of the understanding do not in reality proceed; none the less its serves to give to these concepts the greatest [possible] unity combined with the greatest [possible] extension.[31]

Finally, the end of this section has Kant appealing to the inevitability of a "certain subtle anthropomorphism."[32] Three notions and one operation need to be distinguished and explored here: first, the ideal or archetype, its status formally and materially; second, the relation of the ideal to a possible schema of it, even if only negatively, particularly given the constant use of biblical texts in *Religion;* third, the *focus imaginarius* as it relates to ideal and instantiation; fourth, the tendency toward instantiation, again even if negatively understood by Kant. Sorting out these notions and operation will require an investigation of the first chapter of the transcendental analytic on the schematism, with its albeit cryptic discussion of the role of the imagination and temporal sequence.

Most important, however, are the late works on history and the origin and end of humanity. It seems possible to analyze Kant's use of biblical texts in these works as being more than the occasion for an allegorical reading and to observe some development of his philosophic principles in conversation with those texts, such that the biblical texts and characters have a formative influence on the revision of the rational principles. Whether his use of the persons of Job and Christ in the historical works really does involve a slightly altered use of the text, in which the schematism is not merely informed by a priori principles but can be the agent of the development; even reformation, of the a priori principles, is not entirely clear. There is some evidence, together with the hints from the first critique in particular, that such an interpretation has some validity.[33]

No less difficult but more helpful are a great variety of texts from Hegel which Frei's analysis does not consider. Hegel's comprehensive view of the relation of Christianity to other religions and to philosophy, his incipient understanding of the importance of language to philosophic reflection, and his development of the role of the historic embodiment of the transcendent may indeed be fraught with interpretive difficulties but certainly offer more fruitful occasions for reflection than Kant in a search for understanding realistic narrative.

Frei's assessment of Hegel in *Eclipse* tends to emphasize the movement from representation to thought, the "spiritualizing, universalizing tendency" (214). He adopts the position that

> Hegel and his school were ambiguous on the issues of the dispensability or indispensability of a factual occurrence to the truth of christian faith, and on the possibility or impossibility of deriving factual assessments from speculative or ontological claims.
>
> (236)

Leaving aside the ambiguity introduced into Frei's discussion of Hegel by his use of the term "understanding" as a comprehensive one to cover Hegel's thought (when it actually is a technical term with which Hegel is critical of as an incomplete form of thought), what is clear is Frei's evaluation, positively and negatively, of Hegel's relation to realistic narrative. From the single sustained discussion of Hegel in *Eclipse* (316–18), let me quote just one of several succinct summaries:

> Though Hegel came closer than Schleiermacher to seeing narrative as its own continuity and meaning, it was finally the case for him that the meaning

is the common framework into which the interaction of incident and character is taken up, so that the interaction may be seen to be more than a contingent external relation, and that framework, at the phenomenological or interpretive rather than ontological level, is that of consciousness or knowing.

(317)

If one were to alter the end of this quotation to name the framework as the ultimate eschatological unity of all things in God through Christ and the Spirit, Frei's assessment might be occasion for encouraging a rereading of Hegel rather than not. Such an alteration, of course, is the kernel of Hegelian controversy.

Other of Frei's writings confirm the basic analysis of *Eclipse*. In the Niebuhr chapter, the priority of concept and thought to concrete reality is a primary characterization of Hegel, and in the Strauss essay there are considerable references to Hegel which tend, I think, to be more generous to the solution Hegel offers to the problems of relating *Glaube* and *Wissenshaft*. Frei reiterates Hegel's insight that the traditional doctrine of Christ is of the very essence of true rationality, and that to maintain this required Hegel to try

> to unite and balance the ideas of incarnation and redemption, to preserve the affectively religious within the conceptual aspect of consciousness, and of course to balance the idea of divine-human unity with its individual representation in Jesus of Nazareth.[34]

Frei is quite right, however, to press with Strauss the question of whether the historical manifestation of the divine-human unity in Jesus of Nazareth must indeed be an historical occurrence or only "the temporary, representational, believing consciousness taking this representational shape."[35] Hegel's emphasis on *Vorstellung,* or representation/image, should not be an obstacle to an appreciation of realistic narrative, but rather a quite companionable notion. Similarly, does Christian conceptual redescription need to be considered that different from the passage from representation to thought? The following considerations are the line of interpretation which encourages me to press such similarities.

Hegel makes no bones about what knowledge is essential to his understanding of Christ. In the 1827 edition of the *Lectures on the Philosophy of Religion* he states:

> The reconciliation in Christ, in which one believes, makes no sense if God is not known as the triune God, [if it is not recognized] that God *is,* but also is as the other, as self-distinguishing, so that this other is God himself, having implicitly the divine nature in it, and that the sublation of this difference, this otherness, and the return of love, are the Spirit.[36]

Lest one think such an appeal to the doctrine of the Trinity would only be part of a discussion of the Christian religion, we can note that in a section at the start of the third volume of the *Encyclopedia* where he develops at length the meaning of his comprehensive category, Spirit, Hegel uses the doctrine of the Trinity "to elucidate for ordinary thinking this unity of form and content present in mind (Spirit)."[37] I think it is important to note that it is a doctrine of the Trinity which is important to Hegel, and not only a Christology. Locating the latter in the former is vital for an appreciative reading of how he deals with the historical necessity and eschatological promise of the incarnation of God as one particular individual. For orthodox Christianity, though it may seem strange to put it this way, redemption through the incarnation is not the end of the story, much as realistic narrative is indispensable to the Christian scriptures but neither the whole form nor content of those scriptures.

The ordinary thinking which mistakes God for a merely transcendent dimension, if not an utterly transcendental one, is not a simple mistake. It is to be understood, from Hegel's perspective, within a progression through a series of attitudes or modes of thought (and for an understanding of that we could turn to the *Phenomenology* and observe with Hegel the various stages of human inventiveness in the matter of religion). Less often adverted to, however, are the first volume of the *Encyclopedia,* the *Logic,* and his discussion of the three attitudes of thought to objectivity. These three chapters of the *Logic* position Hegel in relation to a typology not unlike those Frei offered in *Eclipse*. In criticizing dogmatic metaphysics and its theology, Hegel insists that "if we are to have genuine cognition, the object must characterize its own self and not derive its predicates from without."[38] His critique of Deism and rational theology is that they do not follow this principle, and he applies the same criterion in his dismissal of so-called theology which lapses into either merely historical recounting of positions or simple repetition of Christian doctrine. Although Frei may not agree with the ultimate form of Hegel's theology, which Hegel himself says must be a real philosophy of religion as was done in the Middle Ages,[39] they share some common ground about the inadequacy of abstract conceptualizations of God.

In the chapter on the second attitude to objectivity, Hegel gives his critique of Kant. The previous principle is carried forward and to it is added a criticism of the categories of understanding and the limitation of reason as inadequate and unfounded. He follows a summation of Kant's system with the observation that the "plain mind" finds Kant's perspectivalism unacceptable. He continues:

> For the true statement of the case is rather as follows. The things of which we have direct consciousness are mere phenomena, not for us only, but in

their own nature; and the true and proper case of these things, finite as they are, is to have their existence founded not in themselves but in the universal divine Idea.[40]

Hegel thus calls his philosophy absolute idealism in contrast to Kant's subjective idealism. It is quite different from "vulgar realism" for it bears the same insight as religion, namely that it believes "the actual world we see, the sum total of existence to be created and governed by God."[41] Hegel insists not only upon the grounding of reality in the transcendent itself, but also on the revelation of the transcendent through the phenomenal. For Hegel, this move follows from, but is also a theological warrant for, why the positivity of revelation is indispensable.

Finally, the last chapter on objectivity is a critique of immediate or intuitive knowledge as the only access to the transcendent, particularly as put forward by Descartes and Jacobi. Thus, whether from the objective or subjective side, knowledge as unmediated is not knowledge for Hegel, especially knowledge of God.[42] This would be enhanced by a consideration of the importance of the study of language in the *Phenomenology* where it plays an essential role in the forwarding of the exposition and where a theory about language is at work. This is not language philosophy as the twentieth century knows it, but when combined with the discussion of language in the third part of the *Encyclopedia* one has an incipient view of language which clearly ties thought to it.[43]

Now we are in a position to grasp the significance of Hegel's remarks in his *Lectures on the Philosophy of Religion*, in their various editions, particularly the third part on the consummate religion. The task of analysis here could proceed through several stages, beginning with an account of the actual use of the biblical text by Hegel, of which there are many instances. In each edition of this section of the lectures, there are lengthy discussions of Christ's life, teaching, death, and resurrection (quite different from Hegel's early life of Jesus), all of which clearly are based upon the conviction that God is, and in fact had to be, made manifest in one, concrete, human individual, who was equally human and divine. Moreover, as already noted reconciliation in Christ cannot be understood independent of an understanding of God as triune. This doctrinal context may indeed result in Hegel's vocabulary and argument being that of absolute idealism, but I do not see an ultimate incompatibility between Hegel's exposition here and the insight of the indispensability of realistic narrative to Christianity. Frei's efforts to show the indispensability of realistic narrative and its importance for Christian self-description, if read as an inverse search for the essence of Christianity, have some common ground with Hegel in an emphasis on the radical mediation of God in Christ, the knowledge of that mediation in which the agent is known in his acts, the reconciliation it accomplishes once for all as inseparable from the actual life of Christ, narratively rendered for us.

IV

One of the key features of the loss of realistic narrative noted in the "Introduction" to *Eclipse* is the breakdown of the appropriate "procedure" by which realistic narrative can be located and analyzed. The operation such narrative performs is the articulating, rendering, deploying, depicting, and instantiating of the unity of person and action which is normative for Christian belief. The recovery of realistic narrative is the recovery of what is uniquely essential to the presence of Christ and which, given the particular history Frei has detailed, requires the refusal of a substitution of ideas, things, or forms of consciousness for that narrative and its rendered agent. I think this argument would be significantly aided by a broadening of the context of investigation and agenda of import beyond chiefly Protestant developments in the eighteenth and nineteenth centuries into origins in the fourteenth and fifteenth centuries, beyond the preoccupation with the doctrine and theology of Christ's person and work into trinitarian concerns, and beyond the helpful but limited concepts of twentieth-century philosophy. If realistic narrative requires "person" as a primary ontological category, then further explorations might take us to Hegel's appreciation of symbol and language, of the move from universality to particularity to individuality combined with a move from christological to trinitarian problems. None of these expansions are intended to contradict Frei's considerable achievement but to develop it, particularly by relativizing the two presuppositions concerning Christology and philosophy, and expanding and deepening the historical insights.

Essential to the retrieval and refusal which *Eclipse* launches is the recovery of something more than a lost "analytic procedure." Recovering the traditioning of interpretation, the community within which interpretation takes place, and the liturgical and spiritual life forms which embody the vitality of realistic narrative are equally important procedures. Perhaps Frei has already anticipated this suggestion and repudiated it, as is evident in a remark about Calvin in *Eclipse:*

> For Calvin, more clearly than for Luther, not the *act of recital or preaching* of a text, but the cumulative *pattern constituting the biblical narrative* (the identification of God's dealing with the world in the peculiar way depicted in the promise of the law and its fulfillment in the gospel) is the setting forth of the reality which simultaneously constitutes its effective rendering to the reader by the Spirit.
>
> (24)

And in a later writing he states outright:

> Not until the Protestant Reformation is the literal sense understood as authoritative—because perspicuous—in its own right, without authorization from the interpretive tradition.[44]

On both accounts, it would seem that realistic narrative must be somehow independent of liturgical enactment and the community of interpretation, just as it must not be reduced to ostensive or ideal reference, to subject matter, or to states of consciousness. But I can quote another passage which seems more attuned to my suggestions:

> The descriptive context, then, for the *sensus literalis* is the religion of which it is part, understood at once as a determinate code in which beliefs, ritual, and behavior patterns, ethos as well as narrative, come together as a common semiotic system, and also as the community which is that system in use—apart from which the very term ("semiotic system") is in this case no more than a misplaced metaphor.[45]

Even if our approach to realistic narrative remains perpetually asymptotic, my remarks have intended in some small part to explode *Eclipse* into that broader "common semiotic system" so that realistic narrative might shed a bit more of its own light.

NOTES

1. Hans Frei, *The Eclipse of Biblical Narrative* (New Haven: Yale University Press, 1974), 1. All further quotations from *Eclipse* will be noted in the text by page number.
2. George Lindbeck, "The Story Shaped Church: Critical Exegesis and Theological Interpretation," in *Scriptural Authority and Narrative Interpretation*, ed. G. Green (Philadelphia: Fortress Press, 1987): 161.
3. Ibid., 161.
4. The three types of biblical theology Frei discusses in Chapter 9 seem to cut across the other types, the key figures in each type being members of more than one of the major types, all of them of course being unable to deal with realistic narrative on its own terms.
5. It begins in earnest in Chapter 5, although there are references to it in previous chapters, and is located principally in Chapter 6, pp. 118–20, with additional comment in Chapter 7, pp. 124–36.
6. I refer to a typology of contemporary theology in a brief essay entitled "Typology of Modern Christian Thought" which was available only in mimeographed form at the time of writing this article.
7. "It is easy enough to fix (e.g.) Deist and Pietist responses to the consensus about the figure of Jesus; it is more challenging to ferret out what those in between were saying." Cf "Typology of Modern Christian Thought," 4.
8. It would also be extremely illuminating to place David Kelsey's seven types of usage of Scripture along side the typologies of *Eclipse* and the later Frei essay. Kelsey's continuum, from objectivization to subjectivization of the text, in

combination with his discussion of authority and canon, and the importance of the discrimen, provide a lucid and dynamic proposal for theology.

9. Also of importance would be an exploration of the formative influence, and perhaps problematic character, of Frei's reliance on Auerbach and Barth, or on commentators such as Hirsch. Searching out such influences and limiting factors would be a lengthy process.

10. Hans Frei, "Karl Barth: Theologian," in *Reflection* (New Haven: Yale Divinity School), 66/4., (January 28, 1969): 5–9; reprinted in *Theology and Narrative*, 167–76.

11. Ibid., 6. It is interesting to note that the quotation from Farrer occurs again in the 1988 work noted below in the collection of essays edited by McConnell.

12. Ibid., 6.

13. Hans Frei, "Barth and Schleiermacher: Divergence and Convergence," in *Barth and Schleiermacher: Beyond the Impasse?* ed. J. Duke and R. Streetman (Philadelphia: Fortress Press, 1988): 72.

14. Hans Frei, "Theology and the Interpretation of Narrative: Some Hermeneutical Considerations," 10. This essay was available only in mimeographed form at the time of writing this article.

15. Ibid., 16.

16. H. G. Reventlow, *The Authority of the Bible and the Rise of the Modern World* (Philadelphia: Fortress Press, 1985).

17. Ibid., 31.

18. One example familiar to me would be the realistic reading of the Gospels essential to Ignatius of Loyola's *Spiritual Exercises* (a contemporary of Calvin's), and the history of his taking distance from spiritualist tendencies and relating his sense of Scripture to liturgical and ecclesiastical practices.

19. Michael J. Buckley, S.J., *At the Origins of Modern Atheism* (New Haven: Yale University Press, 1987).

20. Ibid., 345.

21. Ibid., 361.

22. See, for example, F. J. van Beeck, *God Encountered* (San Francisco: Harper and Row, 1988), 183. Van Beeck goes on in this section of his work to make reference to and use *Eclipse*.

23. I will not follow Garrett Green's emphasis on *imagination* as a key to the use of Kant and Hegel, but rather will suggest that Kant and Hegel be reread for their incipient appreciation of language, the historical and the symbolic as educative of rational principles, and temporal sequence as associated with both.

24. Hans Frei, "Niebuhr's Theological Background," in *Faith and Ethics*, ed. P. Ramsey (New York: Harper and Row, 1957): 9–64.

25. Ibid., 33.

26. Hans Frei, "David Friedrich Strauss," in *Nineteenth Century Religious Thought in the West,* ed. O. Smart et al. (Cambridge: Cambridge University Press, 1985), vol 1: 215–60.

27. Immanuel Kant, *The Critique of Pure Reason* (New York: St. Martin's Press, 1965), 486.
28. Ibid., 486–7. The reference to a romance, given Frei's analysis of the lack of realism in German letters, would have Kant appear to be perceptive about the unsatisfactory character of that genre as a vehicle for the life of Christ.
29. Immanuel Kant, *Religion within the Limits of Reason Alone* (New York: Harper and Row, 1960), 56–7.
30. Kant, *Critique of Pure Reason*, 497.
31. Ibid., 533.
32. Ibid., 568.
33. I am indebted to M. Martin for his exploration and tentative conclusions on this matter. Cf. M. Martin, "Kant's 'Religion within the Limits of Reason Alone' as Elucidated by His Philosophy of History: The Emergence of an Applied Doctrine of Symbol," unpublished MA thesis, Regis College, Toronto.
34. Frei, *Strauss*, 228.
35. Ibid., 230.
36. G. W. F. Hegel, *Lectures on the Philosophy of Religion* (Berkeley: University of California Press, 1985), vol. III, 327.
37. G. W. F. Hegel, *Philosophy of Mind* (Oxford: Clarendon Press, 1971), 17.
38. G. W. F. Hegel, *The Logic of Hegel* (Oxford: Oxford University Press, 1892), 64.
39. Ibid., 73.
40. Ibid., 93–4.
41. Ibid., 94.
42. In addition, Hegel's early work, *Faith and Knowledge* (Albany: State University of New York Press, 1977), on Kant, Jacobi, and Fichte is an alternate account of these attitudes.
43. Hegel, *Philosophy of Mind*, 221.
44. H. Frei, "The 'Literal Reading' of Biblical Narrative in the Christian Tradition: Does it Stretch or Will It Break?" in *The Bible and the Narrative Tradition*, ed. F. McConnell (Oxford: Oxford University Press, 1986): 42.
45. Frei, "Literal Reading," 70–1.

CHAPTER TWELVE

Meaning and Truth in Narrative Interpretation: A Reply to George Schner

BRUCE D. MARSHALL

George Schner's discussion of *The Eclipse of Biblical Narrative* contains much helpful analysis and suggests some thought-provoking lines of criticism and potential development. In particular, his "seven views" of *The Eclipse* strike me as in many respects an illuminating summary and explication of that important and difficult text. But rather than comment piecemeal on various points in Schner's analysis and criticism, I would like to concentrate briefly on one issue which he raises: the theological force of the "historical study under a thesis" (*Eclipse*, p. 10) which constitutes the argument of *The Eclipse,* and in particular the way in which two different kinds of "philosophic preferences," to use Schner's phrase, might detract from or intensify the theological impact of that argument.[1]

Schner is, I think, right to argue that *The Eclipse* is written "for a theological and pastoral purpose," and that while this is clearly not the only purpose of the book, it can be characterized fairly, to use his term, as the "ultimate" one. The proximate and more obvious theological purpose is the reconstruction of the possibility of a realistic narrative reading of the Bible, and especially of the gospels; for this sort of reading Frei explicitly took "Barth's biblical exegesis" as "a model" (*Eclipse,* p. viii). As Schner suggests, the final but less evident theological purpose is specifically christological. Frei displays the rise to dominance of various non-narrative readings of the Bible as a sequence of historical contingencies which must be understood against the constant background of the alternative possibility, widely recognized but increasingly ignored, of realistic narrative reading. In the final analysis, it seems, he does so in order to provide historical and conceptual support for the development of Christologies quite different from those which have arisen in tandem with the eclipse of narrative reading. The kinds of Christology the argument of *The Eclipse* may be seen as aiming to support can be characterized as those in which that identification of the particular person Jesus of Nazareth uniquely provided by a realistic narrative reading of the gospels is logically basic to and decisive for all of our talk about his significance or "specific messiahship" (*Eclipse,* p. 278), and thus indirectly to all our talk about God and ourselves. Here again Barth is clearly though not explicitly the model. (Whether one could know these things without having read *The Identity of Jesus Christ* I'm not sure, but perhaps the remarks which follow will help it seem plausible that one could.)

Schner suggests that the overall argument of *The Eclipse*, including its aim of supporting a Christology rooted in narrative readings of the gospels, would be promoted by a rereading of Kant and Hegel. I'm happy to join him in rereading Kant and Hegel, although I confess to grave doubts about whether the christological purpose he rightly finds lurking in *The Eclipse* is likely to find much support in either of them. This can be seen, I think, from Schner's own reconstruction of the argument of *The Eclipse*. Along with a number of others, Schner maintains that a key contribution of *The Eclipse* lies in its exposure of a basic tendency in modern biblical interpretation to identify the meaning or sense of a narrative text with its putative, ostensive, or ideal reference. More broadly, this tendency can be described, in language from *The Eclipse* (p. 278) quoted by Schner, as the nearly universal affirmation that "understanding the text's subject matter (*Sache*) has priority over understanding its words, indeed that the text's words have to be interpreted through the subject" (or, as I would prefer to say, interpreted through a *description* of the subject matter which is logically independent of the narrative in meaning, at least in part). This historically contingent interpretive tendency made it virtually impossible to read the gospels as realistic narratives, in which, as Frei puts it, "meaning ... is not *illustrated* (as though it were an intellectually presubsisting or preconceived archetype or ideal essence) but *constituted* through the mutual, specific determination of agents, speech, social context, and circumstances that form the indispensable narrative web" (*Eclipse,* p. 280).

As Schner's quotations from them clearly show, Kant and Hegel shared with almost all of their Enlightenment and Idealist companions in Germany, though not with the Enlightenment in France and England, a continuing fascination with the narrative texts of the Bible, especially the gospels, and with the trinitarian and christological doctrines classically regarded as indispensable to the right interpretation of those narratives. In quite different ways, each writer wanted to make something positive out of both the narratives and the doctrines. But recognizing this is a rather different matter from showing that either one was interested in narrative interpretation of the biblical texts in anything like Frei's sense of the term. Two of the key features of this kind of interpretation, as Schner rightly argues, are the constitution of meaning by the verbal shape of the narrative and the closely correlative identification of the subject matter of a narrative text with its verbal sense. It seems to me that Kant and Hegel both repudiate, with remarkable systematic power, this sort of interpretation. They oppose what Frei characterizes as narrative interpretation on at least three different points: (1) each insists, in both theory and practice, on the separation of the meaning and subject matter of narrative texts from their verbal sense; (2) each maintains that the meaning and subject matter of the "fact-like descriptions" which constitute the biblical narratives can be "known apart" from those narratives, however indispensable the narratives are in "the representation" of what is thus independently known (to use language of Frei from *Eclipse*, p. 340, note 21, also quoted by Schner); (3) the independently described subject matter "gives the rule" for the right interpretation of the narratives themselves (to put the point in Kantian terms).

Showing this would, of course, require an extensive textual argument. For the moment, let me simply call to mind one well-known passage from Hegel, in the *Lectures on the Philosophy of History*. Arguing against those who would allow nothing in Christology except what is permitted by historical criticism (on this point Hegel and Frei have, to be sure, a common enemy!), Hegel maintains that "if Christ is to be looked upon only as an excellent, even impeccable individual, and nothing more, the conception of the Speculative Idea of Absolute Truth is ignored. But this [viz., the speculative idea] is the desideratum, the point from which we have to start. Make of Christ what you will, exegetically, critically, historically"—and, presumably, narratively—"... let all such circumstances have been what they might—the only [question of concern] is: What is the Idea or the Truth in and for itself?"[2] Stephen Crites puts the point of this remark, I think, quite precisely: "The speculative idea is the truth of Christianity, and thus 'the point from which we have to start' in construing Christian doctrine properly. It will stand regardless of what we make historically of 'the Christian fact'"—or, again, what we make of the Christian narrative.[3]

Schner stresses that his appeal to Kant and Hegel is in the service of a more basic aim: to make Frei's argument in *The Eclipse* accessible to contemporary Catholic theologians, and to facilitate a conversation between them and those theologians, mostly Protestant, who are already sympathetic to Frei. With this aim I am in complete agreement—not only for the sake of contemporary Catholic theology, but even more for the future of Frei's work, which very much needs this vast theological audience, and could well find a home in its midst. Thus my skepticism about the way Schner attempts to accomplish his aim coexists with considerable hope for the aim itself. I wonder if there are not other ways in which it might be realized, although I will not speculate about them here.

Moreover, I agree with Schner that precisely for theological purposes the argument of *The Eclipse* can be enriched and strengthened by drawing some further philosophical discussions into its orbit. Among these the lively debate in contemporary Anglo-American philosophy about meaning and truth strikes me as especially helpful. Casting our net in this direction brings us closer to Frei's original "philosophic preferences" than would turning to Kant and Hegel, but it is not this which makes drawing on the current debate about meaning and truth helpful. The value of doing so lies rather in exposing more clearly the logical force latent in Frei's largely historical argument, especially in what that argument suggests about the relationship between the interpretation of narrative texts and the basic truth commitments which inform the interpretation. I will here have time only for a few schematic observations.

As a historical argument, *The Eclipse* makes a detailed case that the modern tendency to interpret narrative texts through an independent description of their subject matter was a dramatic change from earlier Christian interpretation of the Bible. But woven into the historical account is the very strong suggestion that theologically this was not simply a change, but a mistake—and that current theological use of the Bible, especially in Christology, should not continue to accept this tendency but should redevelop genuinely realistic narrative readings of the text.

What is less clear is why the interpretive change should be regarded as a mistake. Simply to observe that it is a departure from earlier Christian practice does not *per se* make it wrong, however much one is attracted to the earlier practice. In *The Eclipse* Frei suggests that the problem lies in a distortion of the distinctive character of narrative texts, in which "the text, the verbal sense, and not a profound, buried stratum underneath constitutes or determines the subject matter itself" (*Eclipse*, p. 280). There is surely something in this. But one of Frei's clear "philosophic preferences" is the broadly Wittgensteinian one for finding the meaning of language by analyzing the way it is used in specific contexts. Given this "philosophic preference," one cannot easily maintain that narratives, any more than other sorts of discourse, have a fixed, intrinsic sense (or subject matter, if the latter is inextricably linked to sense) that cuts across variant contexts of their use. So it remains puzzling what makes the dramatic modern interpretive shift a mistake, and not simply a partial though quite significant change in the meaning of these texts when they are used in new and different contexts for new and different purposes. (One could, of course, appeal to the anticipated theological, and especially christological, results of a reconstructed narrative reading, but since the results are supposed to be based logically on the narrative reading, that would smack of circularity.)

Here is where the contemporary philosophical discussion of meaning and truth can, I think, be helpful. In particular, I have in mind the train of thought perhaps most powerfully represented by Donald Davidson. Developing especially ideas of Tarski and Quine, Davidson argues, in a word, that meaning is truth-dependent. A theory of meaning which is neither circular nor question-begging must proceed without assuming knowledge on the interpreter's part of the intentions (more precisely, what Davidson calls the propositional attitudes) of the speaker (because, as Frei would agree, grasping the meaning of a speaker's or author's situated discourse or action is the only way we can know his or her intentions [cf. *Eclipse*, p. 281]). The only plausible way to construct a workable account of meaning, Davidson argues, is to regard the successful interpreter as holding for truth while testing for meaning, that is, as maximizing the ascription of truth to a speaker's sentences in the effort to discern what they mean. This is clearest in the situation of radical interpretation, where people are uttering sounds that seem to be sentences in a language which is totally unfamiliar to us. The only way to find out what these sentences mean is to identify which ones are held true by the speaker (initially following behavioral clues) and to assign a meaning to them which enables them to be held true by the interpreter as well, according to the only standards available, namely the interpreter's own. If we find ourselves assigning meanings in such a way that we end up ascribing massive falsity to sentences the speakers hold true, then our only plausible course is to regard our interpretations, and not the speakers' sentences, as in the main mistaken. The more unwilling the speaker is to give up holding a sentence true, the more the interpreter should try to assign a meaning to it which enables it to be held true, and to interpret other sentences in a manner consistent with the meaning thereby assigned. Of course it will not always be possible to do this; sometimes, precisely in order to maximize agreement on sentences held true, we will have to interpret some sentences regarded as true by the speaker as having a meaning to the truth of which we the interpreters cannot assent.[4]

This line of thought touches on only one aspect of the way Davidson relates meaning, truth, and belief (sentences held true), and there is, of course, a complex argument behind it. Working that argument out and applying it to the matter at hand (viz., the character of narrative meaning) would be tricky, not least because of differences between interpretation within a natural language and across natural languages, and between written and spoken language. But the upshot, I will venture to guess, would be roughly this: if modern biblical interpretation made a mistake about the meaning of the gospel narratives (or a series of mistakes rooted in a mistake about the way narrative meaning is constituted), it was ultimately because they made a mistake about the truth of the gospel narratives. Or, more precisely, it was because they interpreted the narratives which identify Jesus as a particular person without ascribing primacy or centrality to those narratives in deciding about truth. As Frei shows, what modern interpreters repeatedly did was interpret the gospel texts (from different points on the complex three-dimensional theological map Frei draws) in terms of an independent description of their subject matter. In light of a truth-dependent account of meaning, this is to say (again roughly) that there was a decisive shift in the sentences that modern interpreters were least willing to give up, that is, cease holding true, and thus in their primary or central criteria of truth (i.e., in those sentences with which all the rest of their beliefs had at least to agree). It was no longer the gospel texts, read as identifying Jesus as the central character in a unique and ultimately redemptive narrative plot, which had this function; indeed biblical interpreters in the period Frei covers found it increasingly difficult to hold the texts true at all when they were read in this way. Yet they were almost always unwilling simply to reject the gospel texts as false, and so quite naturally (in good Davidsonian fashion) interpreted them to conform to their various—now at least partly independent—conceptions of what was historically, ideally, or otherwise religiously true and significant. They did this, it is important to stress, precisely in order to find truth in the gospel texts, although in a situation in which they could no longer regard them as true when taken as realistic narratives (and so as texts embodying the unity of verbal sense and subject matter which Frei takes to be a hallmark of such narratives). Without talking explicitly about the relation between truth and meaning, Frei frequently proposes a logically similar analysis of modern interpreters.[5]

So, if modern interpreters did not read the Bible, and especially the gospels, as a realistic narrative, it was not because they failed to notice intrinsic features of the texts which require that they be read that way. Indeed, as Frei often avers, they *did* notice the features which support narrative interpretation, but preferred not to heed them, thinking they had good reasons to interpret the texts differently. (In doing so, to be sure, they did not usually explicitly consider and reject narrative interpretation as an option.) These "good reasons" were simply what I have called their primary truth commitments, with which, as we all do, they tried to make the rest of their beliefs (including their interpretation of the Bible) agree. The interpretations generated by this procedure may be on the whole less plausible than those generated by realistic narrative readings, but they are usually not *impossible,* and their proponents can and do argue that any sacrifice of interpretive plausibility is more than made up for by a gain in the credibility of the result (as, it seems to me, Kant and Hegel basically did).

If, therefore, the general absence of realistic narrative interpretation in modern theology was a mistake, it was so because the various primary truth commitments of most modern theology were mistaken—not that they were necessarily false, but that they were mistakenly taken as primary. Conversely, the only way finally to ensure that the *meaning* of the gospel texts won't shift away from that which they have as realistic narratives is for a narrative reading of these texts to function as epistemically primary, that is, for such a reading to provide the primary criteria of truth, and that on the broadest possible scale. This, to recall my earlier question to Frei, is the *use* of these texts which adequately secures their narrative *sense*. And this, it seems, is also what Frei's theological cognate (in *The Identity of Jesus Christ*) to his claim about the unity of narrative sense and subject matter implies: to grasp the identity of Jesus in the text (the "verbal sense") is to have him (the "subject matter") present in his crucified and living reality; to understand *this* narrative is to know its truth. If this is the case then there are no further criteria of truth to which one need appeal to decide the truth of this narrative and in terms of which one might interpret it; and so it is *eo ipso* the primary criterion of truth, in terms of which all else must be interpreted. Thus, we return to the type of Christology which it seems, *The Eclipse* aims to support. If the moderns made a mistake in biblical interpretation with regard to the narratives, it was ultimately because they made a christological mistake: they failed to see the narratively identified Jesus as epistemically primary and in that sense as logically basic to and decisive for all of our talk about God and ourselves.

NOTES

1. All references to Hans W. Frei, *The Eclipse of Biblical Narrative* (New Haven: Yale University Press, 1974) will be made parenthetically in the text.
2. G. W. F. Hegel, *The Philosophy of History,* trans. J. Sibree (New York: Dover, 1956), 325–6.
3. Stephen Crites, "Dialectics and Apologetics in Yerkes's Interpretation of Hegel," *The Journal of Religion* 60 (1980): 216. The phrase "the Christian fact" comes from Yerkes, of whose book on Hegel's Christology this article is an extended review.
4. The gist of Davidson's argument is perhaps most accessibly presented in "A Coherence Theory of Truth and Knowledge," in *Truth and Interpretation: Perspectives on the Philosophy of Donald Davidson,* ed. Ernest LePore (Oxford: Blackwell, 1986): 307–19; see also Davidson's important "Afterthoughts" to this article in Alan Malichowski (ed), *Reading Rorty* (Oxford: Blackwell, 1990). It is perhaps pertinent to note that this essay was originally published in Germany in a volume entitled *Kant oder Hegel?*.
5. See, for example, his assessment of Strauss: had Strauss considered the possibility of narrative reading more seriously, he would have been forced "to face the possibility that the meaning of the gospel story is that very focus on the narrated enactment of the specific messiahship of Jesus which he found factually incredible and therefore religiously impossible" *(Eclipse,* p. 278). It was, in other words, precisely because Strauss could not hold a narrative reading to be true that, still wanting to find truth in the text, he was impelled to interpret it in another way.

PART FIVE

Hans Frei's Achievement

CHAPTER THIRTEEN

Hans Frei, George Lindbeck, and the Objectivity of Scripture

MIKE HIGTON

ABSTRACT

Scripture's objectivity is its capacity to yield a sense not dictated by its readers. It is scripture's capacity to stand over against those readers, interrupting them and calling them to repentance. George Lindbeck and Hans Frei have often been understood to sit light to or even to abandon such objectivity, and to claim instead that the sense of scripture is constituted by the church's use. Yet both of them believed that a focus on the church's use of scripture was compatible with an insistence upon its objectivity. More than that, they believed that a focus on the church's use of scripture is necessary for a full account of its objectivity. To miss Lindbeck and Frei's double emphasis on objectivity and use is to misunderstand the relationship between them, the nature of their postliberalism, and the contribution that their work might make to current hermeneutical debates.

I developed some elements of the presentation of Lindbeck in this chapter in "Reconstructing *The Nature of Doctrine*," *Modern Theology* 30, no. 1 (2014): 1–31, and in "George Lindbeck and the Christological Nature of Doctrine," *Criswell Theological Review* 13, no. 1 (2015): 47–62. Elements of the argument appear in *The Life of Christian Doctrine* (London: Bloomsbury, 2020), ch. 7. I presented a version of it a seminar at St. Andrew's chaired by Steve Holmes, and another in Cambridge chaired by Simeon Zahl; I am grateful for all the feedback I received.

INTRODUCTION

In *The Drama of Doctrine*, Kevin Vanhoozer wrote—wrongly—of Hans Frei and George Lindbeck that

> There is a palpable tension between their professed intertextuality, on the one hand, and their focus on the church's use of Scripture, on the other. The urgent question for cultural-linguistic theology is whether genuine Christian identity is received through the apostolic witness—mediated by the biblical text—or whether it is produced in and by the community's performance, a social construction.[1]

This is one version of a widespread criticism of Frei and Lindbeck. It is my aim in this article to explain why it misses its mark.[2] Both Frei and Lindbeck, I will argue, insist upon the objectivity of scripture. By "the objectivity of scripture," I mean scripture's capacity to yield a sense not dictated by its readers. It is scripture's ability to stand over against those readers, interrupting them and calling them to repentance. Both Frei and Lindbeck believe that an insistence upon such objectivity is not only entirely compatible with, but is in fact supported by a focus on the church's use of scripture. To miss this double emphasis on objectivity and use (or to construe it as a "palpable tension") is to misunderstand the relationship between Frei and Lindbeck, the nature of their postliberalism, and the contribution that their work might make to current debates.

THE CRITICISM

Vanhoozer's presentation of his "canonical-linguistic" approach to the theological interpretation of scripture includes a sustained conversation with Lindbeck, sprinkled with asides about Frei. Vanhoozer acknowledges that Lindbeck insists upon the authority of the biblical text, but argues that "a closer inspection shows that he relocates authority in the church."[3] Instead of "Scripture as used by God, even, or perhaps especially, when such use is *over against* the church," Lindbeck gives authority to "Scripture as used by the church"[4] and insists that "only church practice gives the text its sense."[5] This is quite wrong, according to Vanhoozer. "Theologians", he says, "should pay less attention to how this or that Christian community uses the Bible (the *sensus fidelium*) and greater attention to the Bible as itself a communicative act of the triune God."[6]

Vanhoozer draws attention to Lindbeck's claim that "the meaning ascribed to texts is underdetermined to the extent that their use in shaping life and thought is unspecified."[7] This means, according to Vanhoozer, that there is, for

Lindbeck "no such thing as 'the' sense of the text."[8] And Vanhoozer thinks he sees the same idea in Frei: "Because a text can have a multiplicity of senses, Frei felt obliged to turn to the tradition of Scripture use in the church in order to secure stable meaning. Frei's argument amounts to the claim that *for Christians*, the biblical narratives render the identity of Jesus Christ."[9] This means, Vanhoozer argues, that for both Frei and Lindbeck "the biblical text ultimately cannot make sense on its own terms." It lacks the independent objectivity it would need to stand over against the life of the church.[10]

The late John Webster offered a similar argument. He acknowledged that, for Lindbeck, scripture does indeed shape the church. It is "a durable linguistic artefact which organises the Christian religious and cultural system, and so shapes Christian thought, speech, and action."[11] But this is, in Lindbeck's presentation, a norm securely possessed by the church, a norm with which the church has settled and made its peace. Lindbeck therefore has (Webster thinks) no serious account of how the text of scripture can serve "the *viva vox Dei*" as it breaks out *against* the life of the church.[12]

For Webster, by contrast, "Attending to Scripture … is not a matter of being socialised, but of being caught up in the dissolution of all society—including and especially church culture—through the word of the one who smites the earth with the rod of his mouth."[13] "Scripture is not," he says,

> the domestic talk of the Christian faith, or simply its familiar semiotic system. It is the sword of God, issuing from the mouth of the risen one. And that is why there can be no 'coinherence of Bible and Church', no 'mutually constitutive reciprocity' between the scriptural witness and the community of the Word, but only of their asymmetry.[14]

GEORGE LINDBECK

Lindbeck is, of course, best known for *The Nature of Doctrine*[15]—though he insisted that the book "was, and still is, peripheral to my main concerns" and that it is "misinterpreted when its purpose of supplying theoretical warrants for ecumenical practice is disregarded, as has often been done."[16] Lindbeck was seeking to do justice to practices of theological reasoning that he had encountered in formal ecumenical dialogues in the 1960s and '70s. His book was an attempt, by means of a new account of the nature of doctrine, to describe, steady, and direct this ecumenical reasoning. It was a book written in service of the basic ecumenical goal of reading the various Christian denominations as diverse forms of faithfulness to the one God who has revealed Godself in Jesus Christ.

One of the distinctive moves that Lindbeck makes in the book is to emphasize the *descriptive* task of theology. He points his readers to the ethnographic work of Clifford Geertz, and to Geertz's practice of "thick description," and suggests that theology will take a similar form. Christian theology should involve, it seems, the description of Christian practice, and the identification of the grammar embodied in it. Doctrines—statements of normative Christian teaching—can be thought of as expressions of such grammar. They are, in other words, rules for Christian practice, and it sounds like they must be rules designed to keep Christian practice in a shape that it already possesses. It is not hard to see how Vanhoozer concluded that Lindbeck "relocates authority in the church." Specifically, Lindbeck appears to relocate authority in the already-achieved shape of the church's practice.

Lindbeck adds to this account the claims that the church's practice is its way of inhabiting scripture, and that the grammar embodied in this practice includes the church's rules for reading scripture. It is not hard to see how he can be read as domesticating scripture within the life of the church, treating it as a possession of the church which (in Webster's words) "organises the Christian religious and cultural system." It does seem that, for Lindbeck, scripture supports the settled shape of the church's life—and is captive to it.

The Nature of Doctrine is, however, a misleading anchor for making good sense of Lindbeck's thought.[17] As I have argued at some length elsewhere, his account in that book is got up in clothes borrowed for the occasion, including in ones borrowed from Geertz. The analogy between postliberal theology and Geertzian ethnography is a lot less close than Lindbeck's text initially suggests—and that is especially true if we ask in more detail what *kind* of description of the church's life Lindbeck's theology actually involves.[18]

If we look at works that Lindbeck wrote before *The Nature of Doctrine*, it becomes clear that Lindbeck's turn to description is theologically driven. The shape of the life of the church, held in place by its doctrinal rules, is the church's response to God. The church is supposed, by the grace of God, to correspond to God's being and will—with as realist a sense of correspondence as one could wish.[19] That is, the church's response to God is true if and only if it is aligned to the being and will of a God whose existence and nature are in no way dependent upon the church.[20]

This is not in itself, of course, enough to undermine the criticism offered by Vanhoozer and Webster. It certainly rules out the idea that truth *consists* in performance (such that to say that some Christian form of life is "true" means no more than that it conforms to the shape of life embodied by the church). It leaves open, however, the possibility that performance might *guarantee* truth. That is, it leaves open the possibility that conformity to the form of life already embodied by the Christian community be sufficient to make one's practice correspond to God—presumably because that form of life is a God-given means for creating such correspondence. Obedience to God and obedience to the church would, in such a view, be functionally equivalent, and Vanhoozer's and Webster's criticism would stand.

If we look at Lindbeck's work after *The Nature of Doctrine*, however, we find an antidote to such thinking. In that work, we can see him deepening and extending an emphasis upon the *sinfulness* of the church, and its need for ongoing reformation. That idea had certainly been present in his earlier work, but it now became one of his dominant concerns. After *The Nature of Doctrine*, Lindbeck associates the theme with discussion of the church's relation to Israel. He insists that Israel and the church are not related as type and antitype (with sinful Israel now superseded by the holy Church) but that "the kingdom already present in Christ alone is the antitype, and both Israel and the church are types."[21] In this pattern, the Jews are acknowledged to be (as portrayed in scripture) a sinful people—but so is the church. The church's story is, we must both acknowledge and expect, a story of fallings away, of disastrous choices, of faithlessness and of necessary repentance—no less than (and perhaps more than) the story of the people of Israel in the pages of the Hebrew Bible.[22]

As well as providing a vocabulary in which Lindbeck can talk in general about the sinfulness of the church, this account provides him with a central example of the church's sinfulness. The pattern that Lindbeck favors—"Israel and the church as type; Christ as antitype"—was not the pattern of thinking that came to dominate the church's imagination or to shape its practice. It is not the pattern that came to give the church its dominant grammar. It was overtaken by another pattern: "Israel as type, church as antitype." In that pattern, Israel is deemed faithless, the church faithful; Israel rejects grace, the church basks in it; Israel lacks the Spirit, but the church is the Spirit's community. This pattern, Lindbeck argues, made possible "the ecclesiological triumphalism of a *theologiae gloriae*."[23] It was a mistake with "monstrous offspring."[24]

This is not simply a matter of a holy church, its life shaped in conformity to the being and will of God, nevertheless suffering a moment of aberration, a stain upon its purity. It is not an error which a turn back to the well-embodied grammar of the church's current existence can correct. Lindbeck is clear that supersessionism is a deep-seated, pervasive, and persistent disordering of the Christian faith. It is an error embedded in the grammar of that faith, and it will require a thoroughgoing reformation before it is undone.[25]

Lindbeck is equally clear about the implications of all this for the church's relation to scripture. It means that the church's ways of inhabiting scripture, of exploring and performing the strange new world within the bible, can (and do) take the form of distortions of that biblical world. And some of those distortions are egregious.[26] "[I]t is no exaggeration", he insists, "to say that the great majority of Christians, not excepting the theologians whom we most honor as our ancestors in the faith, have at this point heard the voice of the devil quoting Scripture when they thought they were listening to God."[27]

Yet if the church's practice, including its reading of scripture, can be distorted, Lindbeck also insists that scripture can be the means by which the church is called by God to repentance. He expresses this most clearly when discussing (as he does throughout his work) the Reformation *solas*—especially the *sola scriptura* and the *solus Christus*.[28] The central point of these *solas*, for Lindbeck, is precisely to hold the church—including the deep doctrinal grammar of its present practice—open to question.[29] "The *sola scriptura*," he says, "and the eschatological Lordship of the coming Christ to which it bears witness, forbids the formal attribution of irreversibility to even the most necessary dogmatic developments."[30]

Taking the *solas* seriously (in a sense to which we will return shortly) should teach the church an orientation to scripture that acknowledges its authority, and accepts that scripture can and must act as "judge of the Church."[31] Acknowledging that we inhabit a sinful church, and that there is no telling in advance how deep are the distortions that mar the church's life and witness, Lindbeck calls the church to turn to scripture as the means by which God will judge and renew its life.

That brings us, finally, to Lindbeck's scriptural hermeneutics. In *The Nature of Doctrine* itself, Lindbeck's hermeneutical comments are very brief, but they are filled out and developed considerably in several later essays.[32] What emerges is a consistent claim that *if* scripture is approached by Christians in the right manner then it can provide the means by which God both forms them for holiness, and speaks out against their continued unholiness. It will be both with *and* over against them. The "right manner" is to approach scripture "as a Christ-centered and typologically unified whole with figural applications to all reality."[33] More fully, it is to approach scripture as "a canonically and narrationally unified and internally glossed (that is, self-referential and self-interpreting) whole centred on Jesus Christ, and telling the story of the dealings of the Triune God with his people and his world in ways which are typologically ... applicable to the present."[34]

It is true that, for Lindbeck, the "right manner" is a manner that we are taught primarily by the faithful practice of earlier generations of Christians. Yet this way of reading is not an invention of the church, nor is it an imposition of a sense on scripture by the church. It does not involve the church deciding what scripture will mean for them. It is the church's acknowledgment of a sense that is not theirs to dictate.

A focus on the church's practice of scriptural reading need not be in any tension with a focus on the ability of scripture to stand over against the practice of the church. Consider, as an analogy, the activity of counting the pages in this book. This book is the length that it is, and that length is in no way subject to my whims. I can nevertheless talk about this activity of page-counting as a practice that has a particular, contingent shape to it. I can talk about the forms of attention and the skills that I need to pursue it. I can talk about the history of the activity (the shift from counting sheets with recto and verso sides to counting pages; the rise of double numbering systems with roman numerals for prolegomena and Arabic for the body, the complications introduced by a shift to online publication, and so on). I can talk about the way in which, at different points in that history, I would actually be asking slightly different questions, and so would come up with different answers—not because the length of the book issue depended upon my practice, but because my changing questions would be getting at slightly different facts about the book. And I can also talk about the process by which I have ended up thinking that this is an important thing for me to be doing with this object—the practical contexts within which numbering pages makes a difference. None of this need be in any competition with a recognition of the objectivity of the answers that this practice yields. Similarly, the bare fact that Lindbeck focuses on the church's practice of reading, speaking of it as a practice that has a particular contingent shape to it, and a history, does not by itself imply that he denies the objectivity of scripture.

The pattern of reading that Lindbeck identifies is one that he believes emerged as the Spirit led the church into the truth revealed in scripture. It was as much learnt *from* scripture as it was brought *to* scripture.[35] Humanly speaking, that history could, of course, have gone quite differently. The church could have adopted some other approach to scripture (a wholesale allegorization, for instance). It was not inevitable that Christians would learn to read in the way Lindbeck describes, and it remains possible for people to approach the text as if it is some other kind of reality (rather than being God's faithful witness to Godself). If they are to be brought up against its Christ-centered objectivity, Christians need to learn this particular way of reading.[36] They need to be guided into it. Without such guidance, they might read in all sorts of ways that would allow them to miss the Triune God's self-testimony.

To accept that the faithful practice of earlier generations of Christians can lead one into the true way of reading does involve some kind of reliance upon that practice. In Lindbeck's terms, it involves, a "confidence that the Holy Spirit guides the church into the truth."[37] Yet the truth into which the Holy Spirit has guided the church is precisely the truth that the church is not the source, standard, or guarantee of truth. It is the truth that the church must look outside itself, to a standard that it does not control, for its guidance and correction. And this truth entails that even the guidance that has led us into this form of reading must itself be subjected to testing by further practice of this form of reading.

Lindbeck fills out what it means for the church to provide this guidance by attending to the *regula fidei*, produced by the early church. He sees the *regula* as comprising a set of "low-level generalizations" about the nature and purpose of scripture, and the approach proper to its interpretation. The emergence of the *regula* was not, however, a matter of Irenaeus (for example) describing the way his community happened to read various passages, and treating those readings as authoritative because they came from his church. Rather, the *regula* is (as Lindbeck reads it) a summary of what Irenaeus believed the church had been shown, by the Spirit, through the medium of the text, to be scripture's overarching message, and what the church had been taught by the Spirit of the disciplines appropriate to reading this text, given its nature and its place in the purposes of God.

When Lindbeck speaks of scripture as "a canonically and narrationally unified ... whole centred on Jesus Christ, and telling the story of the dealings of the Triune God with his people and his world," he is summarizing the *regula fidei* as a rule for reading scripture.[38] And whatever he might have said about ethnographic approaches, this is the only kind of description of the church's use of scripture that Lindbeck actually pursues. This account of scripture's nature, and the practice of reading which yielded it and which it supported, emerged (as Lindbeck understands it) as the church was taught by the Spirit to read. And having been taught to read in this way, the church can be brought up against the action of God working through scripture.[39] "The *regula fidei* which developed into the trinitarian and christological affirmations of the early church," he says, "was needed to make sure that the Bible is not read any old way (as the ancient gnostics and contemporary deconstructionists do), but as testimony to and from the creator God whose Word enfleshed is Jesus Christ."[40]

The *regula fide* does not dictate what the interpretation of the text will yield. Rather, it helps to hold in place a way of approaching the text, as testimony to and from the creator God whose Word enfleshed is Jesus Christ. The actual interpretation of the text is done by faithful Christians in the contexts in which they find themselves, as, so guided, they discern prayerfully and diligently what the text as a whole demands of them in those situations. It is true that such interpretation is, for Lindbeck, made determinate in practice. That does not mean, however, that the church decides what the text means, making a choice between a range of equally plausible possible senses left open by the indeterminateness of the text. Lindbeck is not saying that the church's practice determines what the text means. Rather, it is in practice that the church declares (and can't help but declare) in its most determinate form what it finds the text to mean. The church may well, in the process, *mis*take the text—and, as we have seen Lindbeck insist, it has often done so, sometimes very deeply. And so these determinate lived interpretations are properly subject to correction by ongoing reading. The *regula* helps the church to practice this ongoing reading in such a way as to hold itself open to such correction—to the possibility of finding its conscience "compelled by Scripture itself" toward repentance.[41]

The church's continued reading of scripture as witness to Christ is, in other words, not about preserving some already achieved identity, but about holding open the possibility of "communal self-criticism."[42] Diligent attention to the text is attention to meaning as "constituted by the text, not by something outside of it," emerging from the whole canonical metanarrative centered upon the gospel narration of Jesus Christ. It is a form of attention that involves a constant struggle to avoid our "reflex tendency" to "project our ideas into the Bible."[43] Such diligent reading does, by the grace of God, have the capacity to call the church away from its mistakes (even if it might sometimes take centuries, and the Spirit working upon the church through all kinds of external stimuli, to drive the church back to scripture with re-opened eyes, and for this capacity to be realized). It is as the church goes on reading the text in all the situations in which it finds itself, as it goes on staking itself in practice on determinate readings, goes on testing its readings, and goes on being corrected, that it is led by the Spirit deeper into the true meaning of the text.[44]

The question that Lindbeck's account (if taken on its own) leaves open, however, is just *how* it is that the text, read in the way that he describes, genuinely stands over against the church. It is clear that he takes his focus on the use made of scripture by the church to be, precisely, a focus on the kind of use in which readers yield the priority to scripture, acknowledging that it is God's witness to God's self, and looking for God to use it to guide and correct them. Yet he does not himself provide (at least, not in any detail) an account of *how* the objective sense of scripture appears within this use. Indeed, because he focuses a good deal of his attention on the way in which the church reads scripture as a narrationally unified whole, it is not hard to retain the suspicion that this form of reading *does* involve the church, having grasped the plot, now knowing in advance what all of scripture will mean. That plot, however, centers upon scripture's portrayal of Jesus of Nazareth—and, when it comes to explaining how that portrayal *can* stand over against the church, Lindbeck points us to the work of his friend and colleague, Hans Frei.[45]

Frei's "greatest contribution," Lindbeck says, "has been to make possible the restoration of the christologically centred narrative sense of scripture to its traditional primacy"—precisely by articulating the "primacy of the narrative meaning of the stories about Jesus for scripture as a whole." And it was Frei who had taught him that "The [Gospel] stories in their narrative function unsubstitutably identify and characterize a particular person as the summation of Israel's history and as the unsurpassable and irreplaceable clue to who and what the God of Israel and the universe is." That, for Lindbeck, is where the heart of the objectivity of scripture resides.[46]

HANS FREI

Frei's work as a whole—and especially the work that he did on the literal sense, the *sensus literalis*, in the 1980s—provides the sustained account of objectivity that Lindbeck's work needs. He goes to a level of depth and detail (if not always of clarity) that Lindbeck's own forays in hermeneutics lacked. And Frei himself indicates that he and Lindbeck should be read together at this point: he refers to Lindbeck's "cultural linguistic" and "intratextual" approach when indicating the kind of theology that will be congruent with his own account.[47]

Frei's work on the *sensus literalis* has, however, often been read (as by Vanhoozer) as a turn away from a focus on the text of scripture itself, and on what that text demands, and toward the Christian community's use of the text. In other words, it has often been read as a symptom of the very problem that I am claiming it will help us solve. And as with Lindbeck, it is not hard to see how that misreading has arisen.

Frei's early work—above all in *The Eclipse of Biblical Narrative* and *The Identity of Jesus Christ*—focused on the "history-like" narratives of the Gospels. He focused, in particular, on the passion and resurrection narratives, which are "realistic" or "history-like" in the sense that they depict the interactions of characters and circumstances in a public world. Frei sought to demonstrate that the meaning of those narratives is simply the story that they tell. More specifically, those narratives render their central character's identity to us in such a way that the depiction has a certain objectivity, a certain normativity, over against all the religious and other uses we might want to make of it. We don't need to look "behind" this depiction, to some more real identity of Jesus for which these texts can act as evidence; nor do we need to look "in front" of them, perhaps to some ethic or form of religious consciousness detachable from the story which we can take to be the true subject matter, safe from the fires of historical criticism. Rather, just as, in a somewhat analogous way, *David Copperfield* gives us the identity of David Copperfield, the gospels give us, quite directly, the identity of Jesus Christ. They teach us to recognize him as one who was truly raised from the dead (not in some imaginative or ideal realm, but in this everyday world of ours, leaving his tomb quite straightforwardly empty). And the texts similarly teach us to recognize that this man's life, death, and resurrection are God's climactic action on behalf of the world, and so to recognize this Jesus as Lord.[48] In both *The Eclipse of Biblical Narrative* (by describing their loss) and in *The Identity of Jesus Christ* (by proposing their retrieval), Frei's early work explores in great detail the ways in which the texts can be read for the sake of this realistic narrative sense.

In a letter written in July 1980, Frei looked back on this early work with the benefit of several years' hindsight, and noted that, at the time, he had been "really naively persuaded that there was such a thing as a normative meaning to a narrative text, if not to others." In the same letter, however, he noted that he had in the years since become "a bit more jaded," although he insisted that he was still inclined to dig in his heels in the face of the rising popularity of deconstructionist readings.[49] By October 1981, he was declaring himself "personally doubtful about the persuasiveness of some of the moves I have made in the past," saying that "at the very least they need large-scale qualification."[50] And then, in 1982 and 1983, he gave a pair of lectures, one at Haverford College and one at the University of California, Santa Barbara, in which he made clear the nature of his doubts and the qualifications that they demanded—and in which he is understood by critics like Vanhoozer to have taken leave, if not of his senses, then at least of the objective sense of scripture.[51]

Frei's concerns did not, however, involve him abandoning the idea that there is a literal sense to scripture, capable of rendering objectively to readers the identity of Jesus Christ. His concerns focused, instead, on the answer that in his earlier work he had implicitly given to the question, "*Why* should one attend to that sense when reading scripture?" Scripture has, after all, been read in all sorts of ways, and in some of those ways the literal sense is downplayed or ignored. What can one say to readers who adopt those other ways of reading, if one wishes to persuade them instead to attend to and learn from the literal sense? In his earlier work, Frei now acknowledged, the implicit answer given had simply been: "This text is a realistic narrative, and realistic narratives ought to be read in this way." In other words, his early work appeared to be underpinned by something like a general theory of realistic narrative: the erection of a "general category of which the synoptic Gospel narratives ... are a dependent instance."[52] Had Frei found himself faced, for instance, by a historical critic intent upon using the text as evidence for the reconstruction of a Jesus rather different from the one depicted, a critic for whom the narrative qualities of the text were simply one more bit of evidence to be used in reconstructing the early church's imagination of Jesus, the only response imagined in Frei's early work is, "But it is not that kind of text!"

Frei had now become convinced, however, that such a general and neutral justification of reading for the realistic narrative sense was implausible. It is, simply as a matter of fact, perfectly possible to do other things with such texts, and one is not necessarily by so doing committing a philosophical error—an error identifiable as such by means of generally available concepts. In fact, Frei had become convinced that such a justification was not only implausible, but undesirable. It would provide yet another way in which Christian reading ended up subordinated to a more general hermeneutical theory. It would mean, in particular, that the claim that these texts give us the identity of Jesus Christ became an instance of a more general kind of claim about what realistic narratives as such can do. It would become subject to the limitations, and the changing fortunes, of the field of narrative theory, rather than being recognized as a *sui generis* claim about what the God of scripture does by means of scripture.

Frei nevertheless remained convinced that the kind of realistic narrative reading championed in his early work *was* the appropriate way for Christians to read these portions of scripture. He remained convinced that, so read, these texts do render for us objectively the identity of Jesus Christ, teaching us to recognize him as truly risen and to acknowledge him as Lord. He was equally convinced, however, that the proper justification for reading this way can only be given in theological terms—i.e., in terms that cannot be converted without remainder into the terms of some more neutral, non-theological account. And there is therefore an unavoidable circularity involved in identifying and justifying the kind of reading to which Christians are called. It is only as one participates in this practice of Christian reading that one is put in a position to learn what is meant by the theological terms that are required for articulating its nature, and justifying its priority. One learns, for instance, to read the scriptures as God's witness to Godself, but only as one does so does one learn what is meant by "God" and "witness." It is only as one reads in this way that one can learn to articulate and justify what one is doing, and to explain why this is the way that one *should* read.

There is no way into this circle except by taking the plunge and entering it (or perhaps we should say: except by being drawn into it by the Spirit). No neutral account—i.e., no account that can be framed in terms available to one who has *not* yet learnt to read scripture—can adequately indicate how it is that one should read. No neutral account can indicate what scripture is, nor how it relates to the God and Father of our Lord Jesus Christ.[53]

Frei therefore begins with a descriptive account of the *practice* of Christian reading. That is, he begins with a descriptive account of the life of reading into which one must plunge in order to learn how to read, and so to articulate the reasons for such reading.[54] Some confusion has been caused by the fact that Frei's account of the *sensus literalis* describes the church's practice of reading in two different ways. At some points, he focuses on the formal fact that what he is describing is the kind of reading that, as a matter of fact, Christians have learnt to pursue (and have believed themselves called to pursue). This is the reading that has become for them the "plain sense," the communal sense, the dominant use in Christianity of these texts. That does not yet tell you substantively what kind of reading this is, nor what kind of authority it is taken to have, nor how the Christian community believes it to be grounded, nor what explanation and justification they can offer of it, nor in what ways this tradition of reading is open to criticism. And it certainly does not tell you that scripture is whatever the church makes of it. It simply tells you that Frei is speaking about the kind of reading that the church has, on the whole, and by the grace of God, learnt to regard as central.

Substantively, however, he focuses on the particular shape of the reading of the scriptures to which Christians are committed: a reading that attends to the gospels' rendering for us of the identity of Jesus Christ.[55] Christian reading, Frei argues, is gathered around "a very simple consensus: that the story of Jesus is about him, not about somebody else or about nobody in particular or about all of us; that it is not two stories ... or no story and so on and on."[56] And Christian reading acknowledges that telling us the story of Jesus in this way is the text's true purpose (rather than a misleading surface feature beneath which true reading will seek to penetrate). Or, to put it another way, the text is a fit enactment of its author's intention, and our interest as Christian readers is precisely in acknowledging and responding to that intention.

In other words, Frei offers as his substantive account of the *sensus literalis* a deliberately minimal description of a rough practical consensus that has been visible in Christian reading over the centuries. At least when it comes to the gospels, Christians have on the whole assumed that scripture tells the story of Jesus, and that it means what it says. This is not an exceptionless norm; it is possible to identify all kinds of counter-examples, or contexts in which this practice has not been to the fore of Christian life. It is even easier to identify (especially in the modern period) times when Christian theorists have articulated the nature of scripture and the forms of reading proper to it in ways that have made this practice of reading for the story of Jesus seem dubious or of secondary importance, or which have made it very difficult to recognize. Nevertheless, Frei claims, the consensus is recognizably there.

Frei then argues that if we do want to describe and justify this kind of Christian reading, we will do best to turn not to an independent hermeneutical theory, but to a theological account set out in terms that are themselves given their meaning by this practice of reading.[57] He argues, for instance, that to describe and justify such reading, we will need to turn to the doctrine of the incarnation (which is, precisely, a "partial second-order redescription" of "the synoptic Gospel narratives") as the basis of the idea that Jesus' identity is given to us in textual form.[58] He argues that the doctrine of creation is the basis for insisting that "Language is not fallen, not absent from truth or meaning," so that certain kinds of deconstruction are ruled out.[59] And he argues more fully that

> Any notion of truth such that that concept disallows the condescension of truth to the depiction in the text—to its own self-identification with, let us say, the fourfold story of Jesus of Nazareth taken as an ordinary story—has

itself to be viewed with profound scepticism by a Christian interpreter. The textual word as witness to the Word of God is not identical with the latter, and yet, by the Spirit's grace, it is "sufficient" for the witnessing.[60]

From a human, historical point of view (i.e., leaving out anything we might want to say about the work of the Spirit, or the action of providence), other forms of reading could have come to be the norm for the church. In the contest between Irenaeus and the Valentinians, for instance, the Valentinians could have prevailed, and their pattern of spiritual reading could have become the habitual (the "plain") sense of the Christian community. "There is no a priori reason why the 'plain' reading could not have been 'spiritual' in contrast to 'literal', and certainly the temptation was strong."[61] Had that happened, a lonely heir of Irenaeus in the present would certainly be able to say (on Frei's account) that the text was now being misused, that the true meaning of the text had been missed, and that this meaning was waiting there ready to be rediscovered—but she would have no knock-down argument with which to convince her Valentinian friends of these claims. The very coinage with which she could most fully fund her case would depend for its currency on the kind of reading that the Valentinian church had rejected.[62]

Yet if we do ask, "Why is it that the church catholic should read in the way that, on the whole, it does?" Frei will *not* say that it is simply a sociological fact, and that full membership of this community depends by definition upon compliance with the community's rules. Rather, he will say that the church has learnt to read this way as the Spirit has taught its members how to attend to the scriptures. He will say that they have learnt in that process that the text is God's witness to Godself, graciously assuming a textual form. And he will say that there is no more neutral way of specifying the kind of reading to which the church is called than by describing this knowledge into which the church has been drawn. Only the language learnt in the course of this reading is adequate to explain why Christians should read in this way, whatever analogies we might be able to find to other ways of reading.

CONCLUSION

Lindbeck's work is wide-ranging and multi-faceted, though sometimes rather loosely argued and conceptually imprecise. Frei's work is more cautious and more focused, and he is far more hesitant about drawing out the wider connections and implications of his claims. For all their differences of approach and temper, however, they can be read together, such that each theologian's account supplements the other's.

There is much more that needs to be said about scripture's objectivity. There are other forms that the objectivity of scripture can take than the gospel-focused, identity-depicting form discussed here. There is more to say about the relationship of the gospels' depiction of Jesus to the rest of scripture. Above all, there is much more to say about the ways in which the church's life in the world animates and challenges its reading in unpredictable ways. The church is often taught to re-read scripture—to discover in new ways its objective witness to Christ—by means of prophetic voices speaking at a distance from the church's current centers of power and privilege. The uncovering or illuminating of scripture's rich objectivity, the challenging and overthrowing of our mistaken readings, takes place as scripture's readers are drawn onward and outward by the Spirit into diverse encounters and relationships across the church and out into the wider world. The Spirit's work leading the church into the objectivity of scripture is unfinished.[63]

What Lindbeck's work suggests, however, and Frei's work makes clear, is that there is a double logic in theological hermeneutics: on the one hand a circle, and on the other hand a line. The circular logic is the logic of learning to read; the linear logic is the logic of reading.

On the one hand, then, there is the circle. One learns to read with the help of the practice of the church and rule of faith. Yet that practice and rule are themselves justified only by the results of the very form of reading that they help to inculcate. There is, in other words, a mutually supporting circularity uniting the text and its use.

On the other hand, there is the line. The pattern of reading into which the church has been led is precisely one in which there is a stark asymmetry, a line of authority running from text to reader. The pattern of reading in question is marked by a constant determination to bring all one's thought and practice, including one's hermeneutical thought and practice, to be tested by scripture, in recognition that it is God's instrument in both forming and correcting the church.

To turn away from the line in order to focus on the circle would, as the critics suggest, be to neuter scripture, to turn it into the secure possession of a complacent church. My claim has been that, despite the critics' fears that they have fallen into precisely this trap, both Lindbeck and Frei can, when read together, help us to avoid it—and that they can perhaps do so more surely than those critics can themselves. That is because, as Frei suggests, to downplay the circle for the sake of the line will ultimately be self-defeating. It will mean that our accounts of the nature of scripture and of scriptural interpretation will rely upon (possibly unstated) claims about the possibility, priority, and even necessity of certain kinds of reading, claims not themselves fully rooted in the results of such reading. It will, in other words, immunize our hermeneutics from scriptural critique.

For a robust account of the objectivity of scripture, Frei and Lindbeck teach us, both the circle and the line are needed.

NOTES

1. Kevin J. Vanhoozer, *The Drama of Doctrine: A Canonical-Linguistic Approach to Christian Doctrine* (Louisville, KY: Westminster John Knox, 2005), 170; italics removed.
2. I will be providing a very different account (at least of Lindbeck) from the one I gave in "Frei's Christology and Lindbeck's Cultural-Linguistic Theory," *Scottish Journal of Theology* 50, no. 1 (1997): 83–95—an article I now regard as seriously mistaken.
3. Vanhoozer, *The Drama of Doctrine*, 10.
4. Ibid., 16–17, emphasis original.
5. Ibid., 97.
6. Ibid., 63, emphasis removed; cf. 149–50.
7. George A. Lindbeck, "Postcritical Canonical Interpretation: Three Modes of Retrieval," in *Theological Exegesis: Essays in Honor of Brevard S. Childs*, ed. Christopher R. Seitz and Kathryn Greene-McCreight (Grand Rapids, MI: Wm. B. Eerdmans Publishing Co., 1999): 26–51, 36.
8. Vanhoozer, *Drama*, 172.
9. Ibid., 173.
10. Ibid.
11. John Webster, *Holy Scripture: A Dogmatic Sketch* (Cambridge: CUP, 2003), 48–9.
12. Ibid., 49.
13. Ibid., 50.
14. Ibid., 52, quoting Lindbeck, "Scripture, Consensus and Community," in *Biblical Interpretation in Crisis: The Ratzinger Conference on Bible and Church*, ed. Richard John Neuhaus (Grand Rapids, MI: Wm. B. Eerdmans Publishing Co., 1989): 74–101, reprinted in Lindbeck, *The Church in a Postliberal Age*, ed. James J. Buckley (Grand Rapids, MI: Wm. B. Eerdmans Publishing Co., 2002), 201–22, 205.
15. George Lindbeck, *The Nature of Doctrine: Religion and Theology in a Postliberal Age* (Philadelphia, PA: Westminster, 1984).
16. George Lindbeck, "Ecumenisms in Conflict: Where Does Hauerwas Stand?" in *God, Truth and Witness: Engaging Stanley Hauerwas*, ed. L. Gregory Jones, Reinhard Hütter, and C. Rosalee Velloso Ewell (Grand Rapids, MI: Brazos, 2005): 212–28, 212, 214 n. 4.
17. Both Vanhoozer and Webster primarily focus on texts written by Lindbeck after *The Nature of Doctrine*. My claim is not at all that they have ignored Lindbeck's wider corpus, but that they take *The Nature of Doctrine* as the central statement of Lindbeck's project, and so miss some of the deeper features of his approach.
18. See my "Reconstructing *The Nature of Doctrine*," for a more detailed justification of this claim.
19. See Lindbeck, "Discovering Thomas (1): The Classical Statement of Christian Theism," *Una Sancta* 24, no. 1 (1967): 45–52, 51; "The Infallibility Debate," in *The Infallibility Debate*, ed. John J. Kirvan (New York, NY: Paulist Press, 1971): 107–52, 126; and *The Nature of Doctrine*, 51.

20. All of this is very confusingly expressed in *The Nature of Doctrine* itself (in the "Excursus on Religion and Truth," 63–9), but clarified by Lindbeck in several subsequent comments. See Lindbeck, "Response to Bruce Marshall," *The Thomist* 53, no. 3 (1989): 403–6 (which needs to be read in tandem with the Marshall paper to which it is a response: "Aquinas as Postliberal Theologian," 353–403); and Lindbeck, "Reply to Avery Cardinal Dulles," *First Things* 139 (2004): 13–15.

21. Lindbeck, "The Church," in *Keeping the Faith: Essays to Mark the Centenary of Lux Mundi*, ed. Geoffrey Wainwright (London: SPCK, 1989): 179–208; reprinted in Lindbeck, *The Church in a Postliberal Age*, 145–65: 166.

22. Even when writing against supersessionism, Lindbeck was better at writing about Jews encountered in scripture than about Jews as a living community today. The best account of Lindbeck's work in this area is provided by Peter Ochs in *Another Reformation: Postliberal Christianity and the Jews* (Grand Rapids, MI: Baker Academic, 2011).

23. Lindbeck, "Ecumenical Directions and Confessional Construals," *Dialog* 30, no. 2 (1991): 118–23, 120. I have discussed all this in more detail in "George Lindbeck and the Christological Nature of Doctrine."

24. Lindbeck, "The Story-shaped Church: Critical Exegesis and Theological Interpretation," in *Scriptural Authority and Narrative Interpretation*, ed. Garrett Green (Philadelphia, PA: Fortress Press, 1987): 161–78, 171; see also "The Church as Israel: Ecclesiology and Ecumenism," in *Jews and Christians: People of God*, ed. Carl E. Braaten and Robert W. Jenson (Grand Rapids, MI: Wm. B. Eerdmans Publishing Co., 2003): 78–94.

25. Lindbeck speaking to Peter Ochs, quoted in Ochs' *Another Reformation*, 48.

26. Lindbeck, "Atonement and the Hermeneutics of Social Embodiment," *Pro Ecclesia* 5, no. 2 (Spring 1996): 144–60, 151. (The essay was later published in a revised form as "Atonement and the Hermeneutics of Intertextual Social Embodiment," in *The Nature of Confession: Evangelicals and Postliberals in Conversation*, ed. Timothy Phillips and Dennis Okholm (Downers Grove, IL: IVP, 1996): 221–40.)

27. Ibid., 148.

28. These are a central focus in Lindbeck's ecumenical work on Catholic accounts of infallibility or irreformability. See, alongside the works cited below, Lindbeck, "Reform and Infallibility," *Cross Currents* 11, no. 4 (1961): 345–56; "Ecclesiology and Roman Catholic Renewal," *Religion in Life* 33 (1963): 383–94, reprinted in *New Theology 2*, ed. Martin Marty and Dean Peerman (New York, NY: Macmillan, 1965), 183–97; "The Infallibility Debate" (see n. 20 above); *Infallibility*, the 1972 Pere Marquette Lecture (Milwaukee, WI: Marquette University Press, 1972), reprinted in *The Church in a Postliberal Age*, 120–42; "Papacy and *Ius Divinum*: A Lutheran View," in *Papal Primacy and the Universal Church: Lutherans and Catholics in Dialogue V*, ed. Paul C. Empie and T. Austin Murphy (Minneapolis, MN: Augsburg, 1974): 193–208; "The Reformation and the Infallibility Debate," in *Teaching Authority and Infallibility in the Church: Lutherans and Catholics in Dialogue VI*, ed. Paul C. Empie, T. Austin Murphy, and Joseph A. Burgess (Minneapolis, MN: Augsburg, 1980): 101–19; "Problems on the Road to Unity: Infallibility," in *Unitatis Redintegratio 1964–74: The Impact of the Decree on Ecumenism*, ed. Gerard Békés and Vilmos Vajta = *Studia Anselmiana* 71 (1977): 98–109.

29. This is obscured in *The Nature of Doctrine* by Lindbeck's desire that the book offer an ecumenically neutral framework. He therefore (see 84–8, 98–104) seeks to show that it is compatible with the claim that some doctrinal decisions are irreformable, and with claims about infallibility. He wants the theory of doctrine he sets forth to provide him with a shared ecumenical language within which his arguments about *sola scriptura* can be substantively worked out without having been decided in advance by a biased technical conceptuality.
30. Lindbeck, "The Problem of Doctrinal Development and Contemporary Protestant Theology," *Concilium* 3, no. 1 (1967): 64–72, 69.
31. Lindbeck, "The Reformation Heritage and Christian Unity," *Lutheran Quarterly* 2, no. 4 (1988): 477–502; reprinted in *The Church in a Postliberal Age*, 53–76: 60.
32. See Lindbeck, "Barth and Textuality," *Theology Today* 43, no. 3 (1986): 361–76, "The Story-shaped Church: Critical Exegesis and Theological Interpretation" (see n. 24 above); "The Church" (see n. 22); "The Church's Mission to a Postmodern Culture," in *Postmodern Theology: Christian Faith in a Pluralist World*, ed. Frederic B. Burnham (San Francisco, CA: Harper and Row, 1989): 37–55; "Scripture, Consensus and Community" (see n. 15); and "Atonement and the Hermeneutics of Social Embodiment" (see n. 26).
33. Lindbeck, "Ecumenical Theology," in *The Modern Theologians*, Vol. 2, ed. David F. Ford (Oxford: Blackwell, 1989): 255–73, 266.
34. Lindbeck, "Scripture, Consensus, Community," 203.
35. Ibid., 204–5.
36. That, after all, is why some Christians need to write books like Vanhoozer's *Drama of Doctrine*, or Webster's *Holy Scripture*.
37. Lindbeck, "Atonement and the Hermeneutics of Social Embodiment," 146.
38. Lindbeck, "Scripture, Consensus, Community," 203.
39. Ibid.
40. Lindbeck and Gerhard O. Forde, "Confessional Subscription: What Does It Mean for Lutherans Today?" *Word and World* 11, no. 3 (1991): 316–20, 319. Lindbeck's wider position on doctrinal rules suggests that even these "low-level generalizations" can't be seen as irreformable; they too must be considered to be open to testing by means of the very reading that they support. I am, however, not aware that he ever explicitly pursues this point.
41. Lindbeck, "Atonement and the Hermeneutics of Social Embodiment," 148.
42. Lindbeck, "Confessional Subscription," 320; cf. "Scripture, Consensus, Community," 206.
43. Lindbeck, "Atonement and the Hermeneutics of Social Embodiment," 152.
44. For more on this, see my discussion of Lindbeck's decision-focused "historical situationalism" in "Reconstructing *The Nature of Doctrine*," 19; cf. Lindbeck, "The Problem of Doctrinal Development and Contemporary Protestant Theology," 66–8.
45. Lindbeck had drawn on Frei's work extensively while he was working on *The Nature of Doctrine*. See "The Bible as Realistic Narrative," in *Consensus in*

Theology? A Dialogue with Hans Küng and Edward Schillebeeckx, ed. Leonard Swidler (Philadelphia, PA: Westminster Press, 1980): 81–5.

46. Lindbeck, "The Story-shaped Church," 161, 164.
47. Hans W. Frei, "The 'Literal Reading' of Biblical Narrative in the Christian Tradition: Does It Stretch or Will It Break?" in *The Bible and the Narrative Tradition*, ed. Frank McConnell (Oxford: Oxford University Press, 1986): 36–77; republished in *Theology and Narrative*, ed. George Hunsinger and William C. Placher (New York and Oxford: Oxford University Press, 1993): 117–52, 147–8.
48. Frei, *The Eclipse of Biblical Narrative: A Study in Eighteenth and Nineteenth Century Hermeneutics* (New Haven, CT: Yale University Press, 1974); *The Identity of Jesus Christ: The Hermeneutical Bases of Dogmatic Theology* (Philadelphia, PA: Fortress Press, 1975). For a detailed discussion of Frei's core argument in his early work, see my *Christ, Providence and History: Hans W. Frei's Public Theology* (London: T&T Clark, 2004), especially ch. 3–6.
49. Frei, Letter to Bruce Piersault, July 8, 1980 (Hans Wilhelm Frei Papers, Manuscript Group no. 76, Special Collections, Yale Divinity School Library, box 4, folder 75).
50. Frei, Letter to Mark Ellingsen, October 20, 1981 (Frei Papers, box 1, folder 23). This is, interestingly, part of Frei's response to the suggestion that he is part of a "Yale school"—a suggestion made before the publication of *The Nature of Doctrine*, and before any obvious "turn to practice" in Frei's work.
51. Frei, "Theology and the Interpretation of Narrative: Some Hermeneutical Considerations," in *Theology and Narrative*, 95–116, and "The 'Literal Reading' of Biblical Narrative in the Christian Tradition."
52. Frei, "The 'Literal Reading' of Biblical Narrative," 142.
53. Of course, various neutral accounts might approximate to a proper theological account, in *ad hoc* ways, and so might provide stepping stones toward a Christian reading.
54. Frei is much more cautious about the connection between the kind of description he wants to issue and ethnographic description. It will be "closer to the social sciences than to philosophy" (though "certainly not identical to them") because it will look at the meaning that the practice of reading has for Christians (the ways in which it is described in their language, the sense it has within the wider scheme of their life) rather than relying on more general accounts—and there are some resemblances between such an approach and one, Weberian strand of social science ("Theology and the Interpretation of Narrative," 96–8). More than that he will not say.
55. See Frei, *Types of Christian Theology*, ed. George Hunsinger and William C. Placher (New Haven, CT: Yale University Press, 1992), 3, 16, 141–2, and "The 'Literal Reading' of Biblical Narrative," 122.
56. Frei, *Types of Christian Theology*, 140.
57. He also, I think, continued to regard the kinds of conceptual tools deployed in *The Identity of Jesus Christ*—tools for articulating how it is that a realistic narrative conveys identity, and for speaking about the shape of the identity so conveyed—as appropriate for use in exploring the yield of such Christian reading.

He does not make this explicit, but one of his last writings provides a very similar account of the resurrection to the one offered in *Identity*, with no indication that the basics of Frei's articulation of that account have changed. See "'How It All Began': On The Resurrection of Christ," *Anglican and Episcopal History* 53, no. 2 (1989): 139–45, republished as "Of the Resurrection of Christ" in *Theology and Narrative*, 200–6, and again in Hans Frei, *Reading Faithfully: Writings from the Archives*, I: *Theology and Hermeneutics*, ed. Mike Higton and Mark Alan Bowald (Eugene, OR: Wipf and Stock, 2015), 184–9.

58. Frei, *Types of Christian Theology*, 141–2.
59. Frei, "Theology and the Interpretation of Narrative," 109.
60. Frei, "Conflicts in Interpretation" (the 1986 Alexander Thompson Memorial Lecture at Princeton Theological Seminary), in *Theology and Narrative*, 153–66: 164.
61. Frei, "Theology and the Interpretation of Narrative," 122. This is what Frei meant when he said, in a 1984 letter to Gary Comstock, that "outside of that tradition there is no reason to think of *any* single interpretive move or scheme as *the* meaning of these stories" (*Reading Faithfully*, 35–40: 38).
62. Vanhoozer (as cited above) claims that "Frei's argument amounts to the claim that *for Christians*, the biblical narratives render the identity of Jesus Christ." In one sense, this is quite right—but this claim is of the same logical type as the claim that "For *those who open the Bible and read it*, the biblical narratives render the identity of Jesus." The fact that those who don't open the Bible and read it will not have the identity of Jesus rendered to them by the text doesn't mean that authority in determining the sense of scripture has shifted from the text to the text-opening reader. Similarly, no interesting shift in authority is implied when we say that those who (for whatever reason) don't read scripture for its identity-rendering sense won't have the identity of Jesus rendered to them.
63. I have argued this at length in *The Life of Christian Doctrine*, especially chapters 7 and 9.

CHAPTER FOURTEEN

What Can Evangelicals and Postliberals Learn from Each Other?

The Carl Henry/Hans Frei Exchange Reconsidered

GEORGE HUNSINGER

"All human truth," writes Hans Küng, "stands in the shadow of error. All error contains at least a grain of truth. What a true statement says is true; what it fails to say may also be true. What a false statement says is false; what it means but does not say may be true."[1] This reminder that claims to truth—especially in the midst of controversy—are always fraught with complexities, pitfalls, and ambiguities seems salutary for the enterprise I am about to undertake. For what I hope to do—even if only in the form of a thought-experiment—is to suggest that Evangelicals and Postliberals might actually have something to learn from each other. No enterprise such as mine can hope to succeed, however, if it does not at least try to remain sensitive not only to matters of straightforward truth and falsity, but also to those gray areas that include grains of truth, omissions of truth, and inadequate formulations of truth, assuming of course, as I think we must, that truth in theology, however fragmentarily, can be approximated. Hans Küng continues:

> It is a simplified view of the truth to suppose that every sentence in its verbal formulation must be either true or false. On the contrary, any sentence

can be true *and* false, according to its purpose, its context, its underlying meaning. It is much harder to discover what is meant by it than what it says. A sincere, fearless and critical ecumenical theology, the only kind which can be constructive, must give up throwing dogmas at the other side. Theology today must be actively concerned to try and see the truth in what it supposes to be the errors of the other side, and to see the possibility of error in what it itself believes. In this way we would reach the situation which it is essential that we reach: the abandonment of supposed error and a meeting in common Christian truth.[2]

My hope is that the following discussion will reflect something of what Küng means by "sincere, fearless and critical ecumenical theology," and that it will thereby contribute to the possibility of "a meeting in common Christian truth" between Evangelicals and Postliberals today.

A PREVIEW OF COMING ATTRACTIONS

The centerpiece of my discussion will be an exchange that took place between two figures whose credentials seem impeccable: Carl F. H. Henry for the Evangelicals and Hans W. Frei for the Postliberals. In November 1985, Carl Henry gave a series of three lectures at Yale. One of them offered his critique of what he called "narrative theology," with particular reference, among others, to Hans Frei. Frei himself responded to that lecture, and both contributions later appeared in the *Trinity Journal*. In *Types of Christian Theology* Frei returned to Henry's views, placing them in the unlikely company of David Tracy and other modern theologians. Theologians of this type, Frei argued, approach specifically Christian doctrines and beliefs in a way that seems overly determined by general philosophical considerations.

Among the issues that emerge from the Henry/Frei exchange, the most stubborn seem to involve the place of Holy Scripture within the Christian knowledge of God. Henry not only asks Frei very pointedly about the unity, authority, and inspiration of Scripture in their own right, but also about the extent to which these three need to be grounded in a logically prior doctrine of scriptural inerrancy. Above all, Henry seems concerned throughout about the overly disjunctive relationship, as he sees it, between biblical narrative and historical factuality in Frei's theological proposal.

Frei, on the other hand, frames the issues between him and Henry rather differently. He thinks that they disagree primarily about the "sufficiency" of Scripture as opposed to matters of unity, authority, or inspiration. This disagreement seems connected to a further difference about just exactly what the subject matter or the "factual" referent of Scripture really is. Finally, Frei responds to Henry's question about factuality by posing a counter-question about differing habits of mind and frameworks of understanding. Whereas Henry presents himself as an exponent of historic Christian orthodoxy, Frei wonders whether some of Henry's central contentions do not actually reflect modes of thought that are heavily conditioned by modernity in significant and unfortunate ways. One of Frei's deepest worries is that Evangelicals and Liberals, however much they may see themselves as archenemies, have more in common in thinking about Scripture than anything that sets them apart, so that they end up being "siblings under the skin."[3]

In trying to discern what Evangelicals and Postliberals might learn from each other about Holy Scripture, I will try to uncover various points where concessions might be made from each side. I will look especially for concessions that can be made without compromising the basic convictions that seem definitive of either position. I will therefore be looking for areas of possible convergence rather than for areas of complete or outright agreement. In this thought-experiment, I will grant Frei's point that Henry seems bound by an excessive commitment to modernity. I will go on to argue, however, that other and very different formulations of Henry's concerns have standing within the Evangelical community, formulations that uphold a strong doctrine of "inerrancy" without Henry's modernist excesses. In particular I will suggest that the views of Abraham Kuyper and Herman Bavinck offer a greater possibility for fruitful Evangelical dialogue with Postliberalism than the tendency represented by Carl Henry. (And in order not to make things too easy for myself, I will follow not the interpretation of Kuyper and Bavinck advanced by Jack Rogers and Donald McKim,[4] but instead that by Richard B. Gaffin, Jr. of Westminster Theological Seminary, who subjects the Rogers-McKim interpretation to a full-fledged revision and critique.)[5] Once the encumbrances of excessive modernity are shed and left behind, the real theological issues can emerge with greater clarity, and the differences between Evangelicalism and Postliberalism—though still strong—begin to look more like a matter of degree than a matter of kind.

In the other prong of my thought-experiment, I will grant Henry's point that in general the account of scriptural unity, authority, and inspiration among the Postliberals is, to say the least, fairly thin and unsatisfying so far. This thinness symptomizes the heavily "formal" character of Postliberal theology, at least in the versions of it emanating from Yale. Evangelicalism, after all, is a historic stream of theological reflection that has claims of reaching back to as far as the Reformation or Post-Reformation period.[6] By contrast, Postliberalism, however promising it may be, is little more than a current of recent provenance. Postliberals would do well, I will argue, to pay careful attention to the historic doctrinal concerns of the Evangelicals, however much it may be felt that reformulations are in order. Focusing above all on the historic Evangelical plea for an adequately biblical understanding of the saving death of Christ, I will nominate the work of John R. W. Stott and Alister McGrath as representing the kind of proposals from which Postliberals would have much to learn.

HENRY'S APPRAISAL OF NARRATIVE THEOLOGY

In the course of his critical survey, Henry acknowledges several points of agreement with narrative theology. Although they are not strongly emphasized, they should not be overlooked. The appreciative comments that Henry makes all seem to focus on what might be called the integrity of Scripture. He observes that narrative theologians tend to work with the received scriptural text, taken as it stands. Theologians like Frei, he writes, emphasize "that the entire book is important to the meaning, and not just preferred sections as in nonEvangelical criticism."[7] This acceptance of the received text carries a number of implications. As Henry rightly notes, it means that he and Frei hold significant affirmations in common, namely, that Scripture is a harmonious unity, that historical criticism has not invalidated the relevance of Scripture, that the biblical world is the real world which illuminates all else, and that Jesus is the indispensable Savior.[8] It also means that Scripture can function as Scripture "apart from the question whether we can demonstrate the historical factuality of events to which it refers. The authority of the biblical text is independent of confirmation or disconfirmation by historical critics."[9]

Despite this impressive range of common affirmation, Henry proceeds to subject the work of various narrative theologians to severe and vigorous criticism. In what follows I will summarize the concerns that he sets forth under several headings that are similar to but not identical with those that he uses himself, and I will concentrate only on those points that seem to pertain directly to Frei. Henry sees himself as differing from Frei on four main questions: the unity of Scripture, the authority of Scripture, the factuality of Scripture, and the truth of Scripture.

Although discussed only briefly, the unity of Scripture seems to me to be a point on which Frei is questioned to good effect. Is the category of narrative, Henry asks, really sufficient to account for the unity of the Bible, whether in terms of form or of content?[10] "Not all of Scripture," he continues, "falls into the narrative genre."[11] Because so much of the Bible is not narrative, the narrative category cannot account for the Bible's unity. The point is as telling as it is obvious, for the thinness of the narrative account of scriptural unity seems to suggest a larger problem in Postliberal theology as a whole. As Gabriel Fackre has pointed out, "most proponents of narrative theology are more concerned with method than with theological content."[12] Not much is said about doctrinal substance, and doctrine itself is in danger of dwindling into a set of rules with no more than a regulatory function. Based on such considerations, Henry concludes rather severely that "Frei diverts attention from revelation."[13] I will return to this criticism at the end of my remarks.

A second question that Henry has for Frei pertains to the authority of Scripture. Among the many and diverse points that arise here, I will mention only one, although it seems to be at the heart of Henry's concerns, namely, a perceived drift toward subjectivism in matters of biblical authority. Henry repeatedly accuses narrative theologians of failing to arrive at a consensus among themselves in their interpretation of Scripture.[14] The lack of hermeneutical consensus in narrative theology indicates that it has "no objective criterion for distinguishing truth from error and fact from fiction." This is "the unresolved dilemma facing narrative theology." Its method cannot eliminate "divergent and contradictory theological claims."[15] Although I suspect that when they are together *en famille,* Evangelicals may not be wholly innocent of divergent and contradictory theological claims—if I am not mistaken it has been difficult even to find a definition of the term "Evangelical" around which a consensus can be built[16]—what seems to disturb Henry is a certain absence of objective criteria.

If I do not misinterpret him, Henry seems to hold that if Scripture is really authoritative, then we should be able to arrive at consensus in biblical interpretation by means of objective criteria. Beyond a certain point this seems an odd thing to say. If we take the Nicene-Constantinopolitan Creed and the Chalcedonian Definition as established criteria for the church's interpretation of Holy Scripture—as I think Postliberal theologians like Hans Frei and George Lindbeck are prepared to do—then I don't see how these standards *qua* standards can be said to conform to Henry's canons of "objectivity" in the non-perspectival or value-neutral sense that seems so important to him[17]. There are two points here. First, as is notorious, even these standards will not eliminate all significant theological diversity and contradiction; and second, the standards themselves are articles of faith. Could it be that Henry's concerns about an arbitrary subjectivism, while not entirely without merit, are somehow driven by canons of objectivism so stringent that in this life, fallen and finite as we poor creatures are, none of us can ever really meet them? Note that Henry does not shrink from asking in criticism of Fackre as a narrative theologian: "But is his epistemology immune to critical miscarriage and to perversion of tradition?"[18]

This is an interesting question. Is Henry's epistemology immune to critical miscarriage and to perversion of tradition? Is anyone's? Here we confront for the first time the counter-question about a certain peculiar cast of mind that Frei will pose to good effect in his published response.[19]

A third question has to do with factuality in the biblical narratives. This is undoubtedly the issue in Frei's work that worries Henry the most deeply. Although revelation "is conveyed in and through Scripture," according to Frei, he also holds that realistic narrative "has a loose and unsure connection with historical actuality."[20] This establishes an unhappy "disjunction" between the literary witness of scriptural narrative and the redemptive events it depicts. Positing such a disjunction, laments Henry, has "distortive consequences" in theology as well as being epistemologically "destructive" of the "orthodox heritage."[21] By contrast, writes Henry, "Evangelical orthodoxy routinely affirms" the full "historical factuality" of the biblical narratives along with their "objective inspiration and inerrancy."[22]

Henry rightly sees that for Frei the central question is a question of genre. The Gospels are allegedly misconstrued if they are taken as reliable historical reports whose meaning is to be found in historical events. He also rightly sees that for Frei "the narrative content is not necessarily historical."[23] As Henry does not tire of insisting, however, the relevant question still remains as to whether the events of the history-like narratives—whether miraculous in their depiction or not—"are in fact historical."[24] Again, Henry rightly sees that for Frei the scriptural narration is "realistic" whether or not the depicted action is factual, and that the depicted action functions to render a character in a story. In this sense the narrative form constitutes, not just illustrates, the meaning of the narrative. The meaning is thus located inside not outside the text.[25]

Beyond a certain point, however, Henry unfortunately fails to grasp what Frei is claiming. Henry asks: Wouldn't Frei have to say that faith retained its full validity and saving power "even if historical investigation were to discredit the empty tomb and Jesus' bodily resurrection?"[26] "It is difficult," the critique continues, "to find a categorical statement that if Christ's body disintegrated in the tomb Christian faith would be impaired. ... Narrative hermeneutics embraces uncertainty over historicity."[27] Frei's approach is so open to fictional elements in the narratives that it "clouds the foundations of a stable faith. ... It is incumbent on those who claim that narrative story and history are not compatible to clarify which historical specifics are nonnegotiable."[28] Despite referring to Frei's book *The Identity of Jesus Christ*, Henry does not seem to have read it carefully enough to discover just how Frei has answered these very questions.

Since an account of those answers is better postponed until a later section of this essay, it will be fruitful here to pursue an important theme in Henry's own constructive proposal. This theme concerns how faith in the biblical testimony is related to the question of verifying or disconfirming the events depicted by biblical narratives. This theme is not so much a question of "faith and history" as of "faith and historiography" or of "faith and modern historical investigation." At first glance what Henry has to say on this theme seems fairly straightforward. He states repeatedly that faith is independent of historiography. "The Evangelical belief in the divine redemptive acts does not depend on verification by historical criticism but rests on scriptural attestation."[29]

Or again he states: "The biblical redemptive acts are not established as historical only if historical method confirms them, nor discredited if it does not do so, for empirical investigation is always incomplete and its verdicts subject to revision."[30] Henry even acknowledges that "questions about the supernatural fall outside the method's competence."[31] Were there no more to Henry's position than this, he and Frei, as it turns out, would not widely disagree.

On the other hand, elsewhere in the same essay Henry seems to become strangely equivocal. What are we to make, for example, of the following assertion? "Unless the historical data are assimilated not only to faith but also to the very history historians probe, the narrative exerts no claim to historical factuality."[32] This seems to be a claim, again quoting Henry, that "the factual implications of the text" cannot be upheld "independently of historical criticism."[33] Factual implications must apparently be validated by historical criticism. Faith, says Henry in the same vein, cannot focus merely on the narratives "independently of all historical concerns." If "faith" is split off from "reason" and "history," "that would in principle encourage skepticism and cloud historical referents in obscurity."[34] Most surprising of all, despite what we heard about supernatural matters falling outside the competence of historical-critical method, we are told almost in the same breath that a skillful use of this method "would uncover an objective transcendent revelation, even if confined to historical events or acts."[35]

The principle of charity dictates that one should try to construct a plausible account that would reconcile these apparently contradictory statements. Since my knowledge of Carl Henry's writings is not extensive, the best I can do is to offer the following hypothesis. I suspect that Henry's overall position might plausibly be described as one of "systematic consubstantiation." If so, this position will not only separate him from Postliberals like Frei, but (as I hope to show) also from Evangelicals like Kuyper and Bavinck. "Systematic consubstantiation" between faith and historiography would mean something like the following. Although faith is independent of historiography, it makes systematic use of it in two ways. First, it makes a negative case that events depicted by biblical narratives (e.g., Christ's resurrection) have not in fact been disconfirmed by historical-critical method; and second, so far as possible, it makes a positive case (by means of that method) for the historical factuality of those events.³⁶ Some such position seems to be what Henry means when he writes that Evangelicals "lean on inspired Scripture *more than* on historical research for assurance of past salvific events."³⁷ Faith, according to this statement, seems to substantiate itself and to find assurance not only through Word and Spirit, but also through historical research. It seems to require a reliance on historical-critical method as well as on Scripture itself, though not in the same way or to the same degree. However, if faith were to forego a systematic reliance on historical-critical method as a secondary means of verification and certainty, then the consequences as Henry understands them would be dire indeed. For in that case skepticism would not only be encouraged, but the foundations of a stable faith would remain clouded in obscurity. Here is another point to which we will return.

Henry's questions to Frei about the unity, authority, and factuality of Scripture are finally sealed by a question about the truth of Scripture. Once again we confront a very large topic that can be treated only very briefly. In any case, Henry is clearly concerned about what he calls "objective truth," which seems to be defined as truth that can be known in a value-neutral way apart from any self-involving perspectives or presuppositions.³⁸ This kind of truth—namely, disinterested cognitive truth about objective realities—is what Henry seems to have in mind when he suggests that Scripture has two primary functions: first, it conveys "propositional truths about God and his purposes;" and second, it gives us "the meaning of divine redemptive acts."³⁹ If I understand Henry correctly, it seems that the propositional truths conveyed by Scripture demand our intellectual assent, whereas the meaning of the divine redemptive acts as mediated exclusively by Scripture demands not only our assent but also our personal commitment. More succinctly, whereas the truth demands our assent, the meaning demands our commitment.

When Henry reads Frei what he finds missing is a concern for this kind of objective truth. What he finds instead is simply a set of ungrounded assertions, however commendable some of them may be. "It takes more than strenuous assertion," he states pointedly, "to establish historical factuality and objective truth. ... Really to turn the flank of destructive criticism requires an articulate view of revelation and reason and of revelation and history, and a public test of truth."⁴⁰ The significance of Henry's drive to defeat modern skepticism on its own terrain—really to turn the flank, as he says, of destructive criticism—can scarcely, it seems, be overestimated. Modern skepticism will not be defeated merely by strenuous assertion. A whole array of conceptual weaponry and armor will be required, none of which can be found in Frei's depleted arsenal. To defend the factuality of biblical narrative against the onslaught of modernity, one needs to wield a public test of truth. To fortify the meaning of the facts attested, one throws up a towering theory of revelation. And to safeguard the truth of biblical assertions, one rolls out the ultimate weapon: a doctrine of inerrancy.

Theologians such as Frei are wrong, Henry urges, "to reduce biblical historicity and inerrancy to second-order questions."[41] It is to Henry's insistence on the centrality of inerrancy that we must turn, however briefly. Although I wish to make only a small observation, it will prove to be important when we come to Kuyper and Bavinck. "Evangelical theology," writes Henry, "roots the authority of Scripture in its divine inspiration and holds that the Bible is inerrant because it is divinely inspired."[42] Only the doctrine of inerrancy, he continues, can finally "protect the identity and centrality of Christ" as well as "the authority and inspiration of the Bible."[43] Note the logical order and relation of these ideas. The authority of Scripture is seen as grounded in its divine inspiration, and this inspiration is then seen as the source of inerrancy in all matters of factuality and truth. Whereas inspiration is the source of inerrancy, inerrancy is the ultimate ground of truth. The doctrine of inerrancy thus emerges from Henry's account with a peculiar logical status and conceptual force. Logically, it is the final ground (though not the source) of biblical truth; and functionally, it serves to make that truth objective, certain, and secure.

FREI'S RESPONSE TO HENRY'S APPRAISAL

In responding to Henry's critique, Hans Frei opens with his famous plea for a "generous orthodoxy." He states: "My own vision of what might be propitious for our day, split as we are, not so much into denominations as into schools of thought, is that we need a kind of generous orthodoxy which would have in it an element of liberalism—a voice like the *Christian Century*—and an element of Evangelicalism—the voice of *Christianity Today*."[44] With characteristic modesty, he continues: "I don't know if there is a voice between those two, as a matter of fact. If there is, I would like to pursue it."[45] Frei's opening remark signals that he wants to re-frame the entire discussion. Although he approaches both Liberalism and Evangelicalism with critical sympathy, he will accept neither on its own terms. Only a new framework of understanding, he suggests—one that overlaps both Liberalism and Evangelicalism, while transcending the limits of each—will show the way forward. Henry's critique gives Frei the opportunity to say something about the possibilities and limitations of Evangelical theology, at least as Henry represents it.

Henry's concern about the unity of Scripture elicits no more from Frei than a small concession: "Not all of Scripture is narrative, obviously," he admits.[46] In an early and programmatic essay, Frei had indicated how Scripture's unity might be set forth: "For a beginning," he wrote,

> let's start with the synoptic gospels, or at least one of them, because their peculiar structure as narratives, or at least as partial narratives, makes some hermeneutical moves possible which we don't have available elsewhere in the New Testament. And having started there, I would propose to go on to say, let's see how much more of the New Testament can be coordinated by means of this series of hermeneutical moves.[47]

Although Frei clearly believed that more was necessary than narrative analysis, he unfortunately never got around to making those larger hermeneutical moves. As I have already suggested, this kind of deficit seems to typify the Yale variants of Postliberal theology to this day.

Frei goes on to make a remark in passing that, for all its simplicity, seems to cut to the heart of his disagreements with Henry. Frei states:

> The Bible has a very *particular* story to tell. That doesn't mean all the elements in the Bible are narrative. It only means, so far as I can see, that something like John 1:14—"And the word was made flesh and dwelt among us, full of grace and truth"—is something that we don't understand except as a sequence enacted in the life, death and resurrection of Jesus. The Christian tradition by and large took verses like that to be the center of its story.[48]

This statement implies that Frei departs from Henry's conception of meaning and truth. He does not share the view that cognitive truth is necessarily propositional in form. Remember that for Henry propositions demanding our assent are the only way (or only proper way) that truth is conveyed. As he insists in an essay called "Is the Bible Literally True?" both the metaphors and the stories of Scripture need to be re-stated in propositional form; otherwise, Henry argues, they cannot really be understood.[49] For Frei, however, the stories are not secondary in significance to doctrines. Although Frei thinks that doctrines are indeed conceptual redescriptions of the biblical narratives, it is the narratives themselves that have the priority in conveying meaning and truth. Whereas Henry seems to think the narratives are finally about the doctrines, for Frei it is just the reverse. Although doctrines indeed arise from the narratives and point back to them, it is the narratives that properly convey biblical truth. We don't understand doctrinal statements, Frei argues, except by understanding the stories. A doctrinal statement like "the Word became flesh" is something that we don't understand except through the biblical accounts of Jesus' life, death, and resurrection. A statement like the "Word became flesh" is not a logically prior or independent proposition; it is the center of the gospel *story*.

There are clearly several issues here. Unlike Henry, Frei does not think that cognitive truth is *necessarily* propositional in form, or more precisely, that propositions are the only *proper* form of cognitive truth. Nor does he think that cognitive truth is the only *kind* of truth, or even the primary kind of truth, that the Bible conveys to us—although he certainly agrees with Henry that biblical truth is not non-cognitive. Rather Frei thinks that biblical truth is primarily narrative in form and that this form of truth demands more than just our cognition. In particular, although the doctrines and the stories are inseparable, Frei thinks that in the end the doctrines are understood through the stories rather than holding, with Henry, that the stories are finally understood through doctrinal propositions. On such matters as these, I will argue, Kuyper and Bavinck represent a form of Evangelicalism that seems closer to Frei than is possible for someone like Henry, just because Henry has committed himself more heavily than they have to certain rationalist forms of modernism.

Along with arguing for the primacy of biblical narrative, Frei also argues for the sufficiency of Scripture. Remember that Henry took a position on this matter that was ambiguous or at least complex. Although in principle he did not wish to challenge the idea that Scripture functions independently of modern historical criticism, in practice he insisted that the two must be systematically correlated. What Frei denies is precisely the necessity of systematic correlation. Whereas Henry stands for something like "systematic consubstantiation," Frei pleads by contrast for something like *"ad hoc* minimalism." That is, for Frei faith and historiography are related in a way that is not systematic but ad hoc, and the ad hoc use that faith makes of historiography is not maximal, as Henry proposes, but minimal. Faith needs no more from modern historical criticism, Frei urges, than two very minimal assurances: first, that Christ's resurrection has not been historically disconfirmed;[50] and second, "that a man, Jesus of Nazareth, who proclaimed the Kingdom of God's nearness, did exist and was finally executed."[51] This much and more, Henry could have learned about Frei's position from a careful reading of *The Identity of Jesus Christ*.

Frei presents a complex set of reasons for this stance of *"ad hoc* minimalism."[52] Although they cannot all be pursued here, some of them form the background to what he says in response to Henry about the sufficiency of Scripture. Three points in particular are worthy of note. The first has to do with the actual state of the evidence. Frei thinks the existing historical evidence is so sparse and so indeterminate that it can be given a plausible shape by any number of mutually conflicting positions, ranging all the way from extreme skepticism at one end to measured credence at the other.[53] The indeterminate state of the evidence alone would be enough to rule out any such strong reliance on it as Henry requires. In any case, what little relevant evidence that exists is not enough to disconfirm faith in Christ's resurrection, yet it is enough to confirm a certain historical minimum about his life, teaching and death, and that is basically all that faith needs to know from the use of the historical-critical method.[54]

Second, whereas the possibility of disconfirmation raises one set of issues, that of confirmation raises quite another so that the two ought not to be run together and confused. Whereas in principle the resurrection of Jesus could be disconfirmed by historical evidence (though in fact it is not), in the nature of the case his resurrection could not possibly be confirmed by that means. "Actual belief in the resurrection is a matter of faith," writes Frei, "and not of arguments from possibility or evidence."[55] Confronted by the claim that Jesus Christ rose from the dead, historical-critical method simply reaches its categorical limit. In the nature of the case, Jesus Christ can be known for who he is only through our response of faith to his own self-witness as the Risen Savior, by means of Word and Spirit. "Concerning Jesus Christ and him alone," argues Frei, "factual affirmation is completely one with faith and trust of the heart, with love of him, and love of the neighbors for whom he gave himself completely."[56] Note that the response as Frei describes it is not simply one of assent, but one that involves trust and love. Since the truth of the gospel is fundamentally a person rather than a proposition, our proper grasp of this truth always involves us somehow as whole persons.

Unlike Henry, Frei thinks that we properly grasp the truth of the gospel not just with our heads, but also with our hearts and our hands. Although the term "God" as used by the language of faith is "in some sense referential," Frei writes, "it is also true in some sense other than a referential one."[57] In other words, the truth of the gospel requires more than just cognitive confirmation, because the category of truth has performative as well as cognitive and referential aspects. The truth is not just something to be known but also something to be done. Furthermore, these two aspects of truth—the cognitive and the performative—are so deeply interrelated in practice that this interrelation defies all attempts at strict or systematic conceptualization. Hence the word "God" as used by faith, says Frei, "is true by being true to the way it works in one's life, and by holding the world, including the political, economic and social world, to account by the gauge of its truthfulness."[58] In short, "the word 'God' is used both descriptively and cognitively, but also obediently or trustingly, and it is very difficult to make one a function of the other. ... You have both uses together."[59] As will become clear in a moment, Frei's conception of truth means that in his low-key epistemology the objective and the subjective, the factual and the meaningful, the cognitive and the performative cannot be so neatly separated and detached from each other as they are in Henry's discourse.

Third, Frei understands the genre of the Gospel narratives differently from Henry. He sees them not primarily as reports about historical facts, but rather as depictions of a particular person. By means of these stories Jesus is depicted as the unique and indispensable Savior. The stories seem more like a realistic though mysterious portrait than they do like a historical report. The values governing the construction of this portrait are not necessarily the same as those that would govern a work of modern history. Although some aspects of the narratives are surely factual in the modern sense, other aspects may well be depictions of the Risen Savior in the lineaments of the earthly Jesus. That is, at certain points and to varying degrees, the narratives may actually depict the earthly Jesus in a way that conflates him with the risen Christ, or that superimposes the risen Christ on the earthly Jesus. And yet they may function quite aptly to portray his identity as the Gospel intends to convey it. The validity of the narrative portrayal does not necessarily depend on factuality as narrowly conceived. For the chief "fact" that the narratives wish to convey is precisely that the earthly Jesus and the risen Christ are one and the same.[60]

This understanding of how faith is related to history provides the background for what Frei says to Henry about the sufficiency of Scripture. We refer to Jesus Christ by means of the gospel story, writes Frei, and "the text is sufficient for our reference."[61] Beyond the minimal use of historical method, faith does not need the kind of systematic external validation that Henry so zealously demands. "It is enough," writes Frei, "to have the reference to Christ crucified and risen."[62] To suppose otherwise is not so much to set about refuting skepticism on its own terms—which would in any case be an inordinately ambitious project—as it is to verge toward a kind of practical atheism. Systematic human efforts at independent validation, however well intended, can all too easily overshadow our reliance on the promises and faithfulness of God. Frei's minimalism, I would suggest, is really an epistemological adaptation of "justification by faith alone apart from works of the law." Ad hoc minimalism seems to honor the Reformation principle of *sola scriptura*—of the sufficiency of Scripture—in a way that systematic consubstantiation does not.

The question of validation is a function of the question of reference, and reference in the biblical narratives is a complex matter. "I would say," Frei remarks, "that we refer in a double sense. There is often a historical reference and often there is textual reference; that is, the text is witness to the Word of God, whether it is historical or not."[63] Either way, says Frei, the mode of reference is analogical, not (as Henry would have it) literal or univocal.[64] For Frei the sufficiency of Scripture in matters of reference means being bound to the basic patterns of scriptural usage and depiction, not to the literal details. "We start from the text: that is the language pattern," he writes, "the meaning-and-reference pattern, to which we are bound, and which is sufficient for us."[65] The linguistic patterns of the narratives are what identify Jesus Christ, Frei seems to be saying, and these patterns are sufficient, because they stand in a good enough or analogical relation to what is factually the case. What is factually the case, however, is also complex. For the dual referentiality of the narratives pertains to the twofold factuality of Jesus Christ. In other words, the narratives are so constructed that they refer not only to Jesus in his earthly life (whether we can verify that factuality by modern methods or not), but also and at the same time to the risen Jesus Christ who lives to all eternity, and who attests himself to us through those narratives here and now. Faith in Jesus Christ involves a confidence that the Gospel narratives are sufficient for us in the arresting, complex, and subtle ways that they depict and refer to Jesus Christ in this twofold sense. By contrast, a faith that anxiously seeks to prop itself up by means of systematic and external validation, and to invalidate its opponents by defeating them, seems in danger of ceasing to be faith.

From Frei's point of view, Carl Henry consistently makes a series of category mistakes—mistakes about reference, factuality, genre, and truth—mainly because he is excessively committed to the canons of modernity. "I am looking for a way," writes Frei, "that looks for a relation between Christian theology and philosophy that disagrees with a view of certainty and knowledge which Evangelicals and liberals hold in common."[66] Evangelicals and Liberals, each according to their own kind, subscribe to modernist views of how we obtain certainty and knowledge in a way that ends up either distorting or denying the gospel. Unlike "Dr. Henry," writes Frei, "I think 'reference'—to say nothing of 'truth'—in Christian usage is not a simple, single or philosophically univocal category."[67] Nor does he think that the concept of "fact" is theory-neutral.[68] Such terms "are not privileged, theory-neutral, trans-cultural"; they are not "ingredient in the structure of the human mind and of reality always and everywhere."[69] They are modern terms that depend on modern ways of thinking. While they need not be banned from Christian theology, they ought not to be used systematically.

The alternative to using modern epistemological categories systematically is simply to use them "eclectically and provisionally,"[70] always striving to grant primacy to the witness of the gospel itself. Theories that are logically independent of the gospel ought not to be used as frames of mind that end up distorting its intrinsic mysteries and certainties. When modernist versions of formal certainty and clarity are leavened by a more modest view that allows for an ineffaceable degree of subjectivity, commitment, cultural-historical location, and other forms of self-involvement in all our cognitive judgments, then fact and meaning, cognition and performance, mystery and clarity, humility and certainty need no longer be so radically divorced from one another as they are by the epistemological excesses of modernity. It should then be possible to see with Postliberals like George Lindbeck and Hans Frei that we never have truth—and least of all theological truth—except under a depiction. "The truth to which we refer," writes Frei, "we cannot state apart from the biblical language which we employ to do so. And belief in the divine authority of Scripture is for me simply that we do not need more."[71]

BEYOND EXCESSIVE MODERNITY: THE PROMISE OF OLD AMSTERDAM

At this point my remarks become much more nearly conjectural than analytical. Although I do not know the writings of Abraham Kuyper (1837–1920) and Herman Bavinck (1854–1921) very well, the impression I receive from reading those who do is that these two theologians have not committed themselves as heavily as Carl Henry has to the canons of modernity. Although they hold a high view of scriptural inerrancy, they do not seem as encumbered as Henry does by excessive epistemological anxieties about skepticism, factuality, reference, certainty, and objectivity, even when they also express concern about such matters. In general, their conceptions of scriptural unity, factuality, and truth seem less distorted by the systematic use of theories that are logically independent of the gospel. Above all, their conceptions of inerrancy seem finally to have a different logical status, and to play a different conceptual role in their theologies, than what we find in the case of someone like Henry. The likes of Kuyper and Bavinck therefore emerge as more fruitful dialogue partners, it seems to me, than the likes of Henry for any future discussion between Evangelicals and Postliberals. I can do no more here, however, than hastily to sketch some themes that might be of interest in such a discussion.

One such theme is the unity of Scripture. When Kuyper discusses this question, he highlights two matters that seem to differentiate him from Evangelicals like Henry, while also placing him at the same time within hailing distance of Postliberals like Frei or Lindbeck. The first is that the unity of Scripture is the *presupposition* of a faithful reading of Scripture, not a logical inference independent of faith. Since the contents of Scripture are obviously diverse, faith cannot arrive at Scripture's unity unless it takes that unity as the starting point. Kuyper writes: "He who, in the case of Scripture, thus begins with the multiplicity of the human factor, and tries in this way to reach out after its unity will never find it, simply because he began with its denial in principle."[72] Or again he states: "And however much it is your duty to study that *multiplicity* and *particularity* in the Scripture (both materially and formally), yet from that multiplicity you must ever come back to the view of *the unity of the conception,* if there is, indeed, to be such a thing for you as Holy Scripture."[73] One notes with interest Kuyper's view that Scripture's unity does not efface its real diversity as well as his emphasis on the priority of faith as a necessary condition for perceiving that unity. Kuyper shows no anxiety that he has somehow lapsed into a fatal form of subjectivism.

Nor does he try to present Scripture's unity, as Henry does, as a "logical system of shared beliefs"[74] or as a comprehensive "rational unity."[75] Instead Kuyper stresses that "Christ is the whole of Scripture, and Scripture brings the *esse* of the Christ to our consciousness."[76] He also cautions against restricting the Logos to words, even though the Logos is now embodied for us in Scripture.[77] He almost seems to be following George Lindbeck when the latter recommends reading Scripture "as a Christ-centered narrationally and typologically unified whole in conformity to a Trinitarian rule of faith."[78] By contrast, when Henry writes of scriptural unity, he does not (to my surprise) concentrate on a Christ-centered reading,[79] he comes close to postulating a dichotomy between propositional content and personal encounter with Christ (as though they somehow failed to form a unity),[80] and he finally elevates cognitive propositionalism over the person of Christ in his account of Scripture's "logically interconnected content."[81] I suspect that Kuyper would have had little sympathy with such moves.

Even more interesting, however, is the view taken by Kuyper and Bavinck when they come to the question of Scripture's factuality. For both theologians, according to Richard Gaffin, "the biblical records are impressionistic; that is, they are not marked by notarial precision or blue-print, architectural exactness."[82] Nevertheless, neither theologian thought that "this impressionistic quality" in any way detracted from the certainty of biblical truth.[83] The truth of Scripture, they held, is appropriate to its unique divine authorship.[84] As the ultimate author of Scripture, God is more like an artist than a photographer.[85] "It is not even [Scripture's] purpose," wrote Bavinck, "to provide us with an historical account according to the standard of reliability which is demanded in other areas of knowledge."[86] The historical narratives of Scripture, he also stated, "are not history in our sense but prophecy."[87] They do not intend to convey "historical, chronological geographical data ... in themselves"; rather, what they intend to attest is "the truth poured out on us in Christ."[88]

The doctrine of inerrancy advanced by Kuyper and Bavinck is in accord with their understanding of Scripture's "impressionistic" quality of factuality and truth. Although, as Gaffin demonstrates, inerrancy for them extended to all matters, including historical data, nonetheless they finally understood inerrancy "in an impressionistic, nontechnical sense."[89] They both felt, writes Gaffin, that "pushing infallibility into the limelight is intellectualism" of the kind "that began with the rationalists."[90] Kuyper even went so far as to remark that "If Satan has brought us to the point where we are arguing about the infallibility of Scripture, then we are already out from under the authority of Scripture."[91] Infallibility for Kuyper and Bavinck, it seems, is not the kind of intellectualistic doctrine that it is for someone like Henry. It does not function as the linchpin of objectivity, certainty, and truth. It seems more nearly to be a nontechnical term for the reliability and sufficiency of Scripture.

With these views of scriptural unity, factuality, and truth, Kuyper and Bavinck arguably stand midway on a continuum that begins with someone like Calvin at one end and that stretches to figures like Frei and Lindbeck at the other.

Like any careful reader of the Gospels, Calvin was aware that the evangelists were not overly concerned about strict factual accuracy. "It is well known," he wrote, "that the evangelists were not scrupulous in their time sequences, not even keeping to the details of the words and actions [of Jesus]."[92] What the evangelists were really interested in, Calvin tells us, were not the details so much as the *patterns* by which the identity and significance of Jesus Christ could be disclosed to us. "The evangelists had no intention of so putting their narrative together as always to keep to an exact order of events," he wrote, "but to bring the whole pattern together to produce a kind of mirror or screen image of those features most useful for the understanding of Christ."[93] Kuyper and Bavinck go at least one step further by devising conceptions of factuality, inerrancy, and truth that would seem to conform to the kind of interests and practices that Calvin noticed in the evangelists. In this connection Postliberal theologians like Frei and Lindbeck could then be seen as going at least one step further still. For although they see a greater discrepancy between biblical narrative and historical fact than did their predecessors, they retain a high sense of biblical authority about what they think really matters, namely, the literary patterns of the texts by which Jesus Christ's identity and significance as the risen Savior are really disclosed to us.

What I wish to suggest, therefore, about what Evangelicals might learn from Postliberals is simply this. Although on these matters they may not wish to go as far as theologians like Frei and Lindbeck, they should at least be prepared to go as far as theologians like Calvin, Kuyper, and Bavinck. Freed from the encumbrances of excessive modernity, then the real conversation could begin.[94]

BEYOND POSTLIBERALISM: THE PROMISE OF EVANGELICAL THEOLOGY

Carl Henry, it will be recalled, accused Hans Frei of diverting attention from revelation; and Gabriel Fackre observed (more justly) that theologians like Frei and Lindbeck seem more concerned with method than with theological content. As my thought-experiment now moves into its final phase, I am prepared to grant that Postliberal theology, at least in the versions from Yale, has run up a considerable deficit in producing works of doctrinal substance. In this light the promise of Evangelical theology, at the very least, is that it has never allowed itself to focus on questions of method, so dear to academic theologians, at the expense of the kind of real theological work that the church needs in order to fulfill its task of faithfully proclaiming the gospel.

More importantly, Evangelical theology, it seems to me, has always had an admirable sense of priorities. Within the field of Christian doctrine *per se*, it has consistently been the standard bearer of the Reformation insofar as it has stood—often in a lonely and exposed position—for "Christ alone," "grace alone," and "faith alone" in all matters pertaining to salvation. Although Evangelicalism has not always been so strong in upholding other traditional *loci* such as the doctrine of the Trinity—although the chapter on this theme in Alister McGrath's new book *Christian Theology: An Introduction* makes my observation obsolete[95]—Evangelicalism has historically been of inestimable value right down to the present day for its uncompromising insistence on the saving death of Christ as the very heart of the gospel. The cross of Christ, writes John R. W. Stott, "lies at the center of the historic, biblical faith, and the fact that this is not always everywhere acknowledged is in itself a sufficient justification for preserving a distinctive Evangelical testimony."[96] Stott continues:

> Evangelical Christians believe that in and through Christ crucified God substituted himself for us, and bore our sins, dying the death we deserved to die, in order that we might be restored to his favor and adopted into his family.[97]

Stott is also commendable for his attempt to set forth not only what we were earlier calling the "cognitive" aspects of this doctrine, but also its "performative" aspects or practical implications.[98]

In conclusion, let me suggest not only that Postliberals would indeed have much to learn from Evangelicals in these matters, but also that Evangelicals seem to have run up a deficit directly opposite to that of their Postliberal counterparts: they are more concerned about content than about theological method. If I may, let me put it like this. Although Evangelicals have consistently produced an impressive number of distinguished biblical scholars over the years, especially in the field of New Testament studies, and although more recently they have also produced a distinguished crop of philosophers and of historians of Christianity in North America, they have not done nearly so well in producing truly distinguished theologians, and this shortfall may have something to do with their failure to attend sufficiently to questions of theological method.[99]

It is not surprising, therefore, that when George Lindbeck proposes to widen the scope of Postliberalism beyond what we know from Yale, the theologians, undeniably distinguished, to whom he is drawn are Karl Barth and Hans Urs von Balthasar. Lindbeck observes:

> Here are twentieth century theologians whose use of the Bible is more nearly classical than anything in several centuries and who yet are distinctively modern (e.g., they do not reject historical criticism). Both are wary of translating the Bible into alien conceptualities; both seek, rather, to redescribe the world or worlds in which they live in biblical terms; both treat Scripture

as a narrationally (or, for von Balthasar, "dramatically") and typologically unified whole; and in both the reader is referred back to the biblical text itself by exegetical work which is an integral part of the theological program. In short, these two theologians inhabit the same universe of theological discourse as the fathers, medievals, and Reformers to a greater degree than do most modern theologians.[100]

Most interesting is then the conclusion that Lindbeck draws: "Discussions between them are possible—perhaps even decidable—by reference to the text because they approach Scripture in basically similar ways."[101] If I am not wholly mistaken about the continuum that seems to run from the likes of Calvin through the likes of Kuyper and Bavinck to the likes of Frei and Lindbeck,[102] then it would not seem amiss to suggest that a similar possibility exists also for Evangelicals and Postliberals today.

NOTES

1. Hans Küng, *The Church* (New York: Sheed and Ward, 1967), 442.
2. Ibid.
3. Hans W. Frei, *Types of Christian Theology* (New Haven: Yale University Press, 1992), 84.
4. Jack Rogers and Donald McKim, *The Authority and Interpretation of the Bible: A Historical Approach* (San Francisco: Harper & Row, 1979).
5. Richard B. Gaffin, Jr., "Old Amsterdam and Inerrancy?" *Westminster Theological Journal* 44 (1982): 250–89 and 45 (1983): 219–72.
6. As a movement within Anglo-Saxon Christianity, however, Evangelicalism is best understood as arising in the early eighteenth century. See David W. Bebbington, *Evangelicalism in Modern Britain: A History from the 1730s to the 1980s* (Grand Rapids: Baker, 1989).
7. Carl F. H. Henry, "Narrative Theology: An Evangelical Appraisal," *Trinity Journal* 8 NS (1987): 3–19, on 5.
8. Ibid., 15.
9. Ibid., 4.
10. Ibid., 9.
11. Ibid., 10.
12. Quoted by Henry, ibid., 15. Although I do not mean to equate narrative theology with Postliberal theology, they are closely enough related that what Fackre says of the one applies equally well to the other.
13. Ibid., 15.
14. Ibid., 8, 9, 19.
15. Ibid., 19.

16. See, however, Robert Letham, "Is Evangelicalism Christian?" *The Evangelical Quarterly* 67 (1995): 3–16. Letham not only offers an illuminating account of distinctive "Evangelical" characteristics, but also uses it to explain why Evangelicalism has become increasingly fragmented and diffuse.

17. It is not clear that all who call themselves "Evangelicals" would be willing to subscribe to these ecumenical standards, and in general I would regard this as a serious problem. On the other hand, most such dissenting Evangelicals would probably be willing to rule out the kinds of theological positions that these ecumenical standards are designed to rule out. Even among those who might somehow want to endorse a position that is ruled out, however, it would not always be easy (though sometimes it would) from a Postliberal point of view to reject the endorsed position out of hand. For an incisive discussion of this and related matters, see Letham, "Is Evangelicalism Christian?" (see n. 16).

18. Ibid., 18.

19. Perhaps as another indication of his worry about "subjectivism," Henry strangely misreads Frei's narrative analysis of the Gospels as proposing a merely "linguistic" or "literary" presence of God. "Narrative hermeneutics removes from the interpretative process any text-transcendent referent and clouds the narrative's relationship to a divine reality not exhausted by literary presence" (Ibid., 13). Does God really speak to us through his Word as Calvin taught, Henry asks, or not? "Narrative exegesis is misguided if it leaves problematical the divine authority of its message and its revelatory identity and fails over and above literary affirmation to indicate an adequate test for truth" (p. 13). It is not enough to stay at the level of literary analysis. Frei (along with Brevard Childs) is said to correlate the biblical text with "God's linguistic presence"—a category that has no conceivable bearing on any fair reading of Frei (or for that matter of Childs) (Ibid., 7. See also p. 9.). Henry seems to think, oddly, that if "historical events are not *per se* a medium of revelation," then God's only mode of presence must be "literary" (Ibid., 7). Frei speaks of God's "presence" in relation to Scripture as "mysterious" but never as "literary." See Frei, *The Identity of Jesus Christ* (Philadelphia: Fortress, 1975). There seems to be no good reason to think that Frei viewed the relationship between Word and Spirit fundamentally differently from Calvin.

20. Ibid., 12.

21. Ibid.

22. Ibid., 9.

23. Ibid., 6.

24. Ibid.

25. Ibid.

26. Ibid., 13.

27. Ibid.

28. Ibid.

29. Ibid., 8.

30. Ibid., 12.

31. Ibid.

32. Ibid., 11.
33. Ibid.
34. Ibid.
35. Ibid., 12.
36. This positive move may, in turn, take one of several forms. It may simply argue that the case for historical factuality is *one* plausible position among others. Or it may take the stranger form that historical factuality is *more* plausible than any other position. Or it may take the still stronger form that historical factuality is the *only* plausible position and that all other possibilities are implausible. If I am not mistaken, Henry seems to gravitate toward the latter position.
37. Ibid., 5, italics added.
38. Ibid., 8.
39. Ibid., 3.
40. Ibid., 13, 14.
41. Ibid., 14.
42. Ibid.
43. Ibid., 19.
44. Hans W. Frei, "Response to Narrative Theology: An Evangelical Proposal," in *Theology and Narrative*, ed. Hans W. Frei (New York: Oxford University Press, 1993): 207–12; on 207–8. Reprinted from *Trinity Journal* 8 NS (1987): 21–4.
45. Ibid., 208.
46. Ibid.
47. Frei, "Remarks in Connection with a Theological Proposal," in *Theology and Narrative*, 26–44; on 32.
48. Frei, "Response," 208.
49. Carl F. H. Henry, "Is the Bible Literally True?" in *God, Revelation and Authority*, Vol. IV (Waco, TX: Word Books, 1979): 103–28. See especially the remarks about metaphor on pp. 109, 113 and 120, and about stories on pp. 105–8.
50. Frei, *Identity of Jesus Christ*, 151; cf. 103.
51. Ibid., 51.
52. For a further account see George Hunsinger, "Afterword: Hans Frei as Theologian," in Frei, *Theology and Narrative*, 235–70, especially pp. 265–8.
53. Frei, *Identity of Jesus Christ*, 48, 132, 141.
54. Ibid., 151; cf. 103.
55. Ibid., 152.
56. Ibid., 157; cf. 147.
57. Frei, "Response" (see n. 44), 210.
58. Ibid.
59. Ibid. Whereas Henry seems to make the question of performance a function of cognitive truth, George Lindbeck seems to move in the opposite direction. "The *only* way to assert the truth is to do something about it. ... It is *only* through

the performatory use of religious utterances that they acquire propositional force." See Lindbeck, *The Nature of Doctrine* (Philadelphia: Westminster Press, 1984), 66, italics added. Although Frei agrees with Lindbeck that the cognitive and performative aspects of truth are interrelated, he does not follow him in making the one a function of the other. In "Epilogue: George Lindbeck and *The Nature of Doctrine*," Frei differentiates himself from Lindbeck by giving qualified support to those whom he describes as "moderate propositionalists." Moderate propositionalism seems to be the idea that the cognitive and performative aspects of truth are at once deeply interrelated and inseparable, while also being relatively autonomous and distinct, so that in principle neither has precedence over the other (though in practice either one might assume precedence, depending on the situation). See *Theology and Dialogue: Essays in Conversation with George Lindbeck,* ed. Bruce D. Marshall (Notre Dame: University of Notre Dame Press, 1990), 278–9.

60. Frei, *Identity of Jesus Christ,* 140–1.
61. Frei, "Response," 209.
62. Ibid.
63. Ibid.
64. For Henry's argument against analogical reference, and for univocal reference, see "Is the Bible Literally True?" (see n. 49), especially p. 118.
65. Frei, "Response," 209.
66. Ibid., 211.
67. Ibid., 210.
68. Ibid., 211.
69. Ibid.
70. Ibid., 210.
71. Ibid.
72. Abraham Kuyper, *Principles of Sacred Theology* (Grand Rapids: Wm. B. Eerdmans Publishing Co., 1954), 474. Quoted by Richard B. Gaffin, Jr. "Old Amsterdam and Inerrancy?" *Westminster Theological Journal* 44 (1982): 256–7.
73. Kuyper, *Principles*, 480. Quoted by Gaffin, ibid., 257n. For a somewhat similar view, see David H. Kelsey, *The Uses of Scripture in Recent Theology* (Philadelphia: Fortress Press, 1975), 103.
74. Carl F. H. Henry, "The Lost Unity of the Bible," in *God, Revelation and Authority,* Vol. IV (see n. 49): 456.
75. Carl F. H. Henry, "The Unity of Divine Revelation," in *God, Revelation and Authority,* Vol. II (Waco, TX: Word Books, 1976): 74.
76. Kuyper, *Principles,* 477. Quoted by Gaffin, "Old Amsterdam and Inerrancy?" *Westminster Theological Journal* 44 (1982): 255.
77. Gaffin, ibid.
78. George A. Lindbeck, "Scripture, Consensus, and Community," in *Biblical Interpretation in Crisis,* ed. Richard John Neuhaus (Grand Rapids: Wm. B. Eerdmans Publishing Co., 1989): 83.

79. See the belated and underdeveloped reference in Henry, "Lost Unity," 468–9.
80. Henry, "Unity in Divine Revelation," 74–5.
81. Ibid., 74. See also "Lost Unity," 469.
82. Gaffin, ibid., 278. Cf. 276.
83. Ibid.
84. Ibid., 288–9.
85. Ibid., 281.
86. Herman Bavinck, *Gereformeerdedogmatiek* (4 vols.; Kampen: J.H. Kok, 1895–1901; 2nd revised and enlarged ed., 1906–11; 6th ed., 1976). Vol. I, 356. Quoted by Gaffin, *Westminster Theological Journal* 45 (1983): 229.
87. Bavink, ibid., 361ff. Quoted by Gaffin, ibid., 231.
88. Bavink, ibid., 546f. Quoted by Gaffin, ibid., 259.
89. Gaffin, ibid., 269.
90. Gaffin, WTJ 44 (1982), 272. Cf. 284.
91. Kuyper, *Dictaten dogmatiek*, Vol. 2 (1.66) (Grand Rapids: J. B. Hulst, n.d.). Quoted by Gaffin, ibid., 271–2.
92. John Calvin, *Calvin's Commentaries,* Vol. II: *A Harmony of the Gospels: Matthew, Mark, and Luke* (Grand Rapids: Wm. B. Eerdmans Publishing Co., 1972), 55 (on Luke 8:19). Cited by William C. Placher, *Narratives of a Vulnerable God* (Louisville: Westminster/John Knox Press, 1994), 7.
93. John Calvin, *Calvin's Commentaries,* Vol. I: *A Harmony of the Gospels: Matthew, Mark, and Luke* (Grand Rapids: Wm. B. Eerdmans Publishing Co., 1972), 139 (on Matt. 4:5). Cited by Placher, ibid.
94. Perhaps it might also be mentioned here for the sake of future discussion that, from a Postliberal point of view, American Evangelicals have typically been at least as excessive (and with consequences no less unfortunate for the progress of the gospel) in committing themselves to the pathologies of American nationalism and militarism as they have in encumbering themselves with the excesses of modem epistemology. The common thread in both cases, if I may say so, seems to have something to do with a lack of Christian self-confidence; an inordinate, or insufficiently self-critical, desire for external validation; and an aversion (in practice) to the theology of the cross.
95. Alister E. McGrath, *Christian Theology: An Introduction* (Oxford: Blackwell, 1994).
96. John R. W. Stott, *The Cross of Christ* (Downers Grove, IL: Intervarsity Press, 1986), 7.
97. Ibid.
98. Ibid. See "Part Four: Living Under the Cross."
99. In making this observation, I am using the term "Evangelical" in the somewhat peculiar sense it has acquired in the English-speaking world over the last 250 years or so. A more generous (and more descriptively apt) usage would widen its scope to include theologians often neglected, excluded, or castigated by self-described "Evangelicals": theologians like Thomas F. Torrance, Eberhard Jüngel, and Robert W. Jenson, each of whose work I would regard as distinguished.

100. Lindbeck, "Scripture, Consensus, and Community" (see n. 78), p. 98.
101. Ibid.
102. It may not be amiss to indicate that I don't think there is necessarily a tight fit between one's views of historical criticism and the continuum I am seeking to establish. The continuum pertains to the relationship between *signum* and *res* in Holy Scripture. What the theologians on my continuum all share is a belief that this relationship is positive though not univocal. The rejection of univocity separates them from someone like Henry, just as the affirmation of adequate and reliable reference separates them from modem skeptics. Not everyone who accepts historical criticism believes that it undermines adequate reference or signification (although there may be disagreements about just what constitutes the *res*). The issue that determines the continuum is not whether one accepts the relative validity of modem historical criticism (about which Calvin, of course, knew nothing, and toward which Kuyper and Bavinck were largely negative though not without some ambivalence). The issue is whether one affirms the texts of the Holy Scripture as inspired, authoritative, and sufficient vehicles of reference to their relevant subject matter, including its historical aspects (about which the likes of Frei and Lindbeck agree with the rest).

CHAPTER FIFTEEN

On Being Theologically Hospitable to Jesus Christ: Hans Frei's Achievement

Review article of Hans Frei, Types of Christian Theology*

DAVID F. FORD

Hans Frei (1922–88) was Professor of Religious Studies at Yale University and died before he could complete a major project on the figure of Jesus in England and Germany (in high and popular culture, within and beyond the churches) since 1700. Yet to put his achievement like that could be very misleading. I suspect that he might well be the most significant figure in North American theology and religious studies during the last quarter of this century. His importance is due to a convergence of factors: his way of understanding and carrying forward the Yale theological tradition of his teacher H. Richard Niebuhr; his interpretation of the theology of Karl Barth in a way which allowed Barth to be given a fresh, provocative reading different from most

---

*Hans W. Frei, *Types of Christian Theology* ed. George Hunsinger and William C. Placher (Newhaven and London: Yale University Press, 1992). © Oxford University Press 1995 [Journal of Theological Studies, NS, Vol. 46, Pt. 2, October 1995]

"Barthians" and "anti-Barthians"; his hermeneutical work on the gospels which culminated in his book *The Identity of Jesus Christ. The Hermeneutical Bases of Dogmatic Theology* (1975); his associated historical work on the modern period summed up in *The Eclipse of Biblical Narrative. A Study in Eighteenth and Nineteenth Century Hermeneutics* (1975); his part in an influential group of theologians and scholars at Yale, including George Lindbeck, David Kelsey, and Wayne Meeks; his teaching of many students who have gone on to help shape their field; his role within Yale and beyond in helping to see how those often uneasy bedfellows, theology and religious studies, might face up to their intellectual and institutional problems and possibilities with integrity and also with sociological self-awareness; his concern always to relate his theology to politics—to the end of his life he grappled with this aspect of H. Richard Niebuhr's legacy; and the considerable amount of work done on that final project.

Yet despite having achieved so much and having been, for the many who were deeply influenced by him in person, such an amazingly generous and wise colleague, teacher, or friend, there is a certain appropriateness in the incompleteness of that project. Frei was something of a Moses, going to the edge of the Promised Land, pointing at it but not crossing over. That land was not just the historical project on Jesus, it was also the doing of Christian theology under its classical headings of God, creation, Jesus Christ, salvation, and so on. He did many fragments of such theology, and some of the most valuable have now been published in a posthumous volume, *Theology and Narrative: Selected Essays* (1993, reviewed in *JTS*, NS, 46 (1995) 428–30). But he was deeply aware of the irony of someone with his utter commitment to theology who yet spent most of his academic life in a religious studies post on apparently preparatory matters of historical investigation, conceptual analysis, methodological clarification, categorizing theologies into types, and institutional development of his discipline. It is an achievement that can be taken very differently. To put it in terms of the figuration on which he was such an acute commentator: some see the academic enterprise in relation to religion as quite properly stopping short of any theological Promised Land—its contribution is "second order" and its academic credentials are endangered by direct advocacy of substantive theological positions, so the academic is called to endless wilderness journeys, at best giving to others the opportunity to cross over the Jordan and set up a theological home; others rejoice in Frei having helped them so far and see his life's work as enabling the next generation to do what he would have wanted to do: working out a theology that deals with the big issues of Christian faith in dialogue with a wide range of voices from the past and present, having above all been enabled by his typology to see what the right approach to constructive theology might be; yet others wonder whether it might by possible to be more like Joshua, enduring (and at times even enjoying) those desert journeys alongside Moses, but aiming to do their main work across the Jordan. Figures have their limits, but the prosaic point is that the work of Frei is, in its ambiguity as well as in its authoritative clarity, an extraordinarily helpful focus through which to try to discern what theology and religious studies are about and what the fruitful ways forward might be for specifically Christian academic theology.

In this article I want to focus, in review mode, on the recent publication of the material for his final project that Frei left behind. It has been well edited by George Hunsinger and William C. Placher and published as *Types of Christian Theology*. It consists largely of what was discovered among his papers relating to three sets of lectures: a complete manuscript of the 1983 Shaffer Lectures at Yale Divinity School, parts of the Edward Cadbury Lectures delivered in the University of Birmingham in 1987, and nearly complete manuscripts of some Princeton University lectures delivered later in 1987. Also included are a grant proposal which gives a most helpful summary of his project, and a review of Eberhard Busch's biography of Karl Barth.

I THE "MYSTERY" OF THE MISSING CADBURY LECTURES

The editors say in their introduction: "What happened to other manuscripts, particularly the rest of the Cadburys, remains a mystery" (p. ix). I am in a position to clear up part of that mystery and, for the sake of accuracy and completeness, before discussing the content of the book I will offer my conclusions about the Cadbury material and its relation to what has been presented by the editors. Those who are not concerned with the results of this detective work might wish to skip the next six paragraphs.

I attended Frei's Cadbury Lectures in Birmingham and took notes. The editors used those notes, but there is more information that could have been elicited from them. My reconstruction of the Cadburys in correlation with what the editors have published (hereafter called *Types*) is as follows. There were eight Cadbury lectures. The first, entitled "According to the Text: The Specificity and Universality of Jesus Christ" is all in the Princeton material which appears as Appendix B in *Types*—it has been filled out in places, but is substantially the same. The second, entitled "The Theological Faculty in Modern Universities: Growth of a Profession" is included in the Princeton material appearing in *Types* as part of Appendix A Part 1. The only substantial section of this Cadbury that is not included in the Princeton lecture (or anywhere else in *Types*) is a historical introduction on John Locke's mediating theology. The third Cadbury, entitled "Teaching about Reason and History: The Rational Pursuit of Jesus," is mostly included in the same Princeton material in Appendix

A Part 1—there are additions about Edward Farley and Van Harvey and about the contrast between England, where geology became the paradigmatic science, and Germany, where it was history; and there was also a summary of the five types of the typology. So it seems likely that for his Princeton lectures Frei used the first three of his Cadburys (as well as other material, mainly that in Appendix A Part 2). This might explain why no manuscript of these Cadburys exists—Frei was working with handwritten scripts and he probably integrated those of the first three Cadburys with his Princeton manuscripts; or he may have decided that, after producing the Princeton manuscript, it was not worth keeping the superseded Cadbury manuscript.

The fourth and fifth Cadburys do seem to be missing in written form. The fourth was entitled on the published program: "Mediating between Church and Academy: The Turn to the Subject," but in fact Frei was getting behind schedule (due partly to a good deal of extempore expansion) and that topic was not reached until the fifth lecture. The fourth was largely on the theology of Kant, especially his understanding of incarnation. A tape recording of part of this lecture exists and was transcribed and sent to the editors of *Types*, who decided that it was too fragmentary to use. It has been deposited with the rest of the papers in the Yale library. Other aspects of Kant are treated by Frei elsewhere in the material in *Types*, but there is nothing corresponding to what was delivered in the fourth Cadbury. It is quite possible that a great deal of what he delivered was not written down at all—it was a topic which he knew well, had lectured on over many years, and could well have spoken on using few notes. This would partly explain why he got so far behind his published schedule.

The fifth Cadbury continued with Kant and then discussed the turn to the subject. The historical treatment of this in relation to Pietism, Methodism, idealism, Romanticism, Karl Marx, and others is not reproduced in *Types*, although the substance of the conclusion of the lecture, concerning Strauss on the Jesus of history and the Christ of faith, occurs in Shaffer material.

The final three Cadburys are all included in *Types* chapters 6 and 7. The final Cadbury was advertised in advance of the series under the title "Knowing Jesus and Learning to Live Christianly: The End of Academic Theology." It was intended to be Frei's discussion of his fifth type, but he never caught up on his schedule and the fourth type took up a major part of the lecture. What was actually delivered is accurately reflected in chapter 7 of *Types*, "The End of Academic Theology?" One might ask where the rest of the intended lecture went, but in fact Frei was writing the later ones during the two weeks he spent delivering them. My wife and I watched the hectic process, as he was staying at our home. So by the time he neared the end it was clear that there would not be time for a full lecture on the final topic, and there is no evidence that there was ever anything more than appears in *Types* (pp. 92–4).

In their introduction the editors say that chapter 5 is also Cadbury material. If it is, it was not delivered as such. It is possible that it is undelivered Cadbury material, but there is internal evidence that it was written for an American audience—e.g., the heavy irony about theology in the American Academy of Religion (p. 65).

The overall conclusion is that there is not much mystery left about the Cadburys. Happily, nearly everything of significance in them appears in *Types*. A good deal that does not was probably delivered extempore. The editors are to be congratulated on having done such a competent recovery job on very valuable material and will, I hope, be willing to consider my footnotes to their work if it is ever possible to have a second edition.

II FIVE TYPES OF CHRISTIAN THEOLOGY

Now to discuss the content of the book. As the first chapter, Frei's outline of his major project in a grant application, makes clear, the immediate purpose of this typology was as a conceptual analysis to help in doing better justice than other typologies to the richness of thinking about Jesus Christ and Christianity since 1700. The immense labor Frei put into this aspect of his historical work makes one realize how conceptually inadequate so much of the intellectual history of Christianity is. Without the sort of thorough engagement with the content of theology, past and present, which Frei brought to bear, such histories are, however detailed and broad their research, almost bound to betray an implicit theology and understanding of Christianity which fails to recognize some of the most significant contributions.

He fixed on five types. They can be described from various angles, as Frei does in the sets of lectures making up *Types*, and it is important not to get stuck in a one-dimensional understanding of them. I would argue that, while the typology can at one level be used formally in a fairly clinical way, it is most fully appreciated as itself a substantive theological framework and position which unite the main thrusts of Frei's previous work. I will now try to lay the typology out briefly so as to show, from the diverse, somewhat fragmentary, accounts in *Types*, how that is so.

At its simplest the typology describes five types according to the ways in which they relate to two descriptions of what Christian theology is. On the one hand, Christian theology is seen as subject to "general criteria of intelligibility, coherence, and truth that it must share with other academic disciplines" (p. 2). On the other hand, it is seen as defined by its relation to Christianity as a cultural or semiotic system: it makes first-order statements regarding Christian practice or belief and is also the Christian community's own second-order appraisal of those statements. Type 1 gives the first view complete priority: theology is a philosophical discipline in the academy and all Christian self-description is adjudicated according to its rational criteria. Frei's main examples are Kant and Gordon Kaufman. Type 2 tries to correlate general meaning structures with what is specifically Christian, while giving priority to the former. Frei sees Bultmann, Pannenberg, David Tracy, and Carl Henry as exemplifying this. For them, "external and internal descriptions of Christianity are two aspects whose conceptual convergence is made possible by the same underlying transcendental philosophical structure" (p. 3). Type 3 also attempts a correlation, but without proposing any comprehensive structure for integrating them. Instead, they are related in various ad hoc ways, such as "broadly pragmatic appeals to the character of human experience" (p. 3). Schleiermacher and (to a lesser degree) Tillich are seen to attempt this non-systematic correlation of heterogeneous equals. Type 4 gives priority to Christian self-description, letting that govern the applicability of general criteria of meaning in Christian theology, while nevertheless still engaging, in ad hoc ways, with the broader conceptual and cultural context. Barth, John Henry Newman, and Jonathan Edwards are examples of this. Type 5 takes Christian theology as exclusively a matter of Christian self-description. It is the "grammar of faith," its internal logic learnt like a new language through acquiring appropriate conceptual skills "which are as much behavioral or dispositional as they are linguistic or descriptive" (p. 4). This is seen in D. Z. Phillips and some evangelicals.

As described so far, that typology is well suited to appreciating how theologians handle the unavoidable tension between a religious identity and the array of alternative construals of meaning and reality. It could also just as well apply to other religions and, indeed, other forms of identity. Its originality in comparison with other common ways of categorizing lies in Types 3 and 4. His main effort is expended on these, and especially on Schleiermacher and Barth. The implications are considerable. There is a challenge to the usual ways in which the intellectual history of Western Christianity in the modern period is described. By bringing Schleiermacher and Barth close to each other in adjacent types, not only are many readings of each of these theologians put in question, but a space is created where theology might flourish by being liberated from (though not out of relationship with) the imposition of a set of expectations and demands which can easily inhibit doing justice to the specifically Christian. Frei reinterprets two of the greatest theologians of the past two centuries in the interests of what he sees as the best ways in which theology can engage satisfactorily with both Jesus Christ and the modern context. In discussion after one of the Cadbury lectures he said that he would probably place himself between Types 3 and 4—but that "aesthetically" he found himself participating in all five. That says a good deal about him as a theologian in a religious studies setting: a rigorous "aesthetic" intellectual engagement across the board, together with the ability to make perfectly clear where he considered the most lively, true, and practically appropriate Christian theology might be done.

Now let us develop the initial picture of the types by noting that Frei is not only interested in how each relates to the two basic views of theology. There are further refining questions about representatives of each type. How do they relate specific external description of Christianity to Christian self-description? Even philosophical views of Christianity see it as a specific religion and need to discuss or assume some answer to that. Furthermore, how do they relate "specific description of Christianity to a view of the general criteria for meaningful description" (p. 27)? In other words, Frei is concerned to analyze forms of description, both as regards whether they are internal or external and also by articulating the criteria according to which they are conceived as appropriate descriptions of Christianity. Again and again he claims to find confusions and blurrings whose practical effects tend toward making it more difficult to see just what Types 3 and 4 in particular are up to.

One critical issue is the main cognate discipline of theology. For Types 1 and 2 it tends to be philosophy of some sort, usually biased toward intellectual or experiential content and toward theoretical explanation of it. These easily confuse the descriptive with the explanatory, the internal with the external, and the logic of coming to and exercising belief with the logic of the belief itself. Types 3 and 4 have more affinities with interpretive (rather than explanatory) social science, stressing that Christianity is a social entity and that it is learnt in ways similar to the learning of a language or culture. Categories of practice are primary here and there is a sharp distinction between description and explanation, with the primacy given to the former. Theology reflects on the "ruled use" of the language of the Christian community understood as constituted in "complex and changing coherence" by such elements as sacred text, regulated relations between an elite and other believers, preaching, baptism, celebration of communion, common beliefs and attitudes, and an interpretive tradition (p. 22). The sort of social science which gives a rich description of such elements can lead to close convergence between internal and external description, especially if the logic of coming to and exercising belief is kept separate from the logic of belief.

Frei clearly considers that the social scientific description of Christianity is more adequate than the philosophical, and is also able to do justice to the philosophical in a way that is not reciprocally the case. But the recognition of the importance of a social scientific description cannot stop there: it must also be extended to the community of academic theologians. This leads into another original feature of *Types*: its linking of the five types with the institutional context of academic theology. A crude summary of the institutional "plot" of modern theology reads as follows. Before the foundation of the University of Berlin in 1809 there was a great debate about whether theology should have a place in a university dedicated to *Wissenschaft*, understood as "the inquiry into the universal, rational principles that allow us to organize any and all specific fields of inquiry into internally and mutually coherent, intelligible totalities" (p. 98). This view of *Wissenschaft* meant that the philosophical faculty integrated the university. Fichte (in line with Kant) argued against the inclusion of theology. Schleiermacher argued successfully for its inclusion. But his case was not that theology could fit the criteria of pure *Wissenschaft*. It was rather that, like medicine and law, it was a practical discipline directly useful to the public sector and drawing on many of the pure *wissenschaftlich* disciplines. Theology was then incorporated in a state-run university with a dual responsibility: to the state church, for which it educated the ministers, and to *Wissenschaft*. Schleiermacher had refused any hegemony of philosophy over theology, and the practical orientation of theology toward the Christian community meant that its autonomous character as Christian self-description was balanced unsystematically with its concern to relate to general human experience and to the range of academic disciplines. This delicate balance between the Christian and the academic set up an institutional context in which there was bound to be continuing tension between faith and reason or their various analogues (confessional theology and religious studies is a contemporary version). The University of Berlin was influential in structuring theology not only within Germany but also elsewhere, but even where this pattern did not obtain there tend to be variants of that crucial tension. Frei recognizes that his whole typology might look different in another context, but argues that it holds, in some form, for most modern academic Christian theology. As regards other religions, even whether they have anything corresponding to theology in Christianity would have to be argued case by case—Judaism is the only one he discusses, focusing on Midrash (p. 123).

The practical effect of the Berlin paradigm tends to be that, because theologians are academics in an institution dedicated to *Wissenschaft*, there is a strong bias toward Types 1 and 2 in university theology and other theology influenced by it. Schleiermacher's victory over Fichte made theology one exception to the rule of strict *Wissenschaft*, but it depended in that context on a relationship between the state, the church, and the university in which the ministers of the church were state officials. The wider context is that of the relation of Christianity to Western civilization and its public life, and Frei notes the ambiguity of Christianity's status: "it has been viewed and has viewed itself both as an independent religious community or communities and as an official or at least privileged institution in the general cultural system, including the organization of learning and of thinking about the meaning of culture" (p. 1). In this way Frei's typology connects with some of the most fundamental questions in late modern societies.

The specificity of Christianity both as a religious community and in the institutional form of its academic theology is therefore a crucial pivot of Frei's typology. But so far the key specific has not been spelled out. For Frei it is Jesus Christ. Perhaps the most important of all the features of his typology is the way in which it incorporates (or, perhaps more truly, is generated by) a perception of the essence of Christianity. He makes a daring claim for which the preparatory case is presented in his main previous works, *The Identity of Jesus Christ* and *The Eclipse of Biblical Narrative*. The claim is that the distinctive essence of Christianity is Jesus Christ as portrayed in the New Testament when it is read giving priority to the *sensus literalis*. Jesus Christ under this description is at the heart of Christianity according to the consensus of the Christian community over the centuries, and types of Christian theology should be assessed by their hospitality to this rendering of Jesus Christ. Frei takes Types 3 and 4 as being most hospitable. Many pages of *Types* are concerned with unpacking that claim.

The two central facets of the claim are that there has been a Christian "consensus that in the interpretation of Scripture, especially the New Testament, the literal sense has priority over other legitimate readings, be they allegorical, moral, or critical," and that there is "a strong interconnection (which may even indicate derivation) between this priority of the literal sense and its application to the figure of Jesus Christ" (p. 5). It is vital not to misunderstand what Frei means by the literal sense. It is worth noting his own explanation.

"Literal sense" here applies primarily to the identification of Jesus as the *ascriptive* subject of the descriptions or stories told about and in relation to him—whether the status of this identification is that of chief character in a narrative plot, historically factual person, or reality under an ontological scheme. In other words, "literal" is not referentially univocal but embraces several possibilities. All other senses of the quite diverse and changing notion "literal" are secondary to this (to my mind, basic ascriptive Christological) sense of "literal," that the subject matter of these stories is not something or someone else, and that the rest of the canon must in some way or ways, looser or tighter, be related to this subject matter or at least not in contradiction to it. That is the minimal agreement of how "literal" reading has generally been understood in the Western Christian tradition. The consensus, then, covers the literal reading or meaning of the New Testament stories about Jesus in an ascriptive mode, but not the reality status of the ascriptive subject Jesus.[1]

That means that, for example, it is possible, in relation to the question of the historical Jesus, to have a variety of ways of being "literal." Types 1 and 2 might see only certain critically justifiable New Testament statements as referring to the historical Jesus, and the Christ of faith must be tailored to fit this reconstructed figure. Here historical-critical criteria play the part of the general structure of meaning which dictates the rational meaning of Christian faith. Type 3 might try to correlate a Jesus of history arrived at in the same way as 1 and 2 with a Christ of faith arrived at by reference to the Jesus of the New Testament text as a whole. One of the most interesting results in the intellectual history of Christianity to which Frei's typology leads is his reinterpretation of Schleiermacher's posthumously published lectures on the life of Jesus. They are generally acknowledged to be disastrously inadequate, and David Friedrich Strauss savaged them. Frei does not uphold their adequacy, but makes two main points. First, they are concerned to affirm Jesus as the ascriptive subject of the New Testament texts and also "in his uniqueness and finality for Christian faith" (p. 72). The bottom line was that "*Jesus of Nazareth* can only be demonstrated from the testimony of the record" (p. 75) and this Jesus genuinely "owns his predicates" (p. 76). Second, Schleiermacher failed adequately to distinguish between Jesus as a historical construct behind the text and the Jesus rendered by the text and so laid himself open to Strauss's attack.

Type 4 avoids this confusion by giving priority to the text's realistic portrayal of Jesus and refusing to try to specify how it might be integrated with any historical reconstruction. In a crucial statement, which requires much of his previous work as backup, Frei says:

> To the question, how do we then use the complex term "empirical" or "historical factuality" in relation to the New Testament portraits, Type 4 theologians have no definite answer. Of course, they say, when you do use that category, he was a fact rather than a fiction, but as the ascriptive subject of the portraits it is his relation *to God* that identifies him, and are you seriously proposing that the relation is best specified under the interpretive category "fact"? Surely not, unless you are ready to say that "God" is a historical fact. The category "factuality" is simply inadequate (not wrong) for the interpretation of this text.[2]

That argument has perhaps the most explosive potential of any in contemporary academic theology and religious studies. Its relativizing of what is normally uncritically taken for granted is the obverse of the fundamental hermeneutical proposal which is the topic of Frei's two main books. It is not so much that it claims to solve problems; rather, it both challenges several of the most influential assumptions of scholars and theologians working within and outside Christianity and also suggests a constructive alternative. Chapter 6 of *Types*, in which Frei works out Types 3 and 4 in relation to Jesus and the literal sense, is the most important of the book.

As for Jesus in Type 5, Frei says little (for reasons given above). In his summary of the types in chapter 4 (Shaffer material) as well as in the brief chapter 7 he tends to see the logic of the position being to exclude theology as an interpretive discipline (pp. 54, 93 f.) and to see the literal sense as "logically equivalent to sheer repetition of the same words" (p. 55). This places it outside the consensus in the Christian tradition and, insofar as this is philosophically justified (e.g., by reference to Wittgenstein), it brings Type 5 back to meet Type 1.

There is much more about the types and related issues packed into this dense book, and I have hardly mentioned the discussions of language and reference, theory and practice, intentional agency and social structure, the critique of "meaning" as an objective universal and of "understanding" as its transcendental condition of possibility, and the addition of a concept of the "third-order" to first- and second-order. There is even a condensed Jesus-centered practical wisdom sketched in broad strokes in the opening pages of Appendix B, lightly touching on the severity and humaneness of Jesus; his universality and complex simplicity; the Kierkegaardian theme of Jesus Christ incognito; the manifestation of love in ordinary kindness and natural gentleness; how "the enjoyment of the neighbour in her and his peculiar character, religion, lifestyle, and work—the enjoyment of just the way she or he is—may also be part of the service of Christ" (p. 136); and how the concept of anhypostasis flows from all this. The whole is the distilled thought of an academic lifetime of rumination, wide reading, and intensive pursuit of a few big questions through their ramifications. The more one reads it the more coherent a book it is, both in itself and in relation to the rest of Frei's work. But the coherence is of a peculiar kind, since it is so consistently in the service of insistence on incompleteness, fragmentariness, deliberately non-systematic theology, informal and non-prescriptive "rules," making do without being able to know the conditions for the possibility of what is most important, suspicion of overviews, and frequent acknowledgment of ignorance. To switch to a language that was not Frei's, this is a typology and theology that, in the name of Jesus and with reference to large areas of modern thought, resists any form of "totality" and, positively, has a radical respect for "otherness."

This has considerable implications for theology and religious studies. There is a myth that the academic way to deal with religions is to strive for a detachment, neutrality, and objectivity which are in tension with commitment to any one faith. Frei would not make any general claims for the virtues of commitment, but his work demonstrates that his specific commitment is inextricable from a respect for the particularity of each "other." The classic test case for Christians in this regard is that of Judaism. Frei's own family was of Jewish ancestry and he discussed the relation between Christianity and Judaism with great sensitivity. The logic of his typology and theology points to just the sort of collegiality with Jewish colleagues, dialogue with Jewish thought, and learning from the history of the Jewish community which actually informed his life. By extension, there would be comparable relationships possible with those of other faiths. And reciprocally, it is possible to see scholars with other commitments—not just religious, but also agnostic or atheist—who have worked out ways of handling theology and religious studies that embody a spirit analogous to Frei's. One might add that the whole enterprise is made a good deal less fraught by the priority of respectful description and respect for self-description. He wrote in *Types* of a "simple and delighted generosity" toward others (p. 137) and if his rigorously thought-out typology is applied and criticized in that spirit it allows one to envisage a discipline which does not institutionalize a divide between theology and religious studies and which encourages constructive, as well as critical and descriptive, activity.

The secret lies in Frei's verbal admission, quoted above, that he saw himself doing theology between Types 3 and 4 while aesthetically participating in all five. If adherents of other types or of other typologies were able to embody something analogous, then we might perhaps have the ideal participants in theology and religious studies for the future. There would be no guarantee of agreement (Frei is highly controversial) but there would be the possibility of full and appropriate academic engagement in this deeply divided field.

Yet that is far too anodyne and even naive a conclusion about the institutionalization of this field. Major strategic, staffing, and funding decisions can determine the shape and quality of the subject in ways that the academics in a department can do little to affect. Frei wisely emphasized the social, institutional, and political realities. His work suggests the need for a reconception of the academic setting for theology and religious studies comparable in scope to that of Schleiermacher and the University of Berlin. As in the case of Berlin, for it to be successful it would require that a multitude of contingent factors converge. But also as in Berlin it would be impossible without profound intellectual conceptions coming into strenuous dialogue with a view to actual implementation. Frei's work allows for sufficient analysis of, and critical distance on, the origins and character of our present institutional arrangements to help inspire a self-aware attempt to envision something new. This is not the place to attempt that, but one obvious remark is that it is likely to happen, in the first place, not according to some general pattern but, again as in Berlin, by vigorous thinking in practical engagement with the complexities of a particular situation, including constructive compromises.

The present time seems ripe for such projects, since it is not only the field of theology and religious studies which needs reshaping: the university itself is in a complex period of turmoil and the very meaning of "academic" could be illuminated by a sophisticated typology which does justice to the fragmentary, the non-systematic, and the improvisatory. Even some of the "cultured despisers" of religion have noticed that the religions are not going to disappear (3 to 4 billion disappearances are hard to imagine) and that millions of intelligent people (even perhaps as intelligent and cultured as themselves) are actually practicing members of religious communities and, in many cases, of academic communities too. Many of the traditional modern ideologies which dismiss, reduce, or explain away religions seem less credible than they once did, and the way is open for just such a reconception as Frei could contribute toward.

There is much else to discuss about Frei which will have to take place elsewhere. I have not begun the critical appraisal that is desirable, but it is worth stating some of my questions. Does the focus of the typology on Jesus Christ bias it toward the specificity of Christianity in a way that makes it almost too easy to accommodate in a pluralist social and academic environment? Is it actually an oversimplification? The other main candidate for Christian distinctiveness is the trinitarian God and, while an emphasis on this obviously need not be in tension with Frei's, yet it raises different and often awkward questions about universality, the role of theory in relation to practice, and even the relation of theology to other disciplines. A focus on God would also raise the question as to the effects of making the practice of worship rather than the reading of Scripture the critical communal activity through which the essence of Christianity is characterized. What about Frei's understanding of the human subject, and in particular the role of language in its constitution? Can Frei's conceptions of identity, both individual and social, adequately accommodate the complexities of personal and community boundaries, with all the coinherence, ambivalence, and contradiction that are actually present? Can "rules" as used by interpretive social science do the job Frei demands of them in description? Even though he hedges his concept of rule with qualifications, it is not clear that he meets the sorts of objections to rule-centered accounts of anthropological and sociological fieldwork that Pierre Bourdieu and others make. What about Type 5? Even though it is near neighbor of Type 4 and apparently shares many of its strengths in terms of the priority of Christian self-description, the negative assessment of it is more vehement than of any other. What is the significance of the fact that the critical difference between them is not in any understanding or practice of Christianity but in how they relate to other structures of meaning? How essential to the typology is the priority of the practical, and are there ways of reasserting the theoretical in ways which are still hospitable to Jesus Christ and the literal sense? How might Frei's suggestions of a non-correspondence conception of truth be worked out? What are the consequences for academic Christian theology of its increasingly "lay" character?

The questions could go on, but I want in conclusion to return to the Moses figure. In the light of the intervening discussion there is perhaps more in the comparison. In the form in which the redactors left the books of Moses he is seen, certainly, as not entering Canaan; but especially in the delivery of the Law he is credited with reaching forward to shape life way beyond the crossing. Frei's final project on Jesus post-1700 may have been the Canaan he did not enter. But his typology might have some analogy with a law which helps form life and belief. If its potential is grasped it might yet contribute to a fresh start for the field he worked in. And if it does so it will be in no small measure due to the immense amount of first-order substantive theological thought which, though rarely made explicit in his writing, pervades it and is its constant horizon.

NOTES

1. Hans W. Frei, *Types of Christian Theology*, ed. George Hunsinger and William C. Placher (New Haven and London: Yale University Press, 1992), 5.
2. Ibid., 85.

CONTRIBUTORS

David F. Ford is Regius Professor of Divinity Emeritus in the University of Cambridge.

Garrett Green is Class of '43 Professor Emeritus of Religious Studies at Connecticut College.

Mike Higton is Professor of Theology and Ministry at Durham University.

George Hunsinger is the Hazel Thompson McCord Professsor of Systematic Theology at Princeton Theological Seminary.

David H. Kelsey is Luther A. Weigle Professor Emeritus of Theology at Yale University Divinity School.

John Allan Knight is the Sprigg Visiting Professor of Philosophical Theology and Ethics and Director of Faculty Research at Virginia Theological Seminary

Bruce D. Marshall is Lehman Professor of Christian Doctrine at Perkins School of Theology, Southern Methodist University.

R. David Nelson is director of Baylor University Press.

William C. Placher[†] was Follette Distinguished Professor in the Humanities at Wabash College.

George P. Schner S.J.† was Professor of Philosophical Theology at Regis College, Toronto.

Katherine Sonderegger is William Meade Chair in Systematic Theology at Virginia Theological Seminary.

Jason A. Springs is Professor of Religion, Ethics, and Peace Studies at University of Notre Dame Kroc Institute for International Peace Studies.

Jeffrey Stout is Professor Emeritus of Religion at Princeton University.

John F. Woolverton† was Professor of American church history at Virginia Theological Seminary and editor of *Anglican and Episcopal History* magazine.

INDEX

American Academy of Religion 255
  Narrative Theology group 98
American Christians 23–5, 30
Anglicanism 22, 27–8, 31
Anselmian theology
  Barth's view 82, 84–5, 146
  central task 106
  Christ's identity and resurrection 53, 55, 144
  Festschrift 102–4
  Frei's version 98–102, 106–14, 123, 151
anthropology 31, 34–5, 50, 80, 83, 87, 109–10, 130
anti-Semitism 26
apologetics 15–18, 79, 91, 106–8, 113–14, 123–4, 174–5, 177–8, 185
Auerbach, Erich 15, 33, 35, 91–2, 158
  Mimesis: The Representation of Reality in Western Literature 32
Augustine 28–30, 158
  De Doctrina Christiana 164

Barth, Karl 23, 28, 30, 32, 57, 100, 103
  biblical and dogmatic writing 34–6
  book on Anselm 82
  break with liberalism and relationalism 78–82
  Busch's biography on 253
  Christocentricity 84
  Church Dogmatics 18, 137
  criticism of 80–3
  dissertation on 78–80
  epistemological monophysitism 79
  Frei observation 182–3, 198–9
  Jüngel's relationship 160
  method of *Ineinanderstellung* 82
  misconception in English speaking world 138
  ontology over epistemology 81–3
  post-liberal dialectical method 81–2
  primacy of God, 82–3
  Romans commentary 145
  scripture reading 146
  as *systematic* theologian 24
Bavinck, Herman 229, 233, 235, 237, 241–3, 245
Berger, Peter 18
Berlin, Isaiah 26
Bible
  analogical language 32
  Barth's interpretation 146
  distortion of meanings 15–16
  Frei's deliberations 147–50, 152–3, 162–3, 176
  Hebrew 211
  historical-critical study 119, 198–201, 203
  historical information 14–15
  life and world interpretation 89, 212

literary analysis 17–18
mistake about the truth 202–3
narrative reading 61–2
nonnarrative form 15, 19
preaching Christ 176
radical criticism 30, 32, 36
reading 13–14, 61–2, 145, 214–15
realistic approach 14–15, 203
sensus literalis doctrine 100
stories, use-in-context 65–6
theological use 201
three different points 200
world vision 19
Worterklärung and *Sacherklärung* 177
Boorstin, Daniel 26
Bourdieu, Pierre 263
Brandom, Robert 102
Brunner, Emil 107–8, 159
Buckley, Michael Joseph 185–6
Bultmann 30, 49, 74, 159, 256
Busch, Eberhard 34–5, 98–9, 253

Calvin, John 28–9, 37, 48, 162–3, 174, 179, 185, 194, 242–3, 245
Christian reading communities 63–4
  Bible studying 152
  literal *vs.* plain reading 65
  of Old Testament 163
  reading and interpretation 65
  rule of faith/truth 64–6
  scriptural practices 66–7, 207–20
Christian self-description 20, 79, 99, 106, 193, 256, 258, 262–3
Christian theology
  knowing and following Jesus 151–2
  language use 101–2, 105–9, 112–14, 131, 150–2, 157–61, 165–8
  Latin tradition 159
  life-stance of faith 123
  positivity 178, 200
  problem of faith and history 139–43, 145, 147–51
  scandal of particularity 183
  twenty-one theses 107–14
  types of 105–6, 255–64
Christological reflection
  belief logics 128–34
  category of presence 125–6
  existential-historical 120–2
  God's love 121
  problematic consequences 119, 121–9
  revisionism 119–22, 124–9
  transition to modernity 118–21
church
  reading practice 61–2, 65–8, 210–21
  use of scripture 208, 210–15
Church of England 28
  Creeds and the Thirty-Nine Articles 72–3
Clebsch, William 34
Collins, Anthony 90
Copperfield, David 216
Crites, Stephen 109–10, 200

Danto, Arthur 32
Davidson, Donald 202–3
deconstructionists 18–19, 32, 36, 78, 80, 108, 112, 214, 217
Deism 192
Descartes 193
Dialogical theology 105, 107, 110–11, 114
Donne, John 27
Dostoevsky, Fyodor 27, 29

Ebeling, Gerhard 26, 31, 160, 164
Edwards, Jonathan 28, 30, 256
Enlightenment 34, 140, 162–3, 177, 199–200
Episcopal Church 22, 27
Esperantist theology 105, 107, 112, 114
Evangelicals 23
  historic doctrinal concerns 227–34, 240–1, 243–5
evangelists 165, 243

Farrer, Austin 27, 31, 148, 182
The Fate of Academic Theology 99
Feuerbach, Ludwig 141
Frei, Hans Wilhelm. *See also* works (Frei)
  American citizenship 25
  Anselmian argument 55–6
  Cadbury Lectures 99, 253–6
  Chalcedonian formula 56–8
  characteristic sensitivity 26
  Christology 47–58, 61, 99–104
  concept of presence 49–52, 122, 125–30, 133–4
  early life 16, 37

Greenhoe Lecture 146–8, 150–1, 157, 162–3
interview with 3–10
literal sense or plain sense of scripture 36, 58, 62–9, 89, 91–2
logic of relationalism 48
monastic life 27
philosophic preference 185, 198, 201
as a priest in Episcopal Church 22
Princeton lectures (1986) 57, 99
sensus literalis 100, 162–4, 195, 216, 218–19, 259
Shaffer Lectures 99
teaching career 22–3
theological vocabulary 151
Fuchs, Ernst 160, 164

Geertz, Clifford 18, 62, 210
Genesis, creation stories 146
Gore, Charles
Essays Catholic and Critical 27
Lux Mundi 27
Great War 159
Guder, Darrell 158

Hauerwas, Stanley 18, 110, 112–13
Hegel, Georg Wilhelm Friedrich 49, 179, 182, 184, 186–7, 190–3, 199–201
Lectures on the Philosophy of Religion 191, 193, 200
Phenomenology of the Spirit 31
Vorstellung 191
Heidegger, Martin 158, 160, 167, 186
Henry, Carl Ferdinand Howard 69–70, 73, 227–8, 233, 240–1, 243, 256
Herder, Johann Gottfried 174, 176, 179, 186
Hermann, Weyl 126
hermeneutic theory 24, 33–5, 53, 57–8, 61, 72, 78, 80, 88, 90, 103, 105, 111–12, 128–9, 132–3, 158–68, 175, 177–9, 181, 183, 186, 188, 207, 212, 218–19, 221, 231–2, 256, 260
second naïveté 137–53
Higton, Mike 61–2, 79
Christ, Providence and History 139
Hirsch, Emanuel 26

historical criticism 140, 142, 145–7, 164, 174–9, 183, 200, 216, 230, 233, 237, 244
historical Jesus 14, 17, 21, 118–22, 125–7, 129, 133, 159–60, 165, 178, 181, 259
Hitler, Adolf 5, 26
Holy Scripture 185, 228–9, 231, 241
canonical-linguistic approach 208
dual warrant of text and tradition 68–9
normative constraints 67–8
objectivity 207
orientational witness 67, 69–70
pattern of reading 63–4, 213
Holy Spirit 29, 36, 58, 82, 91, 213
How It All Began: On the Resurrection of Christ (*Journal of Anglican and Episcopal History*) 70
Hunsinger, George 47, 71, 138, 227, 253

interpretative method 54, 65, 78–81, 87–92

Jacobi 193
Jesus Christ
apostolic witness 120
divine-human union 57–8, 82, 85, 178, 182, 191
God's relation to 120
historical *vs.* human 119–20
humanity 120, 127
identity description 36, 47–8, 51–5, 70, 121, 124–5, 128–34
liberation struggle 126–7
Logos 35, 123, 242
pattern of exchange 54, 56, 71–2
physical nature 71
portrayal in Gospels/scriptural narratives 35, 56, 128–34
relationship with disciples 36
resurrection 55, 73
unsubstitutable identity 51, 62, 72, 124–34
Jews 4–5, 7, 9–10, 211
Jung, Karl 36
Jüngel, Eberhard
doctoral dissertation on Paul and Jesus 157, 160

God as the Mystery of the World
  157–63, 167–8
 originality and creativity 156–7
 on parables of Jesus 160–2

Kant, Immanuel 128, 179, 182, 184,
  186–90, 192, 199–201
 Critique of Pure Reason 188–9
 *Religion within the Limits of Reason
  Alone* 188–9
 schematism 190
Kaufman, Gordon 101, 256
Kelsey, David 19, 24, 108–10, 113, 118,
  129, 131, 252
Kermode, Frank 17, 36, 62–3, 69
Kierkegaard, Søren 20, 27–8, 30, 49, 150,
  261
Kissinger, Henry 24–5
Kraus, Hans-Joachim 29
Küng, Hans 227–8
Kuyper, Abraham 229, 233, 235, 237,
  241–3, 245

language. *See* Christian theology, language
  use
Latitudinarians 179
Laurence, David Ernst 30
Lee, David, *Luke's Stories of Jesus:
  Theological Reading of Gospel
  Narrative and the Legacy of Hans
  Frei* 52–3
Lindbeck, George 19, 24, 35, 61, 129,
  150, 157, 175–6, 207–9
 The Nature of Doctrine 209–12
 *Scriptural Authority and Narrative
  Interpretation* 22, 103–4, 110, 113
 theological reasoning 209–16
Livingston, James 141
Luther, Martin King 18, 27, 29, 162–3,
  174, 194

MacIntyre, Alasdair 18
 The Eclipse of Biblical Narrative 19
Malebranche, Nicolas 186
Marx, Karl 181, 254
McClendon, James 18
Meeks, Wayne 19, 252
Meilaender, Gilbert 18

Moltmann, Jürgen 31–2
Mommsen, Theodor Ernst 25

naturalists 132, 147, 179
Neologians 179
New England Puritans 29
New Hermeneutic 159–61, 164, 167–8
Newman, Henry 256
New Testament 17, 29, 44, 52, 58, 68,
  70–1, 73, 109, 119–22, 124, 140–1,
  145–6, 149, 160, 165, 183, 188,
  236, 259–60
 concept of myth 141
 historical-critical study 120, 140
 Jesus' passion and resurrection 145–6
 three inter-related questions 120
Niebuhr, Helmut Richard 23–5, 27, 30,
  35–6, 57, 188, 251
 Christ and Culture 56
 *Faith on Earth: An Inquiry into the
  Structure of Human Faith* 49–50
 The Responsible Self 35

Ogden, Schubert 119–22, 124–7, 129, 134
 The Point of Christology 118
Old Testament 8, 14, 29, 147, 163, 183
Outka, Gene 19, 24, 33, 109–11

Pauck, Wilhelm 25
Phillips, Dewi Zephaniah 179, 256
Pietists 179
Pilgrim's Progress 18
Placher, William 66
Postliberals 19, 207–8, 210
 historical doctrinal concerns 227–30,
  233, 241, 243–5
Presentist theology 105, 107, 112, 114
Price, Charles 33–4
Protestants 8, 26, 30–1, 63, 80, 88, 142,
  185–6, 194, 200
Puritan-Protestant tradition 30

Quine, Willard Van Orman 202

Rahner, Karl 187
realistic narrative 177–80, 182–7, 189–95,
  198–9, 201, 203–4, 217–18, 232
Reformation movements, leftwing 184

Reformers 63–4, 68, 142, 147, 162–3, 176, 245. *See also* Protestants
regula fidei 214–15
Reimarus, Hermann Samuel 177, 179
Ricoeur, Paul 80, 139–40, 146, 150, 168
    Rule of Metaphor 166
    Time and Narrative 166
    triadic schema 140
Ryle, Gilbert 17, 52, 182, 186

Schelling, Friedrich Wilhelm Joseph von 25
Schleiermacher, Friedrich 25, 31, 49, 100, 103, 126, 142, 174, 176, 179, 182, 190, 256, 258, 260, 262
Schner, George 198–201
Schweitzer, Albert 30, 181
    Quest for the Historical Jesus 21, 181
scripture. *See* Holy Scripture
secondary theology 132
second naïveté hermeneutics
    Barth's realistic approach 146
    Ricoeur's vision 140, 146, 150
Segregationist theology 106–7
Sellars, Wilfrid, Some Reflections on Language Games 102
solas 212
story theology 33–4
Stouts, Harry
    Festschrift, Scriptural Authority and Narrative Interpretation 22
    The New England Soul 30
Strauss, David Friedrich 142, 174, 176
    Life of Jesus 141, 147
Supernaturalists 179
Sykes, Stephen 27

Tanner, Kathryn 33, 98, 111
Tarski, Alfred 202
Temple, William, *Nature, Man, and God* 27
thematic submoment
    God's immediate presence to creation 85–6
    meaning of the scriptural texts 87
    primacy of ontology over epistemology 78, 80–5, 91
Thiemann, Ronald 19, 22–3, 110–11
Thiselton, Anthon, *The Two Horizons* 164

Thucydides, *History of the Peloponnesian War* 23
Tillich, Paul 15, 23, 25, 31, 34, 126, 150, 182, 256
Tracy, David 80, 101, 179, 228, 256
triune God 191, 193, 208, 212–14
Troltsch, Ernst 103

Vanhoozer, Kevin 210–11
    canonical-linguistic approach 208
    The Drama of Doctrine 208

Webster, John 138, 161, 209–11
Wiles, Maurice 27, 111
Wissenschaftliche 124
Wittgenstein, Ludwig 32, 62, 150, 165, 179, 201
Wolterstorff, Nicholas 64, 102
Wood, Charles 19, 33, 98, 101, 111–12
Word of God 48, 63, 68–9, 82, 84, 86–7, 91, 124, 127, 131, 152, 161, 165, 209, 220, 239
works (Frei)
    Alexander Thompson Memorial lecture 62
    Barth and Schleiermacher: Divergence and Convergence 183
    The Bible and the Narrative Tradition 16–17, 24
    Doctrine of Revelation in the Thought of Karl Barth, 1909–1922: The Nature of Barth's Break with Liberalism 30, 48, 80
    The Eclipse of Biblical Narrative: A Study in Eighteenth- and Nineteenth-Century Hermeneutics 16, 21, 24, 88–9, 139, 142–3, 145, 147, 157, 162, 172–3
    Faith and Ethics: The Theology of H. Richard Niebuhr 16, 103
    The Genesis of Secrecy 63
    History, Church and Nation 35–6
    The Identity of Jesus Christ: The Hermeneutical Bases of Dogmatic Theology 16, 21, 24, 33, 47, 50–7, 64, 71–2, 118, 121–2, 139, 143–5, 157, 165, 199, 204, 252
    Interpretation and Devotion: God's Presence for Us in Jesus Christ 148

Literal Reading essay 64
The Mystery of the Presence of Jesus Christ 48
Nineteenth-Century Religious Thought in the West 16
Notes on Leaving Things the Way They Are 149–50
On Interpreting the Christian Story 146–7, 157

Proposal for a Project 98
The Range of Subject Matter Proposals 179
Theological Reflections on the Account of Jesus' Death and Resurrection 33, 47
Theology and Narrative: Selected Essays 22, 99
Types of Christian Theology 22, 58, 74, 98–9, 228

www.ingramcontent.com/pod-product-compliance
Lightning Source LLC
Chambersburg PA
CBHW081417230426
43668CB00016B/2266